Get the eBook FREE!

(PDF, ePub, Kindle, and liveBook all included)

We believe that once you buy a book from us, you should be able to read it in any format we have available. To get electronic versions of this book at no additional cost to you, purchase and then register this book at the Manning website.

Go to https://www.manning.com/freebook and follow the instructions to complete your pBook registration.

That's it!
Thanks from Manning!

Terraform in Depth

Infrastructure as Code with Terraform and OpenTofu

ROBERT HAFNER

FOREWORDS BY CHRISTIAN MESH
AND ANTON BABENKO

MANNING
SHELTER ISLAND

Manning Publications Co.
20 Baldwin Road
PO Box 761
Shelter Island, NY 11964

Development editor:	Rebecca Johnson
Technical editor:	Ryn Daniels
Review editor:	Kishor Rit
Production editor:	Andy Marinkovich
Copy editor:	Kari Lucke
Proofreader:	Mike Beady
Technical proofreader:	Lauro Fialho Müller
Typesetter:	Tamara Švelić Sabljić
Cover designer:	Marija Tudor

ISBN 9781633438002
Printed in the United States of America

To my wife (and favorite human), Ali

brief contents

contents

5 *The Terraform plan*   123

9 Testing and refactoring 288

forewords

In theory, we should all have identical production and test systems that are kept in sync every time there is a change. We should also apply updates regularly, track vulnerabilities, perform change management, have backups, and do all this while making sure not everyone has root access to every machine and features are delivered quickly and without a hiccup.

In practice, at least one of these very often suffers when the infrastructure is maintained manually. No matter how many fancy new toys we have been given over the years, be that the virtualization craze of 2010; containers; or, more recently, Kubernetes clusters, setting up and maintaining infrastructure manually is already painful. Setting up and maintaining the same infrastructure multiple times for testing, staging, and other environments is nigh on impossible.

This is where infrastructure as code (IaC), and specifically Terraform and OpenTofu, comes in. IaC promises that it will take a recipe—a blueprint if you will—and apply it to your servers or cloud environment. Configure an SSH key, hit a button, and it will roll out over hundreds of machines. No longer will you need to think about which machines the new colleague needs access to. The best part is that the recipe to do so and all changes to it can live in a version control system, giving you easy access to the history of changes that happened over time.

Additionally, Terraform and OpenTofu go a step further than just providing IaC. While many IaC tools only provide you with a way to automate certain tasks, Terraform and OpenTofu give you a way to remove the infrastructure you created without any additional code. While this may sound like a small feature, it is incredibly powerful for testing updates: you can spin up a complex infrastructure for a few minutes, test what you need to test, and then tear it down. You can provision multiple copies of the same infrastructure for short periods of time without breaking the bank. As a side benefit from using the same code frequently to create and remove infrastructure, bugs will come out immediately rather than days, weeks, or even months later when you next use the automation.

Whether you are starting from scratch or are an experienced user, *Terraform in Depth* is a thorough guide.

As with any complex topic, this book starts at the very beginning. You will start with a clear introduction to IaC with simple, real-life examples. You will learn how Terraform and OpenTofu are different from other IaC tools thanks to their declarative language. You will quickly acquire the skills to use these tools to rapidly and confidently deploy large and complex infrastructure.

With the fundamentals in hand, you will be introduced to more advanced topics, which allow you to leverage what you have learned in team and production environments. As every team and organization is different, a wide variety of tooling and services are explored and compared. Scaling a project from an individual to a whole team or organization requires careful consideration of tooling and workflow, for which this book will have you well prepared.

For those wanting to take their skills to the next level, the final section of the book dives into advanced features. Although limited by a declarative language, Terraform and OpenTofu can be supercharged by building custom providers or integrating with other programming languages using CDKTF. *Terraform in Depth* does an excellent job of breaking down the complexity of these integrations and teaches you how to leverage them to get the most out of your infrastructure.

— CHRISTIAN MESH,
OPENTOFU TECHNICAL LEAD

Robert Hafner is a remarkable contributor in the DevOps and automation fields, known not only for his expertise in Terraform but also for his work with MLOps, GitHub Automation, and Python. His knowledge across these areas gives him a unique approach to infrastructure, which he brings fully to life in this book.

Terraform has become a standard for cloud management and automation because of its flexibility and the strength of its community. Many professionals trust it not just for its capabilities but for the quality that users around the world have contributed to over the years. This book, *Terraform in Depth*, goes beyond the basics and takes a deep dive, making it a powerful guide for anyone who wants to really understand Terraform's potential.

Long before Robert started writing this book, I was following his work, learning from his blog posts that broke down complex topics in simple terms. His ability to explain things clearly is just as present here, making this book useful for both new and experienced Terraform users.

As you go through *Terraform in Depth*, I encourage you to keep asking questions and trying out what you learn. Robert's approach will challenge and inspire you, showing you not only how to use Terraform but how to think about infrastructure in a new way.

—ANTON BABENKO,
AUTHOR AND MAINTAINER OF VARIOUS POPULAR
TERRAFORM & AWS PROJECTS, AWS HERO, AND TERRAFORM INFLUENCER

preface

When I first entered this industry in the early 2000s there was no concept of cloud computing, configuration management, or infrastructure as code. Projects were planned out months in advance, hardware was ordered from suppliers or rented from data centers, and machines were often hand configured. In an attempt to speed up development systems, administrators would build collections of scripts they used to build machines, with scripts being shared on forums and tutorial sites. Building and configuring servers was often a manual process, and servers were important—if a server went down, it would have to be replaced or repaired.

In 2006, Amazon announced a beta of Amazon Elastic Compute Cloud, and by 2008 it had enough functionality that companies were using it for real workloads. Around the same time (2005), Puppet Labs came out with the first version of the Puppet configuration management system and language.

The combination of these two events changed the entire industry. Puppet, and other configuration management tools like it, allowed people to define system configurations with a unified language. Building a new machine image meant running a simple program. Making changes to running machines was possible by applying code changes. At the same time, hardware had been decoupled from the process of running a server—it was now possible to launch hundreds of servers at the click of a button and then throw them away with just another click.

This completely changed how people developed distributed systems. Individual machines stopped being important while deployment times dropped from weeks to minutes. It became easier to simply throw away virtual machines running older software than try to upgrade them in place, and scaling up and down could be done without needing to own every machine in the process.

Terraform was launched in 2014 by HashiCorp, and it did the same thing for infrastructure that Puppet did for virtual machines. Terraform made infrastructure easily launchable and disposable—extremely complex systems could be created and destroyed as simply as running Terraform. Operations that used to rely on kludgy scripts or manual setup could be codified, shared, and built on to create even larger systems.

It's hard to overstate how much this affected the industry. It lowered the barrier for entry for many developers to work on infrastructure, as it gave them a unified language for doing so. Just as configuration management had given developers the power to update fleets of machines, infrastructure as code gave them the ability to manage the components around those machines.

Many of the systems and architectures that are common today would not be possible without this level of abstraction. If we had to manually put up every single microservice for an application, it would naturally push people toward monolithic stacks. If it took several hours of manual work to use an AWS or GCP service, then people would not use them—or if they did, they wouldn't be able to iterate nearly as quickly as high-performing teams do.

acknowledgments

Writing a book is not something I ever would have accomplished on my own. This book was made infinitely better by the support and help of many people.

First and foremost, I want to thank my wife, Ali, for supporting me through this whole process. Over the two years it took to make this book a reality, she was there every step of the way.

Next, I want to thank my technical editor, Ryn Daniels, for reviewing every word written and providing valuable feedback on the technical content in the book. Ryn is an infrastructure engineer leading the Cloud Platform team at Mapbox, whose work focuses on infrastructure operability, sustainable on-call practices, and the design of effective and empathetic engineering cultures. Ryn was also responsible for introducing me to the wonderful folks at Manning and sharing their own experience as an author. It's fair to say this book would not have happened without them.

I also want to thank Lauro Müller for their work as a technical proofreader. Lauro not only tested every single code example in the book but also provided valuable feedback around clarity and consistency.

Of course, none of this would have been possible without the folks at Manning—in particular, my editor, Rebecca Johnson. Rebecca provided feedback every step of the way, while also managing the overall process. Additionally, I want to acknowledge Brian Sawyer, my acquisitions editor, who helped build out the initial proposal and refine it into the structure we have today.

This would also have been a very different book without the army of reviewers who went over every single page. Their feedback, especially in the early stages, resulted in significant changes that really shifted the focus and direction of the book. To all the reviewers—Alceu Rodrigues de Freitas Junior, Alessandro Campeis, Alexis Perrier, Amit

Lamba, Chaithanya Krishna, Chris Kolosiwsky, Cliff Zhao, Daivid Morgan, Dan Sheikh, Dylan Scott, Eric Dickey, Ernesto Cárdenas Cangahuala, Geert Van Laethem, German Gonzalez-Morris, Harsh Gupta, Henry Stamerjohann, Jehad Nasser, José Alberto Reyes Quevedo, Kristina Kasanicova, Leonardo Taccari, Manuel Martins, Michael Bright, Miguel Quintero, Neil Croll, Peter Bishop, Prashant Dwivedi, Rambabu Posa, Roman Levchenko, Ronald Haring, Serge Smertin, Shaun Rust, Tobias Getrost, Werner Dijkerman, and Zachary Manning—your suggestions helped make this a better book.

Finally, I want to thank Blip the Cat. While his grasp of English isn't the greatest, and his constant desire to bang on my keyboard certainly didn't speed things up, he happily sat with me the whole time I was writing and rarely complained when I bounced ideas off him.

about this book

Terraform in Depth is written to give a solid understanding of not only the Terraform language but infrastructure as code as a whole. While Terraform is the language focused on throughout the book, many of the concepts and ideas are important for any infrastructure as code project. After reading this book, you can expect to know not just the Terraform language but how to effectively use it as part of a team or organization.

Who should read this book?

Terraform in Depth was written for software developers, system administrators, and other engineers who build software systems that have to be deployed into production. This book is designed for all experience levels, with an initial focus on building a solid foundation before working into more advanced topics. Whether you've never launched infrastructure before or have decades of experience, this book should have lessons that you can learn from.

How this book is organized: a roadmap

This book is organized into 3 parts over 12 chapters. Each chapter builds off of the contents of the previous chapters.

Part 1 explains the basics of the Terraform language, giving you a basic grounding in the language itself. This portion of the book builds a foundation of knowledge that will allow you to utilize Terraform immediately while laying the groundwork for the rest of the book:

- Chapter 1 is a brief introduction to Terraform itself, including a brief history of the project and its new fork, OpenTofu.

- Chapter 2 focuses on the HashiCorp Configuration Language (HCL) that is the basis for Terraform itself. This includes a breakdown of the most common HCL block types.
- Chapter 3 discusses the basic components of Terraform modules, including the different types of variables in the Terraform language. Modules are a core concept in Terraform that enable code reuse and project composability.
- Chapter 4 expands on the previous chapters by introducing expressions and iteration. This allows for data transformations: constructing strings, data structures, and operators to dynamically configure your resources.
- Chapter 5 closes out the first part of the book by focusing on the plan and apply phases of Terraform. This chapter breaks these topics down and ties them back to their underlying computer science theories, which will allow you to better understand and debug problems that occur.

Part 2 talks about how to bring Terraform into production. It is in this portion of the book that you learn how to test, deploy, and manage your projects in a team setting:

- Chapter 6 discusses Terraform state, which is one of the most important parts of bringing your projects into production. This chapter breaks down what state truly is, including a deep dive into the actual data structures inside of state. Most importantly, we discuss how to properly store, secure, and protect your state to increase your project's resilience.
- Chapter 7 is all about using continuous integration to improve code quality. In this chapter, we discuss how to manage your continuous integration systems while also running through the vast ecosystem of tools that exist for managing code quality. This includes an overview of security scanners, code quality scanners, and documentation tools.
- Chapter 8 is a deep dive into continuous delivery of your projects. While continuous development is often tied into continuous integration (often stated as CI/CD), there are a lot of nuances that make it so delivery deserves its own contents. Here, we talk about method, project structure, and deployment systems.
- Chapter 9 is a comprehensive overview of testing with Terraform, using either Terratest or the Terraform Testing Framework, as well as the nuances that come into play when testing infrastructure as code.

Part 3 covers advanced topics. This includes some of the more esoteric components of Terraform, as well as ways to expand Terraform itself:

- Chapter 10 discusses various features, providers, and design patterns in Terraform that can help manage different edge cases you may encounter.
- Chapter 11 goes into detail about how you can wrap Terraform in your own applications, allowing you to build custom tools to manage or analyze your Terraform deployments.
- Chapter 12 breaks down how to build custom providers, which is the best way to expand the Terraform language to support managing new systems.

This book is meant to be read in order, as each chapter assumes you have the knowledge from the previous ones. Existing Terraform developers may be able to skim the first few chapters, but you may miss some interesting tidbits and ideas if you do so.

About the code

This book contains many examples of source code both in numbered listings and in line with normal text. In both cases, source code is formatted in a `fixed-width font like this` to separate it from ordinary text. Sometimes code is also **in bold** to highlight code that has changed from previous steps in the chapter, such as when a new feature adds to an existing line of code.

In many cases, the original source code has been reformatted; we've added line breaks and reworked indentation to accommodate the available page space in the book. In rare cases, even this was not enough, and listings include line-continuation markers (➡). Additionally, comments in the source code have often been removed from the listings when the code is described in the text. Code annotations accompany many of the listings, highlighting important concepts.

You can get executable snippets of code from the liveBook (online) version of this book at https://livebook.manning.com/book/terraform-in-depth. The complete code for the examples in the book is available for download from the Manning website at www.manning.com, and from GitHub at https://github.com/TerraformInDepth/.

liveBook discussion forum

Purchase of *Terraform in Depth* includes free access to liveBook, Manning's online reading platform. Using liveBook's exclusive discussion features, you can attach comments to the book globally or to specific sections or paragraphs. It's a snap to make notes for yourself, ask and answer technical questions, and receive help from the author and other users. To access the forum, go to https://livebook.manning.com/book/terraform-in-depth/discussion. You can also learn more about Manning's forums and the rules of conduct at https://livebook.manning.com/discussion.

Manning's commitment to our readers is to provide a venue where a meaningful dialogue between individual readers and between readers and the author can take place. It is not a commitment to any specific amount of participation on the part of the author, whose contribution to the forum remains voluntary (and unpaid). We suggest you try asking the author some challenging questions lest their interest stray! The forum and the archives of previous discussions will be accessible from the publisher's website for as long as the book is in print.

Other online resources

Terraform has a vibrant developer community that users can take advantage of to learn more:

- Terraform Official Documentation is a great reference guide to parts of the language: https://developer.hashicorp.com/terraform/docs

- Terraform Internal Documentation is useful if you want to see how Terraform works: https://developer.hashicorp.com/terraform/internals
- OpenTofu has its own documentation, which continues to expand as the project grows: https://opentofu.org/docs/
- Terraform Reddit Community is a great place to ask questions and get support: https://reddit.com/r/terraform/
- Terraform Provider Registry has documentation for every registered provider: https://registry.terraform.io/

about the author

ROBERT HAFNER has spent the last two decades managing infrastructure, security, and architecture for companies ranging from pre-Series A startups all the way to Fortune 30 companies. He is also heavily involved in the open source community, including work on standards groups and steering committees. When he's not working with computers, he's creating resin art or trying something new in the kitchen. He lives in Chicago with his amazing wife, two cats, and one really awkward puppy.

about the cover illustration

The figure on the cover of *Terraform in Depth*, captioned "La Maitresse de Maison de Sante," or "The Health House Mistress," is taken from a book by Louis Curmer, published in 1841. Each illustration is finely drawn and colored by hand.

In those days, it was easy to identify where people lived and what their trade or station in life was just by their dress. Manning celebrates the inventiveness and initiative of the computer business with book covers based on the rich diversity of regional culture centuries ago, brought back to life by pictures from collections such as this one.

Part 1

Getting started with Terraform

This part of the book focuses on the core language itself to build the foundation in Terraform that you need to create and manage infrastructure:

- In chapter 1, we discuss some of the history and high-level concepts of Terraform and OpenTofu.
- Chapter 2 will break down the HashiCorp Configuration Language and how it maps to infrastructure when used with Terraform.
- Chapter 3 focuses on writing reusable components with modules and variables.
- Chapter 4 will help you expand your capabilities by introducing functions and logic, allowing you to create more flexible modules.
- Chapter 5 breaks down the plan and apply process, including diving into the theory behind planning to enable easier debugging.

By the time you complete this portion of the book, you'll have a firm understanding of the Terraform language and will be able to use Terraform to manage your infrastructure.

A brief overview of Terraform

This chapter covers

- Infrastructure as code
- Basic Terraform components
- Declarative languages and graphs
- The Terraform deployment workflow
- The relationship between Terraform and OpenTofu

The first time I set up an Amazon Web Services (AWS) virtual private cloud (VPC; the abstraction AWS uses to isolate networks), it was done by hand, and it took me several days. Even after I gained experience with the system, it still took several hours to manually create and configure a VPC that followed the suggested best practices.

When I first discovered Terraform, I attempted to build a VPC again. Terraform was the first infrastructure as code tool I had used: Terraform promised to let me define infrastructure, such as VPCs, using a simple programming language and then let Terraform handle creating the infrastructure itself. Instead of creating it manually, I wrote code using the Terraform language to describe my VPC and all of the components that it needed.

3

When I first ran the code, I was blown away. Terraform launched over 70 resources needed to create that highly available VPC structure, and it did it in about a minute. From then on, whenever I needed a VPC, it was a simple matter of reusing that code. A task that previously took hours was now an afterthought. Just as importantly, that task was suddenly easy.

This had a huge and immediate benefit. Developers who had no understanding of networking were able to spin up VPCs on their own. Infrastructure turned into a series of building blocks that we could reuse over and over again for completely different systems. Even the quality of these systems improved, as one project making an improvement to the building blocks would cascade out to other projects using it. If someone needed a new feature for the VPC module, that feature became available to every project in the company.

Terraform also led another huge culture shift at the companies I've worked at. Once Terraform is introduced, systems become reproducible. That is to say, if you build out a platform with Terraform, it is really easy to spin up another copy of it. Instead of having a single test environment for our products, each developer could spin up environments whenever they wanted. Developers could work on new features while having the entire real system there while working on new features. If someone wanted to experiment with changes, it was easy for them to apply those changes to their own environment and iterate on them at will.

The goal of this book is to help you learn how to use Terraform so you can bring these benefits to your projects. We're going to start with the basics so you can reap the benefits immediately and then expand on that knowledge with more advanced topics. This book will also include support and examples of OpenTofu, the open source fork of Terraform, and we'll explain the history of that fork later in this chapter.

1.1 Infrastructure as code

Infrastructure as code (IaC) is a class of technology that allows developers to provision infrastructure using coding practices. Terraform is not the only IaC tool. Pulumi is another vendor-agnostic framework, while AWS CloudFormation and GCP Deployment Manager are vendor-specific solutions. That said, Terraform is considered to be the standard when it comes to IaC, as it is one of the most mature projects with the most coverage. Unlike vendor-specific systems, such as CloudFormation, Terraform isn't restricted to just working with a single vendor. Terraform also uses a custom declarative language that makes it much easier to use than other frameworks.

IaC is a natural evolution of how systems get managed. There was a time individual machines would be individually configured for their job. System admins would share scripts or tutorials but mostly worked with machines directly. As cloud computing became more popular, this simply did not scale. Configuration management tools such as Puppet and Chef were developed to configure large groups of machines, while tools such as Packer were created to build golden images of machines for reuse. IaC frameworks take the next step and allow for entire platforms to be codified and repeatedly deployed.

1.1.1 Software development practices with IaC

A huge part of the appeal of IaC is that many of the tools and practices that have been developed over the years for software development can be directly applied to infrastructure. IaC can be versioned with Git, scanned with linters for quality control and security, and automatically tested using speciality continuous integration and deployment (CI/CD) pipelines. Even more than that, teams can apply the principles and practices developed for software engineering directly to infrastructure.

This has benefits everywhere in the stack. The use of a version control system (VCS) such as Git alongside a modern VCS host such as GitHub or GitLab adds numerous benefits, such as audit trails, versioning, automated workflows, and the ability for multiple people to work on the same project without stepping on each other's toes. Branches can be created to test new features, while pull requests can require reviews from different teams and passing tests.

This all adds up to improved quality, particularly for more complex systems. When done right, this also means the ability to develop faster and with higher confidence even as system complexity grows.

1.1.2 Repeatability and shareability

Software allows for repeatability. If you write a program, you can run that program over and over again. Bringing this repeatability to the infrastructure world allows developers to create building blocks that can be used repeatedly across their codebase and even across projects. Terraform does this using modules (which we'll discuss in chapter 3).

In general, configuring a piece of infrastructure—whether it's a VPC (a common component provided by cloud vendors such as GCP and AWS), an autoscaling group, or an orchestration system such as Kubernetes—takes research and work. It also tends to take a lot of time to do manually. Wrapping that knowledge into a reproducible piece of software allows others to take advantage of and build on that work without needing to reproduce that labor. The reusable modules can also be improved over time, which allows those improvements to get pushed out across the stack.

As an example, a company can create a VPC module that gets shared across multiple teams. Over time, they may add more functionality, such as the use of VPC endpoints or increased security monitoring. Terraform and other IaC frameworks allow those improvements to spread across the organization in the same way that software engineers upgrade the libraries they use for development.

1.1.3 Continuous integration and deployment

An important part of software is integrating and deploying changes. Working with IaC is no exception.

There are even CI/CD platforms that are built specifically for running Terraform. These Terraform-specific systems have gotten so popular that they even now have their own name: TACOS (for Terraform Automation and Collaboration Software). HashiCorp, the maker of Terraform, runs a solution called HCP Terraform that works as a software as a service (SaaS) and a self-hosted version called Terraform Enterprise.

There are also third-party vendors like Spacelift and Scalr, which run their own systems. Each of these platforms provides integration with GitHub and GitLab. This allows them to automatically publish modules from Git tags, run speculative plans to see what would happen if the code changes in a pull request were run, and even manage the deployment of changes as they are merged in.

It's common to use both a specialty system such as Terraform Cloud as well as a more traditional CI/CD system (such as GitHub Actions, CircleCI, or Jenkins). The more general systems have the advantage of being more flexible in the types of jobs they can run. This lets developers add jobs for testing, formatting, linting, and more while keeping the results alongside the results for other projects that make up their platform.

Continuous integration and deployment is one of the most important topics in Terraform; chapter 7 is devoted to the topic.

1.2 Terraform overview

Terraform exists to create and manage infrastructure. One of the major reasons it is so powerful is that it provides a single unified interface to thousands of different vendors and software systems. It doesn't matter if you're creating files on a local system, launching machines into the cloud, editing domain name system (DNS) records, or even ordering a pizza. When you use Terraform, there is only one language you need to know.

Terraform accomplishes this by abstracting all of the system-specific components into providers. As shown in figure 1.1, each vendor has their own resources and APIs, but all of that is wrapped up behind the provider where the developer doesn't need to worry about it. Instead, the Terraform core [which lives in the Terraform command-line interface (CLI)] translates between the Terraform language that the developers have written to launch their systems and the underlying providers, and the providers then handle communication back to their vendor systems.

This breakdown of components is powerful. The provider system lets vendors and community members develop their own Terraform interfaces, which can be updated and released independently of Terraform. There are currently more than 3,280 providers in the Terraform Provider Registry (https://registry.terraform.io/browse/providers) that can all be used by developers.

Terraform takes this approach in other areas as well. Terraform has a concept of state, which is a collection of metadata about the resources it manages. Every deployment has its own state. To manage that, Terraform has backends, which tell Terraform where to store the state. Backends are capable of storing multiple deployments, which Terraform breaks up into workspaces. If you were to think about Terraform as a desktop program, like a word processor, then your backends would be like your filesystem and each workspace would be a different file you saved there.

1.2.1 Terraform language

One of the things that makes Terraform particularly unique amongst IaC frameworks is its use of the HashiCorp Configuration Language (HCL). HCL is designed to be easily readable, even by people who may not be well-versed in the language. HCL is also a

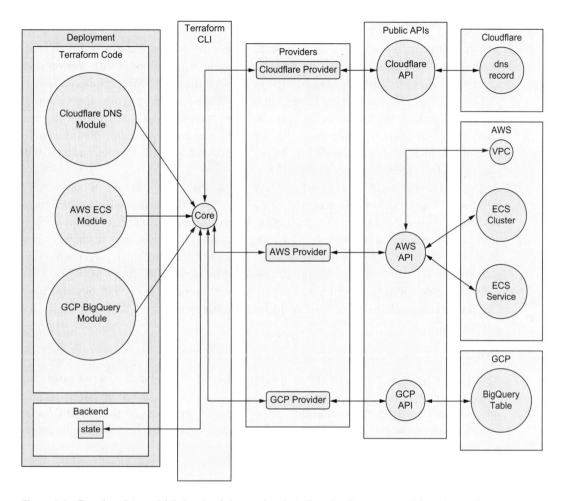

Figure 1.1 Terraform has multiple levels of abstraction that allow developers to get things done without worrying about vendor-specific minutiae.

declarative language, which means that developers define their ideal end state rather than the steps needed to get there.

Other IaC frameworks tend to either use existing imperative languages or try to build on top of data only languages like YAML. Using a data-only language such as YAML has many limitations that are often addressed by using interpolation schemes that work against readability.

HCL was created by HashiCorp and is used by multiple products: Packer, Nomad, and Consul all use HCL. Each HashiCorp project that uses HCL exposes its own resources and functions inside of HCL, with other subtle differences such as how they structure resources. This book focuses on the Terraform flavor of HCL, but once you understand the syntax, it should be easy to jump between HCL flavors. Unless otherwise mentioned, this book uses Terraform HCL in all examples.

1.2.2   *Terraform CLI and core*

The Terraform CLI is the primary way that Terraform projects are run and managed. It contains the engine that bridges the HCL written by developers with the vendor-specific libraries and APIs that are needed to manage the underlying resources.

The CLI is used to create new infrastructure, update it, destroy it, and apply manual changes. The CLI has features that make it easier to run with CI/CD platforms, and many such platforms are built around it. The CLI also has commands meant to help developers, such as a built-in code formatting system and a system for generating visualizations of Terraform-managed infrastructure.

The CLI is very heavily entwined with Terraform itself. The Terraform core is built into the CLI and can only be accessed by the CLI. CI/CD systems that run Terraform (which we'll discuss in chapter 8), such as HCP Terraform or Spacelift, are built around either the Terraform or OpenTofu CLI and call it directly. This differs from other languages like Go or C where you can compile code, but it is similar to interpreted languages such as Python or Node where you need a tool to run the programs.

For most developers, the CLI is going to be used extensively even if they also have CI/CD systems available. This book includes examples using the CLI as new topics are introduced.

1.2.3   *Providers*

A provider is a plugin for Terraform that supplies a collection of data sources, resources (both of which we'll discuss in detail in the next chapter), and functions for managing infrastructure with a particular vendor. These are often wrappers around an API. Some providers are managed directly by HashiCorp while others are released by their specific vendors (see figure 1.2).

Providers are generally written in Go (the same language Terraform is written in) and communicate with Terraform over gRPC (a high-performance remote procedure call framework). They act as an interface between Terraform and the vendor systems the developer is trying to work with. In theory, providers can be written in other languages as long as they implement the appropriate gRPC interfaces, but, in practice, there are only a few very experimental examples out there and none that are production ready.

Don't worry if you've never used gRPC. It is not something you need to know to work with Terraform unless you're making your own custom provider and even then you'll mostly be working with the existing Terraform libraries that work with gRPC. Since most vendors create and manage their own providers, the vast majority of Terraform users will never need to create one on their own (although if you need to, we discuss how in chapter 12).

Figure 1.2   Vendor abstraction in Terraform using providers

Providers tend to have a one-to-one relationship with a vendor or platform. If you want to interact with AWS, then you use the AWS provider. GCP also has a provider, while Azure has released multiple providers to cover their products. Just like when using third-party libraries in another programming language, providers will have their own nomenclature, style, and documentation.

1.2.4 Vendors

The whole purpose of Terraform is to manage infrastructure. Terraform itself is vendor agnostic. It doesn't care what kind of infrastructure it manages, as long as it has a provider that exposes it. Each vendor has its own API, resources, and methodology of working that has to be abstracted behind the provider. There are vendors for just about anything you can think of:

- Cloud service providers
- DNS providers
- Data analytics
- Virtual machine hosts
- Git repositories
- Authentication systems

There are even providers for pizza delivery (https://mng.bz/BXDq) and another that gives read-only access to which McDonald's ice cream machines are currently broken (https://mng.bz/dXPz) Terraform is an extremely well-adopted platform, and as a result, most vendors maintain fairly up-to-date providers.

1.2.5 Backends

Backends are used to customize where a workspace stores its state files. By default, a workspace uses the local backend, which means that if you run a workspace locally with no other changes, then the state files will be stored directly on your local filesystem. This is great for testing, but it means that the only way your workspace can be acted on is from your computer, which really doesn't scale to teams.

Backends solve that problem by allowing the state to be stored in another location. There are backends for the object storage systems for the major cloud vendors (AzureRM, GCS, S3, etc.), for open source databases, and even an HTTP one that can be used to create simple custom services. Some backends (the remote and cloud backends) go further than that and expose APIs that Terraform can use to run special operations.

When using a backend other than local, it is much easier to work as a team. In chapter 6, we'll discuss the different types of backends and their benefits.

1.2.6 Workspaces

A Terraform workspace represents a deployment of a Terraform code base with a specific backend and set of input variables. When comparing Terraform to other software development projects, a workspace can be compared to a specific installation of a program—like other software, you can have as many installations as you want, and each installation is completely independent of the others with its own configuration and saved data.

Every Terraform workspace includes the code base, the configuration for the specific workspace, and a list of all resources currently created in the workspace (this list is known as the state and will be discussed further in chapter 4). Once code has been written, a Terraform workspace can be initialized from that code. Once configured and initialized, the infrastructure from that code can be created, updated, and destroyed.

A Terraform code base can have an unlimited number of deployments. If each of these deployments was using the same backend, then each deployment would be given its own location in that backend. It's very common to have production, staging, and ephemeral feature deployments all sharing a common backend. Some deployments are long-lasting while others may exist for only as long as a feature is being developed. Developers working on Terraform projects will often have a local workspace they use so they can iterate quickly, with their local filesystem as the backend.

1.3   Declarative languages

Terraform uses a declarative language to codify infrastructure. Declarative languages are a class of language where the developer defines how something should look after the code has been run. With a declarative language, the focus is on defining the end state, and then the engine running the language creates a plan of actions to bring the system to the desired end state.

Declarative languages create their plans using a computer science concept called directed acyclic graphs (DAGs), which in this context are basically a list of actions that have to be completed in a specific order. Terraform refers to these as `plans`. We'll discuss DAGs in more depth in chapter 5 when we discuss how to debug problems with Terraform plans.

Declarative languages tend to be more popular among configuration management and IaC frameworks. Terraform HCL, the Kubernetes YAML language, Cloud-Formation's YAML, and Puppet's DSL are all examples of declarative languages.

1.3.1   Declarative vs. imperative languages

Most developers are familiar with imperative languages. When using languages such as Javascript and Bash, the developer uses statements to explicitly change the state of the system. Imperative languages describe how to do something, while declarative languages describe what the outcome should be. Declarative languages focus on the outcome rather than the steps to get to that outcome and are very different from imperative languages.

One way to think about this is that declarative languages primarily use nouns and adjectives, while imperative languages primarily use verbs. With Terraform, you will never say "Check if this machine exists, create the machine if it does not exist, and then apply this configuration." Instead, you will describe the machine that you want and Terraform itself will translate that into actions that result in that machine being created.

In the context of infrastructure, this is extremely powerful. It removes the need to write migrations, allowing developers to focus on what they want the end state to be. When you combine this with versioning, it allows the ability to move back and forth between different versions without having to create specific code paths between them.

1.3.2 Dependency resolution

Modern software systems include a lot of infrastructure. Even a basic web application often has an application, filesystem, database, cache, and DNS record. These components have relationships between them. The application has to read from the database and cache while the DNS record needs to know where the application's host is. Declarative languages make it easier to define these relationships between components, often to the point where they can automatically infer that relationship without the developer having to explicitly define it, as shown in figure 1.3.

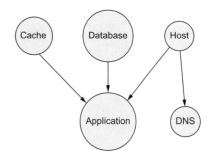

Figure 1.3 A diagram showing the relationship between the components in a web application

This relationship exists regardless of the tool being used to launch the infrastructure. The application needs to know where the database is and what credentials to use or it cannot access the database, which means that the database has to launch first. The relationship between these resources is defined through configuration. The application has to be configured with the credentials that come from the database. The DNS record has to be configured from the IP address that comes from the host.

Declarative languages such as Terraform are built around defining these relationships. When a developer defines resources and runs an IaC tool such as Terraform, the tool converts its code into the actions needed to create its infrastructure in the proper order. It sees where the developer used values from one resource to configure another resource and uses that to figure out what the relationships should look like. This gives Terraform the ability to create resources in the proper order without the developer having to explicitly define that order. The developer of the web application doesn't have to say "deploy the database before the application"—once the developer says that the application is using a value from the database, that relationship is already defined.

1.3.3 Pitfalls of declarative languages

While there are many benefits of declarative languages, there are also pitfalls. The biggest problem most developers will run into is that declarative languages cannot easily define systems that have a circular dependency between resources.

A circular dependency is a type of relationship where a chain of resources creates a cycle in the graph, as shown in figure 1.4:

- Resource 2 needs resource 4 to launch.

- Resource 4 needs resource 3 to launch.
- Resource 3 needs resource 2 to launch.

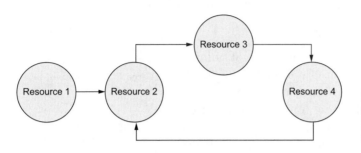

Figure 1.4   An example of a circular dependency in which resources are dependent on one another

All three of these resources end up waiting on the other, and so none of them can launch. Systems such as Terraform cannot create resources that are part of a circular dependency without some sort of manual workaround.

In general, circular dependencies are frowned upon with distributed systems, but there are scenarios where they can come up. In chapter 5, we'll discuss some tools that Terraform has to resolve situations where circular dependencies can not be helped.

1.4   *Terraform deployment flow*

There is a flow to how deploying with Terraform works. As shown in figure 1.5, a change is desired, a workspace is initialized, a plan is created, changes are reviewed, and then if the change passes review, it is applied. The init, plan, and apply phases are all initiated by the Terraform CLI, although there is commonly a CI/CD system actually calling the CLI rather than a person manually doing it.

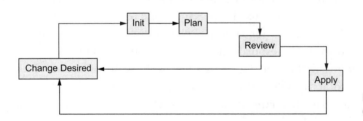

Figure 1.5   The Terraform development flow

1.4.1   *Change desired*

At some point, someone will want to change their system. You might have a new project where the change is simply creating the initial infrastructure, or it may be that new features need to be added, bugs fixed, and dependencies updated on an existing project.

Regardless of what the change is, it needs to be programmed. Depending on the size of that change, it may require some research into the underlying systems as well as experimentation by the developer. Just like any software project, the actual workflow for this phase can vary quite a bit between companies and teams.

A really simple change could be adding a new compute instance to an existing environment. This would mean adding a single Terraform resource (which we'll address in the next chapter) that represents an Elastic Cloud Computing (EC2) instance. Other changes are more complex and might require removing and replacing a resource, while others are simpler and might simply change a few attributes while leaving the resource in place. One of the things that makes Terraform so powerful is its ability to distinguish between these different cases to make the right decision.

1.4.2 *Init*

Once the change is written it is time to run Terraform. The first part of running is the init phase. During the init phase, Terraform downloads any modules or providers that are defined in the job and prepares the local system for development. The modules and providers are downloaded from either the public Terraform registry or, if configured, from a private registry.

The first thing running `terraform init` does is initialize the backend (we'll get into different state backends in a later chapter, but for now, just know that we're following a common development practice using the default local backend to store state). Once the backend is initialized, the `init` command then installs the needed providers. If we were using any modules, these would also be installed here.

In the case of adding a new EC2 instance, we only see the AWS provider being added.

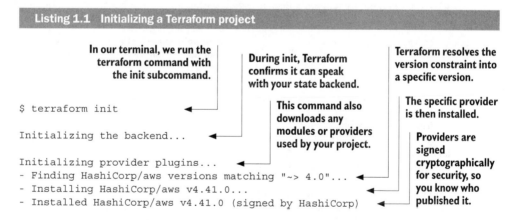

Listing 1.1 Initializing a Terraform project

```
$ terraform init

Initializing the backend...

Initializing provider plugins...
- Finding HashiCorp/aws versions matching "~> 4.0"...
- Installing HashiCorp/aws v4.41.0...
- Installed HashiCorp/aws v4.41.0 (signed by HashiCorp)

Terraform has created a lock file .terraform.lock.hcl to record the provider
selections it made above. Include this file in your version control
repository so that Terraform can guarantee to make the same selections by
default when you run "terraform init" in the future.

Terraform has been successfully initialized!

You may now begin working with Terraform. Try running "terraform plan" to
see any changes that are required for your infrastructure. All Terraform
commands should now work.
```

If you ever set or change modules or backend configuration for Terraform, rerun this command to reinitialize your working directory. If you forget, other commands will detect it and remind you to do so if necessary.

1.4.3 Plan

The Terraform plan is both an action and an output—you run the `terraform plan` command and it calculates a plan that can be used during the apply phase. The planning process itself has three subphases:

- *Refresh*—Terraform reads the real state of the infrastructure directly from the vendor, as well as any data sources that exist in the code, to identify anything that may have changed since the last time Terraform ran.
- *Compare*—Terraform compares the state from the previous step to what it thinks should exist based on the code.
- *Plan*—Terraform creates a DAG of actions to take to bring the infrastructure in line with what the code expects.

In our example of adding a new instance, we can see our code looking up some information from AWS and then presenting the proposed change. This matches up with our expectations—we wanted to add a single instance and the plan shows that Terraform has noticed this change and has scheduled one `create` action in its plan to create the `hello_world aws_instance`.

Listing 1.2 Using Terraform to plan changes

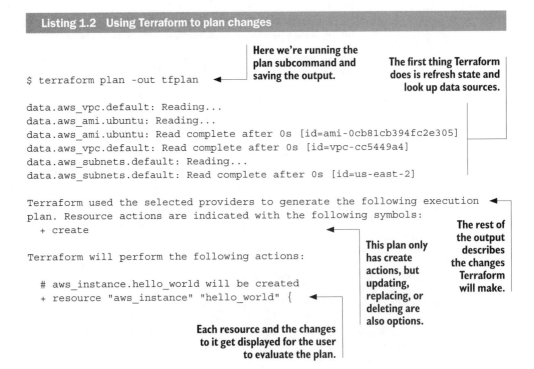

```
$ terraform plan -out tfplan

data.aws_vpc.default: Reading...
data.aws_ami.ubuntu: Reading...
data.aws_ami.ubuntu: Read complete after 0s [id=ami-0cb81cb394fc2e305]
data.aws_vpc.default: Read complete after 0s [id=vpc-cc5449a4]
data.aws_subnets.default: Reading...
data.aws_subnets.default: Read complete after 0s [id=us-east-2]

Terraform used the selected providers to generate the following execution
plan. Resource actions are indicated with the following symbols:
  + create

Terraform will perform the following actions:

  # aws_instance.hello_world will be created
  + resource "aws_instance" "hello_world" {
```

Here we're running the plan subcommand and saving the output.

The first thing Terraform does is refresh state and look up data sources.

The rest of the output describes the changes Terraform will make.

This plan only has create actions, but updating, replacing, or deleting are also options.

Each resource and the changes to it get displayed for the user to evaluate the plan.

```
    + ami                                        = "ami-0cb81cb394fc2e305"
    + arn                                        = (known after apply)        ◄───────┐
    + get_password_data                          = false                              │
    + host_id                                    = (known after apply)                │
    + host_resource_group_arn                    = (known after apply)                │
    + id                                         = (known after apply)                │
    + instance_initiated_shutdown_behavior       = (known after apply)                │
    + instance_state                             = (known after apply)                │
    + instance_type                              = "t3.micro"                         │
## "known after apply" attributes truncated ##                                       │
    + source_dest_check                          = true                               │
    + subnet_id                                  = "subnet-b96b6ed1"                  │
## "known after apply" attributes truncated ##                                       │
    + tags                                       = {                                  │
        + "CreatedBy" = "terraform"                                                   │
      }                                                                               │
    + tags_all                                   = {                                  │
        + "CreatedBy" = "terraform"                                                   │
      }                                                                               │
  }
```

Some fields will only be available after they're created.

At the end of the plan there's a brief summary.

```
Plan: 1 to add, 0 to change, 0 to destroy.    ◄────┐  ┐
```

If any outputs are changed they are listed here.

```
Changes to Outputs:                           ◄────┤
  + aws_instance_arn = (known after apply)     ◄────┘
```

The new value of the output will not be known until after the apply.

Once complete, a plan is created: it is either saved to a file, discarded, or automatically applied if run as part of an `apply` command.

It was mentioned earlier that plans were DAGs, which are just a fancy way of saying that plans have a lot of resources that are dependent on each other. Using the Terraform graph command, you can output graph files that can be converted by tools like GraphViz into visual representations of those resources. Figure 1.6 shows the direct output from Terraform of the plan for the project we're building. It describes the same thing as our `terraform plan` command from earlier but uses graphics instead of text. The `data.aws_subnet_ids` that appears here in the graphic is the same as the one that shows in the plan creation.

1.4.4 Apply

During the apply phase, the Terraform engine runs through all of the actions created during the plan phase. This means creating, deleting, and updating resources in the order that the plan defined. In the apply phase, we supply the plan file we created in the previous section—if no file is provided, then Terraform will create a plan beginning the apply.

Our desired change is only a single resource, so the apply phase is pretty short.

Listing 1.3   Changing infrastructure with `terraform apply`

```
$ terraform apply tfplan      ◄──────
```

Here we run the apply subcommand while passing through the plan file we created earlier.

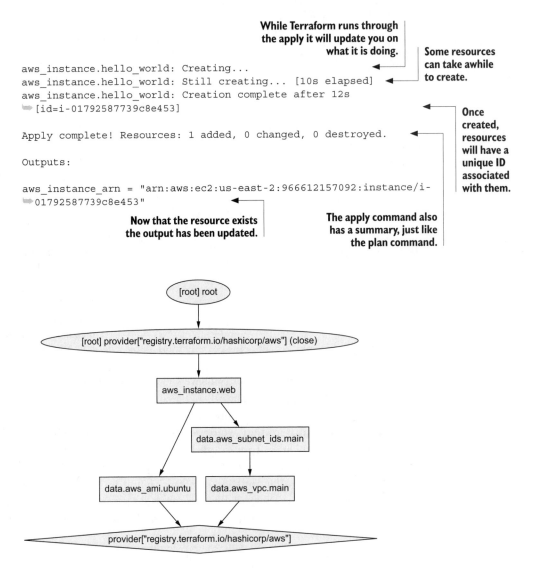

```
aws_instance.hello_world: Creating...
aws_instance.hello_world: Still creating... [10s elapsed]
aws_instance.hello_world: Creation complete after 12s
➥ [id=i-01792587739c8e453]

Apply complete! Resources: 1 added, 0 changed, 0 destroyed.

Outputs:

aws_instance_arn = "arn:aws:ec2:us-east-2:966612157092:instance/i-
➥ 01792587739c8e453"
```

While Terraform runs through the apply it will update you on what it is doing.

Some resources can take awhile to create.

Once created, resources will have a unique ID associated with them.

The apply command also has a summary, just like the plan command.

Now that the resource exists the output has been updated.

Figure 1.6   A graph of the Terraform plan. This graph was directly generated by Terraform using the `terraform graph` command.

Our apply has succeeded and the new instance is launched! You can see the ID of the instance in the `creation complete` message, and since this code defines it as an output, you can see it in the outputs section. The total time to create the instance was 12 seconds.

This process can take some time depending on the resources. Terraform attempts to speed things up by running as many concurrent operations as it possibly can. Regardless, it is almost always faster to launch infrastructure from Terraform than it is to do manually, as the delays that Terraform faces are typically on the vendor side while resources are being provisioned.

Once complete, Terraform displays a status message to let you know how many resources were created, updated, or destroyed as well as any errors that occurred. In the next chapter, we'll go into detail on how to define those resources using the Terraform language.

1.5 What are people using this for?

Terraform is an awesome tool, but what exactly are people doing with it? The thing that makes this question somewhat difficult is that it can really be used for just about anything. In the last few years, I've seen several amazing use cases.

1.5.1 Machine learning training

Machine learning is all the rage right now, but it is extremely expensive to train a model. A common way companies manage this is by renting equipment from cloud providers such as Google, Azure, and AWS. This allows researchers to save money by only using the equipment when they need it.

Training machine learning models normally involves building a cluster. This means creating networking, defining templates for the machines, providing a high-performance filesystem, and finally providing a way to save the models in a high-reliability storage system. Giving the nodes access to the filesystem and storage system means creating and assigning permissions. To take advantage of autoscaling, the number of jobs running needs to be managed as well, which adds in the requirement for a redis cluster and a lambda function to trigger the autoscaling.

This is all super-complicated, right? For most teams, this is a project that can easily take several weeks. Terraform provides two distinct benefits for a project like this:

- The Terraform code itself can be used to collaborate and build out the design of the cluster, allowing for simple components at the start and iterative improvement over time. Maybe the cluster first gets created without autoscaling, and that gets added on later.
- By utilizing Terraform, teams can launch multiple clusters and take them down, all in moments, as shown in figure 1.7. If a team has custom needs, then it's a matter of modifying an existing system, not creating something from scratch.

1.5.2 API and web services

Another extremely common pattern is hosting web applications or APIs, particularly when you want them to scale. Your standard web application tends to have a lot of the same parts: load balancers to direct traffic, a series of "tasks" or instances of your web application, SSL certificates for security, and DNS records to give your site an easy-to-use address. They also often have a caching layer and database.

These components are also built on top of network layers. As you can see in figure 1.8, that means creating subnets, making sure private subnets have internet access and a variety of other smaller components.

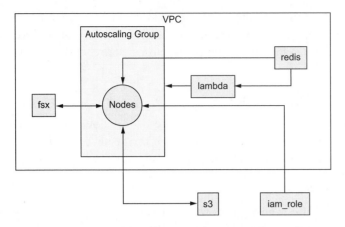

Figure 1.7   An example machine learning training cluster

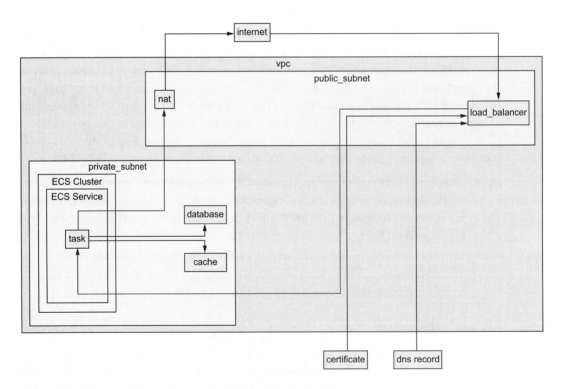

Figure 1.8   Components that are common when deploying web services

By placing all of this in a Terraform module, it makes it very easy for developers to launch their services without having to think about these components. From their perspective, they really only need to worry about their code, and the module takes care of the rest. Although building out a module like this takes some effort, once it's built it can be expanded for more use cases and advanced features that can then be rolled out to everyone using it.

1.5.3 Single sign-on authentication structure

In a very different direction, I've also seen Terraform used to manage large single sign-on systems such as Okta using Terraform. These systems can get pretty complex, with groups, users, applications, policies, roles, and more, as shown in figure 1.9.

Placing these systems into Terraform can make it easier to see and manage permissions, especially in larger organizations. Enforcing the use of Terraform allows for stronger security controls, as it's easier to enforce policies such as multiple people signing off on a change, while also creating a natural audit trail through source control.

Figure 1.9 Single sign-on system resources

1.5.4 Rapid prototyping

This final item isn't about a specific system but about capabilities. I've spent a lot of time working in startups, and one of the things that really made a difference was the ability to experiment and innovate on ideas. Using Terraform allows teams to do that by abstracting away the minutiae of the infrastructure itself.

Think about it in terms of hackathons or other quick projects. If a developer has to spend a day putting an environment together and half a day understanding the different parameters around launching a queuing system and then needs to figure out data storage, then they've already spent a significant amount of time just on the overhead for a project. By comparison, if they start with reusable Terraform modules written and maintained by experts in those systems, then the infrastructure component becomes a tool they can quickly utilize while they focus on their main goals.

Over the course of this book, it is my goal to give you the tools to use Terraform and make this a reality. Over the next few chapters, we discuss the foundational components of Terraform. After that, we expand into more advanced topics, such as making reusable modules and building out CI/CD pipelines. By the end of this book, you should have a solid grasp not only of Terraform itself but of how to utilize it to improve the quality and reliability of your projects and teams.

1.6 Terraform and OpenTofu

In late 2023, the makers of Terraform, HashiCorp, announced that they were changing the license of Terraform and several other tools that they had previously released as open source. This means that versions beyond Terraform starting with version 1.6 are no longer open source but instead use a custom proprietary license. To say that this has caused a stir in the community would be an understatement, and it did not take long before a group of companies came together and forked Terraform into a new open source project named OpenTofu.

1.6.1 HashiCorp's history with open source

Terraform started as an open source project released under the Mozilla Public License (MPL). When companies and developers release software under an open source license, they give the users of the project a variety of rights, such as the ability to view and modify the source code, to release their own versions of the software, and to choose which systems they can run the software on.

Open sourcing software has some major benefits. Since projects that are open source are typically freely available, people are able to try it out themselves without an upfront cost. Other open source developers and companies are also more likely to build tools around open source projects than they are around proprietary projects. With Terraform, this meant a large community of developers building providers, documentation tools, testing frameworks, and modules. It also meant that other companies were incorporating Terraform into their own products. Terraform was not the only open source project at HashiCorp. HashiCorp has products like Vault and Consul that other companies have also built their own products around.

Over the last few years, there seemed to be a new trend with how HashiCorp was looking at some of their open source projects and instead focusing on internal development and new products. This escalated in 2021 when it updated its contributor documentation (https://mng.bz/rKBE) on GitHub to make it clear that it was not reviewing any external pull request to the Terraform project.

In addition to this, many community-requested features were ignored, even if they were fully implemented and tested by third parties. Over time, this discouraged further contributions, as many in the community felt that the open source practices that Terraform started with were no longer as high of a priority to the company.

1.6.2 HashiCorp license changes

In 2023, HashiCorp announced that it was going to stop releasing open source versions of many of its projects starting in 2024 and would instead be releasing the code under the Business Source License (BSL). These projects included not just Terraform but also Nomad, Consul, Vault, and several other HashiCorp projects. Other projects, such as the Terraform providers themselves and many individual libraries that HashiCorp has released over the years, have remained open source under the MPL license.

The BSL is what's known as a shared source license. This means that the source code is still publicly available for review and audit. Unlike open source software, BSL software has additional limitations that are designed to give the owner of the software monopoly power over it. The BSL still allows individuals, and even companies, to use the software, but it restricts the ability to build products on top of it without getting a special license from HashiCorp.

HashiCorp has said that this license change will prevent competitive services from being built on its products, which in turn will help it build better products. The new license is pretty clear about this, as it grants permission to everyone to use Terraform in production "provided such use does not include offering the licensed work to third parties on a hosted or embedded basis which is competitive with HashiCorp's products."

1.6.3 Community reactions

Once it was officially announced, the license change sparked conversation and debate throughout the technology world. Conversations (and arguments) on Reddit, Hacker News, and even LinkedIn over the implications and ethics of the decision by HashiCorp were commonplace and are still ongoing.

The open source community itself was rather vocal about the changes. Many people claimed that Terraform, as well as the other HashiCorp products, would never have gained the popularity they did without the initial support from the open source community. Terraform, even more so than the other HashiCorp products, also depends on third parties to build out the providers that make Terraform valuable. Additionally, groups like Gruntworks have been filling the gaps around Terraform by building out testing frameworks and other tools. For many, the license changes felt like a rug pull.

On the Terraform side of things, the biggest groups that were affected were the companies that made products that were built on the formerly open source project, as well as their customers. There are many third-party products that interact with the Terraform program, from private module registries to full-blown continuous deployment platforms.

The end result of this was a manifesto, published in August 2023, asking HashiCorp to reconsider the change in license. That manifesto was signed by more than 150 companies, 11 software projects, and more than 750 individual software developers. This manifesto was not simply a request: it stated that if HashiCorp did not come to the table for discussion, then a new software project would be created to continue developing an open source version of Terraform.

1.6.4 OpenTofu fork

One of the major benefits of open source software is that any developer can take a piece of open source software and release their own version of it. This is referred to as forking the project. There are a lot of examples of this: MariaDB was created as a fork of MySQL, Jenkins was created as a fork of Hudson, and LibreOffice was created from OpenOffice.

OpenTofu was announced as a fork after HashiCorp did not respond to the manifesto, as shown in figure 1.10. The announcement had a lot of support behind it, with several companies (Scalr, env0, Spacelift, and Harness) announcing that they would cover a total of 18 dedicated developers to work on the new project for at least the next five years. Additionally, the supporters of open source projects based on Terraform, such as Gruntworks (which has created multiple tools we'll be talking about in this book, such as Terratest and Terragrunt) have committed to supporting the new project.

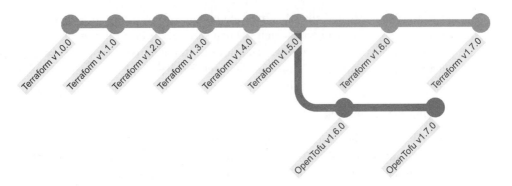

Figure 1.10   Terraform and OpenTofu forking development

OpenTofu has also embraced both open source and transparency. The project has been accepted into the Linux Foundation and is working toward joining the Cloud Native Computing Foundation. By placing the project inside of a foundation, they ensure that it isn't subject to the whims of a single company. As part of its goals around transparency and openness, the OpenTofu project has a public request for comment (essentially a feature proposal system) process that allows developers to submit their own ideas for development.

1.6.5   *OpenTofu and Terraform compatibility*

Of course not everything about forking a project is positive. One of the biggest concerns that many people have is whether their code can be expected to work. If you write something for Terraform, how much attention are you going to have to pay to which program is actually running it?

So far, OpenTofu has remained compatible with code written in Terraform. However, OpenTofu is also starting to implement some long-requested features that the community has been requesting of Terraform for years. As a result of this, OpenTofu can be considered a superset of the Terraform language, with additional features added on top. This does make it easier to switch from Terraform to OpenTofu, but it may make the transition back from OpenTofu to Terraform more difficult if you've started using features that are not available in HashiCorp Terraform.

That being said, while OpenTofu has maintained compatibility with the Terraform language, it has done so at the cost of a slight delay in its releases. For OpenTofu to reimplement a feature that is added to Terraform, it needs to review and evaluate that feature, then come up with a plan to build it on its own. As a result, Terraform will often have new features that are not immediately available in OpenTofu.

1.6.6   *Using OpenTofu*

For the most part, OpenTofu is a drop-in replacement for Terraform. Once installed, the `tofu` CLI will be available on your system. The `tofu` CLI has all of the same commands as the `terraform` CLI, which means you can even create an alias from the `terraform` command to tofu and it should simply work.

One of the interesting repercussions of the license change is that many package managers (the tools used to install software) have stopped carrying new versions of Terraform that are not open source. If you are using Homebrew (a commonly used package manager for MacOS), you won't be able to get any version of Terraform beyond v1.5.7, and the same applies to many Linux distributions. OpenTofu, on the other hand, is supported by most open source package managers.

Every example in this book, unless explicitly stated, will work with both OpenTofu and Terraform. In the cases where there are differences, these will be called out and described. There are very few differences in the language itself between the two versions, but as we get into the latter chapters (particularly when it comes to the chapters on testing and CI/CD), we'll explore the implications and differences between the two versions.

Summary

- IaC allows software development best practices to be applied to infrastructure.
- Declarative languages focus on what the end results should look like and allows the underlying engine to figure out how to get there.
- Terraform is built on top of the HCL.
- Terraform plans are DAGs, which means that actions are done in a specific order and circular dependencies are not allowed.
- Terraform has a generic workflow—init, plan, apply—that developers will use when deploying changes.
- Terraform init is where Terraform downloads any needed providers or modules.
- Terraform plan is where Terraform compares the resources in the workspace with the desired set of resources and configuration in the code to create a plan for aligning the two.
- During the Terraform apply phase, Terraform runs the actions from the plan.
- HashiCorp is no longer releasing Terraform under an open source license, which has resulted in a new open source fork named OpenTofu being created.
- OpenTofu and Terraform are mostly interchangeable, and the differences between them will be called out in this book.

Terraform HCL
components

This chapter covers

- How to configure a workspace and its providers
- The basic syntax of `terraform` blocks
- How to look up data with data sources
- Managing infrastructure with `resource` blocks
- Changing the behavior of resources with meta arguments
- Using modules for reusable components

In the last chapter, we talked a bit about Terraform and declarative languages. Using Terraform's declarative language, you define how you want your systems to look, and then Terraform builds and updates your systems based on that language. One way to look at it is to compare it to construction: an architect creates a plan, and then a construction team builds it based on that plan. In this scenario, you're the systems architect and Terraform is your construction crew.

In this chapter, we talk about how to define those plans. Just like construction workers, Terraform has its own language that it reads and interprets to build things.

In this case, we're not creating buildings but rather systems of interconnected resources hosted by vendors such as cloud providers like AWS, GCP, or Azure. As the systems grow and evolve, the "blueprints" can be updated, which then allows Terraform to upgrade the running systems until they line up with those blueprints.

Defining infrastructure in the language of Terraform has many benefits besides simply letting Terraform know what to build. It provides a source of truth for design decisions and lets other developers see exactly what is being built. Even if they haven't worked with those components before, they can recognize what they are in the language of Terraform.

This chapter is focused on the basic components of the Terraform language, specifically the components that allow you to actually launch and update infrastructure. We're going to start with a basic example of a Terraform module that launches a single AWS instance. From there, we're going to break down the different components of the language, what they do, and how they interact with each other. This will be expanded on with more advanced features of the language in the next two chapters.

2.1 Hello World

Although the focus of this book is on Terraform, it is impossible to discuss Terraform without also discussing infrastructure and systems themselves. Terraform is a framework for manipulating infrastructure. As a developer using Terraform, you are going to use Terraform to convert your own infrastructure designs into code. You are the architect, taking the various components and tying them together into a system.

For our very first project, we're going to launch a virtual machine on AWS together. We'll start by diving right into a real Terraform project, and then the rest of the chapter will be spent going over the pieces of that program.

2.1.1 Research and design

Before beginning, we need to do some research. What infrastructure do we want to launch, and what does that depend on? There are a few places to start:

- The infrastructure we want to launch is an AWS instance (a virtual machine that runs in the AWS Cloud), so we can head over to the AWS website to get the documentation at the source.
- Most services have a web console that can be used to manually create the resources. This idea of manual creation, also known as ClickOps, doesn't scale to production but is great for learning.
- The Terraform provider documentation is an excellent place to learn about different systems as well. By looking up the AWS instance resource documentation (https://mng.bz/VVqr), we can see what parameters are available and exactly which are required.

Reading through the documentation, particularly the Terraform resource documentation, allows us to pinpoint the minimum requirements to get our instance launched:

- `ami`—This parameter is for the Amazon machine image. This is the template, including the operating `system`, that AWS uses when creating an instance.
- `instance_type`—This parameter tells AWS what kind of instance to run. AWS has hundreds of different instance types, with each type having a different number of CPUs, memory ranges, and additional features.
- `subnet_id`—This final parameter tells AWS what network to launch the instance in. It is not required to launch the instance, but if we don't provide it, then AWS will launch the instance in the default subnet, which may not be where we want it.

These three values are what we need to launch this instance, but where do they come from? In some cases, these values can be looked up dynamically using a pattern or parameters. It is extremely common to look up the Amazon Machine Image (AMI) value in this way. Other times the configuration comes from the users themselves, which is something we'll discuss in chapter 3.

2.1.2   *Creating the project*

In the next few sections, and throughout the book, we'll be running commands inside of a terminal. If you are using Windows, you may want to install the Windows subsystem for Linux (WSL), as many tools built for Terraform will work best inside of WSL.

The first thing we need to do is create our new project. In a terminal, we'll create a new folder and initialize a Git repository so we can save our changes as our code evolves. In the future, we'll talk about how to bootstrap your projects from existing templates, but for now, let's start with an empty Git repository to show how things are structured:

```
$ mkdir terraform_aws_modules
$ cd terraform_aws_modules
$ git init
```

Next, we're going to create a few Terraform files: `main.tf`, `lookups.tf`, and `providers.tf`. We can name these files whatever we want as long as they end with the `.tf` extension, which tells Terraform to read them when coming up with a plan. However, it's a good idea to name the files in a way that makes it clear what they contain, as it makes it easier for people to work with your code. Our provider file will contain the basic configuration for the provider we are going to use, such as what versions of the provider we want to use. We're going to put some data sources in the `lookups.tf` file to pull some configuration values into our code, and finally the bulk of our logic will go into our `main.tf` file. In our terminal, we can use the `touch` command to create all of our files, or you can create them using your favorite IDE:

```
$ touch {main,lookups,providers}.tf
```

If you're using Windows with Powershell, you should use the `new-item` command instead.

Now that we've created our Terraform files, we can start building out our program.

2.1.3 *Setup providers*

The first thing we need to do is tell Terraform what providers we want to use. Since this first project is meant to launch an AWS instance, we'll need to use the AWS provider to give Terraform access to the needed resources. To do that, we have to write our first piece of Terraform code.

We talked a bit in the last chapter about Terraform and the HashiCorp Configuration Language (HCL). Terraform HCL groups configuration together under `blocks`, and different block types are used to configure different things. Here we're going to use the `terraform` block, which is used to configure Terraform itself. This is similar to the `package.json` file used by many Javascript projects or the `projects.toml` file used by Python.

Just like those languages use their respective configuration files to define the dependencies they're using, we can use the `terraform` block to set our required dependencies. We're going to use a subblock named `required_providers` inside of the `terraform` block to tell Terraform that we want to install the AWS provider. We're also going to use the `provider` block to tell the AWS provider which AWS region we want to log into when creating our instance. We'll get into the differences between the `required_providers` and `provider` block later in the chapter, but the main thing to know is that the `required_providers` tells Terraform what it needs to install while the `provider` block is used to configure the provider itself.

Listing 2.1 Configuring required providers

```
terraform {                          ◀─── Terraform settings block
  required_providers {                    defines workspace settings.
    aws = {                          ◀─── This subblock tells
      source  = "hashicorp/aws"           Terraform which
      version = "~> 5.0"             ◀─── This project uses the    providers to install.
    }                                     AWS provider.
  }
}

provider "aws" {                     ◀─── Provider blocks are used
  region = "us-east-1"                    to configure providers.
}                                    ◀─── This is typically set as a
                                          variable, not hard coded.
```

The `required_providers` block can be skipped for providers in the HashiCorp namespace, as Terraform will automatically recognize that those resources are used and install the right provider. However, this is not considered a good practice. If you don't explicitly define your providers, you can't specify which versions to use, which could result in your code breaking.

Now that we've told Terraform to use the AWS provider (https://mng.bz/xKJq), we have access to all of our AWS resources and data sources.

2.1.4   *Getting our configuration values*

During our research, we learned that the AWS instance resource needs three parameters: an AMI, an instance type, and, optionally, a subnet.

The easiest of these is the instance type. For now, we're still in development, so we can hard code it to one of the cheaper instance families. The `t3.micro` instance type is a nice option because it is very low cost. In general, hardcoding is not a great practice, and in the next chapter, we'll introduce input variables that can be used to let developers define this value themselves.

The other two parameters are a bit more complicated. It's also important that we launch with the newest AMIs available, as newer machine images have bug fixes and security updates that are really important. For that reason, we really don't want to hardcode the AMI. One of the nice things about using infrastructure as code is that we can look these values up instead of hardcoding them, so we don't need to publish a new version of our code every time an update comes out.

Hardcoding the subnet is also problematic. If we hardcoded the subnet, we'd only be able to run this code in the account with that specific subnet, which means our code wouldn't be reusable. In general, we should always try to make our code portable.

Terraform provides a solution to these problems with data sources. These are special blocks that are used purely to look up data. They are read-only and can never actually make changes, but they can be used to perform lookups and expose data that can be reused in your program.

The first data source we're going to create is to look up our AMI. For that, we have the `aws_ami` data source. To use this, we have to set some parameters so it will look up the value we want:

- `owners` is a list of accounts we want to pull AMI images from. I'm personally partial to the Ubuntu operating system, so I looked up the ID of the Ubuntu publisher to use its public AMIs.
- `most_recent` tells the filter that we want the AMI that was most recently published. This will give us the latest bug fixes and security patches. Since we set this to `true`, it means that this data source will return a new AMI every time a new one is published.
- `filter` is a subblock; in this case, that means we can set multiple filters on the object. The first filter we're going to set tells the data source to only pull images that can be launched on the AWS EC2 infrastructure we're using. The second filter tells the data source to only pull images that match the name we're using, which tend to have publisher-specific formats.

The combination of all of these parameters gives us a single AMI that we can use to launch our instance.

We also need to look up our subnet ID. To look up the subnet ID, we can use the `aws_subnets` data source. For this, we end up in a little trouble though—to look up the subnet, we need to provide a virtual private cloud (VPC). This is one example of how building out infrastructure can cascade into larger systems—to create resource A, you need B, but B may need C. For now, we can use the `aws_vpc` data source to look up the default VPC for the region and then pass that along to our subnets.

We're going to put all of these data sources in our `lookups.tf` file we created earlier.

Listing 2.2 Using Terraform to look up data

```
data "aws_vpc" "default" {                       ◄──── Data sources are
  default = true                                        read-only lookups.
}

data "aws_subnets" "default" {                   This data block uses filter subblocks to
  filter {                                  ◄──── restrict which subnets get returned.
    name   = "vpc-id"
    values = [data.aws_vpc.default.id]       ◄──── The id attribute is computed
  }                                                from the aws_vpc data lookup.
}

data "aws_ami" "ubuntu" {
  owners      = ["099720109477"]           ◄──── This is the AWS account for
  most_recent = true                             Cannonical, the makers of Ubuntu.

  filter {                                 ◄──── Blocks can have subblocks.
    name   = "virtualization-type"
    values = ["hvm"]
  }

  filter {
    name   = "name"
    values = ["ubuntu/images/hvm-ssd/ubuntu-focal-20.04-amd64-server-*"]
  }
}
```

With all of this in place, we have the values needed to make our resource.

2.1.5 Creating an instance

Now for the real magic, we're going to use the Terraform `resource` block to create our `aws_instance` using the values from our data lookups. In our `main.tf` file, we need to add a `resource` block that represents our `aws_instance` and then map the attributes from the data sources to the parameters of our `resource` block.

The `ami` parameter comes from the `aws_ami` data source (https://mng.bz/AQ2F). We pass the `id` attribute of that data source to the `ami` parameter.

Our `subnet_id` is slightly more complicated. The data source we used for that, `aws_subnets`, returns a list of subnet IDs rather than a single ID. We're going to use the first subnet it finds and pass that through to the `subnet_id`. It's also possible to add additional filters here, such as filtering by Tag. It is a common pattern to use and filter on tags for more complex networks that include public and private subnets.

Finally, we hardcode our `instance_type` field to the least expensive instance we can use for testing. Since Terraform manages infrastructure, and infrastructure typically costs money, it's important to be price-conscious of our choices. In this case, that means using less powerful infrastructure by default so that people don't accidentally spend more money than they're expecting. In chapter 3, we'll discuss how to allow our users to override our choice here so they can pick more powerful machines.

Listing 2.3   Defining an AWS instance with code

```
resource "aws_instance" "hello_world" {          ◄──────  Resource blocks map to
  ami           = data.aws_ami.ubuntu.id                  specific infrastructure.
  subnet_id     = data.aws_subnets.default.ids[0]
  instance_type = "t3.micro"                     ◄──────  This is typically set as a
}                                                         variable, not hard coded.
```

With that, our AWS instance is defined and ready to launch.

2.1.6   *Running Terraform*

Now we want to actually run our code and launch our instance!

Before we begin, we need to make sure that we can access our AWS account. Terraform providers do not have a standard set of configurations, but instead, all use their own configuration system. That means we need to head over to the AWS provider documentation (https://mng.bz/ZlZj) to see how it handles configuration. The AWS Terraform provider uses the same standard configuration as other AWS tools such as Boto3 or the AWS command-line interface (CLI), so we can install the AWS CLI and run the `cli` command `aws configure` and plug in our credentials that way.

Once that's done, we have to initialize our workspace. This is when Terraform downloads any configured providers or modules.

Listing 2.4   Terraform initializing with the CLI

```
Initializing the backend...

Initializing provider plugins...
- Finding hashicorp/aws versions matching "~> 4.0"...
- Installing hashicorp/aws v4.41.0...
- Installed hashicorp/aws v4.41.0 (signed by HashiCorp)

Terraform has created a lock file .terraform.lock.hcl to record the provider
selections it made above. Include this file in your version control
repository so that Terraform can guarantee to make the same selections by
default when you run "terraform init" in the future.

Terraform has been successfully initialized!

You may now begin working with Terraform. Try running "terraform plan" to
see any changes that are required for your infrastructure. All Terraform
commands should now work.

If you ever set or change modules or backend configuration for Terraform,
rerun this command to reinitialize your working directory. If you forget,
other commands will detect it and remind you to do so if necessary.
```

After that, we run our plan so we can confirm that Terraform is going to do what's expected. In particular, we want to see that Terraform is going to create a single resource—an AWS instance—for us.

Listing 2.5   Terraform planning with the CLI

```
data.aws_vpc.default: Reading...
data.aws_ami.ubuntu: Reading...
data.aws_ami.ubuntu: Read complete after 0s [id=ami-0cb81cb394fc2e305]
data.aws_vpc.default: Read complete after 0s [id=vpc-cc5449a4]
data.aws_subnets.default: Reading...
data.aws_subnets.default: Read complete after 0s [id=us-east-2]

Terraform used the selected providers to generate the following execution
plan. Resource actions are indicated with the following symbols:
  + create

Terraform will perform the following actions:

  # aws_instance.hello_world will be created
  + resource "aws_instance" "hello_world" {
      + ami                                  = "ami-0cb81cb394fc2e305"
      + arn                                  = (known after apply)
      + associate_public_ip_address          = (known after apply)
      + availability_zone                    = (known after apply)
      + cpu_core_count                       = (known after apply)
      + cpu_threads_per_core                 = (known after apply)
      + disable_api_stop                     = (known after apply)
      + disable_api_termination              = (known after apply)
      + ebs_optimized                        = (known after apply)
      + get_password_data                    = false
      + host_id                              = (known after apply)
      + host_resource_group_arn              = (known after apply)
      + id                                   = (known after apply)
      + instance_initiated_shutdown_behavior = (known after apply)
      + instance_state                       = (known after apply)
      + instance_type                        = "t3.micro"
      + ipv6_address_count                   = (known after apply)
      + ipv6_addresses                       = (known after apply)
      + key_name                             = (known after apply)
      + monitoring                           = (known after apply)
      + outpost_arn                          = (known after apply)
      + password_data                        = (known after apply)
      + placement_group                      = (known after apply)
      + placement_partition_number           = (known after apply)
      + primary_network_interface_id         = (known after apply)
      + private_dns                          = (known after apply)
      + private_ip                           = (known after apply)
      + public_dns                           = (known after apply)
      + public_ip                            = (known after apply)
      + secondary_private_ips                = (known after apply)
      + security_groups                      = (known after apply)
      + source_dest_check                    = true
      + subnet_id                            = "subnet-b96b6ed1"
```

```
      + tags                                 = {
          + "CreatedBy" = "terraform"
        }
      + tags_all                             = {
          + "CreatedBy" = "terraform"
        }
      + tenancy                              = (known after apply)
      + user_data                           = (known after apply)
      + user_data_base64                    = (known after apply)
      + user_data_replace_on_change         = false
      + vpc_security_group_ids              = (known after apply)

      + capacity_reservation_specification {
          + capacity_reservation_preference = (known after apply)

          + capacity_reservation_target {
              + capacity_reservation_id                = (
known after apply)
              + capacity_reservation_resource_group_arn = (
known after apply)
            }
        }

      + ebs_block_device {
          + delete_on_termination = (known after apply)
          + device_name           = (known after apply)
          + encrypted             = (known after apply)
          + iops                  = (known after apply)
          + kms_key_id            = (known after apply)
          + snapshot_id           = (known after apply)
          + tags                  = (known after apply)
          + throughput            = (known after apply)
          + volume_id             = (known after apply)
          + volume_size           = (known after apply)
          + volume_type           = (known after apply)
        }

      + enclave_options {
          + enabled = (known after apply)
        }

      + ephemeral_block_device {
          + device_name  = (known after apply)
          + no_device    = (known after apply)
          + virtual_name = (known after apply)
        }

      + maintenance_options {
          + auto_recovery = (known after apply)
        }

      + metadata_options {
          + http_endpoint               = (known after apply)
          + http_put_response_hop_limit = (known after apply)
          + http_tokens                 = (known after apply)
```

```
            + instance_metadata_tags        = (known after apply)
        }

    + network_interface {
        + delete_on_termination = (known after apply)
        + device_index          = (known after apply)
        + network_card_index     = (known after apply)
        + network_interface_id   = (known after apply)
        }

    + private_dns_name_options {
        + enable_resource_name_dns_a_record    = (known after apply)
        + enable_resource_name_dns_aaaa_record = (known after apply)
        + hostname_type                        = (known after apply)
        }

    + root_block_device {
        + delete_on_termination = (known after apply)
        + device_name           = (known after apply)
        + encrypted             = (known after apply)
        + iops                  = (known after apply)
        + kms_key_id            = (known after apply)
        + tags                  = (known after apply)
        + throughput            = (known after apply)
        + volume_id             = (known after apply)
        + volume_size           = (known after apply)
        + volume_type           = (known after apply)
        }
    }

Plan: 1 to add, 0 to change, 0 to destroy.

Changes to Outputs:
  + aws_instance_arn = (known after apply)
```

```
Saved the plan to: plan.tfplan

To perform exactly these actions, run the following command to apply:
    terraform apply "plan.tfplan"
```

The plan shows us what Terraform is planning on doing. In this case, we're creating a single resource, and since this is the first run, we aren't destroying or changing any existing resources. Since our plan doesn't have any errors and appears to be applying the configuration we were looking for, this looks good and we can go ahead and apply it.

Listing 2.6   Terraform apply with the CLI

```
aws_instance.hello_world: Creating...
aws_instance.hello_world: Still creating... [10s elapsed]
```

```
aws_instance.hello_world: Creation complete after 12s [
   id=i-01792587739c8e453]

Apply complete! Resources: 1 added, 0 changed, 0 destroyed.
```

Success! Our program has created a single resource, an AWS instance with the ID `i-01792587739c8e453`.

This is a really simple example of Terraform, but it is also pretty powerful. It can be used to launch the exact same resource in multiple AWS regions and accounts without having to be changed in any way. Any number of developers could use this in their own accounts: even though one person wrote it, hundreds of people can launch infrastructure from it. By exposing the instance type as a variable, developers can also change the instance type on their own without needing to change anything.

For a single instance, this is interesting, but for an entire software stack, it becomes an invaluable tool in any developer's toolbox. The only difference between launching one instance and a system with multiple containerized services, API gateway, steaming queues, a content delivery network, and a database, is the amount of time put into defining the system in Terraform. Once written, that system can be launched repeatedly just like this single instance script can be.

For the rest of this chapter, we're going to break down all of the components that were discussed in the script, from the block syntax to the individual block types themselves.

2.2 Block syntax

Terraform HCL is built around a construct called blocks. In our previous example, we had several types of blocks:

- `terraform settings`
- `provider`
- `data source`
- `resource`

Blocks are the primary language construct of Terraform, in the same way that statements are the primary language construct in Javascript, Python, or Bash. When you write in Terraform HCL, you're going to either be creating a block or writing inside of an existing block.

A helpful way to think about this is that blocks are the nouns of the Terraform language. They represent concrete items such as configuration or infrastructure. This goes back to declarative languages defining how something should look, rather than the actions that should be taken. Most of your time in Terraform is going to be creating nouns (via blocks) and then describing or linking those nouns together.

This chapter is in many ways a discussion of all the different block types and what they add to the language. All blocks follow the same basic structure, regardless of what they do. This structure involves an outer layer that defines what the block is, with arguments and subblocks that change the behavior of the block.

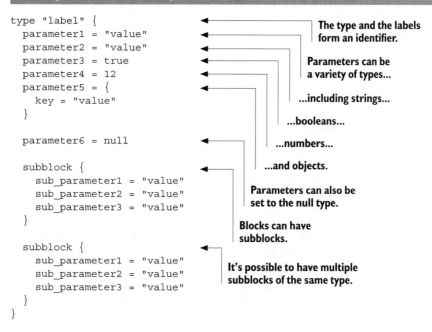

Listing 2.7 HCL block components

```
type "label" {
  parameter1 = "value"
  parameter2 = "value"
  parameter3 = true
  parameter4 = 12
  parameter5 = {
    key = "value"
  }

  parameter6 = null

  subblock {
    sub_parameter1 = "value"
    sub_parameter2 = "value"
    sub_parameter3 = "value"
  }

  subblock {
    sub_parameter1 = "value"
    sub_parameter2 = "value"
    sub_parameter3 = "value"
  }
}
```

The first word that starts a block off is the block type, which defines how everything else is interpreted. The label is included in the quotes next. The rest of the block is enclosed in brackets and includes arguments and subblocks. Blocks can also include separate attributes that can be referenced by other blocks.

Listing 2.8 HCL example with real resources

```
data "aws_subnets" "main" {
  filter {
    name   = "vpc-id"
    values = ["vpc-9ba9b5c6db85a9918"]
  }
}

resource "aws_instance" "hello_world" {
  ami       = "ami-0eeb7197a00865f8a"
  subnet_id = data.aws_subnets.main.ids[0]
}
```

This is a real-world example that includes all of these components. There are two different blocks: a data and a resource block. Both of these have two labels. The first tells Terraform what the subtype of the block is, and the second adds a unique identifier. The data.aws_subnets.main block has a subblock of the type filter, which has arguments. The resource.aws_instance.hello_world block contains only arguments, with the `subnet_id` parameter taking the value of the `data.aws_subnets.main.ids` attribute.

2.2.1 *Block types*

The block type is the most important, as it defines the purpose of the block and how the other components are interpreted.

If you remember from chapter 1, Terraform is built on a language called the HCL. Terraform is not the only tool built on top of HCL. This book is focused on Terraform HCL, but it's important to remember that there are other flavors of HCL in other products: Packer, Consul, and Nomad are other programs made by HashiCorp that also use HCL but that have very different flavors of HCL that fit their intended purpose. Packer, which is a configuration management tool that is used to create machine images (like the AMI we used in our Hello World example) has a completely different set of block types than Terraform.

You do not need to know anything about these other tools to use Terraform, and this book only focuses on Terraform HCL. It is important to know that the Terraform blocks aren't available unless you are specifically using Terraform though, so if you do use some of those other programs, you'll need to read up on their special HCL flavors.

At the time of writing, Terraform HCL had 12 different block types, each with its own purpose:

- `Terraform`—Used to configure Terraform and the current workspace.
- `Provider`—Allows for provider-specific settings.
- `Resource`—Creates and updates a corresponding piece of infrastructure. These blocks have their own subtypes that come from providers. There are potentially hundreds of thousands of resource subtypes.
- `Data`—Is similar to a resource but is read-only and looks up existing infrastructure components. Just like resources, these have subtypes that come from providers.
- `Variable`—Allows for external inputs to be passed into the program or module.
- `Locals`—Contains internal variables that are scoped to a module.
- `Module`—An abstraction that allows HCL code to be reused over and over again.
- `Import`—A way to pull existing infrastructure into Terraform.
- `Moved`—A tool for refactoring that allows you to change the name of resources.
- `Removed`—Allows people to mark an item as removed without causing it to be destroyed.
- `Check`—Used to validate deployed infrastructure.
- `Output`—A way to share data from inside of a module with other modules or workspaces.

The `terraform` and `provider` blocks are normally set when starting a new project—they basically tell Terraform what vendors you're going to be working with (the providers) and other project configurations. The `resource` blocks are likely the most important component in Terraform. It's these blocks that actually create and update your infrastructure. All of the other blocks essentially work to support the `resource` blocks, either by providing configuration values for the infrastructure being created or to help organize `resource` blocks into reusable components.

2.2.2 Labels and subtypes

When you create the instance of a block, you need a way to refer to it. This is important because the attributes, or output, of some blocks can be used in the arguments for others. If you're using a `data` block to look up an AMI, as we did in section 2.1, then you need a way to refer to that `data` block so you can pass that AMI value to the subsequent `resource` block. For this reason, block identities need to be unique, as Terraform has to know the exact block being referred to.

`terraform` blocks have a variety of methods for defining their labels. It is one of the biggest differentiators between blocks. Labels are also the first place where differences between block types come into play—different block types treat labels in different ways. There are several strategies used for block labels.

NO LABELS

The `terraform settings` block is one of two blocks that does not use a label at all. Each module only has a single `terraform`, so there isn't a need to distinguish between them. The `locals` block, which will be discussed in the next chapter, is another block that doesn't use labels.

Listing 2.9 `terraform` block without label

```
terraform {
  required_providers {
    aws = {
      source  = "hashicorp/aws"
      version = "~> 5.0"
    }
  }
}
```

This block doesn't have any labels.

The label in provider blocks will match the key in the required_providers block.

SINGLE LABEL

For `variable`, `provider`, `output`, and `module` blocks, there is only a single label field. With the exception of the `provider` block, this label can be anything the user wants: the `provider` block label needs to map back to a provider inside of the Terraform `required_providers` block.

Listing 2.10 `terraform` block with single label

```
provider "aws" {
  region = "us-east-1"
}
```

This block only has one label.

SUBTYPE AND LABEL

The `data` and `resource` blocks have two labels, with the first one acting as a subtype and the second as an identifier. The subtype is extremely important and will come up often; it tells Terraform how the `data` and `resource` blocks map back to their provider and what they're supposed to do. These are generally just referred to as the resource type and data source type.

Listing 2.11 `terraform` blocks with subtype and label

```
resource "aws_instance" "hello_world" {
  ami           = data.aws_ami.ubuntu.id          ◄──────  Resources have a
  subnet_id     = data.aws_subnets.main.ids[0]            subtype and a label.
  instance_type = var.instance_type
}
                                                   Data sources also have
data "aws_vpc" "default" {                 ◄────── a subtype and a label.
  default = true
}
```

The combination of block type and labels are combined to form a unique reference string for that specific block. This unique reference string has to be unique throughout the module as it refers to one specific block. It is used to reference that block in other places, primarily to share the block attributes with other blocks as an argument (see table 2.1).

Table 2.1   Examples of blocks and their reference strings

Block type	First label or subtype	Second label	Full reference
resource	aws_instance	hello_world	resource.aws_instance.hello_world
data	aws_vpc	default	data.aws_vpc.default
variable	instance_type		var.instance_type

In some cases, the first part of the reference, the block type, is dropped. This happens for arguments that only take a specific block type. We'll see an example of that with the `depends_on` argument, which takes a list of references to other blocks as its argument, in the lifecycle meta argument later in this chapter.

2.2.3 *Arguments and subblocks*

If blocks can be considered nouns, then arguments and subblocks would be adjectives. Every block has its own set of arguments and subblocks that modify their behavior.

Arguments are expressed as assignments, where the argument has a name and a value. The argument name can only be used once inside each block. In other words, you can't define the same argument more than once inside a block. The value can be any Terraform expression: our examples in this chapter use simple assignment expressions, but we'll discuss more complex expression types in chapter 4.

Listing 2.12   Terraform resource with arguments

```
resource "aws_instance" "hello_world" {
  ami           = data.aws_ami.ubuntu.id
  subnet_id     = data.aws_subnets.default.ids[0]
  instance_type = var.instance_type
}
```

These arguments are specific to the aws_instance type.

Subblocks are blocks that are nested inside of another block. They do not have labels, and unlike arguments, subblocks can normally be used multiple times. For `data` blocks, this tends to be used to provide a dynamic number of filters, as different filters may need to be stacked together to get the desired result. One thing that can occasionally get confusing is that subblocks can look very similar to parameters with object values: the big difference is that parameters can only be defined once in a block and use an equals sign between the label and value, while subblocks can be defined repeatedly and don't have an assignment character.

Listing 2.13   Terraform data source with multiple subblocks

```
data "aws_ami" "ubuntu" {
  owners      = ["099720109477"]
  most_recent = true

  filter {
    name   = "virtualization-type"
    values = ["hvm"]
  }

  filter {
    name   = "name"
    values = ["ubuntu/images/hvm-ssd/ubuntu-focal-20.04-amd64-server-*"]
  }
}
```

Arguments can live alongside subblocks.

Subblocks can have their own arguments and subblocks.

Subblocks, unlike arguments, can be called multiple times.

Some resources also take advantage of subblocks to let developers cleanly add multiple configurations of the same type. If a team was working with GCP (Google's Cloud) and wanted to create a firewall for their instance, they'd install the GCP provider and use the `google_compute_firewall` resources. This resource uses subblocks to allow developers to add any number of firewall rules to their firewall. Other block types, such as the resource `lifecycle` block, use subblocks more as a namespace to keep grouped settings together while future-proofing against overlap with new block arguments.

Listing 2.14   A GCP firewall using multiple subblocks

```
resource "google_compute_network" "example" {
  name = "example-network"
}

resource "google_compute_firewall" "example" {
```

This block creates a network.

```
name     = "example-firewall"
network = google_compute_network.example.name
```
◄── **Here we reference the network created above.**

```
allow {
  protocol = "icmp"
}
```
◄── **This rule allows the server to be pinged.**

```
allow {
  protocol = "tcp"
  ports    = ["80", "443"]
}
```
◄── **This second rule allows HTTP traffic.**

```
allow {
  protocol = "udp"
  ports    = ["53"]
}
```
◄── **This third rule allows UDP based DNS traffic.**

```
  source_ranges = ["0.0.0.0/0"]
}
```

Resource and data sources both get their arguments and subblocks from their providers, while modules have their arguments defined by the module developer (more on that in chapter 3). Other blocks that are built into Terraform have a more consistent set of arguments.

2.2.4 *Attributes*

Blocks don't just take in arguments; they also export attributes. This is what allows one block to feed data into another, such as a data source looking up a subnet ID and passing it to an AWS instance resource to launch that instance inside of that specific subnet.

Most blocks, including `data` and `resource` blocks, automatically expose all of their arguments as attributes. Blocks also have additional read-only attributes they can expose. These read-only attributes generally come from Terraform running a plan or apply and getting the results from the underlying provider. (See figure 2.1.)

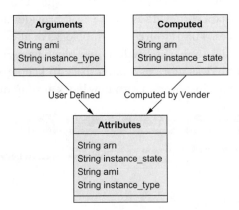

Figure 2.1   The `aws_instance` resource used in our Hello World example has two attributes, `arn` and `instance_state`, that are only exposed after the resource is created. The arguments are also passed through as accessible attributes.

While arguments are passed through as attributes, subblocks are not. Anything inside of a subblock is not accessible as an attribute.

2.2.5 Ordering

We've talked a little bit about Terraform plans in the first chapter. These plans are the order that Terraform executes actions. In a typical programming language, code is run in the order it is written. One statement follows another in the order that they're put down.

With Terraform, the order in which blocks are written is meaningless. Blocks can be written in any order, and it will not affect the plan itself. In our Hello World example, the output could just as easily go to the top of the file or in a completely different file altogether. It is a really common pattern to use multiple files, which we'll discuss when we go into modules in depth. When Terraform runs through the plan phase, it creates a directed acyclic graph of all the resources by figuring out which attributes exposed by resources were later used as arguments for another resource.

Listing 2.15 A data source being referenced by another data source

```
data "aws_vpc" "default" {
  default = true
}

data "aws_subnets" "default" {          ◄──┐  This block depends on the above block
  filter {                                  │  because it uses an attribute from it.
    name   = "vpc-id"
    values = [data.aws_vpc.default.id]   ◄──┐  The argument for this resource is an
  }                                         │  attribute from data.aws_vpc.default.
}
```

In the Hello World example, we create our `data.aws_subnets.default` using an attribute from the `data.aws_vpc.default` block. Although this looks simple, there's a lot happening here. Behind the scenes, Terraform is going to identify the dependency between these blocks: it will map that relationship out and realize that it has to load the `data.aws_vpc.default` block first, and only after it loads can it take the `attribute` block and use it to look up the `data.aws_subnets.default` block. This dependency mapping is one of the more powerful components of Terraform, especially when you have a lot of resources you're managing. Terraform also has a way to directly manage this relationship using the `depends_on` meta parameter that we'll discuss later in this chapter.

2.2.6 Style

Terraform is very specific about how blocks should be styled:

1 Meta arguments, which we'll discuss later in this chapter, are at the top.
2 Block-specific arguments are next. These can be grouped together to place related arguments near each other, with a single empty line separating the groups.

3 Block-specific subblocks come next.

4 Finally, any meta argument subblock should be at the end.

Additionally, blocks of arguments should always line up their "equal" signs so that values are aligned together.

Listing 2.16   `terraform` **block style**

```
resource "resource_type" "unique_resource_name" {
  provider = aws.dns                              ◄──────┤  Meta arguments go at the top.

  string_parameter  = "value"          ◄──────┐
  integer_parameter = 134                      │  Arguments come next, and all
  boolean_parameter = true                     │  equal signs should be aligned.

  object_arguments = {              ◄───────────┐
    key1 : "value"                  ◄───────────┤  Anno arguments can be
    key2 = "value"                              │  separated by empty lines.
    key3 = "value"                  ◄───────────┘
  }                                             Both colons and equal
                                                signs are valid.

  subblock {                        ◄───────────┐  The equal sign is considered
    subargument  = "value"                       │  best practice though.
    subargument2 = "another_value"
  }                                             Resource or data-specific
                                                subblocks come next.

  lifecycle {                       ◄───────────┐  Meta argument subblocks
    ignore_changes = [object_arguments]          │  are always at the end.
  }
}
```

Even though Terraform does have a suggested style guide (https://mng.bz/RVGn), Terraform itself will ignore these code style guidelines when it is creating plans. If these rules aren't followed it will not cause problems running Terraform. However, it is significantly easier for people to jump into a project that follows these standards. The Terraform CLI also comes with a command, `terraform fmt`, which will automatically apply the formatting rules in Terraform (it will not change argument ordering though).

2.3   *Terraform settings*

The `terraform settings` block is the container for Terraform-specific settings. This block holds a variety of Terraform settings:

- Required providers, which we saw in our Hello World example, is basically a list of dependencies.
- Backend and cloud configurations are used for projects that have a centralized backend for their workspaces. These allow developers to work on the same infrastructure at the same time.

- Experimental language features are features you really only need to worry about if you want to test features that Terraform is experimenting with. These features are subject to change rapidly between versions, so they have to be opted into.
- Terraform Version requirements can be used to explicitly define which versions of Terraform your script will work with. This prevents your code from running on versions that may be missing the required features.
- Provider metadata is generally only needed by people distributing providers and something you'll likely never actually encounter.

Listing 2.17 `terraform settings` **block**

```
terraform {
  experiments = [example]          ◀──── Enable optional experiments
                                          for the module.
  required_providers {        ◀────
    aws = {                         Requires providers for the module,
      version = "~> 5.0.0"          Discussed further in section 2.4.2.
      source  = "hashicorp/aws"
    }
  }

  cloud {                    ◀──── Terraform Cloud configuration.
    organization = "example_corp"
    hostname     = "app.terraform.io"

    workspaces {
      tags = ["my-app"]
    }
  }

  backend "s3" {             ◀──── Backend configuration. Note
    bucket = "mybucket"             that only one of backend or
    key    = "path/to/my/key"       cloud should be used.
    region = "us-east-1"
  }
}
```

2.3.1 *Backend and cloud blocks*

Terraform uses backends to store state so that teams can work together in a single workspace even if they are spread out using different machines. There are two blocks inside of the `terraform settings` block that handle this: the `backend` and `cloud` blocks. If one of these blocks isn't defined, then Terraform defaults to using the local backend, which just stores the state as a JSON file on your local computer, which is great for local development but should never be used for production systems.

Backend is the standard block that has been used by Terraform for years now. It supports a variety of backends; S3, GCS, AzureRM, and Consul are just some examples. It also has what Hashicorp calls an "enhanced" backend, `remote`, that is used for backends that provide extra functionality on top of state storage. We'll discuss this further in chapter 6 when we dive deep into state.

Users of Terraform Cloud also have a special configuration that can be used called `cloud`. This is used instead of the `backend` block, and at the moment is only used with the Terraform Cloud product. `cloud` is a newer block that specifically supports Terraform Cloud, including self-hosted Terraform Enterprise instances. At the moment, this block is only usable by Terraform Cloud customers, but it is possible that other providers will adopt it in the future.

Every backend has its own arguments and configuration requirements. It's important to read the documentation (https://mng.bz/6egy) for the specific backend you use. Unlike providers, backends are hardcoded into Terraform. That means that you can't write your own backend directly. However, there is an `http` backend (https://mng.bz/1X7Z) that developers can use to create their own backends following a simple REST API. Creating custom backends is not something a Terraform user will likely need to do.

2.3.2 Experiments

The developers of Terraform and OpenTofu regularly solicit feedback from the community on new functionality, and one of the ways they do this is through the use of experiments. An experiment is essentially a new feature of Terraform that isn't ready for regular production use. They are released with Terraform but are disabled by default so that developers do not accidentally use them. The `experiments` argument of the `terraform` block allows users of Terraform to opt into these experiments.

Listing 2.18   Enabling experimental features

```
terraform {
  experiments = [
    module_variable_optional_attrs        ◀—————  This experiment is
  ]                                               no longer active.
}
```

Experiments are not stable. Their APIs may change between versions, and they may end up being completely removed. Experiments also tend to be short lived as they either get adopted into Terraform as an official feature or discarded. Even if the experiment is adopted, there may be changes in how it gets implemented in the final version. Terraform will give a warning whenever experiments are enabled.

What this means is that a project that uses an experiment is basically locked into a very specific version of Terraform, and upgrades cannot be safely done in an automatic way. Experiments are a great way to familiarize yourself with new features that may be coming and to give feedback to HashiCorp and the Terraform team on how those features work in practice, but experiments should be avoided in most production projects. You can review the current changelog for the version of Terraform you're using to see what experiments are currently available.

2.4   *Providers*

Terraform by itself is essentially just an engine for figuring out the order to create or update components, but it has no idea what those components are. Terraform relies on providers for that.

Providers in Terraform are like vendor software development kits (SDKs) in other languages. If you were using another language such as Java or Python and you wanted to build a script that launched an AWS instance, you'd have to download the AWS SDK, likely from a registry, and install it. You'd also have to look at how that SDK is running the right version, you'd need to make sure it was configured, and then you'd need to familiarize yourself with the functions and objects it exposes.

Terraform providers are very similar. You need to make sure Terraform knows to install the providers you need, at the version you want. You need to configure the provider with credentials, just like you would have to configure the SDK. There may be some other settings you want to run, or you may want to have multiple connections to the service—just like an SDK would allow you to create multiple clients, Terraform will let you configure multiple instances of your provider (see table 2.2).

Table 2.2   Examples of blocks and their reference strings

Vendor	Terraform	Python	Java
AWS	AWS provider (https://mng.bz/Pd82)	Boto3 (https://mng.bz/qxBK)	AWS SDK (https://aws.amazon.com/sdk-for-java/)
GCP	Google provider (https://mng.bz/JY8p)	Libraries (https://mng.bz/7pex)	Cloud SDK (https://cloud.google.com/sdk/)
DataDog	DataDog provider (https://mng.bz/wJE7)	DataDogPy (https://github.com/DataDog/datadogpy)	API Client (https://github.com/DataDog/datadog-api-client-java)

Each provider is tied to a single vendor or system type. There's an AWS provider, a GCP provider, and thousands of others. These providers are each composed of resources and data sources, which are in general mapped one to one with a type of infrastructure component that the vendor offers. In many ways, a provider can be considered a library, but instead of providing functions or classes like in other languages, this library provides components.

When a developer is using Terraform to create a system, the first place they go is to the provider documentation for the vendors they are using. Many projects will have multiple vendors and therefore multiple providers. For example, someone using a system that is deploying machines on Linode, hosting data using Wasabi, and using DNSMadeEasy for their domain hosting will need the providers for Linode, Wasabi, and DNSMadeEasy if they want to use Terraform to manage that system.

There are thousands of providers, with more being added all the time. For popular vendors, providers are regularly updated to support new functionality. Every single data source and resource maps back to a specific provider. In general, you can tell the provider by looking at the resource name, as there's a strong convention toward name-spacing the resource and data source names by prefixing the provider name to the front (i.e., `aws_instance` points to the AWS provider, while `linode_instance` signifies that Linode is the provider).

2.4.1   *Provider registry*

Public Terraform providers are hosted on the Terraform Registry (https://registry .terraform.io/browse/providers). When the `terraform init` command is run, the providers needed for the workspace are downloaded from the registry and configured for use locally.

The Terraform registry also hosts the provider documentation, which for most providers is extensive. In fact, when I am learning a new service that I've never used before, I'll often look at the provider documentation first. Simply seeing the list of resources that a provider exposes can really help build a mental model for how that service works.

2.4.2   *Required providers*

Terraform has a special block inside of the `terraform settings` block that is used to tell Terraform which providers are needed.

Listing 2.19   Requiring the AWS provider

```
terraform {
  required_providers {
    aws = {
      source  = "hashicorp/aws"
      version = "~> 4.0"
    }
  }
}
```

Terraform settings block defines workspace settings.

This subblock tells Terraform which providers to install.

This project uses the AWS provider.

We want the latest in the version 4 line.

The AWS provider comes from the public registry and the Hashicorp vendor.

If Terraform sees a resource or data source that does not have a corresponding provider listed in the required `provider` block, then it will attempt to infer the provider using the name of the resource. When it does this, it assumes that the first part of the resource type is the local name for the provider it needs. Since Terraform also assumes that the namespace for the provider is `hashicorp` as a default, this means that `hashicorp/localname` will be assumed. For example, `resource.random_id` is assumed to come from the `hashicorp/random` provider, while `resource.aws_instance` is assumed to come from the `hashicorp/aws` provider. As mentioned earlier, though, it's best to always use the `required_providers` block and explicitly define the providers you want.

2.4.3   *Provider configuration*

Although provider requirements are defined in the `terraform` block, the actual provider configuration is defined in its own separate `provider` block. Providers have a huge variety of configurations and settings, and it really depends on what the provider is. That said, provider configuration tends to have two important purposes: authentication and scoping.

For Terraform to communicate and send commands to a vendor, it needs to be authenticated, and each vendor has its own way of handling that. Providers have to expose that authentication system to the users, and one way they do that is by exposing configuration through the `provider` block.

Listing 2.20 Using the `provider` block to configure Cloudflare authentication

```
variable "cloudflare_api_token" {                    ◄────  Variables are discussed
                                                            in the next chapter.
}

provider "cloudflare" {                              ┌──  Cloudflare needs an
  api_token = var.cloudflare_api_token      ◄────────┘     API token to connect.
}
```

Many providers also allow you to define configuration settings using files or environment variables. This is not something that is controlled by Terraform, so when using a new provider for the first time, make sure to review the provider documentation.

Although the `provider` block is primarily used for specifying credentials, it can also be used to provide additional context to the provider about where and how it should be operating. AWS uses it to define which region to operate in, while GCP (which names its provider `google`) uses both a project and a region.

Listing 2.21 Using the `provider` block to configure AWS and GCP

```
provider "aws" {                  ◄────────  AWS gets its account ID
  region = "us-west-2"            ◄──────┐    from a configuration file.
}                                        │
                                         │  The AWS provider needs to know
provider "google" {                      │  what region to operate in.
  project = "example_project"   ◄─────┐
  region  = "us-central1"       ◄──┐  │  The Google provider needs to
}                                  │  │  know what project to work on.
                                   │
                                   │  Google also needs a region.
```

Every provider has its own configuration system. Providers typically expose all options through the `provider` block, but many also take environment variables. Our `Hello World` example relies on the AWS provider and relies on environment variables or AWS-specific configuration files for credentials, but we do set the region inside of the program using a `provider` block.

Since most providers have multiple ways they can be configured, a `provider` block is not always required. Many providers read their configuration from specific files or environment variables. In those cases, the `provider` blocks would not provide any value and can safely be skipped.

provider blocks can only be used in the root-level module, as providers are configured for entire workspaces at that root level. In other words, you can only define provider blocks in the files that are in the same directory you are running the terraform or tofu commands in.

2.4.4   *Provider aliases*

You may have noticed a problem in the previous sample. What happens if you want to have a single Terraform program that connects to multiple AWS regions or has multiple Cloudflare accounts it needs to manage? So far we've only seen an example where we set the default provider, but it's possible to define multiple provider blocks using provider aliases.

With a provider alias, you create one provider block for each connection you want. This is like creating separate clients when using an SDK; each "alias" will have its own settings. Then we can tell individual data and resource blocks to use our alias rather than the default.

Building on our example, what if we wanted to create a second EC2 image in another region? This is not an uncommon practice, as multiregion deployments can be built to act as a backup if the primary goes down. To do this, we'd need to create an alias and then use that to do a second set of VPC and subnet lookups for our second region.

Listing 2.22   Using multiple providers and aliases

```
provider "aws" {
  region = "us-east-1"                    ◀─── This provider block does not
}                                              have an alias, so it is the default.

provider "aws" {
  alias  = "west"                         ◀─── This provider block does have an alias,
  region = "us-west-2"                         so it is only used when specified.
}

# Default Subnet Lookup

data "aws_vpc" "default" {                ◀─── No provider is specified, so the
  default = true                               default "us-east-1" is used.
}

data "aws_subnets" "default" {            ◀─── No provider is specified, so
  filter {                                     the default "us-east-1" is used.
    name   = "vpc-id"
    values = [data.aws_vpc.default.id]
  }
}

# Secondary Subnet Lookup

data "aws_vpc" "backup" {                      The AWS provider that points
  provider = aws.west                     ◀─── to "us-west-2" is used.
  default  = true
```

```
}

data "aws_subnets" "backup" {
  provider = aws.west

  filter {
    name   = "vpc-id"
    values = [data.aws_vpc.defabackupult.id]
  }
}
```

The AWS provider that points to "us-west-2" is used.

This example starts with the familiar setup from our Hello World example but then creates a second `provider` block that points to a different region. We then add two more `data` blocks so we can look up the default VPC from the second region to pull the subnets from that VPC. This example also includes a preview of the provider meta argument, which is how we told those two new `data` blocks to use our provider alias.

2.5 Resources

The entire reason for Terraform's existence is to define and manage infrastructure using code. Everything else is just there to make that easier. The `resource` block is the way that this happens. Each `resource` block that a developer creates represents an actual piece of infrastructure that they want to launch and manage using Terraform.

Every `resource` block has its own type. That resource type maps back, through a provider, to a specific type of infrastructure. For a vendor that manages DNS, you might have resources for a domain and another to represent a DNS record, while a provider for a Git host may have resources to represent organizations, repositories, problems, and pull requests. Providers for larger cloud vendors will have thousands of resources that it makes available to represent the actual infrastructure components the Cloud vendor offers.

In some ways, this can be overwhelming: there are literally hundreds of thousands of resources. However, if you know what vendors you're planning on using and have an idea of the type of systems you plan on launching, it is easy to narrow that list down. It helps to architect out what you want the system to look like before putting it down in Terraform, just like most software projects have to have some idea of what is being built before it gets down to code.

2.5.1 Resource usage

Resources consist of their own type, identifier, and arguments. The arguments are specific to the resource type.

Listing 2.23 `resource` block structure

```
resource "resource_type" "unique_resource_name" {
  string_argument  = "value"
  integer_argument = 134
  boolean_argument = true
```

Each argument will have a type and a value.

```
object_argument = {                    ◄─────  Objects can be defined inline.
  "key" = "value"
}
                                       ┌─────  Resources can also have subblocks, including the
lifecyle {                   ◄─────────┘       lifecycle block that exists on all resources.
  create_before_destroy = true    ◄───┐
}                                      └─────  This meta argument is
}                                              present on every resource.
```

The resource type and name combine to make a unique identifier for the resource inside of a module or workspace. This means that two resources cannot have the same name if they also have the same type, but two different resource types can have the same name.

For example, creating an EC2 instance on AWS uses a resource that looks like the following listing in HCL.

Listing 2.24   Example `resource` block

```
resource "aws_instance" "hello_world" {
  ami           = data.aws_ami.ubuntu.id
  subnet_id     = data.aws_subnet_ids.main.ids[0]
  instance_type = var.instance_type
}
```

Here we create a resource with the type `aws_instance` and the name `hello_world`, which combine to make the unique identifier `resource.aws_instance.hello_world`. We also give it the `subnet_id` parameter from our data source (which we'll talk about next) and the `instance_type` from an input variable.

2.6   Data sources

Terraform doesn't just provide the ability to create new resources. You can use another class of object called a data source to pull in information from outside of Terraform. Data sources look very similar to resources. They have types, identifiers, arguments, and attributes just like resources do. The major difference is that they do not create or modify anything; they instead use their arguments to search and filter data from their provider and make that data available to the rest of the program.

Our Hello World example has three data sources. The first two are used to find the subnet to launch our instance into.

Listing 2.25   Data sources for AWS VPC and subnets

```
data "aws_vpc" "default" {
  default = true               ◄─────  AWS creates a default VPC in each region,
}                                       and we want our data source to use that.

data "aws_subnets" "default" {
  filter {                     ◄─────  The AWS provider uses the filter field, but other
                                       providers will have a different parameter.
```

```
name   = "vpc-id"
values = [data.aws_vpc.default.id]
  }
}
```

We want to filter the subnets by the VPC ID.

Now we can get all of the subnets for the default VPC.

The `data.aws_vpc.default` object is using the default parameter to specify that we want the default VPC for the region, which is created automatically when a user creates their account. The `data.aws_subnets.default` resource takes the `vpc_id` from `data.aws_vpc.default`.

Those data sources both use simple arguments to select the data they look for. Some data sources are more complex and require even more filtering. The third data source we use is a great example of that.

Listing 2.26 Data source with filters for AWS AMI

```
data "aws_ami" "ubuntu" {
  most_recent = true

  filter {
    name   = "name"
    values = ["ubuntu/images/hvm-ssd/ubuntu-focal-20.04-amd64-server-*"]
  }

  filter {
    name   = "virtualization-type"
    values = ["hvm"]
  }

  # AWS Account for Canonical, makers of Ubuntu.
  owners = ["099720109477"]
}
```

Since this is a block, not an argument, it can be repeated.

Note that the filter block is unique to this resource type.

The `aws_ami` data source, which we use to get the latest AMI for our `aws_instance` arguments, has an additional `filter` block that can be used to filter down a larger group of resources. We combine this with some standard arguments to make sure we get the latest Ubuntu AMI directly from the company that makes Ubuntu.

One thing you might be wondering is: What happens when a data source can't find a matching resource? In this case, it depends a lot on the specific data source. For most data sources, such as the `aws_ami` data source, failing to find a match will throw an error and prevent the plan from continuing. There are other resources that allow failure. In general, the data sources that look up a dynamic number of resources will be able to return zero results. The `aws_subnets` data source we use is an example of this, as the ID attribute can be an empty list if no subnets are configured.

2.7   *Meta arguments*

`data`, `resource`, and `module` blocks all have arguments that are unique to them. For an AWS instance, this might be the instance type; for an AMI lookup, this might be the operating system. These arguments are very specific to the type of infrastructure that is being managed. These arguments change the infrastructure itself. They map to configuration fields of that infrastructure to change those values. There are times, though, when developers want to change how Terraform processes a block: for this, Terraform has meta arguments.

Meta arguments are arguments that every `data` or `resource` block will always have. They are universal to the block type, regardless of what the underlying provider does. These arguments are built into the Terraform HCL language itself. They exist purely to give Terraform extra instructions for when it makes a plan. This can include telling Terraform to ignore when certain values are changed, having it change the order that resources are created, or even forcing a resource to be replaced when a separate resource changes.

When launching an EC2 instance, like in our Hello World example, it's common to look up the latest AMI version and use that as the basis for the image. Since new AMIs get released often, this can result in the launched instance being replaced by Terraform after a release. It's a common practice to tell Terraform to ignore when the AMI changes—this allows new instances to always launch with the latest image but prevents already-launched instances from getting recreated. Another common method with EC2 instances is to tell Terraform to create the replacement before destroying the old instance—this allows for shorter downtime as services roll to the new instance. We'll go through the meta arguments that allow this throughout this section.

Since meta arguments affect how Terraform creates plans, they are processed very early in the planning cycle. Many of these fields have to have literal values or they will throw an error, while others require that whatever value they use be known at planning time. This means they cannot be set using values that depend on the attributes of resources that won't be known until after the resource is created. If an argument takes `true` or `false` as a value, then it has to literally be `true` or `false`, not just an expression that resolves to one of those.

2.7.1 Providers

In the providers section, we showed how to use provider aliases to allow multiple connections to a single vendor with different settings. Our example included defining `data` blocks using the `provider` argument.

The provider meta argument is meant to help developers when those developers are using multiple provider configurations for the same provider type. Basically, if you've got multiple GCP projects or AWS accounts that are configured as different provider aliases, you need to be able to tell Terraform which alias to use when creating resources. Since Terraform always has one provider of each type that it considers a default, this field is optional—it really is only useful when you need to manage multiple connections to a single vendor.

2.7.2 Lifecycle

The `lifecycle` subblock acts as a container for several arguments that affect how Terraform manages resources. As Terraform has evolved, more arguments have been added to this block. By putting them in a subblock, Terraform allows the language to expand in future versions without having to worry about new arguments conflicting with the vendor-provided arguments.

Each block that uses it can define the `lifecycle` block once—it cannot be declared multiple times for the same resource or data source. We'll review some of the common parameters of this block here and talk about some of the more advanced options later in the book.

CREATE_BEFORE_DESTROY

When Terraform decides that an object needs to be replaced, it defaults to destroying the existing object before creating the new one. This is a really good default behavior, as creating a resource before destroying the resource it is replacing can be dangerous. Many types of infrastructure have unique identifiers or resources that can't be shared by multiple objects, and attempting to create the replacement object first would result in an error. In general, two separate identity and access management roles can't have the same name, and you can't share an elastic IP address among two separate AWS instances. For both of these cases, `create_before_destroy` would cause errors—and there are a lot more examples of this.

There are times when this default isn't desired, though, especially in high-availability environments where the loss of a resource even for a short time can cause problems. The `create_before_destroy` argument gives developers the ability to change this behavior and create new resources before the old ones are destroyed.

Listing 2.27 `create_before_destroy` example

```
resource "aws_instance" "hello_world" {
  ami           = data.aws_ami.ubuntu.id
  subnet_id     = data.aws_subnets.default.ids[0]
  instance_type = var.instance_type

  lifecycle {                              ◀──── If a replacement is needed, it will be
    create_before_destroy = true                 created before the old instance is removed.
  }
}
```

PREVENT_DESTROY

The `prevent_destory` argument is, at first glance, pretty straightforward—when set to true, the resources created will cause any plan that destroys the resource to automatically fail. However, this argument should be used exceedingly rarely as it presents several problems:

- Like other lifecycle rules, it can only take literal (i.e., hardcoded) values. This cannot be enabled for production environments while being disabled for development environments.
- It prevents destroy plans from succeeding, which makes it harder to use Terraform to spin up temporary development environments.

- Deleting the `resource` block, which is one of the more common ways a resource gets destroyed, also removes this setting. That's because removing the block also removes the arguments for the block, so Terraform will no longer consider it to have `prevent_destroy` set when the block is gone.

Listing 2.28   `prevent_destroy` **example**

```
resource "aws_instance" "hello_world" {
  ami           = data.aws_ami.ubuntu.id
  subnet_id     = data.aws_subnets.default.ids[0]
  instance_type = var.instance_type

  lifecycle {                                    It is now impossible to
    prevent_destroy = true        ◄───┘          destroy this resource.
  }
}
```

While there are certainly cases where this field can be useful (e.g., you may want to prevent certain logs from being deleted for compliance reasons), in general, it's better to guard against accidental destruction of a resource using the `ignore_changes` field.

IGNORE_CHANGES

The `ignore_changes` argument tells Terraform not to update a resource if the only attributes that changed are in the list. The `ignore_changes` argument takes in a list of argument names and tells Terraform not to update a resource just because those arguments have been changed and to ignore those fields when doing an update. This basically tells Terraform to ignore the specific arguments completely after creation.

This may be the most common `lifecycle` block used in practice as there are a lot of different cases where it comes up. Some attributes force replacements instead of updates, which may not be desired. We discussed the AMI example earlier, where a new AMI release may not be the best time to replace an existing running instance. There are also many systems that add or remove tags from resources, and being able to ignore those changes prevents errors from occurring. This is common with orchestration systems like AWS Elastic Kubernetes Service or Elastic Container Service.

Listing 2.29   Ignoring changes for a specific attribute

```
resource "aws_instance" "hello_world" {
  ami           = data.aws_ami.ubuntu.id
  subnet_id     = data.aws_subnets.default.ids[0]
  instance_type = var.instance_type

  lifecycle {                                    If the AMI changes, this
    ignore_changes = [ami]        ◄───┘          resource will not be replaced.
  }
}
```

This argument can also take in a special value, `all`, that tells Terraform to ignore any change to the resource. This essentially means that Terraform will create the resource and then never change or update it. Terraform will still read the values to generate attributes for the resource, but it essentially makes the resource read only after launch.

```
resource "aws_instance" "hello_world" {
  ami             = data.aws_ami.ubuntu.id
  subnet_id       = data.aws_subnets.default.ids[0]
  instance_type = var.instance_type

  lifecycle {
    ignore_changes = all          ◄──────── This resource will never be changed. Note
  }                                          that the all keyword is not in brackets.
}
```

The `ignore_changes` field is often used to prevent a resource from being replaced. Since only some fields require replacement (e.g., you can't change the AMI used by an AWS instance without replacing the instance completely), those fields can be added to `ignore_changes` to keep the resource from being replaced while still allowing other fields to be updated. This tends to be preferable over the `prevent_destroy` argument, as this will not prevent a `destroy` plan from being generated.

REPLACE_TRIGGERED_BY

The `replace_triggered_by` argument allows you to force replacements on resources when other resources change. This argument expects a list of resource attributes or references to the resource itself. For attributes, the resource will only be changed if that specific attribute changes, while references to resources themselves will result in a replacement if the triggering resource has any change at all.

In our Hello World example, we exposed a variable, `instance_type`. When an `aws_instance` has its type changed, this triggers an update in place—the machine is shut down, the instance type is changed, and then the same instance is powered up again. We can use the `replace_triggered_by` field to force the instance to be replaced instead of updated when that variable changes.

```
resource "null_resource" "replace_instance" {  ◄──── The null resource is a "state
  triggers = {                                        only" resource. Here it lets us
    instance_type = var.instance_type          ◄──── trigger a replacement when
  }                                                   instance_type changes.
}

                                               Replace this resource when the
resource "aws_instance" "hello_world" {        instance type variable changes.
  ami             = data.aws_ami.ubuntu.id
  subnet_id       = data.aws_subnets.default.ids[0]
  instance_type = var.instance_type           ◄──── Normally, changing this field
                                                     does not replace the instance.
  lifecycle {
    replace_triggered_by = [
```

```
        null_resource.replace_instance
    ]
  }
}
```

> This field has to be a resource or resource attribute—it can not be variable.

The `replace_triggered_by` argument is one of the newer features to be added to the Terraform language. There are many providers that expose resources with arguments that have the same purpose but that are specific to that provider. The `random` provider uses an argument named `keepers`, while the `null` provider uses an argument named `triggers` (both of these providers will be discussed in chapter 8). This is one example of how functionality that exists in providers can make it back into Terraform itself for use by all resources.

2.7.3 Explicit dependencies

So far we've shown that Terraform will map dependencies between different blocks based on how attributes and arguments are linked together. These are implicit dependency links—Terraform infers them based on those attributes and arguments. It is also possible to explicitly define dependencies with the `depends_on` argument.

Listing 2.32   An explicit dependency between two resources

```
resource "aws_internet_gateway" "main" {
  vpc_id = aws_vpc.main.id
}
```

> This resource doesn't export anything needed by the NAT Gateway.

```
resource "aws_nat_gateway" "example" {
  subnet_id = aws_subnet.example.id
```

> There are no arguments that take in attributes from resource "aws_internet_gateway. "main". However, the NAT Gateway will not work until the Internet Gateway is up.

```
  depends_on = [
    aws_internet_gateway.main
  ]
}
```

> depends_on takes the block reference itself an argument, not an attribute.

> Only resource blocks can be depended on so the resource part of the block reference is dropped.

When two resources have a dependency between them but don't require information from each other, the only option is the `depends_on` argument. One example of this is the AWS Internet Gateway and the AWS Network Address Transation (NAT) Gateway. These resources work together to provide internet access to private subnets. However, since there is only ever one Internet Gateway for a VPC, the NAT Gateway does not have an argument for it—there's only one it can use, so it attempts to use that. The problem is that it cannot launch without the Internet Gateway, which could lead to errors if Terraform attempts to launch it first. The `depends_on` argument solves this by letting developers explicitly define dependencies between these resources.

When used in a `module` block, the `depends_on` argument is passed on to all resources in that module.

2.8 Modules

Modules are the primary way that Terraform allows developers to share and reuse code. Modules are an extremely complex topic that we focus on in chapter 3. For now, we briefly show how the `module` block is used.

Modules have their own block type that is used to create the resources inside of a module. This block is pretty similar to resources and even accepts some of the same meta arguments, but modules are written by developers using Terraform HCL.

Modules have a few new meta arguments that are not used by other block types:

- `Source` tells Terraform where to get the module from and is a required argument. This can be a URL pointing to a module in a hosted registry, a path pointing to the module on the filesystem, or a Git reference to a local or remote repository.

- `Version` tells Terraform what the allowed version range is. This is used when the source is a registry and allows the developer to lock into a specific version range for a module. This way, developers can control when their modules get updated so they can ensure new changes don't break their expectations.

- `Providers` allow the developer to specify which provider aliases from the outer module get passed to the called module.

Let's say we wanted to add a virtual private network service to our VPC so we can connect our laptop to the resources in our account. Rather than build it ourselves, we could use a module someone else built. We can pull a module from the Terraform Public Registry that builds the virtual private network for us.

Listing 2.33   Module example

```
module "vpn" {
  source  = "tedivm/dev-vpn/aws"
  version = "~> 1.0"

  identifier = "my-vpn"
  subnet_ids = data.aws_subnets.default.ids
}
```

This tells Terraform to download the tedivm/dev-vpn/aws module from the public registry.

Modules can have version specifications, just like providers.

This module also needs a list of subnets to attach to.

Modules have their own arguments, in this case a user-provided identifier.

Modules get their arguments from the `variable` block and its attributes from the `output` block. Modules are covered in a lot more detail in chapter 3.

2.9 Import, moved, and removed

In the Terraform v1.5.0 release, two new blocks were added to help aid refactoring: the `import` and `moved` blocks. In Terraform v1.7.0, the `removed` block was added. The `import` block helps people move resources into Terraform or from one Terraform project to another, while the `moved` block allows developers to move resources around inside of a single Terraform project. For example, if someone previously created a resource in the AWS console, they could use the `import` block to bring that resource into Terraform without having to re-create it. We'll discuss all of these more in chapter 9.

The `import` block was originally added to work around limitations in the `terraform import` command. Putting the `import` statements in code allows the import to be reviewed during the plan phase and makes it easier to automate imports across multiple environments. For example, if you were migrating a project into Terraform and had staging and production environments, the `import` block would allow you to codify the resources you wanted to import in and then (starting with Terraform v1.6) use variables or even data sources to identify which resources to import.

Once all the resources you want to import have been imported, you can remove the `import` blocks. You don't have to do this immediately, as they will essentially be ignored once they've done their job and the resource is saved. However, leaving them in will make it harder to reuse your Terraform code in new environments where there are no resources to import.

Listing 2.34   `import` **block**

```
import {
  to = aws_instance.main
  id = "i-1234567890abcdef0"
}

resource "aws_instance" "main" {
  # Required Arguments
}
```

The to argument should point to a resource block.

In v1.5 the ID had to be hardcoded, but v1.6 allows variables and attributes.

The `moved` block exists to tell Terraform that a resource isn't in the same place inside of your code anymore. This can happen when the code for a resource is moved into a module or simply when developers decide to rename the `resource` block. The `moved` resource lets Terraform associate the existing resource with the new location without having to re-create it.

Unlike the `import` block, there's really no downside to leaving the `moved` block in place even after it's been run. If Terraform does not find a resource to move to the existing state, it will create a new one to replace it. This allows it to be used on new projects without any conflict. As a result, this block is very safe to use inside of modules that have been published for reuse.

Listing 2.35   `moved` **block**

```
moved {
  from = module.bad_unclear_name
  to   = module.better_name
}

module "better_name" {

}
```

The from argument should be the old resource or module location.

The to argument should point to the new resource location.

At this point, we've gone through the basics of a Terraform program, starting with our example and going through all of the core components. With this knowledge, you can start defining infrastructure using Terraform. In the next chapter, we're going to discuss variables and how they allow for great customization when using modules.

Summary

- The Terraform language is largely centered around blocks.
- A `terraform settings` block is used to configure providers and workspace settings.
- Data sources are read-only blocks used for looking up data.
- `resource` blocks are the primary reason Terraform exists and are used to manage infrastructure.
- Data sources and resources can be abstracted into reusable modules, which are the building blocks of large systems.
- Lifecycle arguments can change how a resource is managed.

Terraform variables and modules 3

This chapter covers

- Reusable components through the use of modules
- The three different types of variables in Terraform: local, input, and output
- How Terraform handles typing
- Validating inputs for more resilient code
- Dealing with sensitive data such as passwords
- Variable files and workspaces

One of the big promises of infrastructure as code is reusability. Being able to write something once and then allowing it to be used throughout a project has a huge number of benefits. Developers can use components they aren't as familiar with, experts can expand and configure the components in the best possible way even as needs grow, and everyone can see how the system is being built. Terraform promotes reusability through the use of modules.

Modules are different from providers in a few ways. Modules are pure Terraform HashiCorp Configuration Language (HCL), so there's no Go provider. In fact, a module cannot define new types or resources itself and instead uses the resources and data sources provided by individual providers. Modules do not have to be vendor specific—they can incorporate resources from multiple providers. While providers expose resources that are extremely low-level, mapping to a specific infrastructure component, modules can be used to create higher-level abstractions over systems composed of multiple components.

In the last chapter, we discussed how companies might abstract their network stack into a reusable building block that can be reused throughout the company. A module is how they would accomplish this. It's also common for companies to have modules for services, such as having a module that launches a Kubernetes cluster that developers can use. The use of modules allows teams to create building blocks of systems that can be composed together to create a larger platform.

NOTE Module development and management is a complex topic that is expanded on throughout this book.

3.1 Modules

Modules are the standard way of sharing Terraform code between projects. Unlike providers, modules are made using the Terraform language and are meant to be called by other Terraform programs. A Terraform module is similar to a package in Python Package or a module in Javascript. In all three cases, you have a collection of related code that can be reused throughout a software project. This isn't a perfect metaphor, though, as modules can also be considered similar to functions where you have input parameters, internal logic, and return statements (or outputs).

DEFINITION A module is, at its core, a collection of data sources, resources, and any assets (configuration files, templates) that are bundled together into reusable components. They are reusable libraries that can be packaged up and distributed for reuse.

Terraform modules come in several flavors:

- *Root modules* are where all Terraform projects start. They configure providers and call any other modules that are needed. When the `terraform init` command is run inside of a root module, it creates a workspace. Our Hello World example is a root module.
- *Shared modules* are modules that are pulled down from a Git repository or Terraform Module Registry. They can be public modules made by third parties or part of a private registry of modules developed and maintained by your team.
- *Submodules* are modules that are distributed as part of another module. They might be part of a root module or a shared module. In general, they tend to be coupled to their parent module, which is why they aren't distributed separately.

3.1.1   *Module usage*

Modules have their own block type that is used to create the resources inside a module. This block is pretty similar to resources and even accepts some of the same meta arguments, but modules are written by developers using Terraform HCL.

Modules have a few new meta arguments that are not used by other block types:

- `source` tells Terraform where to get the module from and is a required argument. This can be a URL pointing to a module in a hosted registry, or it can be a path pointing to the module on the filesystem.
- `version` tells Terraform what the allowed version range is. This is used when the source is a registry and allows the developer to lock into a specific version range for a module. This way, developers can control when their modules get updated so they can ensure new changes don't break their expectations.
- `providers` allow the developer to specify which provider aliases from the outer module get passed to the called module.

Let's say we wanted to add a virtual private network service to our virtual private cloud (VPC) so we can connect our laptop to the resources in our account. Rather than build it ourselves, we could use a module someone else built. We can pull a module from the Terraform Public Registry that builds the virtual private network for us.

To do this, we create a `module` block and use the two meta parameters `source` and `version` to tell Terraform how to download the module. The source can vary, from local filesystems to Git repositories and even special registries. In this case, we can use the `tedivm/cloudinit` (https://mng.bz/mGmn) module, which is published on the Terraform Public Registry. Modules can also be published in third-party registries (such as Artifactory) or directly on GitHub.

Listing 3.1   Using a public module

```
module "vpn" {
    source  = "tedivm/cloudinit/general"
    version = "~> 1.0"

    services = ["consul", "nomad"]
}
```

This tells Terraform to download the tedivm/cloudinit/general module from the public registry.

Modules can have version specifications, just like providers.

Modules have their own arguments, in this case a list of services to launch.

Modules get their arguments from the `variable` block and their attributes from the `output` block. These blocks are the main topic of the next chapter.

3.1.2   *Module file structure*

Modules typically are made up of several Terraform files, all in the same directory. Terraform has a specific file structure (https://mng.bz/5gA4) that it proposes and that the community follows, but from a technical standpoint this structure isn't required. Developers will sometimes create one-file modules that break this structure, and they work just like any other. If you want to stick with the standard format, you should create your files using the names in table 3.1.

Table 3.1 Terraform module files

File	Purpose
variables.tf	Module inputs should all be defined here.
output.tf	Module outputs should all be defined here.
main.tf	Main entry point for module. Simple modules may only use this file to define resources.
*.tf	Terraform files that define resources. How these are named depends on the specific project.
README.md	Documentation for the project. This will be pulled into any module registry the module is published to.
modules/	Submodules that are part of this project should have their own folders here that follow this structure.
templates/	If the project uses templates, they should be in their own folder.
examples/	Examples of how to use the module should be stored here.

3.1.3 Root module

The root-level module is the entry point for your code. When you run commands like `terraform init` or `terraform apply`, Terraform looks in your current working directory for any `.tf` files. Those files comprise your root-level module.

As we've already talked about a bit, the root-level module is special as it is the only place where you can configure providers using the `provider` block. A root-level module will typically have a combination of resources and modules that it controls.

3.1.4 Submodules

Submodules are modules that exist inside of a larger parent module. They are stored in the `modules` directory of the parent module (they aren't required to be in this directory, but it's a very strong convention). They are used to divide up functionality into smaller, more manageable pieces.

Submodules follow the same structure as any other module. They store their files in the same place, expect some level of documentation, and can even be called and tested individually. In theory, it is also possible for submodules to have their own submodules, but this is considered to be a bad practice as it raises the level of complexity of a project.

3.1.5 Module registries

Modules can be stored directly in Git or saved locally on a filesystem, but it is much more common to use a module registry. Module registries generally tie into version control and issue new releases when a tag is created.

Registries can be public or private. The largest public module registry is at Terraform .io (https://registry.terraform.io/browse/modules), where it sits alongside the provider registry. It hosts roughly 12,000 different modules. Some of them are produced and managed by companies while others are open source projects from individuals.

When using a package from a public registry, it is important to understand what it is you are using. Important factors are how regularly the package is updated, whether it commits to backward compatibility or has solid upgrade documentation, whether it's managed by a group or an individual, and whether the code quality itself is good and free of any malicious or weird design decisions.

Private registries tend to be run by companies for their development teams. Sometimes they are self-hosted, but many come from specialty Terraform services such as Terraform Cloud or Spacelift. The `terraform login` command is used to get a login token to store on the system to download modules, while pushes are generally managed by a connection to the company's Git provider and triggered on a tag.

3.2   *Input, output, and local variables*

In most languages, including Terraform, variables are placeholders for reusable values. Terraform has three different components that it calls variables. The differences all relate to how the variable interacts with modules.

Input variables, generally just called `inputs`, are used by developers to send information into a module. In our chapter example, we used input variables to let the users of our module specify the subnet they wanted to attach the instance to and the instance type of the machine. Inputs create parameters that can be used on the `module` blocks in the same way that parameters are passed to resources and data sources.

Output variables, or `outputs`, are used by module developers to get information out of a module. Output variables get exposed as attributes to the user that they can then map to resource parameters, similar to how resources expose their own attributes. Our chapter example uses output variables to share the IP address and instance ID of the instance we created. These attributes are accessed in the same way that resource and data source attributes are.

Local variables, or `locals`, exist inside of a module. They have a lot of uses, including acting as intermediary logic variables (that was a mouthful, but we'll talk about it in just a minute) or saving values that need to be reused a lot inside the module. They are defined with the `locals` block. Just like with resources, local variables cannot have circular dependencies. We'll discuss this more in chapter 5.

If you are familiar with languages that use functions, you can think about this another way. In languages that use functions, you have function arguments to send information into the function and a return value that is used to take information out of the function, and then all of the variables inside of the function only exist in that function. In our case, the input variables are the function arguments, the output variables are the return values, and our local variables are the ones that exist only inside the module.

The only variables from outside of a module that is available are the input variables, and the only internal variables in a module that can be accessed from outside of it are the outputs. Locals can only be accessed inside the module (see figure 3.1).

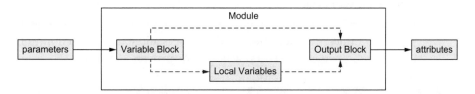

Figure 3.1   Module scope for inputs, outputs, and locals

Terraform variables have another unique feature that makes them very different from most other languages: all Terraform variables are constants. That means that their value can only be set once during a program, and then it cannot be changed or altered during that run. This is because Terraform is a declarative language, not an imperative one. Since it runs the program based on the order of dependencies, not based on the order the code was written, Terraform would have no way to know what order to apply or use variable changes. Don't worry though: it is possible to implement logic and transforms using local variables, and we'll tackle that problem in this chapter.

3.3   *Input variables*

Input variables are what allow modules to be customized without having to change the source code of the module. Module developers provide input variables for their modules, and users of the module can alter what they provide for the input variables to trigger different behavior. Many times, this is a simple configuration, such as our example where we used input variables to change the instance type of our AWS instance. They can also trigger more complex behavior, such as optionally adding load balancers or autoscaling rules, depending on what the module developer needs (we'll discuss these more complex use cases in chapter 8).

3.3.1   *Defining and using inputs*

Inside a module, a developer defines input variables using the `variable` block. This block has a unique name for its label and takes several arguments:

- `description` is an optional argument that is used to provide documentation about the variable. It can be picked up by external tools, such as the Terraform Docs (https://terraform-docs.io/) project, to generate documentation in different formats.
- `type` adds restrictions on what kind of value can be passed to the variable. By default, the variable will accept any type. We'll discuss the different variable types later in the chapter.

- `default` can be used to set a value to use when one isn't provided.
- `sensitive` is used to tell Terraform to be extra careful not to display the value of this variable in any logs. This defaults to `false`.
- `nullable` specifies whether the variable can be assigned the special null value. This defaults to `true`.
- `validation` is a special subblock that can be used to add extra checks on any passed-in values. This lets module developers add extra protection to their variables so users can catch errors earlier in the process.

Listing 3.2   Example variables

```
variable "ami" {
  type        = string
  description = "The Amazon Machine Image to use when launching the EC2
⇒Instance."
}

variable "subnet_id" {
  type        = string
  description = "The ID of the Subnet to launch the instance into."
}

variable "instance_type" {
  type        = string
  description = "The type of instance to launch."
  default     = "t3.micro"
}
```

Variables can be restricted to specific data types, such as strings.

Inputs can have descriptions, and it's a good practice to always add them.

Inputs can have default values so users don't have to explicitly define all of them.

Inside a module, a variable can be referred to using the `var` keyword followed by the variable name. In our example, we referenced the `subnet_id` variable as `var.subnet_id` when passing it to the `aws_instance` resource.

Listing 3.3   Example variable usage

```
resource "aws_instance" "hello_world" {
  ami           = var.ami
  subnet_id     = var.subnet_id
  instance_type = var.instance_type
}
```

The three variables defined in listing 3.2 each used here to configure our instance.

3.3.2   *Marking variables as sensitive*

There are times when a developer using Terraform will have to deal with sensitive data. This can include passwords, API keys, or even credentials meant to be passed to a provider. Terraform has special tools that make dealing with sensitive data easier.

Terraform itself is pretty loud; that is, it tends to log and display a lot of information, including changes in parameters during the planning phase. In general, this is great because it makes it easier to verify changes. This has some pretty big security implications though. If a variable contains data that is supposed to remain private, such as a password or API key, then displaying (and likely logging) those values could be considered a pretty severe breach.

Terraform allows developers to mark input variables as `sensitive`, which tells modern Terraform versions to avoid displaying it. Terraform keeps track of this property on the value itself, so when the input variable is passed to a resource argument or used to calculate a local variable, the value will still be masked in logs.

Listing 3.4 Marking variables as sensitive

```
variable "logging_api_key" {
  description = "The API Key for our logging service."
  type        = string
  sensitive   = true              ◄──────── This prevents Terraform from
}                                            printing or logging the API Key.
```

Once a variable is marked as `sensitive`, Terraform will avoid logging its value. This `sensitive` attribute will follow the value around, so if the value is used to create another value, then that value will also be `sensitive`.

It's important to note that this `sensitive` value can still be stored in the Terraform state. This is one of the reasons keeping your state's security is so important. We'll come back to this topic in depth in chapter 6.

3.3.3 *Using types for robust code*

Terraform allows input values to be restricted by their type. Types are essentially categories of data: a value can have a type of `String`, `Number`, `Boolean`, `List`, `Object`, `Maps`, `Sets`, `Tuples`, or the special `Null` type. If someone attempts to use the wrong type for a variable, it will throw an error. For example, if you accidentally provide a string where a boolean is expected, Terraform will throw an error.

The use of types helps to make programs written in Terraform more robust and easy to debug. If a provider is expecting a boolean but gets a string, it will throw an error with a message describing both what it expected and what it received.

The `variable` block has a `type` argument that takes type `constraints` for the variable. A type constraint is a special Terraform construct that is used to define the type. Some type constraints are really simple: if you want to specify a string, you simply write "string" for the constraint. Other types of constraints, such as those for objects, are much more complex. In section 3.7 we'll go through the constraints for every type.

Listing 3.5 Defining variables with types

```
variable "strings_only" {
  type    = string
  default = "This has to be a string."     ◄──────── The type argument is used to restrict
}                                                     the kinds of values accepted.
```

```
variable "numbers_only" {
  type    = number
  default = 3.14
}

variable "booleans_only" {
  type    = bool
  default = true
}

variable "list_of_strings" {
  type    = list(string)
  default = ["list", "of", "strings"]
}
```

Some types are more complex and allow for subtypes.

By default, a variable can be any type, as Terraform does not require a type. In this way, Terraform can be said to be loosely typed, at least at the module level. Type constraints are optional, but they are also a sign of high-quality code. It's also possible to add custom validation rules to inputs, which we'll discuss in section 3.8.

3.4   *Outputs*

Modules are used to create resources that are expected to be used alongside other modules and resources. For developers to do that, they need to be able to pull information out of a module. The `output` block makes this possible by giving module developers a way to explicitly define the values they want their module to return.

Listing 3.6   Example outputs

```
output "aws_instance_arn" {
  value = resources.aws_instance.arn
}

output "my_favorite_string" {
  value = "Hello World"
}
```

Outputs let us pass information out of our module back to the user.

Any expression or value can be an output.

Outputs are a core part of Terraform. VPC modules return subnets that machines can launch in them, while instance modules (like our EC2 one) return IP addresses and machine IDs so other services can reference them. Part of designing and building distributed systems is linking these independent services together to form a larger platform, which means taking the output of one module and using it as the input of another.

3.4.1   *Defining and using outputs*

Module developers can use the `output` block to return data from inside of their module. This block is much less complex than the input module, with only a few arguments:

- `description` is an optional argument that lets a developer document their outputs. This can be picked up by external tools to create documents in different formats.

- `value` is the actual return value for the module. These are normally populated with attributes from resources created by the module.

- `sensitive` is used to tell Terraform to avoid logging or printing the value. It will still get saved in any state files.

- `depends_on` is an argument that allows the module developer to explicitly create a dependency between the output and another object.

The `output` blocks are pretty simple. There are also some advanced features you can use with outputs known as `preconditions`, which we'll talk about in chapter 10. Outputs are normally stored in a file named `outputs.tf`, so let's create that file in our module to add in a few `output` blocks.

Listing 3.7 Adding `outputs.tf` **to our module**

```
output "aws_instance_arn" {
  description = "The AWS Resource Name for the instance."  ◀── Like inputs,
  value       = aws_instance.hello_world.arn            outputs can also
}                                                          have descriptions.

                                    Outputs can take in any value
                                    local to the module, including
                                    resource attributes.

output "aws_instance_ip" {
  description = "The IP Address for the private network interface on the
➥instance."
  value       = aws_instance.hello_world.private_ip
}


output "aws_instance" {
  description = "The entire instance resource."
  value       = aws_instance.hello_world
}
```

It doesn't require a special keyword to use `output` blocks. Instead, outputs of modules are accessed as attributes of the `module` block that created it. These attributes work just like their counterparts in the `data` and `resource` blocks. Once a `module` block is created, you can access the output as an attribute and use it inside of other resources.

Go ahead and push your code up to GitHub. In this case, you're going to want to name the repository with the pattern `terraform-aws-instance` to describe what it does. In the following example, we take our IP address and apply it to an AWS Security Group (which is the resource AWS uses to allow or deny network traffic between different systems).

Listing 3.8 Using module outputs

```
module "my_instance" {
  source    = "github.com/YOU_USERNAME/terraform-aws-instance"  ◀──
  subnet_id = var.subnet_id
}                                                    We're using our
                                                     published module from
resource "aws_security_group" "allow_instance_access" {   earlier in the chapter.
```

```
    name    = "my_instance_access"
    vpc_id = aws_vpc.main.id
}
```
This is a security group rule that allows our instance to access machines using this security group.

```
resource "aws_vpc_security_group_ingress_rule" "allow_access" {
    security_group_id = aws_security_group.allow_instance_access.id
    description       = "Allow traffic on port 443 from MyInstance"
    from_port         = 443
    to_port           = 443
    ip_protocol       = "tcp"
    cidr_ipv4         = "${module.my_instance.aws_instance_ip}/32"
}
```
This is the port for HTTPS traffic.

We take the output from our module and use it to make a new string.

3.4.2   Sensitive outputs

Outputs can be declared as sensitive, just as inputs can. By declaring an output as sensitive, you explicitly prevent its value from being logged or output by the command line interface. A module that creates a password, for instance, would want to mark it as sensitive to prevent Terraform from displaying it.

Listing 3.9   Adding `variables.tf` **to our module**

```
output "super_secret_password" {
    description = "The password created by this module"
    value       = resource.random_password.id
    sensitive   = true
}
```
The random provider can be used to generate random data, like passwords.

Terraform will avoid displaying this value.

It is really important to mark any output as sensitive if it has a value that comes from another sensitive value. If you don't, then Terraform will assume you are accidentally exposing sensitive data, which will trigger an error.

It is also extremely important to note that sensitive values are still stored in the Terraform state. We'll discuss techniques to minimize this in later chapters, but it is important to remember that marking something as sensitive does not prevent Terraform from remembering that sensitive value.

3.4.3   Output dependencies

Outputs already have a dependency on their own value. They can't return it until it is calculated. There are times when it may be desirable to have an output depend on another resource as well. For example, a module developer may not want to return an instance as an output until it has also configured firewall rules.

Listing 3.10   Output dependencies

```
output "load_balanced_aws_instance" {
    description = "The entire instance resource."
    value       = aws_instance.hello_world
```

```
    depends_on = [
      aws_lb_target_group_attachment.instance_attachement
    ]
}
```

This prevents the output from being returned until the instance_attachement resource finishes processing.

This is very much an edge case, and it's possible to completely avoid this feature for years. That said, it's useful to know about on the off chance it is needed.

3.5   Locals

Local variables only exist inside of the module where they are defined. Earlier in the chapter we compared modules to functions inside of other languages, with `inputs` acting as function arguments and `outputs` acting as return values. If we expand that example, then `locals` are the variables that only exist inside the function themselves. Local variables exist so modules can do their own internal processing and logic, so there's no reason for them to be accessible outside of the module. If for some reason a module author wants to expose a `local` variable, they would do so by passing it as the value of an `output`.

3.5.1   Defining and using locals

Locals are defined using the `locals` block. This is a very weird block compared to other Terraform and HCL components. Unlike most Terraform blocks, the `locals` block does not take a name or label, and it can also be used as many times as you'd like inside a module. At the moment, there is no other block quite like it.

Each `locals` block can take any number of arguments. Each argument is considered an independent `local variable` and takes the assigned value. In other words, if you have a `locals` block with arguments `alpha`, `bravo`, and `charlie`, then you've created three local variables with those respective names.

Listing 3.11 `locals` blocks

```
locals {
  alpha   = 1
  bravo   = "two"
  charlie = false
}

locals {
  delta = ["four", "five"]
  echo = {
    "foxtrot" = "six",
    "golf"    = "seven"
  }
}

locals {
  hotel = local.bravo
}
```

Each of these locals will be available through the whole module.

These locals will also be available throughout the whole module.

Local variables can reference other local variables.

Local variables can be created in any number of blocks. Instead of defining `alpha`, `bravo`, and `charlie` in a single block, they could be defined in three separate blocks spread across multiple files. This doesn't change their behavior at all. However, you cannot reuse argument names, either in the same or a different block, without Terraform throwing an error.

Listing 3.12   `locals` **block duplicate declaration error**

```
locals {
  alpha   = 1
  bravo   = "two"          ◄─────   Even though this is in the top block it
  charlie = false                   will still conflict with the other alpha.
}

locals {                          Since there are two alpha values
  alpha = 2        ◄─────         an error will be thrown.
}
```

Terraform uses the `local` keyword followed by the name to refer to the local (i.e., `local.alpha`, `local.bravo`, `local.charlie`). Locals are only visible inside their own module.

Listing 3.13   `locals` **usage**

```
locals {
  tags = { "Author" : "Rob", "ManagedBy" : "Terraform" }  ◄─
}                                                             Here we use a local
                                                             variable to define a
resource "aws_instance" "first_instance" {                   reusable object to
  subnet_id     = var.subnet_id                              reference below.
  instance_type = "t3.micro"
  tags          = local.tags     ◄─────   Here we use the local tags
}                                          variable we created above.

resource "aws_instance" "second_instance" {
  subnet_id     = var.subnet_id
  instance_type = "t3.small"
  tags          = local.tags     ◄─────   We also use it here.
}
```

3.6   *Value types*

As we discussed in section 3.4.3, all values in Terraform have a corresponding type. Types make programming with Terraform more robust by enforcing the expected data types and structures (in the case of objects), stopping execution before errors occur, and giving rich error messages when problems do occur.

If you've programmed with other languages, you have probably encountered some or all of the types that Terraform has, but there are still some nuances you may need to think about. Next, I give a brief overview of the types that Terraform supports.

3.6.1 Strings

A string is a group of zero or more characters that make up a chunk of text. Strings can be simple labels, complex configurations, or encoded data. Terraform strings are encoded with unicode, so your strings can include characters from other languages and even unicode emojis if you need them.

The keyword for strings is simply `string`.

Listing 3.14 String type constraint

```
variable "name" {
  type        = string
  description = "The name to apply to resources in the module."
}
```

Terraform allows for string interpolation: that is, when you define a new string, you can embed variables in it. This makes it easier to construct smaller dynamic strings. There are easier ways to manipulate and construct larger strings, such as the `templatefile` function that we'll discuss in chapter 4 alongside other string manipulation functions.

Listing 3.15 Interpolated string example

```
variable "prefix" {
  type        = string
  description = "A prefix to be added to the identifiers used in the
  modules."
}

locals {
  identifier = "${var.prefix}-service"        ◀──── The prefix variable is used to
}                                                    create a new local that can be
                                                     reused in the module.
```

3.6.2 Numbers

Terraform has a single type for all numeric values, whether they're whole numbers, fractions, or negative numbers. The keyword for all of these is `number`.

Listing 3.16 Numeric type constraint

```
variable "any_number" {
  type    = number
  default = 1            ◀──── Numbers can be integers.
}

variable "another_number" {
  type    = number
  default = 1.31         ◀──── Numbers can also be floats.
}

variable "a_negative_number" {
```

```
type    = number
default = -1                          Numbers can even be negative.
}
```

Having a single type for all numbers is somewhat rare in programming languages, where it is pretty common to have a separate type for integers (whole numbers) and floats (numbers with a decimal component). This can be a source of errors when a module specifies a number but doesn't further verify that the number is appropriate for the context.

3.6.3 *Booleans*

A boolean, often just referred to as "a bool," is a value that is either true or false. The keyword for booleans is `bool`.

Listing 3.17 Boolean type constraint

```
variable "enable_flag" {                Booleans can be either
  type    = bool                        "true" or "false".
  default = true
}                                       If no value is passed, this
                                        variable will be true.

variable "enable_flag_disabled" {
  type    = bool                        If no value is passed, this
  default = false                       variable will be false.
}
```

3.6.4 *Lists*

Lists are values with multiple values known as elements. Every element in a list has an index that specifies the element's place in the list, starting with zero.

The keyword for lists is `list`. When used as a type constraint, it is expected to be `list(type)`, although, for backward compatibility reasons, Terraform will also accept just `list` and convert it to `list(any)`.

Listing 3.18 List type constraint

```
variable "list_of_anything" {
  type = list(any)
  default = [                           Lists can be flexible and allow the any
    "string",                           keyword, but this is generally discouraged.
  ]
}

variable "list_of_strings" {
  type = list(string)
  default = [                           In this case only strings
    "us-east-1",                        will be allowed in the list.
    "us-west-2",
  ]
```

```
}

variable "list_of_lists" {
  type = list(list(string))          This variable expects a list of
  default = [                        lists, with strings in the sublists.
    ["one", "two", "three"],
    ["red", "green", "blue"]
  ]
}
```

Lists require that every element be the same type. You can have lists of strings, lists of numbers, even lists of lists or objects—but you can't have a list that contains both numbers and strings.

Listing 3.19 List type limitations

```
variable "list_of_anything" {        All elements in a list
  type = list(any)                   have to be the same.
  default = [
    "string",                        This list can have any subtype as
    2.3                              long as all elements are the same.
  ]
}                                    Mixing a string and a
                                     number will cause an error.
```

3.6.5   Sets

Sets are very similar to lists, with two major differences:

- Sets do not have duplicate elements. If you attempt to put duplicate elements into a set, the duplicates will be discarded.
- Sets have no order. If you define a set with the elements in a specific order, you won't be able to get them back out in that order.

Sets are very useful when you need a group of elements that have no repeats in them and when you don't care what their order is.

The keyword for sets is `set`, and, like a list, the constraint takes a type argument.

Listing 3.20 Set type constraint

```
variable "set_of_names" {
  type = set(string)
  default = [
    "Natalya",
    "Serena",
    "Angelica",
    "Brayden",
    "Maddison",
    "Ulises",
    "Blaze",
    "Margaret",
    "Cailyn",
```

```
        "Leonel",
        "Caylee",
        "Brooks",
    ]
}
```

3.6.6   *Tuples*

A tuple is a series of elements similar to a list. Each element has an index starting at zero, and they are accessed in the same way that lists are. Tuples differ from lists in several important ways:

- Tuples have a set length. They have to have the exact number of elements that were defined in the type constraint.
- Each element in a tuple can have a different type. These types should be defined in the type constraint, and the values for each element must match that constraint.

Listing 3.21   Tuple type constraint

```
variable "example_tuple" {
    type    = tuple([string, string, number])   ◄────   This tuple is required to have three
    default = ["alpha", "bravo", 42]                     elements, with the first two being
}                                                        strings and the third a number.
```

3.6.7   *Objects*

Objects are collections of data organized by key. Every key in the object has a corresponding value, and keys are always unique strings. With an object, each key can have values of different types.

Objects have the keyword `object`, as well as the most complex type constraints of any type. Object type constraints allow each key to be defined with a specific type and allow for nested object types.

Object type constraints take an object themselves as an argument. This type constraint argument should have one key for every key that the input variable has, and each of those keys should point to the expected type. An object type of `object({name=string, count=number})` would describe an object with a "name" key that was a string and a "count" key that was a number.

Listing 3.22   Simple object type constraint

```
variable "my_object" {
    type = object({                    Objects contain one or more
        name    = string,       ◄────  keys, each with their own type.
        enabled = bool       ◄───┐
                                 │     The keys in an object do not
    })                                 have to be the same type.
```

```
    default = {
        name    = "default"
        enabled = false
    }
}
```

Object values are
declared with brackets.

It's possible to mark values in an object as optional. The optional type constraint can be used to set a default for when the key doesn't exist inside of the passed input.

Listing 3.23 Object with optional values

```
variable "optional_keys" {
  type = object({
    alpha   = string,
    bravo   = optional(string)
    charlie = optional(string, "default_string")
  })

  default = {
    alpha = "example"
  }
}

locals {
  delta   = var.optional_keys.alpha
  echo    = var.optional_keys.bravo
  foxtrot = var.optional_keys.charlie
}
```

Only alpha is defined as the
other two are optional.

delta will be "example"
or a user-provided value.

echo will be null or a
user-provided value.

foxtrot will be "default_string"
or a user-provided value.

Objects can have keys that point to other objects. This allows for the creation of complex data structures with multiple levels of values.

Listing 3.24 Nested objects

```
variable "nested_object" {
  type = object({
    key = object({
      subkey = object({
        nested_string = string
        nested_tuple  = tuple([string, string, string])
      })
    })
  })

  default = {
    key = {
      subkey = {
        nested_string = "hello world",
        nested_tuple  = ["one", "two", "three"]
      }
    }
  }
}
```

Keys can reference
other objects...

...which can also
reference other objects.

This allows for
arbitrarily complex
data structures...

...including mixing in
other complex types.

In general, you want to avoid making your variables too complex. Deep nesting and complex objects can make it harder to follow and modify code. If you see yourself defining very complex inputs, you should consider whether it would be clearer if the input was broken up into multiple simpler inputs.

3.6.8 Maps

Maps are very similar to objects, especially when it comes to the format for defining them (the curly brackets and key value pairing). There are two major differences though, and that's in how Terraform treats them. Unlike objects, all values inside a map have the same type. If your map is a map of strings, then every value will be a string without exception.

The other difference is that Terraform doesn't enforce the structure of a map the way it does an object. If your object has a defined constraint, then Terraform will drop any key that isn't in that constraint. With maps, Terraform will allow you to have an arbitrary number of keys. This is useful when you're trying to add input variables for fields like tags, which are typically key/value pairs of strings with an arbitrary number of keys.

Other than that, maps and objects are the same. They are defined with the same syntax and are referred to in exactly the same way. When reading the official documentation on the Terraform website, you will regularly see "map" and "object" used interchangeably.

Since maps only allow one type, their constraints are much easier to describe. They have the keyword map and take a subtype as their only argument (i.e., `map(type)`).

Listing 3.25   Map type constraint

```
variable "map_of_strings" {
  type        = map(string)                                This map will only
  description = "This value takes in a map where all values are strings."    allow strings.
}

variable "map_of_objects" {
  type = map(object({                    Maps can refer to complex
    string_key = string,                 objects, but each element
    number_key = number                  will need to match this.
  }))
}
```

3.6.9 Null

The null type is a very special type that only applies to a single value: null. It represents a value that has not been set. A value that has been set to null has basically not been set at all.

It is very common to set optional input variables to null as their default. This allows module developers to easily check that a value has been set: if it is anything other than null, then they know that the user has set the property.

Listing 3.26 Setting a default of null

```
variable "description" {
  type        = string
  default     = null
  description = "A description field to apply to resources."
}
```

This makes the field optional without setting an explicit value.

```
variable "flag" {
  type        = bool
  default     = null
  description = "A flag that can be disabled, enabled, or unset."
}
```

The default isn't true or false even though this is a boolean.

```
locals {
  flag = var.flag != null ? tostring(var.flag) : "default"
}
```

Use the string version of the boolean or the string "default".

The null keyword can not be used as a type constraint, as it would not allow the value to be set to anything at all.

3.6.10 Any

The any keyword is used to specify that a value of any type is accepted. It can be used directly to state there are no restrictions on type, and it can be used inside other type constraints such as lists.

Any is the default for variable types and as the constraint for lists, objects, sets, and other types that have children types. As such, you don't technically need to specify it; however, it makes code much clearer.

Listing 3.27 Allowing any

```
variable "json_blob" {
  type        = any
  description = "This can be any value at all."
}
```

The any keyword can be applied to lists and maps, but it does not change the fact that all elements in both of those types have to be of the same type. This means that a list that specifies a child type of any can be all strings or all numbers, but it can't combine strings and numbers.

Listing 3.28 Maps and lists of any

```
variable "map_of_anything" {
  type        = map(any)
  description = "This can be a map of any type as long as all elements are
the same type."
}
```

```
variable "list_of_anything" {
  type        = list(any)
  description = "This can be a list of any type as long as all elements are
the same type."
}
```

3.7 *Validating inputs*

One of the most important things in programming is input validation. For web services and server daemons, this is a huge security concern, as unexpected input can lead to compromise. With Terraform, the concern is that systems could be misconfigured, leading to outages, security incidents, or just a frustrating experience when an unexpected value gets placed somewhere and can't easily be traced back to the source. This can be particularly frustrating as Terraform's plan and apply steps can take quite a bit of time to run, and some errors won't be caught at all in the plan phase. As a result, being able to catch misconfigurations early is extremely useful.

Terraform has a special mechanism for input validation named, appropriately enough, the `validation` subblock. This block is part of the `variable` block and can be used as many times as needed inside of a block. The `validation` block has two fields: a `condition` field that has to be evaluated as true or false and an `error_message` that will be displayed if the condition fails.

Before Terraform 1.9.0, `validation` blocks had a major limitation where the block could only access attributes from itself, not any other inputs or attributes. This limitation can complicate some of the more complex validation that a user may want to do, particularly the kind where multiple variables interact with each other. As of Terraform 1.9, the `condition` field can take almost any expression that evaluates to a boolean, with the only caveat being that the expression has to also include the variable being tested.

There are also some limitations around the error message. According to the Terraform documentation, they require "at least one full English sentence starting with an uppercase letter and ending with a period or question mark." Although it's not likely they validate the English portion of that requirement, it probably means you are limited in the characters you can include.

Listing 3.29   Simple validation

```
variable "description" {
  description = "An optional description to apply to resources."
  type        = string
  default     = ""                        ◄──────┐  By default, this is an
                                                  └─ empty string.
  validation {
    condition     = length(var.description) <= 125        ◄────────────┐
    error_message = "The name can not be longer than 125 characters."  │
  }                                                                     │
}                                               Restrict the name to keep
                                                 it from being too long.
```

The `validation` block can be used to

- Check for a minimal length on a string or list
- Match a regular expression to confirm a string
- Confirm that a number is an integer
- Test that a number is within a specific range

Since the `validation` block can be used multiple times, it's possible to mix and match these. A developer could specify that a list has to be a certain length and then validate that all the values in the list match a regular expression.

Listing 3.30 Multiple validations

```
variable "my_integer" {
  description = "An integer between 0 and 10 inclusive."
  type        = number

  validation {                                          Our first rule displays an
    condition     = var.my_integer <= 10                error if the value is too high.
    error_message = "The value must not be greater than 10."
  }
                                                        Our second rule displays an
  validation {                                          error if the value is too low.
    condition     = var.my_integer >= 0
    error_message = "The value must not be less than 0."
  }
                                                        Our last rule displays an error if
  validation {                                          the number is not an integer.
    condition     = can(parseint(tostring(var.my_integer), 10))
    error_message = "The value must be an integer."
  }
}
```

Having in-depth validation rules with descriptive error messages is one of the hallmark traits of a great module. Validation rules make it easier to catch problems before they cause problems and make debugging them much easier.

3.8 *A reusable instance module*

Now that we've got a bit more knowledge about modules, let's put that knowledge into practice. In the last chapter, we built a simple program that launched an AWS instance. This program could be reused by directly running it, but what if we wanted to launch multiple instances as part of the same system or pick different instance types? With our current program, we'd have to create unique workspaces for each of those instances, which is not ideal. This is because our current code can only create a single instance of a single type and has no way to expand that.

For the rest of this chapter, we focus on turning that program into a reusable module. Our main goal is to make a reusable module, and to do that we need to understand where the current code is holding us back. In this case, we need to make a few changes:

- We want users to be able to specify a subnet instead of always using the default one. This way, people who have custom VPC setups can still use the module.

- The instance type, which describes the capabilities (such as CPU and memory limits) of the instance, is currently hard coded. Different workloads benefit from different machine types, so making this a selectable option means we support more workloads.

- Once the instance is created, users of the module will need to know metadata about the instance such as its ID or IP address. This allows developers to use the module to integrate the machine they created into other parts of their system.

3.8.1   *Refactoring into a module*

Our original program was a root-level module. This means that it is a module meant to be turned into a workspace and called directly. Root-level modules are turned into workspaces and act as an entry point into your Terraform program. This does not refer to where the module resides in the repository structure; rather it is the module that Terraform starts from. If you've programmed in C or Java, then you can compare the root-level module with the main method or function in each of these languages.

In this chapter, we're going to restructure our code to act as a module. This means creating some new files, moving blocks around, and even creating a quick example of how to use our module. At the end of this, our project should look like figure 3.2.

Root-level modules have some subtle differences from the more standard reusable modules, so we're going to make some simple changes. The first thing we need to do is update our `providers.tf` file. This is where we defined

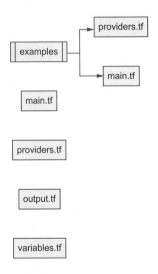

Figure 3.2   Module file structure

our required providers and their configuration. The required provider's section inside of the `terraform` block will stay, as it tells Terraform what provider versions the module needs. We will need to remove the `provider` blocks though, as they can only be used at the root-level module.

Listing 3.31   `Providers.tf` changes

```
terraform {                             ◄─────┐  This block should stay.
  required_providers {
    aws = {                             ◄─────┐  Modules should also specify
      source  = "hashicorp/aws"               │  their required providers.
      version = "~> 5.0"
    }
  }
}
```

```
provider "aws" {
  region = var.aws_region
}
```

This whole block should be deleted
as provider blocks should only be
in the root module.

3.8.2 *Using input variables to customize behavior*

Using our requirements from the start of the chapter, we need to give our users the ability to change the instance type and subnet. This is done by using input variables, which are defined with the `variable` block. Input variables give developers a way to specify behavior and configuration for the module without having to edit the module itself. We're going to create two variables for our module: one for the instance type and another for the subnet.

We want our module to be easy to use, though, so we're going to put some restrictions on our inputs to prevent people from making mistakes. The first thing we're going to do is restrict the type of values we want. By default, the value can be anything that Terraform uses—a string, number, boolean, object, or list. The resources we're planning on using these variables with expect strings for these values though, so we can specify that here. This will cause Terraform to give a useful error if the wrong type is passed through.

This isn't the only restriction we can add. For the `subnet_id` variable, we know that AWS is expecting a string with a certain format. We can add a `validation` subblock to our variable declaration and use that to make sure the string matches what AWS is expecting. To do this, we're going to use the length and regex functions to make sure that the string matches a regular expression we wrote that matches what AWS wants for this string. In chapter 4, we're going to talk a lot more about functions and expressions, but for now you should create a `variables.tf` file to start adding variables.

Listing 3.32 Adding `variables.tf` to our module

```
variable "instance_type" {
  type        = string
  description = "The type of instance to launch."
  default     = "t3.micro"
}

variable "subnet_id" {
  type        = string
  description = "The ID of the Subnet to launch the instance into."

  validation {
    condition    = length(regexall("^subnet-[\\d|\\w]+$", var.subnet_id))
== 1
    error_message = "The subnet_id must match the pattern ^subnet-[
\\d|\\w]+$"
  }
}
```

We limit the possible values
to the string type.

A description helps
users know what
our input does.

Providing a default value
makes this input optional.

We also want a string here.

This message is displayed if
the validation check fails.

Here we use functions to run a
regular expression check. Functions
are covered in the next chapter.

This
validation
block lets us
ensure the
subnet id is
the right
format.

Once our inputs are defined, we can refer to them anywhere else in our module. In our particular use case, we want to pass the variables to our `aws_instance` resource so that our module users can tell the resource what subnet to launch in and what instance type to use. This way, our module gains a lot of reusability as users aren't locked into specific configurations.

Listing 3.33   Using input variables

```
resource "aws_instance" "hello_world" {
  ami           = data.aws_ami.ubuntu.id
  subnet_id     = var.subnet_id
  instance_type = var.instance_type
}
```

The subnet_id input has to be provided by our module users and then gets passed to our resource.

The instance_type input could be our default value or a custom value from our module users.

3.8.3   *Adding output variables to encourage reuse*

At this point, our module can be used to create AWS EC2 instances in any subnet and of any instance type. Outside of our module, though, there's no way to know about the resource that was created. If a user wanted to point other resources at our instance, they currently have no way to do so. That's where output variables come in. Output variables let module developers export data out of their module as attributes. This allows developers to take those attributes and use them elsewhere, such as when configuring another module. With this, developers can compose larger systems out of smaller modules, tying them together as needed for their project.

Listing 3.34   Adding `outputs.tf` to our module

```
output "aws_instance_arn" {
  value = aws_instance.hello_world.arn
}
```

This output lets module users access and reuse the instance identifier.

```
output "aws_instance_ip" {
  value = aws_instance.hello_world.private_ip
}
```

This output exposes the IP address for the instance.

```
output "aws_instance" {
  value = aws_instance.hello_world
}
```

It is also possible to return the entire resource, not just an attribute.

3.8.4   *Testing our changes*

Testing Terraform is a large topic that can (and will, in chapter 9) take up its own dedicated space, but for now, we want to make it easy to do the most basic test possible: actually running the module. In the previous chapter, we were able to run the module directly, as we were also using it as a workspace. However, we've removed the `provider` blocks from our module and have added some variables that have to be set. We're going to need a new workspace for this.

Inside our project, create a new folder named `example`. We're going to build out our new root-level module inside of this folder and then use it to run our code. The first thing we need to do is configure our provider, since that no longer happens in our reusable module. This means both setting up the Terraform-required `providers` block and adding in the variable and `provider` blocks so we can select a region. To do this, we're going to create a new `providers.tf` file in our `example` folder.

We're using input variables to set provider values, which is a common way to allow people to have different values in different workspaces using the same set of code. These values often never change once set for a specific environment: for example, you wouldn't change the region the provider uses to log in and deploy stuff after you've already launched resources.

Listing 3.35 Providers for our test workspace

```
terraform {
  required_providers {
    aws = {                                    ◄──┐  Our workspace needs to set
      source  = "hashicorp/aws"                   │  its own required providers.
      version = "~> 4.0"
    }
  }
}

variable "region" {                            ◄──┐  We add a single variable
  type        = string                            │  to configure the provider.
  default     = "us-east-1"
  description = "The AWS Region to connect and run the tests in."
}
                                               ◄──┐  Since this is a root-level module
provider "aws" {                                  │  we can use the provider blocks.
  region = var.region                          ◄──┐  Our region variable
}                                                 │  gets passed to AWS.
```

Next, we need to call our module. Create a file named `main.tf` inside of the workspace and add the `module` block there. For the module source, we can use a relative path to point up a directory to our module, and for some of the arguments we can rely on the default values. At this point, we run into a problem though. How do we populate the `subnet_id`? For that, we can use a `data` lookup on the default VPC and its subnets, just as we originally had in the module itself.

Listing 3.36 Testing our local module

```
data "aws_vpc" "default" {                     ──┐  These are the same data lookups
  default = true                                  │  we did before, only now we're
}                                                 ▼  calling it from our workspace.
```

```
data "aws_subnets" "default" {
  filter {
    name   = "vpc-id"
    values = [data.aws_vpc.default.id]
  }
}
```

These are the same data lookups we did before, only now we're calling it from our workspace.

```
module "test_instance" {
  source    = "../"
  subnet_id = data.aws_subnets.default.ids[0]
}
```

We pass the first subnet found to the module, which then passes it our resource.

```
output "aws_instance_arn" {
  value = module.test_instance.aws_instance_arn
}
```

Root-level outputs are displayed when Terraform runs.

Now we're ready to go! Inside of the workspace, run `terraform init` to turn the folder into a proper workspace, and then `terraform apply` to run the plan, and after review, apply it.

3.8.5   *Publishing*

The final step toward making our module reusable is to publish it somewhere that other people can grab it. Terraform can pull modules from a variety of sources, such as registries, filesystems, Git repositories, and Git hosts such as GitHub, GitLab, or Bitbucket. For now we'll use GitHub, as it is easier to get started with, but we're going to devote some time in chapter 8 to discuss the nuances of publishing packages.

In your GitHub account, create a new public repository. It's considered a best practice to name module repositories with the format `terraform-PROVIDER-NAME`, where `PROVIDER` is the provider that is focused on. In our case, we're going to put several modules inside of a single repository, so we'll name this repository `terraform-aws-in-depth`.

Now locally you need to push your code up to GitHub. When you create a new repository, GitHub gives you instructions on how to upload a local repository. Once you follow those instructions, you'll be able to push the code up to GitHub.

Now that it's published, we can use it! Inside any of our projects, we can use the `module` block to reference and use our new module. When we run `terraform init`, Terraform will download and install the module for us.

Listing 3.37   Using our published module

```
variable "subnet_id" {
  type        = string
  description = "The Subnet to launch this resource in."
}
```

We previously used the data object to look this up, but it's also common to use variables for things like network settings.

```
module "my_instance" {
  source       = "github.com/YOU_USERNAME/terraform-aws-in-depth//modules/
ec2_instance"
```

Point this at your Git repository, and make sure you keep the folder to point at the ec2_instance module. The double slash is used to reference a submodule inside of the repository.

```
   subnet_id      = var.subnet_id
   instance_type = "t3.large"
}
output "instance_arn" {
  value = module.my_instance.aws_instance_arn
}
```

We left this as a variable this time so you can set it to any subnet in the aws region.

The instance type is configurable now.

In the next chapter, we'll discuss how to write complex expressions using operators and functions. This will allow you to add deeper validation to your inputs and teach you how to transform your data in useful ways.

Summary

- Modules are the primary way that code is shared amongst developers using Terraform.
- Input variables are used to customize module behavior by passing data into a module.
- Output variables allow module users to pull information out of a module for reuse.
- Local variables exist only inside modules and are used for internal data and logic processing.
- All values have a type, and inputs can be restricted to a specific type.
- Terraform has many types, such as strings, numbers, booleans, lists, sets, tuples, objects, and maps.
- Input variables can have additional validation checks using custom logic.

Expressions and iterations

This chapter covers

- Modifying data through the use of expressions and functions
- Operators and their uses
- Some of the most commonly used functions
- String generation using templates
- Multiplying resources with `for_each` and `count`
- Iterating over and transforming objects and lists

So far in our quest to learn Terraform, we've focused on the objects of the Terraform language: the `resource`, `data`, `variable`, and other blocks. We've used those blocks to define and provision infrastructure and have even done a small amount of validation using input `validation` blocks.

With what we've learned up until this point, we can do quite a bit, but we're still mostly using Terraform to define infrastructure and make copies of it. Our variables have given us some ability to customize our setup but only in the sense that we're exposing a few variables to our users.

Terraform is capable of a lot more than that. It can be used to create dynamic features that can be enabled or disabled. It can calculate, derive, and transform values for use as configuration. Terraform has a rich library of reusable functions for transforming data, and it even has a templating language that can be used to build complex strings.

In this chapter, we focus on the features of Terraform that allow us to include more logic inside our code. We're going to break down expressions (pretty much everything to the right of an equal sign is an expression in Terraform), discuss the operators that are available in Terraform, and consider some of the more commonly used functions. From there, we'll explore how Terraform handles iteration, both in the context of transforming data as well as around creating a dynamic number of resources.

Throughout this chapter, you'll see examples of different types of expressions. If you want to test any of these out yourself, you can use the `terraform console` command. This command creates an interface console where you can type in functions, formulas, and other types of basic expressions to see how they work.

4.1 Expanding our module

The EC2 module that we built over the last two chapters has shown continued success! Success comes at a price though, and as more teams adopt the module, feature requests are starting to come in. This time we've got a few requests from four different teams:

- Our first team wants to give their AWS instance permission to access several other AWS services such as S3 (an object storage solution). They want to have some control over this and change it without needing to request more changes to the module.
- The second team has heard about a feature of AWS called Session Manager that lets them log into instances without the need to manage SSH keys.
- A third team wants to launch multiple instances.
- The final team wants to be able to give their instances names for when they're looking for them in the AWS Console (the website for managing AWS services).

This looks like a lot of work, but before panicking let's dig into what it would take to add all of this to our module. Before we start coding, we're going to make a plan, and it's okay if we go into it without knowing exactly what that plan will look like. A lot of times feature requests can seem daunting, but then when you start digging into the specifics it turns out that they're simpler than you realized. That's why, even for small things, it's important to do some initial research before diving in.

4.1.1 Research

Before you can make any changes to your module, you need to understand what it is you're trying to accomplish and what the best path forward is going to be, and that always requires some research. You are not expected to know everything. The world of infrastructure has grown to the point where there are tens of thousands of different systems out there, and not a single person knows all of them. Even for systems you're familiar with, there may have been changes, new features, or even deprecation of features that mean your knowledge is out of date.

In this case, we've got some interesting requirements that you may not have encountered before, and if you have, you may not have used Terraform to implement these features. Before even attempting to write any code for them, we should make sure we know what we want our result to be, and for that, we need to learn a bit. For us, that means

- Reading through the documentation for the service itself—in this case, EC2
- Looking up the Terraform resources and features that might be needed
- Searching for blogs, social media posts, Stack Overflow questions, or tutorials about the topic

For instance, we know that we're working with the AWS instance resource. So we'll want to make sure we've reviewed the Terraform documentation for this resource itself since the Terraform documentation tends to be really solid. We also want to use our favorite search engine with a query like "How do I set the name of an instance in the AWS Console," which will lead us to a Stack Overflow question. In the case of naming an instance, all the answers and searches lead us to the same place: names are controlled with the AWS "name" tag.

If we've never used tags before, then this will also be something we need to research. In this way, our research phase could expand as we learn about new systems and functionality (see figure 4.1).

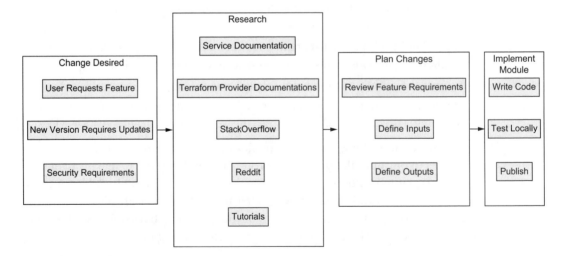

Figure 4.1   Example development process for a new module feature

4.1.2   Adding a name and tags

During the first stage of research, we looked into how to add a name to the AWS Console for our instances, and what we learned was that AWS uses tags to provide the names. Tags are key/value pairs of arbitrary strings (you can create your own keys and values for tags) that are associated with an AWS resource, and it turns out that if you use a tag with the key of "name," then AWS will display that name for you in the console. This means we can resolve our first problem by letting a user set that tag.

At this point, we could just provide a variable for the name. However, tags look like a really useful feature for our users. Since we're already working with tags, we should consider exposing a new variable to let users add their own tags. For that, we're going to add a variable named tags to our module and pass it along to resources that accept tags.

This raises a new question though: What should we do about the name? We could skip it altogether and just let our users assign a name using the tag variable we're providing. Although that is perfectly reasonable, our other feature requests make it a bit more complicated. We know that one of our users wants to be able to launch multiple instances from the module, and they'll likely want unique names for each instance. We also know that other resources that might need names could come up. For that reason, we should create a new variable called name_prefix that will be used to generate the names for all of our resources. It's a prefix, rather than a dedicated name, to accommodate the idea of launching multiple instances from the module. Let's see how that looks in the following listing.

Listing 4.1 Addding tags and name to our instance

```
variable "name_prefix" {
  type        = string
  description = "The prefix to apply to the beginning of names generated
by this module."
}

variable "tags" {
  type        = map(string)
  description = "Key/Value pairs to pass to AWS as Tags."
  default     = {}
}

resource "aws_instance" "hello_world" {
  ami           = data.aws_ami.ubuntu.id
  subnet_id     = var.subnet_id
  instance_type = var.instance_type

  tags = merge(var.tags, {
    Name = "${var.name_prefix}-instance"
  })
}
```

Tags in AWS are key/value pairs, with both the key and the value being strings.

We use the merge function to combine the user-provided tags with our own.

Our research showed that the Name tag is used to add labels in the AWS Console.

Using the prefix might seem a little weird at this point, since we're simply passing it through without changing it. Once we add in our next feature request to create multiple instances, we'll end up changing this section of code to allow for unique names for all the instances.

4.1.3   *Allowing multiple instances*

Our next feature request was to allow the creation of multiple instances from the same module. During this research, we learned about a Terraform feature that will come in handy: the `count` meta parameter! This is a feature of Terraform that exists on the `module` and `resource` blocks that tells Terraform how many of those items you want to create; in this case, we can use it to let the users of the modules create any number of instances.

The `count` meta parameter also gives us access to a `count` index. This is a special variable that exists only inside the block where the `count` meta parameter is set that acts as an index for the created object. Each created resource from this block will have a unique index starting at zero and counting upward one at a time. We can use this to give each of our instances its own unique name so they can be identified in the console.

To allow multiple instances to be created in our module, we need to use the `count` meta parameter on our `aws_instance` resource, and to do that we need to add a new input variable. We want to make sure that this input variable is a whole number, and since it's not possible to create a negative number of resources, we'll verify that a positive number was passed in. This way, if our user provides something that would cause an error with the `count` meta parameter, they'll get a clear error message from our input validation.

> **Listing 4.2   Launching a dynamic number of instances with our module**

```
variable "instance_count" {
  type        = number
  description = "The number of instances to launch."
  default     = 0
  validation { A
    condition     = can(parseint(tostring(var.my_integer), 10))
    error_message = "The instance count must be a whole number."
  }

  validation {
    condition     = var.instance_count >= 0
    error_message = "The instance count can not be negative."
  }
}

resource "aws_instance" "hello_world" {
  count         = var.instance_count
  ami           = data.aws_ami.ubuntu.id
  subnet_id     = var.subnet_id
  instance_type = var.instance_type

  tags = merge(var.tags, {
    Name = "${var.name_prefix}-${count.index}"
  })
}
```

Since Terraform doesn't distinguish between integers and floats we can add a validation rule for safety.

A negative number would throw an error, so we catch it here to give a better error message.

Terraform will create this many resources with these configuration settings.

We use the count index to give each instance a unique name.

You may have noticed that I mentioned modules as well. The `module` block can also take a `count` argument, which means that our module already could have created multiple instances by using `count` on the `module` block calling it. In this particular case, we want to push it inside the module so we can reduce the number of duplicate resources created.

> **Listing 4.3 Using the `count` meta parameter on our module**

```
module "my_instances" {
  source    = "github.com/YOUR_GITHUB_NAME/terraform_aws_instance"
  count     = 5
  subnet_id = var.subnet_id
}
```

Since this count is on the module itself, **EVERY** resource in the module will be deplicated.

4.1.4 Creating a role

One of the requests we received was from a group that wants to use the instance created by our module to access other AWS resources.

AWS manages permissions through a system called IAM, which stands for Identity and Access Management. AWS uses what is known as a role-based access control system, often shortened as RBAC, for permissions. These systems create permissions by creating policies (which combine resources with allowed actions) for roles. The role then gets assigned to users or machines. By creating a role for our instance, we can let other developers add their policies for the machine. This allows our module users to do things like give their instance the ability to access S3 buckets (which are commonly used to store data), provide secret management systems (which could contain database credentials or API keys the developer needs on the system), or any of the other hundreds of services offered by AWS.

IAM for any vendor can be complicated. It may be tempting to try and account for every possible set of permissions right in our module: we could expose variables for S3 buckets, create policies that incorporate them, and then add additional services and features. This is an impossible task though. Every cloud provider has hundreds, if not thousands, of services, and developers need the flexibility to create custom and complex permissions.

Instead of accounting for every possibility, we should focus on giving users of our module the ability to customize their permissions. This makes our task much simpler while also making our module more powerful.

So how do we keep it simple while still letting our users control permissions? In our research, we learned that IAM needs two resources for every instance to work: `aws_iam_instance_profile` and `aws_iam_role`. To customize permission, we can then add new policy documents to the `aws_iam_role` resource. Since every single AWS instance needs those two resources to allow IAM permissions, it makes sense that we would include that in our module. Since the policies themselves are going to be custom for different projects, we shouldn't try to define that. Instead, we can return the `aws_iam_role` as output and allow users to attach policies to it themselves. This makes our module useful without it being restrictive.

Our research also turned up another fact about IAM that wasn't so obvious. For an IAM role to get passed to an instance, we need to give AWS itself the permission to grant the role to EC2. This is done using an `assume_role` policy, which is a special policy that tells AWS who is allowed to use the role. To build that, we're going to use the `aws_iam_policy_document` data source, which is a fancy little helper for building policies that are easy to read and follow the latest formatting standards from AWS.

Listing 4.4   Creating a role

This data source helps us build custom IAM policies. We could use a template or JSON string, but that is more error prone.

```
data "aws_iam_policy_document" "instance_assume_role_policy" {
  statement {
    actions = ["sts:AssumeRole"]

    principals {
      type       = "Service"
      identifiers = ["ec2.amazonaws.com"]
    }
  }
}
```

AWS Services need permission to use the roles we create.

We are giving the EC2 service permission to use this role, but no other services can.

We're using the name prefix to ensure that the role has a unique name. Creating two modules with the same name will cause an error.

```
resource "aws_iam_role" "main" {
  name                 = "${var.name_prefix}-instance-role"
  assume_role_policy = data.aws_iam_policy_document.instance_assume_role_
policy.json
}
```

This is the json generated by our data source.

```
resource "aws_iam_instance_profile" "main" {
  name = aws_iam_role.main.name
  role = aws_iam_role.main.name
}
```

AWS Instances need a "profile" attached to the "role" to use them with AWS Instances.

It's best practice to name the profile the same as the role that it works with.

```
resource "aws_instance" "hello_world" {
  count                = var.instance_count
  ami                  = data.aws_ami.ubuntu.id
  subnet_id            = var.subnet_id
  instance_type        = var.instance_type
  iam_instance_profile = aws_iam_instance_profile.main.name

  tags = merge(var.tags, {
    Name = "${var.name_prefix}-${count.index}"
  })
}
```

Update our aws_ instance definition with our new profile.

Now that our role is created, it can be used to grant permission to the instances by creating and attaching policies. It is impossible for us to think of every possible policy and put it in our module, so we return the role from the module as an output. This way, users of our module aren't limited to only what we've thought of and can use the module for things we haven't considered.

Listing 4.5   Role output

```
output "aws_instance_role" {
  value = aws_iam_role.main
}
```
> Now our role can be accessed by others, who can then attach their own policies to it.

4.1.5   *Enabling the session manager*

The final feature request is to enable the session manager for our instances. Before starting, we had no idea what this was, which is where research came in again. After doing a quick search we found the AWS Systems Manager documentation, which let us know that the system manager is a system with many small tools that help maintain AWS instances. This has the session manager that was requested by our users.

Our research says that we need to install a special agent on our machines and then give it permission to access the AWS Systems Manager service. Since we're using provided machine images (our data lookup from chapters 2 and 3 looked up an AMI for us), it turns out the agent is already installed, so there's nothing for us to do there. That just leaves the permissions.

Fortunately, we set up our role for the last feature, so now we have something to build on for adding permissions. AWS has a predefined IAM policy that grants the permissions needed for the session manager, as well as other systems manager features, to run on an instance. Since we're using the AWS managed policy, we don't have to create our own, but we do need to use a data source named aws_iam_policy to pull in the policy to our program.

Listing 4.6   Using a data source to find the AWS managed policy

```
data "aws_iam_policy" "ssm_arn" {
  arn = "arn:aws:iam::aws:policy/
    AmazonSSMManagedEC2InstanceDefaultPolicy"
}
```
> This looks up the AWS-managed IAM policy so we can apply it to our instances.

Now we can use the aws_iam_role_policy_attachment to attach the policy to the role. We use our variable along with the ternary statement, which is a one-line if/else statement, to switch the count between 0 if the input is false and 1 if the input is true. Using the count meta parameter in this way allows a resource to be toggled on and off.

Listing 4.7   Session manager

```
variable "enable_systems_manager" {
  type        = bool
  description = "When enabled the Systems Manager IAM Policy will be
    attached to the instance."
```

```
    default     = false
}
```

> This resource will only create an attachment if enable_systems_manager is true.

```
resource "aws_iam_role_policy_attachment" "ssm_attach" {
  count       = var.enable_systems_manager ? 1 : 0
  role        = aws_iam_role.main.name
  policy_arn  = data.aws_iam_policy.ssm_arn.arn
}
```

> The count meta parameter lets us define how many resources to create. We switch between one and zero.

With this functionality in place, our module allows users to enable or disable Systems Manager for their instances using a single variable on our module. In theory, we could have left it to the users to attach the policy to the role we've exported, but since this is a fairly common use case, we save our users the trouble and provide a simple interface to use this feature. This is one of the powerful features of Terraform: by providing this functionality in an easy-to-use way, we encourage users to take advantage of this feature they may not have previously even known about.

4.1.6   *Reviewing our work*

At this point we've evolved our module from controlling a single simple instance to building a series of dynamic resources. Our module can launch multiple instances, supports connecting using Systems Manager, and lets our users grant permissions to any number of AWS systems (see figure 4.2).

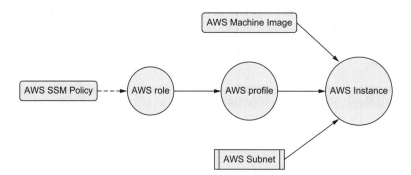

Figure 4.2   The resources we create are circles. We also pull in the AWS subnet as a variable and look up the AWS Machine Image and SSM policies.

Our users can access all of that with a simple `module` block that points to our module and defines a few input variables.

> Listing 4.8   Using our updated module

```
module "my_instances" {
  source                = "github.com/YOUR_GITHUB_USERNAME/
```

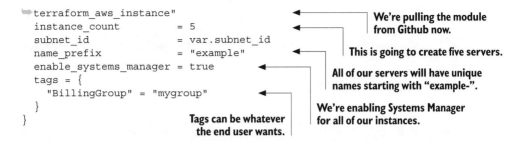

```
terraform_aws_instance"
  instance_count       = 5
  subnet_id            = var.subnet_id
  name_prefix          = "example"
  enable_systems_manager = true
  tags = {
    "BillingGroup" = "mygroup"
  }
}
```

We're pulling the module from Github now.

This is going to create five servers.

All of our servers will have unique names starting with "example-".

We're enabling Systems Manager for all of our instances.

Tags can be whatever the end user wants.

What's even more exciting about this is that these upgrades will roll out to everyone using the module. Although our features were requested by specific users, they are able to be used by anyone and may even inspire a few ideas from the teams that are benefitting.

To accomplish this, we relied on a lot of new functionality. We used functions to merge our tags, used conditional statements to toggle functionality on and off, and introduced the count meta parameter. Throughout the rest of this chapter, we're going to dive deep into those features and similar functionality that is used to dynamically adjust our parameters. This will include different operator types, functions in general as well as some specific important functions that you'll use often, and new expressions that help us transform groups of data.

4.2 Operators and conditionals

In software development, context operators are symbols (one or more characters) that represent an action or process. The most common place people see operators outside of programming is in math, where symbols like the addition and subtraction signs are used to create equations. Operators in Terraform work in similar ways and indeed even include some of the same symbols seen in math.

Operators let us create equations, compare values, evaluate boolean logic, and create branching logic.

4.2.1 Math

One of the common uses of operators is to create mathematical expressions—to literally do math. Terraform has all of the basic mathematical operators, allowing developers to handle most basic arithmetic without the need for special functions. This allows users to perform math right in their Terraform programs (see table 4.1).

Table 4.1 Mathematical operations

Operator	Description	Example usage	Example value
+	Addition	5 + 4	9
–	Subtraction	10 – 5	5
*	Multiplication	5 * 5	25

Table 4.1   Mathematical operations (*continued*)

Operator	Description	Example usage	Example value
/	Division	40/10	4
%	Modulus	50/9	5

Listing 4.9   Math with functions and operators

> **Pick the lowest number using the min function, so availability_zones can't be higher than 3.**

```
locals {
  availability_zones = min(var.active_availability_zones, 3)
  needed_subnets     = local.availability_zones * 2
}
```

> **In this example, each availability zone will have two subnets.**

Other mathematical operations are available using functions. We'll talk about functions in section 4.3, but if you need to calculate exponents, round numbers, or get absolute values, you can do that using functions.

4.2.2   Comparison

Operators are also used to compare values. This can mean comparing the quantity of the value, such as with the greater than and less than operators, or checking whether the values are the same using the equality operator (see table 4.2).

Table 4.2   Comparison operators

Operator	Description	Example usage	Example value
==	Equality	true == "true"	false
!=	Inequality	"This" != "That"	true
<	Less than	15 < 20	true
<=	Less than or equal	20 <= 20	true
>	Greater than	12 > 19	false
>=	Greater than or equal	10 >= 10	true

When comparing using the equality operator, it's important to note that the value has to be the same type to be equal. Terraform does a lot of type conversation behind the scenes, so this doesn't come up often, but the string "12" and the number 12 will return false with an equality check.

One way to use the equality operator and avoid errors is to explicitly cast the values you're comparing to the same type. Alternatively, if you know that the items are both of the appropriate type (if they are both input variables with a defined type, for instance), you can do the comparison without converting.

Listing 4.10 Examples of comparison operators

```
locals {
  alpha   = 15 > 15
  beta    = 15 >= 15
  gamma   = 14 >= 15
  delta   = "15" == 15
  epsilon = "15" != 15
  zeta    = tonumber("15") == 15
}
```

Resolves to false
Resolves to true
Resolves to false
Resolves to false because the type is different.
Resolves to true because the type is different.
Resolves to true due to type coercion.

4.2.3 Boolean operators

You may remember from our discussion on types that booleans are values that are either true or false. The AND, OR, and Negation operators are known as boolean operators, and they always resolve to boolean values (see table 4.3)

Table 4.3 Boolean operators

Operator	Description	Example usage	Example value
||	OR	true || false	true
&&	AND	true && false	false
!	Negation	!true	false

Listing 4.11 Examples of boolean operators

```
locals {
  is_true         = true || false
  is_false        = true && false
  is_also_false   = (true || false) && false
  complex_example = var.servers > 15 || var.feature_enabled
}
```

4.2.4 Conditional (Terraform's ternary operator)

What Terraform calls the conditional expressions is often referred to as a ternary operator in pretty much every other language. Unlike most operators, which have one or two values that it acts on, conditional expressions operate on three values (hence "ternary"). The first value has to resolve to a boolean; if it is true, the second expression is returned, and if it is false, the third expression is returned. This, in essence, makes the conditional statement an "if-then" statement.

As a result, this is perhaps one of the most powerful operators in Terraform, as it allows branching logic. We've already seen this used at the start of the chapter to enable or disable the Systems Manager integration of our AWS instance. Using the ternary operator to enable or disable a resource based on a variable input is an extremely common pattern when working with Terraform. When building modules, you can accept a boolean variable, such as our `enable_systems_manager` example, and convert that boolean (which is always either `true` or `false`) into the number `1` for `true` or `0` for `false` and pass that into `count`. Compared to asking for a number, this provides a much nicer interface for users for resources that can only be turned on and off.

Listing 4.12   Condition expressions to enable a resource

```
resource "aws_iam_role_policy_attachment" "ssm_attach" {
  count      = var.enable_systems_manager ? 1 : 0
  role       = aws_iam_role.main.name
  policy_arn = aws_iam_policy.policy.arn
}
```

If enable_systems_ manager is true, then one resource is created; otherwise none are.

Another common use case is to switch between two different modules depending on settings. For example, if you're setting up networking on AWS you can pick between NAT Instances and NAT Gateways to connect your private subnets to the internet. Both of these do the same thing (let your instances connect to the internet) but do it in different ways. If you made a module that configured networking in AWS, you may want to let people switch between these two methods using a simple variable.

Behind the scenes, two submodules would each hold the respective logic for the service, but only one would be enabled at a time. This allows a simple boolean variable the ability to switch between complex configurations, which is what makes conditional expressions so powerful.

The condition expression, like other expressions, is not limited to the `count` meta parameter and can be used anywhere an expression can be used. When using it to toggle between resources, you can also use it to control the outputs to the module.

Listing 4.13   Conditional expressions to toggle modules

```
variable "use_nat_instance" {
  description = "When enabled a NAT Instance will be used instead of a
NAT Gateway"
  type        = bool
  default     = false
}

module "nat_instance" {
  source = "./modules/nat_instance"
  count  = var.use_nat_instance ? 1 : 0
}
```

This resource is only enabled if use_nat_instance is true.

```
module "nat_gateway" {
  source = "./modules/nat_gateway"
  count  = var.use_nat_instance ? 0 : 1
}
```

◄── **This resource is only enabled if use_nat_instance is false.**

```
output "nat_ip_address" {
  value = var.use_nat_instance ? module.nat_instance.ip :
➥module.nat_gateway.ip
}
```

◄── **Switch between the different module outputs depending on which one is used.**

The Terraform conditional has one feature that makes it very unique among programming languages: it evaluates both return results even though only one is going to be used. Most programming languages only evaluate the expression that is being returned, but Terraform will evaluate both of them. In most cases, this isn't a problem, but if you're trying to choose between two items and one of them doesn't exist, you'll end up with a potential error. A way to avoid this is with the `try` function, which is discussed later in the chapter.

4.2.5   Order

Just like algebra, Terraform operators have their own order of operations. If an expression contains multiple operators, then they will be evaluated in this order:

1   `!, -` (when used to multiply by –1)

2   `*, /, %`

3   `+, -` (when used as subtraction)

4   `>, >=, <, <=`

5   `==, !=`

6   `&&`

7   `||`

You can also use parentheses to override the order of operations and ensure that the expressions you want to evaluate are evaluated in the order you desire. While you can rely on the order of operations, it can be difficult to read and error-prone when editing. For the sake of clarity, if you're using multiple operators in an expression, consider putting parentheses in even if they don't change the logic.

Listing 4.14   Operator ordering and readability

```
locals {
  confusing = 2 + 4 / 5 * var.multiple ? 4 : 9 - 7
  clearer   = 2 + ((4 / 5) * (var.multiple ? 4 : 9 - 7))
}
```

◄──┘ **Although this code is perfectly legal, it is not readable.**

◄── **This code is identical but easier to follow.**

4.3   *Functions*

Functions in Terraform are familiar to functions in languages such as Python, Javascript, and C: they have a name, take in parameters, and return a value. Where Terraform functions are different from other languages is in their purpose. Terraform uses functions primarily to transform data. This could be by running special math functions, converting types, building complex strings, or even converting errors into booleans.

With imperative languages, functions will not only transform data, but they'll "do" things. That could mean opening a socket, saving a file to disk, running an API call to a service, or even making physical changes such as turning on a light or unlocking a door. Terraform is a declarative language though, so the type of operations that would change the state of a system are reserved for resources and data sources. Functions exist to support creating and configuring those resources and data sources, which really means altering data to be used as arguments when creating those block types.

4.3.1   *Calling and using functions*

Functions have a name, may take in arguments, and always return values. A function has the format of `function_name(arg1, arg2, …)`, with the specific arguments depending on the function itself. Functions aren't required to have arguments, and some even take in a dynamic number of arguments:

- The `timestamp` function doesn't have any arguments.
- The `file` function needs a path, so it has one argument.
- The `concat` function needs at least two arguments but can take any number on top of that.

Function arguments can themselves be expressions, which will be resolved before being passed to the function.

Listing 4.15   **Using functions to transform data**

```
locals {
  is_dev    = startswith(var.environment, "dev-")
  env_name  = split(var.environment, "-")[1]
  env_label = upper(local.env_name)
}
```

These are examples of string functions.

Startswith returns true if the passed value matches the passed prefix.

Split breaks a string into a list using a custom delimiter. Here we grab the second value to get the name.

This function returns a new string with all letters being in the upper case.

4.3.2   *The standard library*

Terraform has a standard library of functions (https://mng.bz/6ewG) that it ships with, and before the release of Terraform 1.8 those were the only functions available. Starting in Terraform and OpenTofu v1.8, it is possible to build functions directly into the providers.

It may seem weird that it took so long to add support for third-party functions, and it would certainly be a problem if Terraform was an imperative language. Terraform is a declarative language though, and the vast majority of the work in the language is done with resources and data sources.

Terraform divides the functions into categories, although these categories are mostly for documentation's sake (see table 4.4).

Table 4.4 Terraform function categories

Function categories	Category descriptions
Numeric	Mathematical functions that are too complicated to have operators for
String	String and template manipulation, including regex and pattern-matching functions
Collection	Functions that manipulate lists, objects, and maps
Encoding	Converting data into strings and back, such as encoding into JSON
Filesystem	File manipulation functions, including `templatefile`
Date and time	Functions for formatting and manipulating dates, including pulling the current timestamp
Hash and cryptography	Functions for creating cryptographic hashes of data as well as some cryptography functions
IP network functions	Functions that help automatically calculate subnets (extremely useful for setting up dynamic IP address spacing)
Type conversion	Functions for converting data from one type to another

It's worth looking through and reviewing the list of functions now and then, as it does occasionally grow as new features are added. This chapter goes over the most important functions to immediately know, and others will be introduced and used throughout the book.

4.3.3 *Pure vs. impure functions*

In computer science terms, functions can be pure or impure. A pure function will always have the same return value for the same inputs. For example, if a function adds two numbers together, then you would always expect it to return the same result from the same numbers (2 plus 2 is always 4). Most functions in Terraform are pure functions and don't need any special consideration.

An impure function, on the other hand, can have different results each time it is called. Two really common examples of impure functions are random functions and functions that return the current time. Since time is always moving forward, you can always expect a different return value from a function that gets the current time. A random function that always returns the same value wouldn't be very random.

In most languages, the difference between impure and pure functions can be ignored, but in a declarative language like Terraform, the difference is extremely important. If an impure function is used to generate the configuration of a resource, then the function will always cause Terraform to think that the resource needs to be updated. To put it another way, when impure functions are part of the configuration, then the second the Terraform apply is run, the workspace is already out of date.

If you find yourself in a situation where your code is registering changes immediately after you've already applied all of the updates. then you should look for cases where you may be using impure functions. If you find yourself depending on functions like uuid or timestamp, then you may want to look at the random and time providers in Terraform, which we'll discuss in chapter 6.

Listing 4.16   Example of UUID function forcing constant changes

```
resource "aws_instance" "example" {
  tags = {                          This will have a new value every plan,
    id = uuid()              ◀──    so changes will always be required.
  }
}
```

4.4   Strings and templates

In the last chapter, we talked about strings and introduced string interpolation, which is one method for building strings from a group of variables and attributes. This is a great method for smaller strings, such as when we used it to turn our name_prefix variable into indexed names for our instances at the beginning of the chapter. This can be burdensome for larger strings, so Terraform provides a system for managing large strings using files and templates.

4.4.1   The file function

If you have a large string that you don't need to change at all, then one convenient way to manage it is by storing it in files. The file function (https://mng.bz/oKmN) takes in a path and returns the contents of the path as a string. This way, you don't have to put extremely long strings directly in your code.

When using the file function it's common to use the special path value provided by Terraform. This is an object that contains three values:

- path.module contains a path to the module that it's being called from.
- path.root contains the path to the root module.
- path.cwd contains the path to the current working directory. This is often, but not always, the same as path.root.

The path.module value makes it easier to pull files from inside of your module.

Listing 4.17   file_function example

```
resource "aws_instance" "cloud_init_file" {
  user_data = file("${path.module}/files/cloud-init.txt")    ◀──
}
                                              Cloud Init scripts can be really
                                              long, so we store it in a file.
```

4.4.2 *The templatefile function*

The `templatefile` function (https://mng.bz/nRvv) is similar to the `file` function except it also supports string interpolation and basic iteration using the file as a template. This is used quite often to define complex configuration files to supply to programs or systems. If you're configuring a service that uses Nginx (a common HTTP reverse proxy), you can use a template to generate the configuration file it expects.

The `templatefile` function takes two arguments. Like the `file` function, it takes in a path that it uses to load a template file.

The second argument is a map of strings. The keys are the names of the interpolated variables, which should also be present in the template. When `templatefile` is run, it will replace the variables in the template with the values passed in from the map.

> **Listing 4.18** `templatefile` **function example**

By switching from file to templatefile we can add logic and variables to our configuration.

```
resource "aws_instance" "template_file" {
  user_data = templatefile("${path.module}/templates/cloud-init.tftpl", { ◄
    services = ["nomad", "consul"],
    backups  = var.enable_backups,
    hostname = "${var.name}-nomad"
  })
}
```

These variables will be available inside of the template.

OpenTofu also added support for a function called `templatestring` (https://mng.bz/vKlx) that works like the `templatefile` function, but instead of loading a template from a file, it takes the string directly. This allows you to build templates as variables. Terraform followed their lead and added the same function to Terraform v1.9.0.

4.4.3 *String template language*

So far we've seen a lot of interpolation—that is, expressions that create a larger string by incorporating many smaller ones. In these cases, we're taking the smaller string directly and including in the larger one without any transformations or logic.

Terraform strings and templates allow for more than just string interpolation. With string templates, you can also call expressions and take advantage of logic branches and iteration. This allows for arbitrary complex strings to be generated from a smaller set of inputs.

String interpolation is represented with the "dollar brackets" symbol, while directives such as if/else statements use the "percentage brackets" symbol. In the simplest example, we can include between two branches depending on whether a flag is enabled. This can be used to turn a feature on and off or switch between two different options.

> **Listing 4.19** **Using branches in templates**

```
%{ if enable_feature }
  feature_flag = 1
```

This line is printed if the enable_feature variable is true.

```
%{ else }
  feature_flag = 0
%{ endif }
```

← **This line is printed if the enable_feature variable is false.**

We can also call functions inside of our expressions. The only limit here is that Terraform will not allow us to call the `templatefile` function from inside of a template, but other than that all of the functions are available. We can do math, run type conversations, and encode data right from in our templates.

Listing 4.20 Expressions in templates

```
${value * 2}
${max(OptionA, OptionB)}
```

← **This will multiply the value by two, convert it to a string, and print the new string.**

This runs the function max on the two values to get the largest one, which it converts to a string and prints.

Even cooler, we can apply iteration in our templates. If we have a map or a list, we can iterate over all of the values in our template.

Listing 4.21 Iterating over collections in templates

```
%{ for key, value in variable_object }
${key}   ${value}
%{ endfor }

%{ for value in variable_list }
${value}
%{ endfor }
```

← **This block prints the key and value separated by a tab.**

← **This block will print each value in the list.**

4.4.4 The template_file resource

The `templatefile` function is not the only way to access templates, although it is the recommended way. Terraform does have a deprecated `template_file` resource as part of the `template` provider, although since it is deprecated they are pushing people toward the `templatefile` and `templatestring` functions. It's still good to know about as many older modules still use this resource.

Listing 4.22 The `template_file` resource example

```
data "template_file" "main" {
  template = file("${path.module}/example.tftpl")
  vars = {
    service_name = var.name
    other_config = var.feature_enabled
  }
}
```

← **This data source is deprecated and the templatefile function should be used instead.**

This is the same as the first parameter of templatefile.

This matches the second parameter of tempplatefile.

There is no reason to ever use the `template_file` resource with new code, and if you see this in a module that you're using, you should remove it and replace it with the `templatefile` function. By marking it as deprecated, the Terraform team has made it clear that they do not plan on maintaining it in the long term, and it will likely be removed from the language at some point in the future. The only reason that it's even mentioned here is that a lot of older code uses it, so you're likely to see it when reading examples or when using code that hasn't been updated in a while.

4.4.5 *When not to use templates*

Templates are an amazing feature in Terraform, but there are situations where they are not appropriate. In particular, if Terraform has a way to natively deal with the format you're trying to work with, you are always better off using that method. Since Terraform has a way to natively work with JSON and YAML, for instance, you should avoid building templates to create JSON and YAML files and instead rely on Terraform to encode your data for you.

For example, it may be tempting to store IAM policies as templates and fill in their values from variables. This can result in malformed data that can create errors down the line and in general makes it harder to expand your module. You are normally much better off storing the data directly in code as a variable and then using the `jsonencode` and `yamlencode` functions to handle turning it to the appropriate string.

Listing 4.23   JSON and YAML encoding with strings and functions

```
locals {
  json_string = <<EOT
  "{
    \"name\": \"${var.name}\"
  }"
  EOT

  config_object = {
    name = var.name
  }

  yaml_config = yamlencode(local.config_object)
  json_config = jsonencode(local.config_object)
}
```

◄─── **Trying to write JSON is both ugly and error prone.**

◄─── **Instead, make an object that matches what you want your data to look like...**

| **...then use the built in encoding functions to convert it.**

For specialty documents like IAM policies, there are even data sources (https://mng .bz/4aeB) that can be used instead of templates for even deeper validation. These are nice because they enforce the same structure as the documents they represent and are able to give you better feedback when errors occur.

4.5   *Regular expressions*

Regular expressions are a small language used to match string patterns. Pretty much every commonly used programming language supports regular expressions in one way or another. Terraform supports the use of regular expressions through the use of the `regex`, `regexall`, and `replace` functions.

Regular expressions are powerful. We've seen examples in previous chapters of using regular expressions alongside the `validation` block to throw errors when input variables are set to invalid values. Another common use is to extract a smaller string from a bigger one, such as pulling an account number out of an Amazon Resource Name (the standardized identifier AWS uses for resources).

Listing 4.24   Regular expression with named capture groups

```
locals {
  arn            = "arn:aws:ec2:us-west-2:123456789012:instance/
i-1234567890abcdef0"
  arn_parts      = regex("^\\w+:(?P<partition>\\w+):(?P<service>\\w+):(
?P<region>[\\w-]*):(?P<account>\\d{12}):", local.arn)
  arn_partition = local.arn_parts["partition"]
  arn_service   = local.arn_parts["service"]           Since our regex pattern uses named
  arn_region    = local.arn_parts["region"]            capture groups it returns an object
  arn_account   = local.arn_parts["account"]           with keys matching our group names.
}
```

When writing regular expressions in Terraform, it's important to remember that Terraform was written in Golang and uses the Golang regular expression syntax. If you're using tools such as Regex101 to test your patterns out (which is highly recommended), then you'll want to set them to use the Golang syntax for regular expressions.

4.5.1 Regex

The `regex` function is useful when you absolutely have to get the results out of a string or otherwise fail. With this function, if no matching string is found, it will raise an error.

The return results of the `regex` function depend on whether you use capture groups, which are a feature of regular expressions that allow you to return multiple strings from the same pattern. Regular expressions support unnamed capture groups, where the results come back in the order the capture groups are defined, as well as named groups where each capture group has an explicit name. Capture groups can be named or unnamed as long as the pattern is consistent (you have to use one or the other; you can't mix them together). Depending on your use of capture groups, you'll get a different return value:

- If you don't use capture groups at all, you'll get back a string matching your pattern.
- If you use unnamed capture groups, you'll get a list of the substrings in the order they were defined in your regular expression pattern.
- If you use named capture groups, you'll get back a map, with the keys of the map being the name of the group and the value being the substring.

Listing 4.25 Regular expressions with `regex`

```
variable "name" {
  type    = string
  default = "dev-local"
}

locals {
  env_type = regex("^[a-z]+", var.name)

  env_name = regex("^[a-z]+-(.*)", var.name)[0]

  env_error = regex("^[A-Z]", var.name)
}
```

When no matching groups are used regex will return the matched pattern. Returns "dev".

When capture groups are used then a list of results comes back, even if only one is expected. Returns ["local"], and then we select the first item.

If your pattern doesn't have a match, then regex will throw an error.

4.5.2 *Regexall*

The `regexall` function is very similar to the `regex` function, except instead of finding one match, it can find all the matches from a string in the form of a list.

Just like `regex`, the return value types will vary depending on your use of capture groups. It follows the same rules, only it returns a list of all the results instead of just a single result:

- If there aren't any capture groups, you get a list of strings.
- If there are unnamed capture groups, you get a list of lists.
- If there are named capture groups, you get a list of maps.

Unlike the `regex` function, the `regexall` function will not throw an error if no results are found. Instead, you get an empty list.

Listing 4.26 Regular expressions

```
variable "aws_region" {
  type    = string
  default = "us-east-1"
  validation {
    condition     = length(regexall("^[a-z]{2}-[a-z]*-\\d$",
      var.aws_region)) == 1
    error_message = "This value must match the aws region format."
  }
}
```

The regexall and length functions can be used to confirm a variable matches the expected pattern.

4.5.3 *Replace*

The `replace` function (https://mng.bz/nRzg) is used to alter a string by searching for a pattern and replacing it with a new string. The `replace` function can take pure strings or regular expressions, which it recognizes by the wrapping slashes in the regular expression pattern.

Listing 4.27   Using the `replace` function with plan strings

The replace function can be used to
replace exact match strings.
Returns "Goodnight World!"

```
locals {
    simple_swap = replace("Hello World!", "Hello", "Goodnight")  ◄

    flexible_swap = replace("Hello World", "/^[a-zA-Z]*/", "Goodnight")  ◄
}
```

It can also be used with regular expressions. This one replaces
the first continous block of letters, regardless of what it is.
Returns "Goodnight World!". Notice that the pattern is
wrapped in slashes to signify that it is a regex pattern.

If capture groups are used in the pattern, then the captured strings are available for use in the replacement string. If they are unnamed capture groups, the replacement text accesses them by index number ($1, $2, etc.) while named groups have variables with the same name.

Listing 4.28   Using the `replace` function with regular expressions

We can reuse the data we captured
in our replacement string. Here we
add a suffix to our IP address.

```
locals {
    reuse_swap = replace("ip_address: 192.168.0.1;", "/(?P<ip>\\d+\\.\\d+\\.
    ➥\\d+\\.\\d+)/", "$ip/32")  ◄
}
```

Returns "ip_address:
192.168.0.1/32;"

4.6   *Type conversion*

We've talked about type a few times now, mostly in the context of defining input variables. Outside of that case, type can mostly be ignored, as Terraform itself will handle conversion between one type and another automatically if possible. That said, Terraform does have a few ways to change the type as well as the sensitivity of a value.

4.6.1   *Implicit type conversion*

Terraform attempts to convert types automatically if possible. If a string is passed in where a number is expected, Terraform will try to convert that to a number. If the string contains only numbers and a decimal point, this will work pretty well. Terraform will also convert the booleans `true` and `false` into the strings `"true"` and `"false"`, which works in the other direction as well.

If Terraform cannot convert a value into the needed type, an error will be thrown. Terraform also won't convert types when using the equality operators, == and !=. This is why explicit type conversion, which we discuss next, should be preferred.

> **Listing 4.29 Implicit type conversion from number to string**

```
locals {
  long_pi  = 3.14159
  pi_string = substr(local.long_pi, 0, 4)
}
```

Returns the string "3.14".

The substr function expects a string as its first argument, so Terraform will implicitly replace the value with the equivilent string.

4.6.2 The toType functions

Terraform also has a way to explicitly convert the type using functions. Basically, every type has a toType function: tobool, tolist, tomap, tonumber, toset, tostring.

In general, the Terraform developers recommend that these functions only be used to normalize output of modules, so that modules have a consistent type on their outputs. It is also somewhat common to convert lists to sets so that they can be used with the for_each meta argument.

> **Listing 4.30 Explicit type conversion with `totype` functions**

```
locals {
  enable_flag = "true"
}

output "feature_enabled" {
  value = tobool(local.enable_flag)
}
```

Create and pass back a new boolean value from our string.

4.6.3 Sensitive and nonsensitive

Values can be marked as sensitive, which Terraform uses as a signal to prevent the value from being displayed or logged. This sensitive flag doesn't just apply to the initial value but can also apply to values derived from it. For example, if you embed a sensitive string inside of another string, it can mark the new string as sensitive.

As this system is rather conservative and marks all sensitive-derived values as sensitive themselves, there will be times when innocuous values will get marked as sensitive when they aren't. Other times, you may have a value that isn't sensitive but you think should be. Terraform offers a way to explicitly change the sensitive flag using the sensitive and nonsensitive functions.

Since Terraform is a declarative language, and declarative languages do not allow variables to be changed, these functions do not actually change an existing variable. Instead, the functions return a new value with the corresponding sensitivity flag. In other words, if you pass a value that is sensitive to the nonsensitive function, the function will return a new value that is identical but no longer marked as sensitive.

> **Listing 4.31 Sensitive and nonsensitive**

```
resource "random_uuid" "visible_uuid" {

}
locals {
  sensitive_uuid = sensitive(random_uuid.visible_uuid.result)
}
```

The random provider is a state-only provider with resources that generate random data, such as UUIDs.

All of the arguments for this resource are optional, which is why it is empty.

This creates a new variable with the same value, only marked sensitive.

If you use either of these functions, you should review and document why you're using them. If you are making a value sensitive, it may be a sign that you're using a variable that should have been assigned as sensitive but wasn't. At the same time, if you're removing the sensitive flag with the `nonsensitive` function, then you should make sure you aren't going to leak information that is better kept out of logs.

4.7   *Try and can*

The `try` and `can` functions are both useful in situations where you potentially, or even purposefully, expect an error to occur.

The `try` function takes in any number of arguments and returns the first one that isn't an error. A common use case is to provide a default value for an expression that can fail with some input: for that, the `try` statement takes the expression as the first argument and the default value as the second. It is also pretty common to see `try` statements used to prevent errors while looking up attributes of optional resources (where the count is either 0 or 1 depending on input).

> **Listing 4.32 Using the `try` function to test a dynamic resource**

```
output "instance_id" {
  value = try(aws_instance.main[0].id, null)
}
```

If aws_instance.main has no resources, then the output will be null.

The `can` function converts an expression into a boolean, returning `false` if that expression triggered an error and returning `true` for all other results. The main purpose of this function is to test validation rules in variables, and it is recommended not to use the `can` function outside of that use case. If you want to use `can` somewhere else, chances are you should be using `try`.

> **Listing 4.33 Using `can` to give specific error messages**

```
variable "number_string" {
  type = string
  validation {
```

```
    condition     = can(tonumber(var.number_string))
    error_message = "Although this variable is a string, it is expected to
⮑be numeric."
  }
}
```
If the user passes in a string that can't be converted to a number, then can will return false.

These functions are great for normalizing data, but do not use them to hide real errors. If there's a place where errors are occurring, you should always try to eliminate the error itself rather than cover it up. One area where these functions are great is validation blocks, as they let you catch the errors and replace them with better error messages. They can also be useful inside some output blocks. Outside of those scenarios, you should make sure to document your reasoning for using it in a comment.

4.8 count and for_each

Terraform supports iteration a bit differently than other languages. The typical do and while loops really don't make sense outside of imperative languages, but there are still cases where it makes sense to iterate over objects or attempt to do something more than once. Terraform has two forms of iteration:

- Creating multiple resources at once
- Transforming groups of data from one type to another

The for_each and count meta parameters accomplish the first goal. These two meta parameters each give a slightly different way for a single block to define multiple resources. At most, one of these parameters can be used in a block, as attempting to use both will trigger an error. Accomplishing the second goal can be done with the for expression, which we'll discuss in the section after this.

4.8.1 count

The count meta parameter makes it possible for module and resource blocks to create multiple objects from a single block. It is a simpler method for creating multiple objects. It takes in an integer and creates that many items. If you pass in 5, it will create five; if you pass in 0 as a value, it won't create any.

Blocks that use count get access to a special variable named count that is only valid inside of the block. This variable has one attribute named index, which is a zero-indexed identifier for each item created. If you use this to create multiple AWS instances, such as in the beginning of the chapter, then the value of count.index will be a different number (starting with zero) for each of them.

Listing 4.34 Using the count meta parameter to create resources

```
variable "subnet_ids" {
  description = "A list of subnet ids to launch instances into."
  type        = set(string)
}

variable "num_instances" {
```

```
description = "How many instances to launch."
type        = number
default     = 0
}

resource "aws_instance" "instances" {
  count         = var.num_instances
  subnet_id     = var.subnet_ids[count.index % length(var.subnet_ids)]
  instance_type = "t3.micro"
  ami           = data.aws_ami.main.id
}
```

The count.index is used to spread the instances over multiple subnets.

Data source left out for brevity

The `count` meta parameter can be used with the conditional statement to define a resource that can be toggled on and off with a boolean. This is especially useful inside of modules, as it provides a very nice interface for users to turn on optional features.

Listing 4.35 `count` **as a toggle**

```
variable "enable_resource" {
  type    = bool
  default = true
}

resource "resource_type" "resource_name" {
  count = var.enable_resource ? 1 : 0
}
```

This resource is only created if the enable_resource input is true.

4.8.2   *for_each*

The `for_each` meta parameter services a similar function as `count`, except that it takes in an `object`, map, or `set` instead of an integer and gives developers access to the `each` variable instead of the `count` variable. This `each` variable is an object with two items: a `key` and a `value`. For objects, the `key` and `value` map to the object's own keys and values. When using a `set`, each element is passed to both `each.key` and `each.value`.

This structure lets each object created from the block have its own configuration. Let's say we wanted to create many instances, each with its own name, instance type, and subnet. We can create a local object that has the instance names as a key and the custom variables for each instance as the values. Then, using the `for_each` parameter alongside our module, we can use a single block to create all of these instances.

It's also possible to use `for_each` with `sets`. This can come in handy when you have a group of resources that only differ on one field. AWS has a resource called VPC Endpoints that can be a good example of this. These endpoints create AWS APIs inside your VPC, so you can access AWS services without going over the internet (saving money in transfer fees while also making your services more resilient). It's possible to create a module that takes a list of services you want to enable these endpoints for and create them from that list.

If you attempt to pass a list to `for_each`, it will return an error, but you can use the `toset` function to convert a `list` to a `set` (just understand that any duplicate values will be removed, and the `list` will no longer be ordered once it turns into a `set`).

Listing 4.36 Using `for_each` to create resources with different parameters

```
locals {
  machine_configs = {
    "web_server" = {
      type = "t3.nano"
    }
    "background_processor" = {
      type = "t3.micro"
    }
  }
}

resource "aws_instance" "for_each" {
  for_each      = local.machine_configs
  subnet_id     = var.subnet_id
  instance_type = each.value.type
  ami           = data.aws_ami.main.id
  tags = {
    Name = each.key
  }
}

locals {
  vpc_endpoints = [
    "s3",
    "dynamodb"
  ]
}

data "aws_region" "current" {}

resource "aws_vpc_endpoint" "main" {
  for_each     = toset(local.machine_configs)
  vpc_id       = var.vpc_id
  service_name = "com.amazonaws.${data.aws_region.current.name}.${each.
    value}"
}
```

This will create the two servers defined in our config local.

The subnet_id will be the same for all instances since it's pulled from the same input.

each.value.type will resolve to "t3.large" for the first instance and "m3.large" for the second.

Data source left out for brevity

each.key will resolve to "web_server" for the first instance and "background_processor" for the second.

We're using locals for the example, but in a module this would be an input variable.

This is a list of AWS services we want to create VPC endpoints for.

We need the current region to construct the proper service_name for our endpoints.

AWS VPC Endpoints allow you to access AWS APIs inside of VPCs without going over the internet.

We use the aws_region data source and the value from our list to construct the endpoint name.

We have to convert our list to a set.

4.8.3   Accessing attributes

Resources and modules that use count still have outputs and attributes. Instead of accessing them directly though, they are accessed like you would a list. You can access them individually using their index value, or you can iterate over all of the values like any other list or object.

Listing 4.37 Accessing attributes from resource with `count` or `for_each`

```
resource "aws_instance" "main" {
  count = var.count
}
```

```
output "first_instance" {
  value = aws_instance.main[0]
}
```
◄───── Resources that use count or foreach can be accessed by index.

4.8.4   *Limitations and workarounds*

The values passed to `for_each` and `count` have to be known to Terraform at the start of the plan phase. This means the values cannot rely on data from resources to calculate their values or on data sources, which themselves rely on resource attributes (data sources that can be looked up during the initial refresh phase of the plan should work). There are even some functions, such as the `timestamp` and `uuid` functions, that cannot be used here. When either `for_each` or `count` needs information that isn't available to it at the early planning phase, then Terraform will throw an error.

These limitations are especially painful when working with `for_each`. With `count`, you're dealing with a very simple value, so it's easier to find ways to calculate it without remote values. When using `for_each`, you generally are passing in more complex configurations, and if any part of that configuration comes from a resource attribute or "impure function," then it can't be used.

There are some workarounds to this behavior. Since `count` is often simpler and less prone to this error, it can be used in places where `for_each` would give an error. The configuration values that are needed can be stored in an intermediate local variable, and then that variable can be referenced by the `count.index` value. This works because it's only the meta parameter that needs to be known by Terraform in advance, so we can use `count` as the meta parameter and pull out our local values for configuration during a later part of the planning phase.

Listing 4.38   **Working around** `for_each` **limitations**

```
variable "num_resources" {
  type = number
}

variable "subnet_ids" {
  type = list(string)
}

resource "aws_instance" "distributed_servers_error" {
  for_each  = var.subnet_ids
  subnet_id = each.value
}

resource "aws_instance" "distributed_servers_workaround" {
  count     = var.num_instances
  subnet_id = element(var.subnet_ids, count.index)
}
```

◄─── If subnet_ids are being created in another module this may fail.

◄─── We can use the built-in element function to pull out our subnets, so it doesn't matter how var.subnets was generated.

It is also possible to break up the Terraform plan to create resources in batches so the ones depending on the `count` or `for_each` value will be created later in the process after the information is loaded. Terraform will even mention this as a possibility when the error occurs.

This is, to be blunt, a horrible practice. Part of the beauty of Terraform is the ability to easily launch and tear down the environment while Terraform handles your ordering for you. If you try to work around limitations by complicating your deployment process, you're going to make Terraform more painful to work with. Instead, look at ways you can refactor your code to remove the problem itself.

4.9 For

The for statement allows developers to run a transformation on every item in a group and then return a new group with those transformations. It can also be used to filter items out of the group.

As a very simple example, let's say you have a list of strings and you want to add a prefix to each item in the list:

```
[for item in var.list : "prefix-${item}"]
```

This statement can be translated into English as "for each item in this list create a new string." The statement takes each string in the list, places its value into the item variable for use by the transformation section, and then packages all the results up into a new list.

The for statement can be complicated because it has different options depending on what types you put in and what types you take out. You can put in anything that converts to a list or object (so sets, maps, tuples), and you can return either a list or an object.

4.9.1 List and object inputs

The biggest difference between using a list or an object as your input is that Terraform will give you access to the key and the value when iterating over an object, while you only get access to the values when using a list.

Listing 4.39 Using for expressions with different input types

```
locals {
  object_example = [for key, value in var.object : "${key},${value}"]
  list_example = [for x in var.list : x * 2]
}
```

Input objects provide both a key and a value.

Convert an object into a list of comma-separated key/value pairs.

Input lists only provide a value. Create a new list from var.list where the values from var.list are doubled.

4.9.2 List and object outputs

So far our examples have all returned lists. The for expression can also return objects. A for statement that returns an object will be surrounded by curly brackets, while statements that return a list will be wrapped with square brackets. With objects, you also have to return a key, not just a value like with a list. To make this work, Terraform has a special operator that is only used in this specific case: the `=>` operator.

Listing 4.40   Using for expressions with different outputs

> **The for function will return objects if bounded with curly brackets instead of square ones.**

> **The return format is slightly different as well, since both a key and a value are needed. Create a new object using the items from var.list as the key and their md5 hash as the value.**

```
locals {
  objects = { for x in var.list : s => md5(s) }
}
```

4.9.3   *Filtering*

The `for` statement can support filtering objects with an optional `if` statement. When this statement isn't present, then every item is included, but when it is present, then it only includes items if the statement returns true.

Listing 4.41   Using `for` expressions to filter lists and objects

> **Filter out any null items.**

> **Create a new list with only even numbers.**

```
locals {
  filtered_list = [for x in var.inputs : x if x != null]
  evens_only    = [for x in var.numbers : x if x % 2 == 0]
}
```

4.9.4   *Grouping mode*

Grouping mode is an interesting feature of the `for` expression. It can be used to create new objects, where each key in the new object points to a collection of values (such as a list of strings). What makes this interesting is that the values are built up over multiple iterations, not just through one assignment.

When using grouping mode, you define your output like normal, with a key and a value. To turn on grouping mode, you add three dots (an ellipsis) after your value. Now you can use the same key multiple times, and the results from each iteration will get merged with the other outputs of the same key.

Listing 4.42   Grouping data with `for` expressions

> **This expression creates an object with the subnets as keys that point at lists of server ids.**

```
locals {
  servers_by_subnet = {
    for server in aws_instances.main[*] : server.subnet_id => server.id...
  }
}
```

4.9.5 *Splat*

The `splat` expression is a simple way to turn expressions into lists. Everything that's possible to do with the `splat` expression can be done with the `for` expression, but the `splat` expression removes a lot of boilerplate around a fairly common operation.

Listing 4.43 Removing for boilerplate with `splat` expressions

```
variable "object_config" {
  type = list(object({
    id   = string
    type = string
  }))
}

locals {
  config_id_for   = [for x in var.object_config : x.id]
  config_id_splat = var.object_config[*].id
}
```

Both of these examples are functionally identical.

These examples both return the same output—a list of IDs.

A common pattern is to use the `splat` operator to take the output of a module or resource that uses `count` or `for_each` to turn that output into a list. For example, our instance example has an output for the `aws_instance_ip`. We can use the `splat` operator to get a list of `aws_instance_ip` values, which we can then pass to a security group.

Listing 4.44 Simple `splat` use cases

Both of these examples are functionally identical.

Both expressions return a list of IP addresses.

```
locals {
  instance_ids_for   = [for x in module.instances : x.aws_instance_ip]
  instance_ids_splat = module.instances[*].aws_instance_ip
}
```

The `splat` expression can also be used to turn a single value into a list that contains that value. This is useful if you have arguments that expect a list but you only plan on sending one item to it. By putting the `splat` operator after the variable, it will return a one-item list.

Listing 4.45 Using `splat` to convert single items to lists

```
variable "security_group_id" {
  type = string
}

resource "aws_instance" "sg_example" {
  vpc_security_group_ids = var.security_group_id[*]
}
```

The splat converts our string into a one-item list.

4.10 *Dynamic blocks*

Going back to our second chapter, we know that HashiCorp Configuration Language objects have both arguments and subblocks. Arguments can only be used once inside a block, but subblocks can be used repeatedly to build up a set of configurations.

What if you want to optionally define a block or use a different number of blocks depending on the circumstances? For example, many providers use subblocks to define their network access rules. These rules can change based on need. Someone may want multiple ports open or none at all. API gateways and content delivery networks also tend to use subblocks in their resources, and making a reusable module would be difficult if all the subblocks had to be defined in advance.

Terraform has a construct called `dynamic` blocks that uses a special subtype named `dynamic` that is used to create subblocks. It uses the subblock name as a label and takes a `for_each` parameter similar to the one used by resources and modules. For each of the values passed in, it creates a unique block, and it makes those values available when defining the block config.

`dynamic` blocks have the most confusing syntax in all of Terraform. Rather than using the `each` or `count` keyword like other iterators in the language, the `dynamic` block creates a new keyword each time it is used, named after the subblock the `dynamic` block is creating. This allows for nested `dynamic` blocks, where the subblocks can refer to the ones above it, but this is not something you'll see often. It also puts all of the configuration inside of a sub-subblock named `content`. As a result, many new (and even experienced) Terraform developers end up looking this up often.

Listing 4.46 `dynamic` **block**

```
variable "security_group_rules" {
  type = list(object({
    description = string,
    from_port   = number,
    to_port     = number
    protocol    = string
    cidr_blocks = list(string)
  }))
}

resource "aws_security_group" "main" {
  name        = "${var.name}-sg"
  description = "The security group for an AWS Instance."
  vpc_id      = var.vpc_id

  dynamic "ingress" {
    for_each = var.security_group_rules

    content {
      description = ingress.value.description
      from_port   = ingress.value.from_port
      to_port     = ingress.value.to_port
      protocol    = ingress.value.protocol
      cidr_blocks = ingress.value.cidr_blocks
```

This dynamic block creates "ingress" blocks.

This tells the dynamic block to iterate over the security_group_rules variable.

The "ingress" object is a copy of one of the items in our list.

```
    }
  }

  ingress {
    description = "HTTPS"
    from_port   = 443
    to_port     = 443
    protocol    = tcp
    cidr_blocks = ["0.0.0.0/0"]
  }
}
```

◄── **This is an example of an ingress block on its own. Dynamic and direct blocks can be mixed in the same resource.**

Although `dynamic` blocks are based on the `for_each` parameter rather than the `count` meta parameter, it is still possible to use it to toggle a block on and off. In this case, we use the conditional statement to switch between an empty list and a list with a single placeholder value. If the empty list is provided, the block won't be enabled, while the value from the placeholder list is enough to create the block even if the value isn't used.

Listing 4.47 `dynamic` **block toggle**

```
resource "aws_security_group" "dynamic" {
  name        = "${var.name}-sg"
  description = "The security group for an AWS Instance."
  vpc_id      = var.vpc_id

  dynamic "ingress" {
    for_each = var.enable_public_https ? ["placeholder"] : []
#B
    content {
      description = "Enable global access to port 443 (HTTPS)."
      from_port   = 443
      to_port     = 443
      protocol    = "tcp"
      cidr_blocks = ["0.0.0.0/0"]
    }
  }

  egress {
    from_port        = 0
    to_port          = 0
    protocol         = "-1"
    cidr_blocks      = ["0.0.0.0/0"]
    ipv6_cidr_blocks = ["::/0"]
  }
}
```

This dynamic block controls a single block, turning it either on or off.

for_each expects a list of parameters to pass to each block.

This is the HTTPS port.

The "0.0.0.0/0" network means any network.

AWS requires explicit permission for outgoing traffic.

In this chapter, we learned how to use more of the logical components of the Terraform language. We've expanded our toolset to include the operators, standard library of functions, and iteration—tools we can use to make modules that are far more flexible. In our next chapter, we're going to spend more time focused on how Terraform takes our code and converts it into a plan that it can then execute, which in turn will help us understand how to write more efficient code and the types of problems we can run into and how to avoid them.

Summary

- Terraform has a variety of operators that can be used to perform math, boolean operations, and comparisons (such as greater than/equals to).
- There is a rich standard library of functions built into Terraform, and starting with Terraform v1.8, providers can also add their own functions.
- Functions in Terraform are primarily used to transform data, not to take action.
- Larger strings can be stored as either files or templates, with templates having their own small language that can be used to generate complex strings from developer input.
- Resources and modules can have multiple instances of resources created from the same block through the use of `count` and `for_each`.

The Terraform plan

In the last few chapters, we focused on the Terraform language. This included a heavy focus on the components of the language itself, resources and data sources, the providers they come from, and how we could use functions and expressions to create a variety of configurations. Terraform is more than a language though: it is also an engine that takes your code, compares it to the state of your infrastructure, and then comes up with a dynamic plan to change your infrastructure so it matches your program.

We introduced this concept back in chapter 1 when talking about the development cycle in Terraform (see figure 5.1). You code, plan, review, and apply your changes.

In this chapter, we focus very heavily on the plan and apply portions of this cycle, with an emphasis on how Terraform turns your code into real-world infrastructure changes. One of the most powerful parts of how Terraform functions is the fact that you don't have to explicitly define migrations or paths between the versions of your code. This makes life a lot easier for developers, but it also hides a lot of the complexity behind what Terraform is doing. Most of the time hiding away that complexity is a benefit, but it is still important to understand what is happening (especially when something goes wrong).

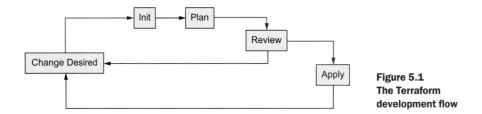

Figure 5.1
The Terraform development flow

This chapter is a bit more theoretical than some of our other chapters. We talk a bit about graph theory and how Terraform uses it to internally represent your code and a lot about the different stages that Terraform goes through to launch and maintain infrastructure. Understanding how Terraform works makes it easier to debug problems and write more efficient code.

5.1   *Directed acyclic graphs*

This next section is the most theoretical portion of the book, as we discuss the concept of directed acyclic graphs (DAGs). DAGs are a type of data structure that comes up occasionally in computer science. A simple but powerful insight is that infrastructure, and in particular the relationships between different components in infrastructure, can be represented by DAGs. This insight has really enabled the development of infrastructure as code (IaC) tools.

Terraform is not unique in its use of DAGs. Most declarative languages, both in and outside of the infrastructure world, use DAGs for figuring out what needs to be done and in what order. Although it isn't necessary to have a deep understanding of graph theory, knowing the basic structure of graphs and how they work will make understanding Terraform plans easier, especially in cases where things go wrong.

5.1.1   *DAGs*

A graph, in computer science terms, is essentially a collection of connections (called edges) and resources (called nodes). These connections and resources can represent any type of relationship you'd like. They show up in the real world all the time: family trees, corporate organization charts, and social media followings are all examples of graphs. Basically, any time you have things that have relationships between each other, you can represent them as graphs (see figure 5.2).

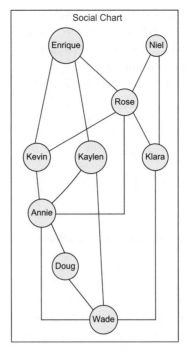

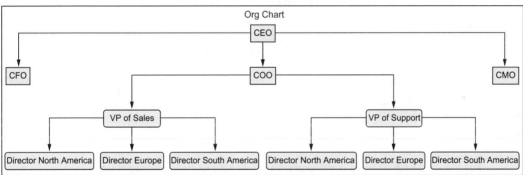

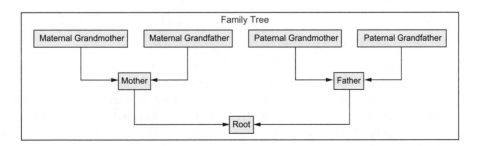

Figure 5.2 Examples of real-world graphs

The relationship between nodes is called an edge (although they're also called links or connections), and these edges in a graph can have a direction. Graphs that have a direction in their relationships are said to be directed, while graphs without a relationship are undirected. The meaning of the direction varies based on the graph, but with IaC frameworks it typically defines a dependency between resources (see figure 5.3).

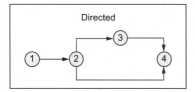
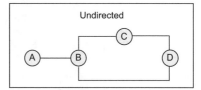

Figure 5.3   For a graph to be directed, the connections between nodes should have a direction: one should point to the other.

A graph can also be acyclic or cyclic. With an acyclic graph, the connections between nodes cannot create a circle, while cyclic graphs do allow circular relationships between nodes. Our organization chart and family tree examples were both acyclic and directed, while our social media example was an undirected cyclic graph (see figure 5.4).

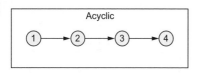
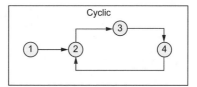

Figure 5.4   An acyclic graph is one where the graphs have no circles between them

5.1.2   *A Transport Layer Security example*

The idea of infrastructure as a DAG is not just an abstraction that we use to understand Terraform: it is directly built into the concept of Terraform itself. One of the recurring themes of this book has been that Terraform will automatically understand the dependencies between your infrastructure. This was discussed first in chapter 1 where we first introduced declarative languages and first introduced the example shown in figure 5.5.

At some point while working on a module, you are going to find yourself needing a Transport Layer Security (TLS; a standard for encrypting traffic between services) certificate. These are used to allow encryption between clients and servers. Every time you go to a website, you are most likely using TLS. Alongside web servers, they are also used for a huge variety of services.

TLS works using asymmetric encryption. It's honestly not necessary to understand the underlying math to take advantage of it. What you need to know is that you have key pairs and certificates. Key pairs are sets of cryptographic keys: a private key that has to be kept secret but can be used to sign documents and a public key that can be used to verify signatures.

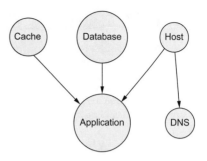

Figure 5.5   The DAG from chapter 1

Certificates are created by using a private key to create a certificate request, which then gets signed by the private key of a certificate authority (CA). This allows people to use the public key of the CA to validate the certificate (see figure 5.6).

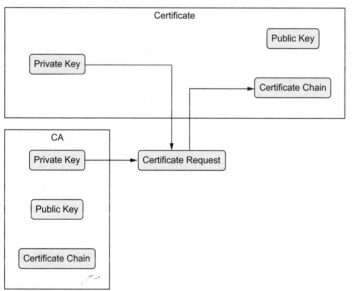

**Figure 5.6
The components of
generating certificates**

Although services such as Let's Encrypt or the various cloud CAs (such as the AWS ACM service) make it easy to get validated certificates, there are many times during development when it's easier to spin up a temporary certificate authority; creating a virtual private network service (https://github.com/tedivm/terraform-aws-dev-vpn) is a particularly common example of this.

Terraform has a provider for just about everything, and TLS is no exception. This provider gives us the resources needed to generate our own development CA that we can use for testing our modules.

Listing 5.1   Example TLS module

```
variable "domains" {
  type = set(string)
  default = [
    "example.com",
    "bravo.example.com",
    "charilie.example.com",
  ]
}
```
In general, we wouldn't set a default, but it makes for a nice self-contained example.

```
resource "tls_private_key" "ca_key" {
  algorithm = "ED25519"
}
```
Our certificate authority needs a private key.

```
resource "tls_self_signed_cert" "ca_cert" {
  private_key_pem  = tls_private_key.ca_key.private_key_pem
  is_ca_certificate = true

  subject {
    common_name  = "TiD CA"
    organization = "Terraform in Depth"
  }

  validity_period_hours = 24

  allowed_uses = [
    "digital_signature",
    "cert_signing",
    "crl_signing"
  ]
}
```
The private key is used to create the root certificate.

We want this certificate to be a certificate authority.

Since this is just for development we give it a lower time to live.

These are the permissions needed for a certificate to be a CA.

```
resource "tls_private_key" "child_key" {
  for_each  = var.domains
  algorithm = "ECDSA"
}
```
We're creating a private key for each domain

```
resource "tls_cert_request" "child_request" {
  for_each        = var.domains
  private_key_pem = tls_private_key.child_key[each.value].private_key_pem

  subject {
    common_name  = "example.com"
    organization = "Terraform in Depth"
  }
}
```
Each of the private keys needs a certificate request.

We are using the private keys created above.

```
resource "tls_locally_signed_cert" "child_certificate" {
  for_each          = var.domains
  cert_request_pem  = tls_cert_request.child_request[each.value].
    cert_request_pem
```
We pass the certificate request for each domain.

```
ca_private_key_pem = tls_private_key.ca_key.private_key_pem
ca_cert_pem        = tls_self_signed_cert.ca_cert.cert_pem

validity_period_hours = 12

allowed_uses = [
  "key_encipherment",
  "digital_signature",
  "server_auth",
]
}
```

The CA certificate is needed to build the certificate chain.

The CA private key needs to be used. It will sign the certificate request.

Since this is just for development we give it a lower time to live.

What's important about this module (and something we're going to explore more throughout this chapter) is that this module is a DAG. Every resource depends on the TLS provider, and with the exception of the `tls_private_key.ca_key` resource, they all depend on other resources. Additionally, none of the dependencies form a circle, so the graph is an acyclic one.

5.2 The Terraform resource graph

Internally, Terraform refers to the graph that it uses as the resource graph (https://mng.bz/pKBG). This graph is the central data structure that all Terraform operations revolve around. Terraform state is essentially a snapshot of the resources in that graph. As mentioned a few times, these graphs are directed and acyclic. This means that there's an order to the dependencies and that the dependencies cannot form a circular relationship.

The dependencies define how the resources Terraform manages relate to each other and is what Terraform uses to launch and modify resources in the proper order: you're essentially defining those relationships yourself in your code by linking resources together through attributes and parameters. The acyclic nature of those dependencies places a limitation on those relationships that you must be careful about, since if you do introduce a cyclic dependency, it will result in Terraform failing with an error.

5.2.1 Nodes

The Terraform resource graph has three types of nodes:

- Resources map to specific resources in your code. These each represent a single resource, so if you are using a `count` or `for_each`, then each resource will be represented in the graph. Despite the name, resources can include things like data sources.
- `Provider Configuration Node` is defined once for every provider configuration, and every resource has a direct dependency on one provider. If you have multiple configurations for a single provider, such as when using multiple AWS provider configurations to connect to different regions, they will each have their own `Provider Configuration Node`.

- Resource Meta Node is essentially a group of resources and is used when the count meta parameter is greater than 1. It's pretty much there for convenience and prettier representations of the graphs.

Now remember, this is the internal representation for Terraform. You're not going to be thinking about these things every day, so don't worry if it seems a little disconnected from the day-to-day usage, which it absolutely is. However, understanding how this works makes debugging a range of problems (that we'll discuss later in this chapter) a lot easier.

5.2.2   *terraform graph command*

Understanding the graph that Terraform created can be useful for debugging. It can help you see where dependencies between resources exist, which in turn can help you understand how changing one resource can affect resources that aren't obviously connected. There are also certain errors, such as circular dependencies, that can be really difficult to find without reviewing the graph itself.

The best way to explore the graph that Terraform builds for your configuration is with the terraform graph command. The terraform graph command can be used alongside a program called GraphViz to create visualizations of the graph that you can directly view. These visualizations are often easier to understand than reading text from the Terraform command-line interface (CLI). Before we can really discuss the terraform graph command though, we need to talk about GraphViz.

GraphViz is an open source program that is made to visualize graphs, and it has a standard file format that is used by a variety of tools (including terraform graph) to save representations of graphs. Since it is open source, it is available free of charge on pretty much every system you're likely to use, including MacOS, Windows, and Linux (https://graphviz.org/download/). The GraphViz program also installs a CLI tool named dot that can be used to manipulate and convert GraphViz files. As a result, it's common to name GraphViz files with the extension dot.

When using terraform graph, you are going to want to use GraphViz, and more specifically dot, to view the generated graph. The command directly outputs a dot file so you can pipe the command (see table 5.1).

Table 5.1   Outputting graphs in different formats

File output	Command
GraphViz dot file	terraform graph > graph.dot
SVG	terraform graph | dot -Tsvg > graph.svg
PNG	terraform graph | dot -Tpng > graph.png

This command has a few different modes for generating graphs. Using the -type flag, you can switch between plan, plan-refresh-only, plan-destroy, and apply.

To see what this looks like in action, let's revisit our TLS module. Going into the directory where that code is stored and running `terraform graph | dot -Tpng > graph` `.png` gives us the graphic shown in figure 5.7.

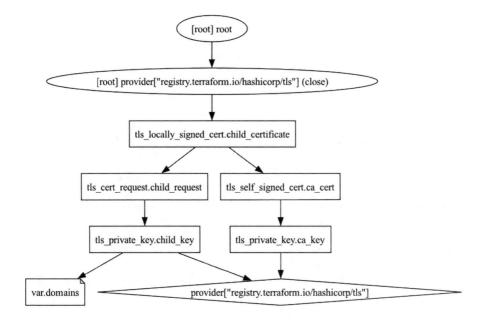

Figure 5.7   A Terraform graph in plan mode of the TLS module from 5.1.3

The `terraform graph` command can also be used to generate apply graphs. The `apply` graphs have to use a saved plan; otherwise, due to a bug, they show an empty graph. Using a fresh copy of our TLS module, we're going to create a plan file with the command `terraform plan -out create.tfplan`, and then generate an apply graph with the command `terraform graph -type=apply -plan=create.tfplan | dot -T png >` `graph.png` (see figure 5.8).

Before Terraform v1.7.0, running this command would give a much more complicated output (see figure 5.9).

As you can see, these graphs both contain a lot more information. Unlike the plan mode, this shows all of the individual resources that are going to be created. It's important to note though that, despite the name, this is still showing a diagram of the plan. The difference is that this shows how Terraform is going to apply that command, while the default plan mode shows a simplified version of the plan.

This command, and the generated images, can be really helpful for visualizing the systems you've built. This is great for debugging but can also be helpful when trying to share system architecture between teams. For example, if you need a quick diagram to share with an outside security team, you can use `terraform graph` to generate it.

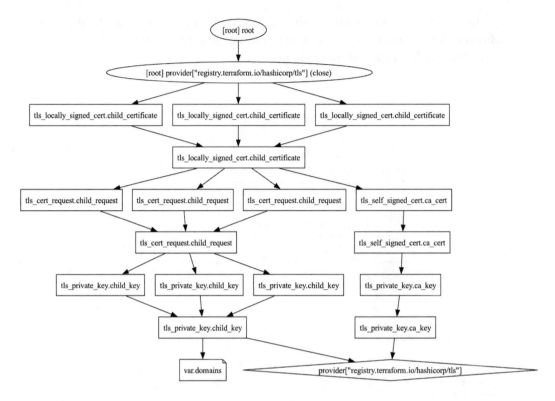

Figure 5.8   A Terraform graph in apply mode after Terraform v1.7.0

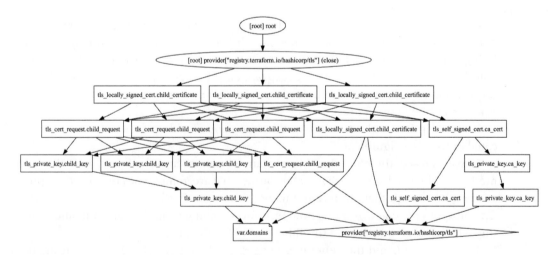

Figure 5.9   A Terraform graph in apply mode using Terraform before v1.7.0

5.2.3   Modules in the graph

One of the things you may have noticed when looking at the type of graph nodes used by the resource graph is that there is no concept of a module. Despite the fact that modules are a core part of how Terraform manages code structure and reuse, the module is not part of the main data structure that actually drives how Terraform functions.

This can have very counterintuitive results and is one of the things that newer Terraform users can struggle with. Most users who have worked with other languages are likely used to the idea of functions, modules, and classes (depending on what language is being referred to) as being self-contained units where their processing is done in one chunk. Although Terraform presents modules like that, under the hood, the boundaries between modules disappear. This means that if module B depends on module A, it is still possible for resources in module B to be created before module A. Terraform only adds the resources to the graph, and if it sees that the underlying relationships between resources allow it to create a resource sooner, it will.

5.3   Plan

The Terraform plan stage is where Terraform does its most important work: comparing your configuration against the real infrastructure and coming up with a plan to bring your infrastructure in sync with your code. To do this, Terraform creates an internal representation of your code (the resource graph), walks the graph to identify changes, and creates a new graph composed of the actions that are needed.

At its simplest, the plan can be run with the `terraform plan` command. It's more common to invoke it with the `out` flag to save the plan to be applied later, such as `terraform plan -out=example.tfplan`. If you don't save the plan to a file, then you're running what is generally called a speculative plan, which is a fancy way of saying you're running a plan that you do not intend to actually apply. Speculative plans are very common during development and testing, especially when working with teams. Speculative plans will be discussed in chapter 7.

To see this in action, let's run `terraform plan` against our TLS module.

Listing 5.2   Plan execution

```
$ terraform plan
```
This plan only has creations since it is the first run.

```
Terraform used the selected providers to generate the following execution
plan. Resource actions are indicated with the following symbols:
  + create
```

```
Terraform will perform the following actions:
```
For all plans, except destroy mode plans, the first actions listed will be the last ones executed.

```
  # tls_cert_request.child_request["bravo.example.com"] will be created
  + resource "tls_cert_request" "child_request" {
      + key_algorithm    = (known after apply)
```
Terraform will not know what this value is until after it is applied.

```
        + private_key_pem = (sensitive value)    ◄─────┐    This value is hidden
                                                        │    because it is sensitive.

        + subject {                                          These values are known at plan
            + common_name  = "example.com"                   time and are not sensitive, so
            + organization = "Terraform in Depth"            they are displayed.
          }

        + truncated attribute list          ◄──────┐   To save space we're skipping a
      }                                             │   bunch of the listed attributes.
```

```
# tls_cert_request.child_request["charilie.example.com"] will be created
+ resource "tls_cert_request" "child_request" {
    + truncated attribute list
  }
```

```
# tls_cert_request.child_request["example.com"] will be created
+ resource "tls_cert_request" "child_request" {
    + truncated attribute list
  }
```

```
# tls_locally_signed_cert.child_certificate["bravo.example.com"] will
be created
+ resource "tls_locally_signed_cert" "child_certificate" {
    + truncated attribute list
  }
```

```
# tls_locally_signed_cert.child_certificate["charilie.example.com"] will
 be created
+ resource "tls_locally_signed_cert" "child_certificate" {
    + truncated attribute list
  }
```

```
# tls_locally_signed_cert.child_certificate["example.com"] will be created
+ resource "tls_locally_signed_cert" "child_certificate" {
    + truncated attribute list
  }
```

```
# tls_private_key.ca_key will be created
+ resource "tls_private_key" "ca_key" {
    + truncated attribute list
  }
```

```
# tls_private_key.child_key["bravo.example.com"] will be created
+ resource "tls_private_key" "child_key" {
    + truncated attribute list
  }
```

```
# tls_private_key.child_key["charilie.example.com"] will be created
+ resource "tls_private_key" "child_key" {
    + truncated attribute list
  }
```

```
# tls_private_key.child_key["example.com"] will be created
+ resource "tls_private_key" "child_key" {
    + truncated attribute list
```

```
  }

# tls_self_signed_cert.ca_cert will be created
+ resource "tls_self_signed_cert" "ca_cert" {
    + truncated attribute list
  }

Plan: 11 to add, 0 to change, 0 to destroy.   ◀──┐
```

Terraform displays a summary once the plan is complete.

```
Note: You didn't use the -out option to save this plan, so Terraform can't
guarantee to take exactly these actions if you run "terraform apply" now.
```

Terraform is giving us a warning because we did not save the plan to a file, so Terraform may not be able to replicate it perfectly.

Although it isn't obvious, there is an order to the output. If you read the resources from the bottom of the output up to the top (which is common when reading terminal output from CLI commands), you may notice that you start with the resources that have no dependencies and work your way up to those that are deeper in the dependency tree. In other words, the resources at the bottom are the ones that are going to be created before the ones at the top.

It's important to note that this output is just a representation of the plan. When you save the plan as a `tfplan` file or pass it directly to the `terraform apply` stage, you're saving the full plan. That plan file is not human readable though: it's a bunch of binary data that is really only interpretably by Terraform. That's why we rely on the output from `terraform plan`, as well as commands like `terraform graph` and `terraform show`, to present the plan in a human-readable way.

5.3.1 Planning modes

There are three different planning modes for a Terraform plan: `default`, `destroy`, and `refresh-only`. Each of these modes creates a different type of plan with very different outcomes, although they essentially function in the same way.

The `default` planning mode (which really needs a fancier name) is what you'll be using the vast majority of the time. As its name implies, it will always run unless you explicitly specify another mode. When this book discusses planning, this is generally what we're talking about, unless stated otherwise.

The `destroy` planning mode is what you will call when you want to tear down all of the infrastructure you've deployed through that specific Terraform configuration. The destroy mode is invoked by passing the `-destroy` flag to the plan `terraform plan -out=destroy.tfplan -destroy`. One of the biggest benefits of Terraform is the ability to rapidly spin up development environments, and as you develop more with Terraform, you'll find yourself running `destroy` plans fairly often in your development cycle.

We can see this in action with the TLS module. Like the other examples, we'll be truncating the attributes to keep it from wasting paper.

Listing 5.3 `destroy` **plan execution**

> Refreshes look for changes in the resources
> that may have occurred outside of Terraform

> Plans start with a refresh. This wasn't visible in the first plan
> we ran this chapter because there wasn't anything to refresh.

```
$ terraform plan -destroy -out=destroy.plan

tls_private_key.child_key["charilie.example.com"]: Refreshing state...
 [id=0338f1f23ab58b83e877d55b841552f13702f7b6]
tls_private_key.child_key["example.com"]: Refreshing state...
 [id=a2c8fa2c3a818ba5ef4d99a7a51f751e029cfd15]
tls_private_key.child_key["bravo.example.com"]: Refreshing state...
 [id=df0cff0803f57bf5eb1380531b6178eac6cb19ae]
tls_private_key.ca_key: Refreshing state...
 [id=95620e32b90ced2c05168a07a25ec75a0af0b983]
tls_self_signed_cert.ca_cert: Refreshing state...
 [id=117817192417241439818976748081836574055]
tls_cert_request.child_request["example.com"]: Refreshing state...
 [id=accc4eb462d733ff3bedb71a66f3777ce3492854]
tls_cert_request.child_request["bravo.example.com"]: Refreshing state...
 [id=dd2cee83947cd28e4ab196d2092e3ce7f83a4ee5]
tls_cert_request.child_request["charilie.example.com"]: Refreshing state...
 [id=033387e9bf462ef1e38144a86cf5db1ff5a1932b]
tls_locally_signed_cert.child_certificate["example.com"]: Refreshing
 state... [id=258074287008428441024989806985225872849]
tls_locally_signed_cert.child_certificate["charilie.example.com"]:
 Refreshing state... [id=217404218134389469028230247658658593694]
tls_locally_signed_cert.child_certificate["bravo.example.com"]:
 Refreshing state... [id=88882504996108895505660070803996339310]

Terraform used the selected providers to generate the following execution
plan. Resource actions are indicated with the following symbols:
  - destroy
```

> Since this is a destroy mode
> plan, Terraform is only going to
> use the destroy action.

```
Terraform will perform the following actions:

  # tls_cert_request.child_request["bravo.example.com"] will be destroyed
  - resource "tls_cert_request" "child_request" {
      - id              = "dd2cee83947cd28e4ab196d2092e3ce7f83a4ee5" ->
 null
      - key_algorithm   = "ECDSA" -> null
      - private_key_pem = (sensitive value) -> null
```

> Since Terraform is deleting
> the resources, it expects
> their values to be removed.

```
      - truncated attribute list
    }
```

> Just like in other examples, we're going to
> truncate the attribute lists for readability.

```
  # tls_cert_request.child_request["charilie.example.com"] will be destroyed
  - resource "tls_cert_request" "child_request" {
      - truncated attribute list
    }

  # tls_cert_request.child_request["example.com"] will be destroyed
```

```
  - resource "tls_cert_request" "child_request" {
    - truncated attribute list
  }


# tls_locally_signed_cert.child_certificate["bravo.example.com"] will
be destroyed
  - resource "tls_locally_signed_cert" "child_certificate" {
    - truncated attribute list
  }


# tls_locally_signed_cert.child_certificate["charilie.example.com"]
will be destroyed
  - resource "tls_locally_signed_cert" "child_certificate" {
    - truncated attribute list
  }


# tls_locally_signed_cert.child_certificate["example.com"]
will be destroyed
  - resource "tls_locally_signed_cert" "child_certificate" {
    - truncated attribute list
  }


# tls_private_key.ca_key will be destroyed
  - resource "tls_private_key" "ca_key" {
    - truncated attribute list
  }


# tls_private_key.child_key["bravo.example.com"] will be destroyed
  - resource "tls_private_key" "child_key" {
    - truncated attribute list
  }


# tls_private_key.child_key["charilie.example.com"] will be destroyed
  - resource "tls_private_key" "child_key" {
    - truncated attribute list
  }


# tls_private_key.child_key["example.com"] will be destroyed
  - resource "tls_private_key" "child_key" {
    - truncated attribute list
  }


# tls_self_signed_cert.ca_cert will be destroyed
  - resource "tls_self_signed_cert" "ca_cert" {
    - truncated attribute list
  }

Plan: 0 to add, 0 to change, 11 to destroy.
```

◄— **For this plan, the summary only includes destroy actions.**

As you can see, this is remarkably similar to a normal plan, with the big difference being that resources are being destroyed instead of created. You may also have noticed that there are a lot of data lookups at the start of the plan. This is the Terraform plan running a refresh so I can identify changes (or drift) between the state Terraform has stored and the actual infrastructure.

Just like with the `default` planning mode, the resources here are ordered such that the resources with the least amount of dependencies are on the bottom. Unlike the `default` plan, however, resources will be destroyed in the opposite order than the one that they were created in. This is because deleting a resource that has dependencies before the dependents themselves will often result in errors [for instance, you can't delete an AWS Virtual Private Cloud (VPC) until you've already deleted the subnets in it].

The `refresh-only` planning mode is a bit more niche. It's used to update the local state without making any changes to any of the controlled infrastructure. When running in this mode, the initial lookups are done, but no other changes are going to occur. Since the `default` and `destroy` modes also run a refresh, this command isn't needed to create updated plans. The major difference that this mode brings is that it only runs a refresh and does not follow up with other changes. This command can be useful when you know that manual changes were made to infrastructure or if you want to detect state drift (which we'll discuss more in the next chapter).

5.3.2   *Replace (previously known as taint)*

Sometimes you have a piece of infrastructure that you want to replace. A database may have been corrupted, or you might have made manual changes to a virtual machine while testing (hopefully in a developer environment) and you want to replace that with a fresh instance. Terraform has the ability to target specific resources for replacement so you do not have to do it manually.

The best way to do this is by creating a new plan using the `-replace` flag and then reviewing that plan and any repercussions it has before applying it. This flag can be used as many times as you need in a single plan, allowing you to tell Terraform to replace a large number of resources in one go.

It's important to remember that the `-replace` flag may target a single resource, but the repercussions of that replacement will often go beyond that. To demonstrate, let's look at what happens if we replace one of the private keys in our TLS module. As a small, but important, note, make sure to put the resource address in single quotes before calling it to prevent your shell from misinterpreting it.

Listing 5.4 Replace plan execution

```
$ terraform plan -replace 'tls_private_key.child_key[
⇝ "charilie.example.com"]'
```
> The replace flag lets us specify a resource to destroy and re-create.

```
tls_private_key.child_key["example.com"]: Refreshing state...
⇝ [id=938ed55a0b4b79de19515e4786ef132bb74a0d61]
tls_private_key.child_key["charilie.example.com"]: Refreshing state...
⇝ [id=c3aa6b04762e95df38fe3db11a844e3c5461dfa9]
tls_private_key.ca_key: Refreshing state...
⇝ [id=044212e8419b555765ab31e0ba95a82618668b40]
tls_private_key.child_key["bravo.example.com"]: Refreshing state...
```
> Terraform is running the refresh here.

```
⇨ [id=d0ab07eef6f7c558ac18ab7693221b9b628dc90d]
tls_self_signed_cert.ca_cert: Refreshing state...
⇨ [id=69838284311976884473259975997369053150]
tls_cert_request.child_request["charilie.example.com"]: Refreshing state...
⇨ [id=8e90ba484854ed7477646b4a15c3f1a56a1f66f2]
tls_cert_request.child_request["bravo.example.com"]: Refreshing state...
⇨ [id=e5c98bec8c2df7f52f5d232d862b6ad16d492c96]
tls_cert_request.child_request["example.com"]: Refreshing state...
⇨ [id=35c5f93644b2aa5c801319a3db024a3da11148e4]
tls_locally_signed_cert.child_certificate["bravo.example.com"]:
⇨ Refreshing state... [id=29478532274442113470358034777726746148]
tls_locally_signed_cert.child_certificate["example.com"]:
⇨ Refreshing state... [id=46604884906036841274762289860009749958]
tls_locally_signed_cert.child_certificate["charilie.example.com"]:
⇨ Refreshing state... [id=24813774051315396104451485743251799830]
```

Terraform is running the refresh here.

```
Terraform used the selected providers to generate the following execution
plan. Resource actions are indicated with the following symbols:
-/+ destroy and then create replacement ◄

Terraform will perform the following actions:
```

For this plan, we have the re-create action.

Although this isn't the resource we specified, it has to be replaced as part of our change.

```
  # tls_cert_request.child_request["charilie.example.com"] must
⇨ be replaced
-/+ resource "tls_cert_request" "child_request" { ◄
    ~ cert_request_pem = <<-EOT
          -----BEGIN CERTIFICATE REQUEST-----
          MIHaMIGKAgEAMDMxGzAZBgNVBAoTElRlcnJhZm9ybSBpbBEZXB0aDEUMBIGA1UE
          AxMLZXhhbXBsZS5jb20wTjAQBgcqhkjOPQIBBgUrgQQAIQM6AASXBlt4uRJnsB6G
          cmmDisA8EcP/2XWMGJqTuD4kA/tzc9fpu7xnqTJl3jYD5AgxGizFdxsFhtIslKAA
          MAoGCCqGSM49BAMCAz8AMDwCHB59NX3D7M4JTazjlpOdjbcEmidilx2/01570oYC
          HCaps8M9e/vnlWgzKdXlhYpWddyvCG7upMiLMoo=
          -----END CERTIFICATE REQUEST-----
      EOT -> (known after apply)
    ~ id                = "8e90ba484854ed7477646b4a15c3f1a56a1f66f2" ->
⇨ (known after apply)
    ~ key_algorithm     = "ECDSA" -> (known after apply)
    ~ private_key_pem   = (sensitive value) # forces replacement

      # (1 unchanged block hidden) ◄
  }
```

The -/+ signifies that this resource is being re-created.

The tilde lets us know that this value is going to change.

Terraform hides anything that will remain the same. Since we aren't changing the subject block it gets hidden.

```
  # tls_locally_signed_cert.child_certificate["charilie.example.com"] must
⇨ be replaced
-/+ resource "tls_locally_signed_cert" "child_certificate" {
    ~ truncated attribute list
  }

  # tls_private_key.child_key["charilie.example.com"] will be replaced, as
⇨ requested
-/+ resource "tls_private_key" "child_key" { ◄
    ~ truncated attribute list
  }
```

This is the resource we wanted to replace. It's at the bottom of the plan because it's the first action to take place.

```
Plan: 3 to add, 0 to change, 3 to destroy.
```
The summary includes the resources erased and the ones created.

```
Note: You didn't use the -out option to save this plan, so Terraform can't
guarantee to take exactly these actions if you run "terraform apply" now.
```
We didn't save this to disk so Terraform is giving us this warning again.

Attempting to replace the single private key results in three total resources being destroyed and re-created. Here, Terraform is helpfully showing how the attributes for these resources are going to be affected, and we can see that while some resources attributes stay the same, others get changed as part of the update.

The `-replace` flag was added in Terraform v0.15.2. Before that, you had to use the `terraform taint` command. This command exists for backward compatibility, but it has been deprecated, which means it will be removed in future versions. The problem with the `terraform taint` command is that it immediately changes your state, rather than presenting a plan that shows you the repercussions of your change. It is essentially impossible to test the changes of `terraform taint` in advance of changing state. There's really no good reason to run it, and you should instead use the `terraform plan` command with `-replace` flags.

5.3.3   *Resource targeting*

I start off this section with a warning: resource targeting should only be used in very exceptional circumstances, and it is not something you should depend on for normal operations. Terraform modules that require resource targeting to work are a massive antipattern, as they mean you can't simply use the module like any other module. In my entire career, I have never had a valid resource to use this outside of development purposes. Unfortunately, Terraform will sometimes include information about resource targeting in some error messages, but, really, if you see that message it means you have other problems to deal with and should not rely on resource targeting to get past it.

With that out of the way, let's get into resource targeting. This is a feature of Terraform that lets you specify which resources you want to focus on in a Terraform plan and then to generate only the changes needed to modify those resources. For example, if you have a module that generates a web service, you might target just the load balancer for a change. If Terraform needed to change other resources that the load balancer depends on, it will, but it won't change anything else.

The primary reason to use this is when debugging or attempting to fix a problem. If someone made changes to a resource manually, outside of Terraform, it could put you into a place where Terraform isn't able to calculate a valid plan. In that case, you might be able to fix the problem by targeting the changed resources and getting them back into a place where Terraform can properly run.

Another common use case for this is when a developer knows a change will take a long time, so they target the changes in batches. Although this is somewhat common, it is a sign that your project is too large and should be broken up. This is a topic we'll touch on more in chapter 9.

5.3.4 *Disabling refresh*

When creating a Terraform plan, you have the option to skip the refresh phase by passing in the `-refresh=false` flag. This is pretty much the opposite of the `-refresh-only` flag. This flag should come with a giant DANGER sign when used, as not refreshing the state means your plan isn't going to have the most up-to-date information when it runs. If you use this, you can expect to have failed apply runs.

The one time where it might be valid to use this flag is when you're working in a development environment and know that you are the only one making changes. In that case, it may be tempting to use it to speed up your development cycle. Even then I would recommend using caution though, because even if you are the only human working in an environment, it's possible that automation in the systems you're building on could change things without you realizing it.

5.3.5 *terraform refresh command*

The `terraform refresh` command is one of two ways to update the state file without making any changes to your infrastructure. It is extremely dangerous, as it does not allow you to validate the changes before it updates your state. The `terraform refresh` command is deprecated and only exists for backward compatibility, but it's often the first result you'll see when you search for refreshing Terraform state. Despite the warnings in the Terraform documentation, people still tend to use this command.

As an example of how this command can go wrong, imagine that the credentials you are using with your provider expire. When the `terraform refresh` command runs and it cannot authenticate, there is a chance that Terraform will detect resources controlled by that provider as missing, and it could remove them from the state. Then, in future runs, your code will try creating new resources instead of updating the ones that are there.

If you find yourself wanting to update your state without updating any resources, you should run `terraform apply -refresh-only`. Unlike `terraform refresh`, this command will tell you what it is going to change and request approval first. This allows you to validate those changes and work around any errors.

Let's look back on our TLS example. If we change the name of our organization from Terraform in Depth to OpenTofu in Depth, this should trigger a change in the plan. However, if we run it with refresh only turned on, Terraform ignores the change.

Listing 5.5   Refresh-only plan

```
$ terraform plan -refresh-only          ◄───┐ Run Terraform plan in
                                             │ refresh-only mode.
```

```
tls_private_key.ca_key: Refreshing state...
➡[id=4c9b44687d30a59610287574ea4efccbfda02f52]
tls_private_key.child_key["bravo.example.com"]: Refreshing state...
➡[id=8ec2521d90a08a519a726f138b19199d6ed6437a]
tls_private_key.child_key["charilie.example.com"]: Refreshing state...
➡[id=435155292c21a131097fcceb9a766e665f2f8ebc]
tls_private_key.child_key["example.com"]: Refreshing state...
➡[id=9d9c8317f875a36b5bc57e670fd47635492d2d68]
tls_cert_request.child_request["charilie.example.com"]: Refreshing state...
➡[id=a2cf771109b74a9aac1f5e53e6315541b6f0ce87]
tls_self_signed_cert.ca_cert: Refreshing state...
➡[id=12130143203772277739991525625097530930]
tls_cert_request.child_request["example.com"]: Refreshing state...
➡[id=7167dd2d7a84a0e93649fe8da51d4a09242f41c1]
tls_cert_request.child_request["bravo.example.com"]: Refreshing state...
➡[id=8a9ed6e21bdf631b6fa5eae4ee1a19054b18c83f]
tls_locally_signed_cert.child_certificate["charilie.example.com"]:
➡Refreshing state... [id=26135442977519668733009038434655883204l]
tls_locally_signed_cert.child_certificate["example.com"]:
➡Refreshing state... [id=197151303769940224413374914269052138442]
tls_locally_signed_cert.child_certificate["bravo.example.com"]:
➡Refreshing state... [id=697784343292722853390858530653849740027]

No changes. Your infrastructure still matches the configuration.
```

Terraform stops here. Even though we made changes to our code Terraform is ignoring them in this planning mode.

Terraform is letting us know there were no changes.

Terraform is checking to see if any resources have changed.

That being said, accidents do happen. In the next chapter we discuss how to manage and safeguard your state so that you can recover from problems when they come up.

5.3.6   *Reviewing plan files with terraform show*

The `terraform show` command is a nifty little command that lets you review Terraform plan files. It is a very simple command, taking only the path to the plan file as an argument. If you run `terraform plan -out test.tfplan`, then `terraform show test.tfplan` will give you a nice human-readable display of what is in the plan file.

A secondary use for this command, which may not have been intended but is certainly useful, is that it can convert Terraform plan files from their binary format into JSON. This is extremely useful if you want to create programs to review Terraform plans, as most languages have built-in JSON support. This is a fairly advanced use case that isn't likely to come up often, but if you ever find yourself wanting to programmatically review Terraform plans, this is the easiest way to do it.

5.4   *Root-level module input variables*

The most common way to modify a plan is through the use of root-level module input variables. These inputs get read by your code and change the generated resource graph. Terraform then compares that resource graph to your state and uses it to generate a plan. This is what allows Terraform to use the same code to generate different environments.

Terraform modules are expected to be used over and over again to generate different environments. The root-level module should expose variables that tell Terraform how one environment differs from another. This often includes identifying information for the environment, such as a base domain to use for generating hostnames. It can also be used when different environments need different features. For example, a SaaS company that sells customers clusters of their software (like Atlassian selling Jira instances) may be using a Terraform module to control their different tenant environments. In that case, the input variables can be used to turn features on and off in those environments.

Terraform has several different ways to set input variables for the root-level module. Input variables can be assigned interactively, through a `command line` flag, using a variable file, or by using environment variables.

5.4.1 *Interactive*

The default behavior for Terraform is to ask you for any input variables it doesn't have an answer for when you run the `plan` command. This means that if you set the input variable using another method, including simply defining a default value for it in your code, then Terraform will not ask about it.

This behavior can be really useful during testing, especially if you plan on changing the values often. Outside of testing, this can be really problematic. Relying on individuals to correctly type out all of the values for an environment every time they deploy is a great way to introduce errors in your pipeline, and it's not even an option for automated workflows.

Even in testing, it can often be tedious to repeatedly type in options each time, and so it's much more common to use variable files instead.

It is possible, and even recommended in many cases, to disable interactive input. Passing the `-input` flag with a value of `false` (i.e., `terraform plan -input=false`) will have Terraform return an error if it is missing inputs instead of directly asking for them. This flag is basically required when running Terraform inside of automated environments, which we discuss more in chapter 7.

5.4.2 *Variable flag*

Input variables can be defined directly in the command line using the `-var` flag. This flag can be used as many times as needed to define all the variables the developer wants:

```
terraform plan -var 'vpc=vpc-01234567890abcdef' -var 'num_instances=2'
```

With this method, the command can be copied and pasted or pulled out of your shell history to rerun at will. This reduces the errors you'd see from typos and makes the command far more shareable.

That said, the `-var` flag has some flaws. Since you're running your command inside of a shell, you have to worry about the formatting between both your shell and Terraform, where there can be conflicts occasionally. You also have to worry about the differences in your shells: if you're running on a Linux machine and share a command with a Windows user, you may find that the different quoting style gets in the way.

Perhaps the biggest problem with using the `-var` flag is that it simply does not handle complex data types well. You essentially end up writing what looks like JSON objects into your script, except you then have to worry about escaping the right characters (which again looks very different on Windows and Linux) and typing out a lot of text without the benefit of syntax highlighting that you'd get from an editor.

5.4.3   *Variable files*

One of the best ways to store your input variable values is through the use of variable files. These files use a slightly different version of the HashiCorp Configuration Language (HCL) format to store input variable values. Unlike most HCL we've seen so far, there are no blocks—just simple "key equals value" expressions. These files can only specify literal data: that is, you can't use any functions or other transformations. Instead, you can define any data type, such as objects and maps, using the same general syntax you're used to and without having to worry about escaping parameters.

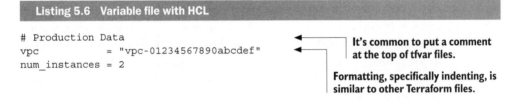

Listing 5.6   Variable file with HCL

```
# Production Data
vpc            = "vpc-01234567890abcdef"
num_instances = 2
```

> It's common to put a comment at the top of tfvar files.
>
> Formatting, specifically indenting, is similar to other Terraform files.

Terraform isn't restricted to only HCL for variable files. Variable files can also be formatted in JSON. This is particularly useful if you're generating the variable files using some sort of automation, such as pulling the variables from a database integrating Terraform itself into another system you're building. If this is the case, then the large number of JSON parsers out there for different languages makes it an ideal choice. That being said, HCL has a lot of benefits for files managed by humans, such as the ability to put comments in your variable files.

Terraform is able to tell which method is used by the file extension. This means that Terraform is pretty strict about what extension is used, because it needs that extension to figure out how to understand your file. The `tfvars` extension is used for HCL, and the `tfvars.json` extension is used for JSON.

Listing 5.7   Variable file with JSON

```
{
    "vpc": "vpc-01234567890abcdef",
    "num_instances": 2
}
```

> JSON files do not support comments.
>
> JSON is not very forgiving: leaving a trailing comma will result in an error.
>
> There aren't any rules in Terraform on JSON formatting as long as it is valid.

The `-var-file` flag is used to tell Terraform what files to load (i.e., `terraform plan -var-file=production.tfvars`). This flag can be used multiple times to specify different files to include. There are also specific file patterns that will tell Terraform to load a file automatically, without needing to pass the `-var-file` flag through. Files that are named Terraform (`terraform.tfvars` or `terraform.tfvars.json`) or files that add `auto` to the extension will get loaded by Terraform if they exist (see table 5.2).

Table 5.2 Terraform variable files

File extension	Format	Usage
`*.tfvars`	HCL	`-var-file` flag
`*.auto.tfvars`	HCL	Automatically loads
`terraform.tfvars`	HCL	AUtomatically loads
`*.tfvars.json`	JSON	`-var-file` flag
`*.auto.tfvars.json`	JSON	Automatically loads
`terraform.tfvars.json`	JSON	Automatically loads

There are many benefits to using variable files. Since they are actual files, you can save them in version control and track how they change over time. People are also far less likely to create problems with typos, and it's possible to put restrictions such as requiring a pull request review on the files before they get merged in. That being said, if you do use variable files, you should not put any sensitive values in them, especially if they're in source control, as anyone with access to the files will be able to see those values.

5.4.4 Environment variables

The final method for setting input variables is through the use of environment variables. You can do this by defining environment variables with the prefix `TF_VAR_` followed by the variable name. This environment variable name should match the case of the input variable, so if you have a variable named `num_instances`, your environment variable should be named `TF_VAR_num_instances`.

In most cases, other methods are better for defining variables. Environment variables tend to be used more when configuring providers, especially for provider authentication, as these values aren't necessarily part of your Terraform configuration and don't need to be tracked in the same way: unlike configuration data, which should be visible and trackable by the team, provider data often includes secrets that the team should not have. Provider authentication values are generally controlled by the shared systems that run Terraform [your continuous integration/continuous delivery (CI/CD) systems], which will often pass the data through as environment variables. This is a complicated topic that we'll touch more on in chapter 7, but for now just keep in mind that other methods for defining your input variables are probably easier to manage for most cases.

5.4.5 *Input precedence*

All of the aforementioned methods for defining input variables can be used together. When Terraform loads the initial variables, it will use the first defined value from this list:

- The first case is if the `-var` and `-var-file` arguments take the highest precedence and will always be used before any other option. If the same variable is defined multiple times, then the value from the last flag in the command line will be used.
- Terraform will use any values from the `auto.tfvars` and `auto.tfvars.json` files. If there are multiple files, they'll be processed in "lexical order" (which is basically what you'd see if you ran `ls -la` in your terminal).
- If `terraform.tfvars.json` exists, this will then be checked.
- If the input still hasn't been found and `terraform.tfvars` exists, it will be used.
- If none of the other methods have worked, then Terraform will look at environment variables.
- Finally, if the variable wasn't found and doesn't have a default set, then Terraform will ask the user for it. If you've disabled interactive inputs using the `-input =false` option and any inputs without a default are defined, Terraform will fail with an error.

This order of precedence is important to remember if you want to avoid frustration. It can be really annoying to change a variable but not have it take effect because something with a higher precedence is defining it instead. The easiest way to avoid this is by picking one method, such as always using variable files, and sticking with it.

5.4.6 *A note on secrets and inputs*

If you have a security background, you may have noticed something disconcerting about each of the methods mentioned: pretty much every one of them can be used to leak data. If you pass variables through using `-var-flag`, then they're stored in your shell history and with anyone you share the command with. Variable files aren't much better, as anything in them is likely to end up in version control. Even environment variables can leak through logs or other methods. In a way, the interactive input is the safest, except it can't really be automated and requires sharing secrets that shouldn't really be shared. There are two ways to get around this problem.

If you're using a generic CI/CD system such as GitHub Actions or a Terraform-specific one such as Spacelift, Scalr, Env0, or Terraform Cloud, there is likely already some type of secret support in that system. For the generic systems, these secrets are often passed in as environment variables, while the Terraform-specific systems each have their own way of passing through variables and masking them as sensitive. In both cases, the systems will then do their best to avoid having the value of those variables displayed or saved in logs.

Another way, and one of my favorites, is to rely on a secrets manager to hold your sensitive values. There are a variety of secret managers, from Hashicorp's Vault to cloud-specific systems like the GCP Secret Manager, AWS Secret Manager, or Azure Key Vault. The details of how these systems work vary, but, in general, they allow you to store a secret with a path that can be used to retrieve it. If you have a variable that is looking for a secret, you could change your code around to have it take in a path to a secret instead.

One of the benefits of this method is that many systems are able to integrate directly with secret managers. If you're using an orchestration system such as Kubernetes or ECS, for example, it's possible to specify a path to a secret and have that secret get embedded into your containers by your orchestrator. If you design your code to work this way, then Terraform never even has to be aware of your secret value, which can add an extra level of security for really sensitive data. If you do need to pull the value into Terraform for some reason, you can still do so with data sources.

5.5 Apply

Finally, the moment we've all been waiting for: it's time to apply our plan! In this phase, Terraform will walk through the graph created by a plan to create the changes to your infrastructure needed to bring the code in line.

Using our TLS module, let's create a plan and then pass it to the `apply` command.

Listing 5.8 Applying a plan

The private keys have no dependencies, so they all get created at the same time.

```
tls_private_key.child_key["example.com"]: Creating...
tls_private_key.child_key["charilie.example.com"]: Creating...
tls_private_key.ca_key: Creating...
tls_private_key.child_key["bravo.example.com"]: Creating...
tls_private_key.child_key["bravo.example.com"]: Creation complete after 0s
⟹ [id=df0cff0803f57bf5eb1380531b6178eac6cb19ae]
tls_private_key.child_key["example.com"]: Creation complete after 0s
⟹ [id=a2c8fa2c3a818ba5ef4d99a7a51f751e029cfd15]
tls_private_key.child_key["charilie.example.com"]: Creation complete
⟹ after 0s [id=0338f1f23ab58b83e877d55b841552f13702f7b6]
tls_private_key.ca_key: Creation complete after 0s
⟹ [id=95620e32b90ced2c05168a07a25ec75a0af0b983]
tls_cert_request.child_request["example.com"]: Creating...
tls_cert_request.child_request["charilie.example.com"]: Creating...
tls_cert_request.child_request["bravo.example.com"]: Creating...
tls_cert_request.child_request["example.com"]: Creation complete after 0s
⟹ [id=accc4eb462d733ff3bedb71a66f3777ce3492854]
tls_self_signed_cert.ca_cert: Creating...
tls_cert_request.child_request["bravo.example.com"]: Creation complete
⟹ after 0s [id=dd2cee83947cd28e4ab196d2092e3ce7f83a4ee5]
```

The CA is using a different kind of resource to create its certificate.

The certificate signing request can be created now since the private keys are available.

The "creation complete" message includes the new ID for the resource. These IDs are created by the providers.

```
tls_cert_request.child_request["charilie.example.com"]: Creation complete
⇒after 0s [id=033387e9bf462ef1e38144a86cf5db1ff5a1932b]
tls_self_signed_cert.ca_cert: Creation complete after 0s
⇒[id=117817192417241439818976748081836574055]
tls_locally_signed_cert.child_certificate["charilie.example.com"]:
⇒Creating...
tls_locally_signed_cert.child_certificate["bravo.example.com"]:
⇒Creating...
tls_locally_signed_cert.child_certificate["example.com"]: Creating...
tls_locally_signed_cert.child_certificate["charilie.example.com"]: Creation
⇒complete after 0s [id=217404218134389469028230247658658593694]
tls_locally_signed_cert.child_certificate["bravo.example.com"]: Creation
⇒complete after 0s [id=888825049961088955056600708039963393310]
tls_locally_signed_cert.child_certificate["example.com"]: Creation
⇒complete after 0s [id=258074287008428441024989806985225872849]

Apply complete! Resources: 11 added, 0 changed, 0 destroyed.  ◄────┐
```

Terraform displays a summary
message once it finished an apply.

Now that the CA certificate is available the
other certificates can all be created.

Here, you can see we have created 11 different resources. Since the TLS provider is all local, these resources were created very quickly.

5.5.1 *Plan and apply in a single command*

If the `terraform apply` command is called without a plan file, then Terraform will run a plan for you. This is basically a nice shortcut around having to save a file and then load that file in a separate command. Terraform will, by default, ask you to confirm before applying the plan it comes up with so you will still get a chance to review any changes before moving forward.

If you are running `terraform apply` without the plan file, then you can also use the same flags you would use if you called `terraform plan`. This means you can pass through variables using any of the variable input methods mentioned earlier, and you can also use resource targeting or the alternative planning methods such as `destroy` or `refresh-only`.

It's also possible to run in this combined mode with no user input. If you add the flag `-auto-approve`, then Terraform will immediately apply the plan rather than ask for approval first. This is not a great idea though, as it means that if there is an error there's no way to catch it and correct it before your infrastructure is changed. Even if you think running `terraform plan` and then `terraform apply -auto-approve`, without saving a plan file in between, will work, you could be wrong if there were other changes made outside of your workflow.

One question you may be asking is if this applies to CI/CD processes as well as when manually running Terraform. Although we'll discuss this further in chapter 7, for now know that this is an area where different people have different opinions, and you'll need to find what works for your project and team. Most Terraform collaboration and automation tools do include an approval step before running, but there are cases where it may be valuable to auto approve.

5.5.2 Using a plan file

If you don't want to run the plan and apply in the same step, you can save the output from the `terraform plan` and pass it to the `terraform apply`. This is the most common way to run Terraform in automation, as it allows the `plan` and `apply` steps to be broken up and gives users the ability to actually review their plans.

Providing a plan file to Terraform is really straightforward, as it's an optional argument for the command, so running `terraform apply plan.tfplan` will let Terraform know to use the file. When you provide a plan file, Terraform will not ask you to approve the plan, as it assumes you already did that after running the `plan` command. Terraform also does not care about the file extension of the plan, although `tfplan` has become a bit of a de facto standard for it.

5.5.3 Destroy

The command `terraform destroy` is an alias for `terraform apply -destroy`. It does not take a plan file, so it will run the `plan` in `destroy` mode and then run the `apply` on the generated plan. Just like all other `terraform apply` commands that run their own plans, it will, by default, ask for confirmation after the plan, before it is applied.

When you're running a destroy, you know what to expect. As such, it is far more common to use the `-auto-approve` flag when running a destroy locally. However, just because it's common doesn't mean it's a good idea. If you're working in an isolated account using your own developer resources, you can get away with this, but considering the consequences you should probably avoid using auto approve and take a few seconds to confirm your plan is running on the accounts and against the resources you expect.

Listing 5.9 `terraform destroy` with `-auto-approve`

> We're running a destroy with auto approve enabled.

> Like other examples, we start here with a refresh to look for changes.

```
$ terraform destroy -auto-approve
tls_private_key.child_key["charilie.example.com"]: Refreshing state...
➥ [id=0338f1f23ab58b83e877d55b841552f13702f7b6]
tls_private_key.child_key["example.com"]: Refreshing state...
➥ [id=a2c8fa2c3a818ba5ef4d99a7a51f751e029cfd15]
tls_private_key.child_key["bravo.example.com"]: Refreshing state...
➥ [id=df0cff0803f57bf5eb1380531b6178eac6cb19ae]
tls_private_key.ca_key: Refreshing state...
➥ [id=95620e32b90ced2c05168a07a25ec75a0af0b983]
tls_self_signed_cert.ca_cert: Refreshing state...
➥ [id=117817192417241439818976748081836574055]
```

```
tls_cert_request.child_request["example.com"]: Refreshing state...
[id=accc4eb462d733ff3bedb71a66f3777ce3492854]
tls_cert_request.child_request["bravo.example.com"]: Refreshing state...
[id=dd2cee83947cd28e4ab196d2092e3ce7f83a4ee5]
tls_cert_request.child_request["charilie.example.com"]: Refreshing state...
[id=033387e9bf462ef1e38144a86cf5db1ff5a1932b]
tls_locally_signed_cert.child_certificate["example.com"]:
Refreshing state... [id=258074287008428441024989806985225872849]
tls_locally_signed_cert.child_certificate["charilie.example.com"]:
Refreshing state... [id=217404218134389469028230247658658593694]
tls_locally_signed_cert.child_certificate["bravo.example.com"]:
Refreshing state... [id=888825049961088955056600708039963393310]
```

```
Terraform used the selected providers to generate the following execution
plan. Resource actions are indicated with the following symbols:
  - destroy
```

Since this is a destroy plan we
are only taking this one action.

```
Terraform will perform the following actions:

  # tls_cert_request.child_request["bravo.example.com"] will be destroyed
  - resource "tls_cert_request" "child_request" {
      - truncated attribute list
    }

  # tls_cert_request.child_request["charilie.example.com"] will be destroyed
  - resource "tls_cert_request" "child_request" {
      - truncated attribute list
    }

  # tls_cert_request.child_request["example.com"] will be destroyed
  - resource "tls_cert_request" "child_request" {
      - truncated attribute list
    }

  # tls_locally_signed_cert.child_certificate["bravo.example.com"] will
be destroyed
  - resource "tls_locally_signed_cert" "child_certificate" {
      - truncated attribute list
    }

  # tls_locally_signed_cert.child_certificate["charilie.example.com"] will
be destroyed
  - resource "tls_locally_signed_cert" "child_certificate" {
      - truncated attribute list
    }

  # tls_locally_signed_cert.child_certificate["example.com"] will
be destroyed
  - resource "tls_locally_signed_cert" "child_certificate" {
      - truncated attribute list
    }

  # tls_private_key.ca_key will be destroyed
  - resource "tls_private_key" "ca_key" {
      - truncated attribute list
```

```
    }

 # tls_private_key.child_key["bravo.example.com"] will be destroyed
 - resource "tls_private_key" "child_key" {
    - truncated attribute list
    }

 # tls_private_key.child_key["charilie.example.com"] will be destroyed
 - resource "tls_private_key" "child_key" {
    - truncated attribute list
    }

 # tls_private_key.child_key["example.com"] will be destroyed
 - resource "tls_private_key" "child_key" {
    - truncated attribute list
    }

 # tls_self_signed_cert.ca_cert will be destroyed
 - resource "tls_self_signed_cert" "ca_cert" {
    - truncated attribute list
    }
```

Terraform still displays the summary, even with auto approve enabled.

Terraform immediately starts an apply phase.

```
Plan: 0 to add, 0 to change, 11 to destroy.
tls_locally_signed_cert.child_certificate["charilie.example.com"]:
Destroying... [id=217404218134389469028230247658658593694]
tls_locally_signed_cert.child_certificate["bravo.example.com"]:
Destroying... [id=88882504996108895505660070803996339310]
tls_locally_signed_cert.child_certificate["example.com"]: Destroying...
[id=258074287008428441024989806985225872849]
tls_locally_signed_cert.child_certificate["bravo.example.com"]:
Destruction complete after 0s
tls_locally_signed_cert.child_certificate["charilie.example.com"]:
Destruction complete after 0s
tls_locally_signed_cert.child_certificate["example.com"]:
Destruction complete after 0s
tls_cert_request.child_request["charilie.example.com"]: Destroying...
[id=033387e9bf462ef1e38144a86cf5db1ff5a1932b]
tls_cert_request.child_request["bravo.example.com"]: Destroying...
[id=dd2cee83947cd28e4ab196d2092e3ce7f83a4ee5]
tls_cert_request.child_request["example.com"]: Destroying...
[id=accc4eb462d733ff3bedb71a66f3777ce3492854]
tls_self_signed_cert.ca_cert: Destroying...
[id=117817192417241439818976748081836574055]
tls_cert_request.child_request["charilie.example.com"]:
Destruction complete after 0s
tls_cert_request.child_request["example.com"]: Destruction complete after 0s
tls_cert_request.child_request["bravo.example.com"]: Destruction
complete after 0s
tls_self_signed_cert.ca_cert: Destruction complete after 0s
tls_private_key.child_key["charilie.example.com"]: Destroying...
[id=0338f1f23ab58b83e877d55b841552f13702f7b6]
tls_private_key.ca_key: Destroying...
[id=95620e32b90ced2c05168a07a25ec75a0af0b983]
tls_private_key.child_key["example.com"]: Destroying...
[id=a2c8fa2c3a818ba5ef4d99a7a51f751e029cfd15]
```

```
tls_private_key.child_key["bravo.example.com"]: Destroying...
➥ [id=df0cff0803f57bf5eb1380531b6178eac6cb19ae]
tls_private_key.ca_key: Destruction complete after 0s
tls_private_key.child_key["example.com"]: Destruction complete after 0s
tls_private_key.child_key["charilie.example.com"]: Destruction complete
➥after 0s
tls_private_key.child_key["bravo.example.com"]: Destruction complete
➥after 0s

Destroy complete! Resources: 11 destroyed.        ◄──────  Terraform is finished
                                                           destroying the resources.
```

With that one command, we've now destroyed all of the resources that we were managing with Terraform. Running `terraform destroy` is one of the scariest things you can do. You are going to wipe out a lot of infrastructure very, very quickly. Reviewing the plan is one way to prevent mistakes. Using a centralized CI/CD system for managing your production environments, and then removing any direct logins to those environments from your machine, is another way to prevent you from accidentally making a very bad mistake when running a `destroy` command. If you can't even access the infrastructure from your development machine, you can't accidentally destroy it.

5.6   Apply and plan options

There are some flags that are used by both the `apply` and `plan` commands. For the most part, these won't be used in your day-to-day flow, but they can come in handy in very specific situations.

5.6.1   Parallelism

Parallelism is an interesting topic. By default, Terraform will attempt to run up to 10 actions at a time. Actions are, in general, provider calls such as updating, deleting, creating, or even reading the status of a resource or data source. You can change the parallelism using the `-parallelism=n` flag, where n is the number of actions you want to run at the same time.

At first you might think that this is great: if you increase the amount of parallelism, you should make things faster. This makes sense in general. If you can split an action up into smaller pieces and run more of them at once, you should see improvement. There are several things that limit this though.

The first, and the most relevant to this chapter, is dependencies. For many resource changes there are things that have to happen first. If you're creating subnets for a VPC, then that VPC has to actually exist first. If you're trying to tell a service which database to connect to, you need to have the database. This means that there are often bottlenecks inside of projects that naturally limit the amount of parallelism that is possible.

The second problem is one that is completely out of your control: rate limits. When using a provider to talk to an infrastructure vendor via their APIs, you have to deal with all the limitations of those APIs themselves. Most APIs have rate limits that prevent you from using them too quickly, which in turn is going to make parallelism less useful. The good news is that you don't really need to think about rate limits yourself, as most providers are smart enough to reduce their requests and retry failed ones when rate limits are hit.

The parallelism feature can be really useful for debugging though. Not every provider has the same level of quality when it comes to error messages, and trying to read through logs where up to 10 things are happening at once is extremely difficult. If you raise the logging level and lower the parallelism, it will be much, much easier to read through the detailed logs to find your problem:

```
TF_LOG=debug terraform plan -parallelism=1
```

5.6.2   Locking

Running operations on Terraform will often cause the state to lock. What this means is that Terraform will tell the backend that only the currently running process can use the state. This makes it so that if two people attempt to run at the same time, they will fail. This is critical, as running two apply runs at the same time can create conflicting errors and corrupt your state. Terraform does a pretty good job of managing locks on its own, so it's generally not something you need to think about often.

You can tell Terraform not to lock the state using the `-lock=false` flag. The vast majority of the time, this is a horrible idea. The one exception, which we'll discuss further in the next chapter, is when you're creating `speculative plans`. This is where you run a plan knowing that you are not going to actually use it. This is useful for testing, pull requests, and simply seeing what the effects of code changes are. In this case, disabling locking is acceptable because you are not going to make changes and there's no chance of a corrupted state file as a result. When using automation to generate speculative runs, it is very common to disable locking.

5.6.3   JSON

One of the really interesting things about Terraform, which we touched on a bit in the first chapter, is that the Terraform CLI really is the engine for Terraform. There isn't a separate SDK for Terraform that you can use to plan and apply Terraform code. This means that if you want to run Terraform in automation, you have to use the CLI itself. To make that easier, Terraform has the ability to return all of its results in JSON, which is much easier for languages to parse than the normal human-readable text.

Interfacing with the CLI using JSON is a bit out of scope for this chapter, but we'll discuss it in considerable detail in chapter 11.

5.6.4   Formatting flags

There are a few flags that are meant to modify how Terraform returns output. These are pretty simple flags that don't change the behavior of Terraform itself—just the formatting that it returns:

- `-compact-warnings` reduces the text you see when warnings appear.

- -no-color strips any color from the output, which can be useful for systems that don't support color.

These aren't particularly fancy, and there isn't a whole lot to be said about them.

5.7 *Common pitfalls and errors*

When using Terraform, there are certain errors that you may run into that are a little different from what you'd see in other languages. Many of these situations come because of the use of the resource graph, which has a lot of powerful benefits but also presents its own downsides. Here, we're going to use our knowledge of graphs to talk about how we can work around these problems when they occur.

5.7.1 *Circular dependencies*

Terraform's use of DAGs has benefits, but it can also lead to some problems. One of these is circular dependencies, which happens when a chain of resources depends on each other in a way that forms a loop.

Imagine you have several microservices running. You might have an authentication service, which depends on a logging service. Now imagine that the logging service depends on the authentication service as well. In this case, if you were to draw the dependencies out, you'd see a circle (see figure 5.10).

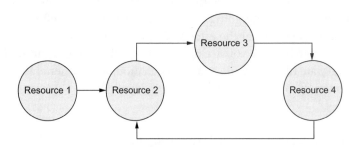

Figure 5.10   Circular dependencies

In most cases, the dependencies aren't so clear. You may have a service that depends on another service, which depends on another service, which ultimately depends on the first service.

Terraform does not handle circular dependencies well. The "acyclic" in directed acyclic graphs explicitly means that the data structure cannot have a circular, or cyclic, relationship. If you attempt to do so, Terraform will throw an error.

This may sound like a huge problem, but it's actually fairly uncommon. With system architecture (as with many types of programming or engineering), the simplest solution to a problem that meets the requirements is typically the best solution, and more complex systems tend to be harder to manage and debug. Systems with large and complex dependency chains are an antipattern, so when circular dependencies come up, it's often a sign that the architecture needs to be revisited.

So the question is: What should you do when you encounter a circular dependency error? The first thing to do is look at the resources involved in the error and identify how they are connected. In many cases, you may find that they simply share an attribute and that it's possible to pass that attribute around in another way such as by generating a variable or local value that creates the same value without depending on a resource.

We're going to demonstrate this using the `null provider`. This is a special provider that gives access to the `null_resource`, which is a resource that doesn't do anything. In other languages this might be referred to as a NOOP (for no op or no operation). We'll talk a bit more about why this is used in chapter 10, but one very common usage of it is for development or to demonstrate different patterns. We're going to use that here to show how Terraform responds to circular dependencies.

Listing 5.10   Services with circular dependencies

```
resource "null_resource" "alpha" {
  triggers = {
    rebuild = null_resource.charlie.id
  }
}

resource "null_resource" "bravo" {
  triggers = {
    rebuild = null_resource.alpha.id
  }
}

resource "null_resource" "charlie" {
  triggers = {
    rebuild = null_resource.bravo.id
  }
}
```

The null resource doesn't do anything, which makes it useful for testing.

The trigger is an object with arbitrary values. If it changes, then the resource is re-created.

This creates a dependency between alpha and charlie

Now bravo depends on alpha.

With this charlie depends on brava, which depends on alpha, which depends on charlie.

Attempting to run `terraform plan` on this code will result in an error:

```
$ terraform plan
| Error: Cycle: null_resource.alpha, null_resource.bravo,
  null_resource.charlie
```

The first time most people see an error like this can be confusing, especially if they're not familiar with graphs and cycles. The good news is that everything we need to at least identify the problem is present in the error itself. When a cycle error occurs, Terraform lists out the resources that are defined there.

To resolve this problem, you need to break the dependency. In general, this can be done by identifying any of the resources in the chain, reviewing how they link, and trying to find another way to accomplish the same goal without that link. In our case, we are trying to re-create all of the `null_resources` if any of them change. We can do that by creating a higher level variable to trigger that change.

Listing 5.11   Removing circular dependencies

```
variable "build_id" {
  default = null                      Create a variable that can be
  type    = string                    changed to trigger a rebuild.
}

resource "null_resource" "alpha" {
  triggers = {
    rebuild = var.build_id            Now use the variable instead of
  }                                   references to the other resources.
}

resource "null_resource" "bravo" {
  triggers = {
    rebuild = var.build_id
  }
}

resource "null_resource" "charlie" {
  triggers = {
    rebuild = var.build_id
  }
}
```

There are other options too, such as creating the resource independently of Terraform and importing it in. These methods break the spirit of infrastructure as code, though, and remove a lot of the benefits of using Terraform. If you find yourself in a position where you can't work around your circular dependencies with small changes like the ones mentioned previously, then you should really revisit the structure and architecture of the project to see if it can be simplified a bit.

5.7.2   Cascading changes

Terraform, and its use of graphs to represent infrastructure, means that you have to think about how your changes may affect downstream dependencies. The `terraform graph` command can be useful to see how all of the resources in your project relate to each other and should be looked at occasionally to help give you an idea of the scope of your overall system.

Even with that, it may not be obvious that a change to one resource will result in another resource being changed. This can be compounded by the fact that some changes can be applied in place, while others will require a resource to be destroyed and re-created. There are three things you can do to reduce this problem:

- Review your plans and pay particular attention to resources that are going to be replaced.

- If you see that a resource you want to preserve is going to be replaced (destroyed and re-created), try to understand why. Normally, it's because a specific attribute has triggered the replacement, which should be visible in the plan. Then add that attribute to the `ignore_changes` portion of the `lifecycle` meta parameter and it will no longer trigger the replacement.

- Try to reduce the dependency chain in your systems, as the fewer dependencies there are, the fewer places you have to worry about. That being said, this is often easier said than done and can involve a review of your overall architecture rather than simple fixes.

Going back to our TLS example, let's see what happens when we make one small change. In our `tls_private_key.ca_key` resources, let's change the algorithm from `ECDSA` to `ED25519`. When we run `terraform plan` again, that one small change is going to result in every one of our certificates being re-created.

Listing 5.12 Cascading changes

```
$ terraform plan -out cascading_changes.tfplan

tls_private_key.ca_key: Refreshing state...
➥[id=4c9b44687d30a59610287574ea4efccbfda02f52]
tls_private_key.child_key["bravo.example.com"]: Refreshing state...
➥[id=8ec2521d90a08a519a726f138b19199d6ed6437a]
tls_private_key.child_key["charilie.example.com"]: Refreshing state...
➥[id=435155292c21a131097fcceb9a766e665f2f8ebc]
tls_private_key.child_key["example.com"]: Refreshing state...
➥[id=9d9c8317f875a36b5bc57e670fd47635492d2d68]
tls_cert_request.child_request["example.com"]: Refreshing state...
➥[id=7167dd2d7a84a0e93649fe8da51d4a09242f41c1]
tls_cert_request.child_request["bravo.example.com"]: Refreshing state...
➥[id=8a9ed6e21bdf631b6fa5eae4ee1a19054b18c83f]
tls_cert_request.child_request["charilie.example.com"]: Refreshing state...
➥[id=a2cf771109b74a9aac1f5e53e6315541b6f0ce87]
tls_self_signed_cert.ca_cert: Refreshing state...
➥[id=309484103170820270480956366529397861852]
tls_locally_signed_cert.child_certificate["bravo.example.com"]:
➥Refreshing state... [id=204072872684390236721245131254840137061]
tls_locally_signed_cert.child_certificate["example.com"]:
➥Refreshing state... [id=78866308622325048575924014004743394875]
tls_locally_signed_cert.child_certificate["charilie.example.com"]:
➥Refreshing state... [id=132895264876037149366012245488140588707]

Terraform used the selected providers to generate the following execution
plan. Resource actions are indicated with the following symbols:
-/+ destroy and then create replacement

Terraform will perform the following actions:

  # tls_locally_signed_cert.child_certificate["bravo.example.com"] must
➥be replaced
-/+ resource "tls_locally_signed_cert" "child_certificate" {
```

The CA key algorithm, which is what we changed, is also being detected by this resource.

The cert PEM is changing, which forces this resource to change.

```
     ~ ca_cert_pem            = <<-EOT # forces replacement
          truncated certificate
       EOT -> (known after apply) # forces replacement
     ~ ca_key_algorithm       = "ECDSA" -> (known after apply)
     ~ ca_private_key_pem     = (sensitive value) # forces replacement
     ~ cert_pem               = <<-EOT
            -----BEGIN CERTIFICATE-----
            truncated certificate
            -----END CERTIFICATE-----
       EOT -> (known after apply)
     ~ truncated
   }
```

The private key changing forces this resource to change as well.

```
  # tls_locally_signed_cert.child_certificate["charilie.example.com"] must
be replaced
-/+ resource "tls_locally_signed_cert" "child_certificate" {
     ~ truncated
   }
```

This certificate has the same changes detected by the others.

```
  # tls_locally_signed_cert.child_certificate["example.com"] must
be replaced
-/+ resource "tls_locally_signed_cert" "child_certificate" {
     ~ truncated
   }
```

This certificate has the same changes detected by the others.

```
  # tls_self_signed_cert.ca_cert must be replaced
-/+ resource "tls_self_signed_cert" "ca_cert" {
     ~ truncated
   }
```

This certificate has the same changes detected by the others.

```
  # tls_private_key.ca_key must be replaced
-/+ resource "tls_private_key" "ca_key" {
     ~ algorithm                        = "ECDSA" -> "ED25519" # forces
replacement
     ~ truncated
   }
```

The change we made is forcing this private key to be replaced instead of updated.

```
Plan: 5 to add, 0 to change, 5 to destroy.
```

Our one change has caused five resources to be replaced.

As you can see here, even a small change in code or even input variables can result in significant changes downstream. If the TLS certificates in this example were actually in use, this could have resulted in even more changes, such as services being reloaded or load balancers getting changed in place. When running plans, always look for the `forces replacement` warning to identify when your changes may be doing more than expected.

If you do notice unexpected replacements, one question you can ask yourself is whether you really think the resource should be replaced or whether it's okay to leave existing resources in place. This is where the ignore changes lifecycle rule we discussed in chapter 2 comes in handy. If you want your changes to apply to new resources but don't want the changes to force replacements, you can always ignore the attribute causing the replacement.

5.7.3 *Hidden dependencies*

A similar problem to cascading changes is that of hidden dependencies. Hidden dependencies occur when infrastructure depends on other infrastructure but there is no link in the code (no attributes being taken from a resource and passed to another). Without these links, Terraform may attempt to create resources before their needed dependencies exist.

Sometimes this doesn't matter. If you have a microservice architecture with a lot of different services talking to each other, they may depend on each other to run, but they will most likely still launch even if they aren't all available. The first time the system is launched, a service may give errors until the other services it depends on are up, but ultimately that problem resolves itself.

There are cases that are less forgiving. A somewhat more common example is internet access. If you're using Terraform to manage a network inside a cloud provider (AWS, Azure, GCP), then you have to grant your networks internet access in some way. The way you do that varies, but it tends to be disconnected from the rest of your resources: that is to say, there's no direct dependency in Terraform. This can result in the resources failing to get created altogether.

The way to handle this is to create explicit dependencies between these resources, typically using the `depends_on` meta argument. For example, if you know that NAT Gateways (a resource used to give private networks access to the internet) cannot launch without the Internet Gateway (a resource that enables internet access for a VPC) being up, you can define the relationship explicitly; otherwise it's possible that the NAT Gateway will fail to launch.

Detailed readers might have noticed that this is the exact opposite of the advice from the previous section about cascading changes. This is one area that is always going to be a balancing act: the simpler the system, the easier it can be to understand and manage, but the more features a system needs to support, the more complex it ends up being. How this plays out in practice often requires experimentation and an understanding of the specific system being built.

5.7.4 *Always detected changes*

I like to think of this category of bug as eternal drift, where no matter how many times you run a plan and apply, Terraform continues to detect changes. This is one of my least favorite bugs, and I do consider it a bug on the provider level. It occurs because the provider isn't translating properly between Terraform and the API it used.

For example, you might set an attribute to the number 45. When Terraform runs a refresh, the API returns a float, 45.0, and Terraform detects this as a change. There are a lot of ways this can happen:

- Converting integers into floats
- Converting booleans into strings
- Changing the order of a list
- Changing a mixed-case string to lowercase
- Change a missing argument to an empty string or 0

This used to be a lot more common, but changes to the underlying Terraform plugin framework and providers themselves becoming more mature have really improved this. These days, this error is pretty rare. When it does happen though, it can be annoying. The solution is to match your input to what the API returns, if possible (some APIs are inconsistent with their responses, making that difficult). If the API returns a lowercase string, then use lowercase strings for your input; if it returns a list in a specific order, then sort your list into that order. Then go to the problem tracker for the provider, and if no one else has reported the problem, you can file it so the developers are aware.

5.7.5   *Calculated values and iterations*

One of the biggest limitations you're likely to run into with Terraform is in calculating your `for_each` and `count` meta arguments. As a reminder, these meta arguments are used to define how many resources you're attempting to create and manage. With the `count` parameter, you specify a number, while the `for_each` parameter takes in a `map`, `set`, or `object`.

The problem is that the values passed to either of these meta arguments have to be known at plan time and cannot depend on values that are only known after the plan has been applied. What this means in practice is that any value that comes from a resource, such as the resource ID or IP address, can't be used when calculating a `count` or `for_each`.

To put it another way, Terraform needs to know what the `count` and `for_each` values are to generate the resource graph. Without that knowledge, Terraform won't be able to create the appropriate resource nodes. If the `count` or `for_each` value depends on a value that Terraform doesn't know about during the planning phase, it won't be able to generate the graph beyond that point.

What makes this potentially confusing is that in Terraform there are a lot of dependencies calculated, and it may not be obvious whether a value was calculated from a resource attribute. This is especially true when using modules. You may find that a module works when you're using it directly but that if you pass some attributes in, then it changes the `count` or `for_each` in a way that Terraform can't calculate at the right time.

Another example is you might have a module that creates a virtual machine, creates a DNS record based off that virtual machine, and then attaches an elastic IP address if the DNS record is in a specific domain. If you attempt to use the domain from the DNS record resource to control the security group attachment, it will fail.

Listing 5.13 Accidental use of computed value for `count`

```
                                  We're referencing resources that are defined    If the domain is
                                  below, but that's okay because Terraform    example.com, then
                                  doesn't care about the order.    use an EIP. Note
variable "domain" {                                                              that it's pulling the
  description = "The base domain to use for DNS records."                        value from the DNS
  type        = string                                                           record resource,
}                                                                                which introduces a
                                                                                 dependency.
locals {
  use_eip     = endswith("example.com", aws_route53_record.name)
  ip_address = local.use_eip ? aws_eip.example[0].public_ip :
➥aws_instance.example.public_ip
}                                                    If we are using an EIP, then use
                                                     it's IP address; otherwise use
                                                     the machine's IP address.

data "aws_ami" "ubuntu" {              As a reminder, this is how we look
  most_recent = true                   up the AMI for an instance type.

  filter {
    name   = "name"
    values = ["ubuntu/images/hvm-ssd/ubuntu-focal-20.04-amd64-server-*"]
  }

  filter {
    name   = "virtualization-type"
    values = ["hvm"]
  }

  owners = ["099720109477"]
}

resource "aws_instance" "example" {        Here we create our instance.
  ami           = data.aws_ami.ubuntu.id
  instance_type = "t3.micro"
}

resource "aws_eip" "example" {
  count  = local.use_eip ? 1 : 0           This is where we run into problems.
  domain = "vpc"                           The use_eip local uses the domain
}                                          from the DNS record, which isn't
                                           available during planning.
resource "aws eip association" "eip_assoc" {
  count         = local.use_eip ? 1 : 0          The error is also going
  instance_id   = aws_instance.example.id        to show up here.
  allocation_id = aws_eip.example[0].id
}

data "aws_route53_zone" "example" {
  name         = var.domain
  private_zone = true
}

resource "aws_route53_record" "example" {
```

```
  zone_id = data.aws_route53_zone.example.id
  name    = "instance.${data.aws_route53_zone.example.id}"
  type    = "A"
  records = [local.ip_address]
}
```

The easiest way to solve this is to try and replace the use of the computed value with one that isn't computed. Here, we can do that by relying directly on the input variable instead of relying on the attribute of `aws_route53_record` resource.

Listing 5.14 Avoiding the computed value in `count`

```
variable "domain" {
  description = "The base domain to use for DNS records."
  type        = string
}
```
                                                          **Rather than depend on the
                                                          resource, we're using the
                                                          variable directly.**
```
locals {
  use_eip    = endswith("example.com", var.domain)  ◀
  ip_address = local.use_eip ? aws_eip.example[0].public_ip :
➥aws_instance.example.public_ip
}


data "aws_ami" "ubuntu" {
  most_recent = true

  filter {
    name   = "name"
    values = ["ubuntu/images/hvm-ssd/ubuntu-focal-20.04-amd64-server-*"]
  }

  filter {
    name   = "virtualization-type"
    values = ["hvm"]
  }

  owners = ["099720109477"]
}

resource "aws_instance" "example" {
  ami           = data.aws_ami.ubuntu.id
  instance_type = "t3.micro"
}
```
                                         **Now this will work, as the
                                         value can be resolved during
                                         the planning phase.**
```
resource "aws_eip" "example" {
  count  = local.use_eip ? 1 : 0   ◀
  domain = "vpc"
}

resource "aws_eip_association" "eip_assoc" {
  count         = local.use_eip ? 1 : 0      ◀    This will also work.
  instance_id   = aws_instance.example.id
  allocation_id = aws_eip.example[0].id
```

```
}

data "aws_route53_zone" "example" {
  name         = var.domain
  private_zone = true
}

resource "aws_route53_record" "example" {
  zone_id = data.aws_route53_zone.example.id
  name    = "instance.${data.aws_route53_zone.example.id}"
  type    = "A"
  records = [local.ip_address]
}
```

The problems that come up with `for_each` are similar. If any of the values inside of an object or list are generated from a resource attribute, then they can't be used with `for_each`. If you know how many keys are in the object, or items in the list, you can use `count` and its index to accomplish the same thing as using `for_each` without depending on retrieved values.

There is another way to work around this problem, but I really recommend never doing it. You can use resource targeting (discussed in the Plan section of this chapter) to create the resources that are needed before the `for_each` or `count` that depends on them. This lets Terraform create those resources, and then when it runs another plan it will be able to calculate the iterator based off the existing values. The problem with this is that it means your Terraform modules can't be run without having additional bootstrapping logic to get things working. This complicates usage and maintenance of your code. It's much better to refactor around the problem than to use this workaround.

5.7.6 *Failed state updates*

One of the most annoying and unpredictable errors that you can encounter with Terraform is when a change is made but the state is not updated to reflect it. These types of errors are pretty rare and generally happen when there's a fault in the underlying system that Terraform is running: either the system is crashing or the state backend is responding with an error instead of saving changes.

How you resolve this depends on what the changes were. If there were only updates and deletions, then you can normally work around the problem by doing a refresh-only apply, at which point Terraform will notice the changes and save them for you. It's a good practice to run a plan afterward to confirm that everything is properly aligned with your code.

If Terraform created resources and they weren't added, you have two options: import the resources into the state or manually delete the resources and then run a refresh-only apply like in the previous cases. This is because Terraform will have no concept that the resources exist. With an update or deletion, Terraform will know what resources to look for because it will have an ID already saved for them, but if Terraform fails to save the state while creating resources for the first time, then there's nothing for it to look up in subsequent runs.

Managing state is one of the most important parts of using Terraform. The next chapter is focused around how Terraform manages state, and it delves into how you can prevent these types of errors to begin with.

Summary

- Graphs are a data structure used to represent relationships between nodes.
- Terraform uses graphs to represent the systems defined with it.
- Terraform also uses graphs to represent Terraform plans.
- The `terraform graph` command can be used to visualize Terraform configurations and plans.
- The `terraform plan` command creates plans and can be run with a variety of modes and options.
- The `terraform apply` command runs plans, either passed in as a saved plan file or by running its own plan.
- While being extremely powerful, Terraform's use of DAGs presents some pitfalls and potential error types.

Part 2

Terraform in production

Now that you understand the Terraform language, it's time to put it into production. In this section, we focus on everything it takes to run Terraform as a high-performing team:

- In chapter 6, we focus on managing the Terraform state, diving deep into what state actually is and how to manage it in a team setting.
- Chapter 7 introduces continuous integration, where we'll use open source projects in the Terraform ecosystem to test for code quality, standards, and security.
- Chapter 8 jumps into continuous delivery systems, which can be used to manage your Terraform deployments.
- Chapter 9 breaks down testing with Terraform and Terragrunt, helping developers build guardrails and safety into their systems.

The chapters in this section are crucial for building and maintaining high-quality code. By mastering the techniques in this portion of the book, you'll reduce the amount of time you spend on maintenance while increasing the resiliency of your deployments and decreasing outages.

State management

This chapter covers

- Reasons that state exists
- Considerations when managing state
- Storing state in centralized backends
- How state is structured
- Fixing common state errors
- Cross project state access
- Resources that exist only in state

When using Terraform, the concept of state comes up quite often. We've talked about it a little so far, defining it back in chapter 1 as "a collection of metadata about the resources that Terraform manages." What is state though, and why do we need it?

One of the easiest ways to talk about state is to talk about what it looks like to have a system without state (also referred to as a stateless system). When you're working with programming languages and protocols, a stateless system is one that has no memory of past runs. Every interaction is a standalone interaction that does not depend on the interactions before it. If you've ever worked with web-based APIs, you may be familiar with the HTTP-based REST protocol, which is a stateless system: every request to the API has to contain everything it needs for that request.

Systems that have state are a bit different. Stateful systems have a memory of what has happened before that they used to drive their current actions. This means that they have to keep track of the current state of the system (hence the name). Terraform is an example of a stateful system: it keeps a record of all the resources under its control and refreshes that record as part of every plan.

Maintaining state has benefits and drawbacks. On the one hand, it allows Terraform to improve performance and reduce the complexity of its engine. On the other hand, it requires users of Terraform to store and manage that state. This chapter discusses the implications and tradeoffs of this decision. We're going to break down why Terraform uses state, what the data structures behind state look like, and how you can manage your state in the most secure and resilient ways possible.

6.1 Purpose of state

Just as the use of a declarative language instead of an imperative one, the choice to use a stateful system instead of a stateless one is a core design choice that touches every part of Terraform. As with any decision, there are tradeoffs that have to be considered. Before we get into the downsides of state, let's take a look at the benefits that it brings to Terraform.

6.1.1 Real-world linkage

A common question that people learning about Terraform ask is why Terraform needs state to function. Maintaining state allows Terraform to always identify resources by their true identifiers (for example, in AWS this would be the Amazon Resource Name of a resource) in a way that can be reliably repeated even when users modify their infrastructure manually. Without state, Terraform would have to find a way to identify every resource under its control, and this turns out to be a surprisingly difficult task.

At first glance, the idea of identifying resources may not sound too complicated, as many vendors have systems that enable tags or descriptions for their resources. If you are using AWS, GCP, or Azure, you can easily tag resources and then use those tags to look them up later. However, not every resource that you could control with Terraform supports tags, which means Terraform would have to start doing additional lookups and inferring what resources are or aren't controlled by Terraform. People also regularly change tags independently of Terraform, which means that relying on them can be brittle and error prone.

Tags are just one example by a few vendors, and other vendors may not support them. Even the ones that do support tags don't use the same APIs for searching them. This complicates the task of automatic identification: any solution would stop being a generic Terraform solution and is pushed onto the providers.

6.1.2   *Reduced complexity*

Although the use of state does make running Terraform slightly more difficult, it also makes Terraform a more robust and feature-rich project by making it easier to develop and extend. The last section alluded to the complexity it would take to automatically look up and associate infrastructure to Terraform resources. There would have to be multiple paths to support lookups, as different vendors have different capabilities.

It's a common saying in development practices that if you take two potential solutions to a problem, the one that is the simplest is the ideal choice. Complexity makes it harder to add features without breaking things, as complex systems have more surface areas and edge cases to worry about. It also makes debugging harder, as there are so many different paths in the code. There are certainly cases where complexity is needed to meet the requirements of a project, but it should be handled with care.

Removing state from Terraform would dramatically increase the complexity of the project. It would do so for Terraform itself, and it would make provider development significantly harder. That last point may be even more important, as Terraform depends heavily on provider developers to cover the vast number of platforms that exist. The harder it is to write high-quality providers, the fewer people who will be able to do so, and that makes the entire ecosystem weaker.

6.1.3   *Performance*

Storing state has a significant, and positive, effect on performance. Any method of automatically identifying and linking infrastructure to resources is going to be slower than simply looking up the resource from a saved identifier. Storing the state also makes it easier to run many of the subcommands, such as `terraform graph`, as those subcommands can use the state instead of running a full refresh to identify everything.

One of the most important things when developing software is not wasting your developers' time. Developers work best when they can have a fast debugging cycle: make a change, test the change, and make more changes based on the results. Reducing the number of interruptions, including interruptions like waiting for Terraform to run, allows developers to keep a mental model of their project in their head while they work, which in turn makes them more efficient (and generally happier).

This is one of the things that makes Terraform so powerful. I spoke in the first chapter about the magic of being able to spin up complex systems in minutes, which previously took days of effort, and this also translates to developer time as well. When working on new modules, it's common to run Terraform plans over and over again between changes to code, and any delay at that point slows down the developer and risks breaking their concentration.

6.1.4   *State-only resources*

Terraform's usage of state opens up some interesting opportunities, such as the ability to define and manage resources that only exist inside of state. Resources that exist only in state are, by themselves, not particularly useful, as they don't have any infrastructure that they directly manage. They can, however, generate data to feed other resources, allow for advanced logic and patterns, or even generate secure credentials.

You've already encountered one state-only provider. In the last chapter, we used the Transport Layer Security (TLS) provider to create a certificate authority. This involved creating keys, signing requests, and certificates. The interesting thing is that we didn't need to use APIs accessed over a network, and we didn't save the data generated to disk. The only place that the resources exist is inside the state itself.

TLS is just one example of resources that exist only inside the state. The `null`, `random`, and `cloudinit` providers are other examples of state-only providers that we'll discuss later in the chapter. Terraform would not be able to support these types of providers without state unless the providers were changed to the point that they lost their usefulness.

6.2 *Important considerations*

Introducing state is not without downsides. Although the benefits of Terraform's decision to use state outweigh the negatives, it does introduce another level of complexity that developers have to consider. When working with any system that maintains data of any kind, it's important to think about how that data is used and what you're going to do if that data isn't available, and Terraform state is not an exception to this rule. When you think about state storage, it's important to consider how your users (other developers) are going to interact with the system. Although state storage can be complex, there are three general areas you can focus on when choosing a state storage system: resiliency, security, and availability.

6.2.1 *Resiliency*

One of the worst possible situations to be in as a Terraform developer is to have your state get lost or corrupted. Terraform has to have the state to run any sort of upgrade plan. Without it, Terraform will either fail to complete a plan or create a plan that assumes it's creating everything from scratch.

Recovering from a loss of state is not trivial. It involves either manually deleting resources from your vendors (such as erasing DNS records and destroying virtual machines) or importing those resources back into Terraform. Either way, it's a tedious process that can take a lot of time simply looking up identifiers and running commands.

This is why it's important to consider how reliable your state storage system is, and just as important is what you'd do if it fails. When reviewing backends, you should look at what their historic data loss is, how often they've had incidents, and whether they offer any commitments on durability. Consider AWS Simple Storage Solution (S3) as an example. They claim to have a durability for each object in storage of "99.999999999%," which means that each year they expect to lose an average of 1 out of every 100 trillion objects they store.

You should also assume that even with a perfect record, accidents and mistakes can happen. It isn't enough to have a resilient backend—you also need to have reliable backups that you are absolutely confident in. Even with an incredibly reliable storage system, there is always the chance that you will lose data. Considering the importance of state, you should be prepared for that to occur. Even if a system doesn't fail on its own, there is always the chance for human error: a system like AWS may promise to never lose or corrupt a file, but that doesn't prevent an engineer from accidentally erasing a bucket, for example.

6.2.2 Security

It's extremely important to take security into account when deciding how to store your state. Poor security can have very negative consequences. If you don't maintain proper security around your state, then malicious actors may gain access to that state by exploiting poor security practices. The only thing worse than losing your state to corruption or a hardware failure is having your state get leaked. Terraform state includes not just identifiers for resources but all the attributes as well. This means that every attribute, even the ones marked as sensitive, would be exposed if the state was ever stolen or leaked.

Poor security can mean a number of things. If your developers have access to state but there isn't any multifactor authentication, such as using a phone app to create a one-time code that has to be entered to log in, then it's possible someone could use a brute force or credential stuffing attack to access state. Another possibility is that a storage backend is misconfigured to allow public access. These are both real examples that have occurred and resulted in larger problems in the past. It's important to not only consider the overall security posture of the vendors you work with but also your own responsibilities for configuration and management of these systems.

There are ways to mitigate the damage. You could have a policy of reducing or eliminating sensitive values from code by utilizing secret managers like Vault. Even with that, there will be limitations, as many systems aren't built to read from secret managers and will need values passed directly to them. Even if you manage to remove all of the sensitive values from state, having a copy of that state will still expose your entire architecture to anyone with access to it.

6.2.3 Availability

The final thing to think about before finalizing your plans for state storage is availability. This refers to how often a system is up and accessible. In some ways, it's similar to resiliency, but it's a bit more than just making sure your data can survive an incident. If a system never destroys data and is completely secure but is accessible for an hour a day, that system isn't going to be particularly useful to you.

When using Terraform, this is especially important to consider as you need the state to be accessible to use Terraform and manage your infrastructure. Being blocked from running deployments is one of the worst things that can happen to a company. On a normal day, it may just be an inconvenience that lowers productivity, but in the event of an emergency, it's important that teams can deploy changes rapidly to deal with the problem. If your state management system is inaccessible, you can't deploy at all while using Terraform.

> **NOTE**   Availability is normally measured in "nines." A 99.99% uptime is called "four nines," while a 99.999% uptime is called "five nines." The website https:// uptime.is/ can be useful to see how those values translate to real time.

When evaluating a company's availability, you need to consider both its historical record and its corporate commitments. Most vendors have some form of service-level agreement that the vendor promises to meet, typically with some level of refund or financial penalty on the company if they don't meet it. Companies that aren't transparent about their own outages, or that aren't willing to commit to a service-level agreement, should be avoided.

For something as important as state storage, you want to have a very high uptime. Personally, I would expect at least 99.99% (four nines) of uptime, which translates to less than 4 minutes and 30 seconds of downtime a month. Your state storage system should be considered absolutely critical infrastructure by your company since any lack of access means that you are locked out of deploying.

6.3   Dissecting state

State is a data structure and a database all rolled into one. As a general rule, you shouldn't ever need to manually edit state, and if you do, you want to be extremely careful. Terraform provides tools, such as the `import` command or the `refresh only` plan, to help deal with problems that come up with state.

That being said, it's a good idea to understand what state is so you can understand the limitations of working with it. Some errors you might receive while working with Terraform backends make a bit more sense once you understand the underlying state data structure. For example, if you get an error about Terraform lineage not matching, or if you ever need to restore state from a backup and need to figure out which version is the latest one, understanding how Terraform state is structured will be very helpful.

6.3.1   State as JSON

State can be represented with JSON (a serialization format used to take data structures and represent them as text). JSON is the default format that Terraform uses when storing `tfstate` files using the local backend, which gives us an opportunity to see what Terraform is doing.

Before we can look at the state itself, we should look at the example code that generated it. To try and keep things simple, we're going to use a single resource from the `random` provider, the `random_password` resource. We'll talk a bit more about the `random` provider later in the chapter, but what makes it a useful example is that it only exists in state and does not require us to configure authentication for a provider.

Listing 6.1   A simple Terraform module

```
data "null_data_source" "values" {


}
```

◄—— The null provider doesn't do anything, which makes it useful when writing examples.

```
resource "random_password" "new_password" {
  length = 12
}
```

> The random provider is used to generate random data such as passwords.

```
output "password" {
  value     = random_password.new_password.result
  sensitive = true
}
```

> We have to mark this output as sensitive because the random_ password result attribute is sensitive.

```
check "password_strength" {
  assert {
    condition     = length(random_password.new_password.result) >= 12
    error_message = "random_password.new_password.id should return a
password at least 12 characters long."
  }
}
```

> The check block is a new feature of Terraform that we'll discuss in chapter 10.

> We're using this block to validate that our generated password is long enough.

> The check block lets you make assertions while running Terraform.

Instead of calling this directly as a root-level module, we're going to call this as a child module. This will allow us to look at how Terraform handles modules inside of state.

Listing 6.2 Calling our Terraform module

```
module "my_password" {
  source = "./modules/password"
}
```

> Our example module is local and not published in a registry.

```
output "password" {
  value     = module.my_password.password
  sensitive = true
}
```

> We're taking the output from the child module and returning it as an output from this root-level module.

> Since the password field is sensitive we have to mark it as such here as well.

For this example we're using the local backend, as we haven't configured any other backend. This allows us to read the state directly from the `terraform.tfstate` file, which stores it in a convenient-to-read JSON structure. All we have to do is run `terraform init` and then `terraform apply` to generate the file.

On the top level, the state includes several different fields:

- `version`—This is the version of the state data structure itself. It allows newer versions of Terraform to read older state files and update them.
- `terraform_version`—This is the version of Terraform that generated the state.
- `serial`—The serial is the version of the state for the project. It gets incremented by 1 every time a change is made to the state.
- `lineage`—The lineage is a universally unique identifier (UUID) that is created the first time `terraform init` is run and creates a state. This will never change for a project and makes it possible to tell if Terraform is looking at the wrong state for a project.

- resources—This is a list of objects that represent the Terraform resources being managed. Every resource that is under Terraform's control should be represented here.

- outputs—The outputs list contains objects representing the outputs from the top-level module. This allows cross-state data lookups (which we'll discuss later in this chapter).

- check_results—Checks are a new feature of Terraform that allow for simple asserts and tests to occur in a Terraform run, and the results are saved to state. Chapter 9 will discuss checks in further detail.

Listing 6.3 Terraform state as JSON

```
{
    "version": 4,
    "terraform_version": "1.5.4",
    "serial": 6,
    "lineage": "7490ef49-8634-ac56-596b-6f2f4259bece",
    "outputs": {
        "password": {
            "value": "[-Cz\u003em@XQnZc",
            "type": "string",
            "sensitive": true
        }
    },
    "resources": [
        {
            "module": "module.my_password",
            "mode": "data",
            "type": "null_data_source",
            "name": "values",
            "provider": "provider[\"registry.terraform.io/hashicorp/null\"]",
            "instances": [
                {
                    "schema_version": 0,
                    "attributes": {
                        "has_computed_default": "default",
                        "id": "static",
                        "inputs": null,
                        "outputs": null,
                        "random": "1249756966943803081"
                    },
                    "sensitive_attributes": []
                }
            ]
        },
        {
            "module": "module.my_password",
            "mode": "managed",
            "type": "random_password",
            "name": "new_password",
```

This version is for the state data structure itself.

This is the version of Terraform that generated this file.

The serial is the version of the file itself. This is the sixth state file version for the project.

The lineage is a UUID created when the project is initialized for the first time. The lineage should never change.

Outputs are from the root-level module. The output from our child module is not included.

Every resource and data source in the project will have an associated object here.

```
        "provider": "provider[\"registry.terraform.io/hashicorp/random\"]",
        "instances": [
          {
            "schema_version": 3,
            "attributes": {
              "bcrypt_hash": "$2a$10$DxQHHtRQY9.I.vGpLGLjV..
  c9pbvfh2vFDax0OFRag1TN4Om44t0.",
              "id": "none",
              "keepers": null,
              "length": 12,
              "lower": true,
              "min_lower": 0,
              "min_numeric": 0,
              "min_special": 0,
              "min_upper": 0,
              "number": true,
              "numeric": true,
              "override_special": null,
              "result": "[-Cz\u003em@XQnZc",        This value was generated
              "special": true,                      by the resource itself.
              "upper": true
            },                                       In theory, the result should have been
            "sensitive_attributes": []              flagged, but the sensitive_attributes field
          }                                          does not appear to be used anymore.
        ]
      }
    ],
    "check_results": [                   Results from check block
      {                                  are stored in state.
        "object_kind": "check",
        "config_addr": "module.my_password.check.password_strength",
        "status": "pass",
        "objects": [
          {
            "object_addr": "module.my_password.check.password_strength",
            "status": "pass"
          }
        ]
      }
    ]
}
```

Although state seems like a complicated topic, as you can see here it really is a simple data structure. We'll break down how the different fields are used by Terraform over the rest of this section.

6.3.2 State versions

The state has two different versions associated with it. The `version` field defines the version of the data structure itself. Over time, as Terraform has evolved, fields have been added, removed, and modified. Terraform maintains backward compatibility with older state versions and will update them automatically when a change is made.

To maintain this compatibility, it needs to know what version it's working with so it can make changes.

The state version is different from the `terraform_version` field. As the name suggests, this field records the version of Terraform that was used when the state file was last updated. In theory, Terraform can use this field to apply version-specific bug fixes, but most of the time it is simply an informational field.

6.3.3   *Lineage and serial*

The `lineage` and `serial` fields describe the specific instance of state. The lineage field is a UUID, which is a special kind of extremely large number that is mathematically guaranteed to be unique (you'd have to generate trillions to have a duplicate). The serial field is a simple integer.

The lineage field is used as a safety mechanism. Since UUID fields are extremely unique, the odds of two separate environments having the same ID is very low, to the point where it's practically impossible. This can be used by backends to prevent Terraform from overwriting the state of one project with the state of another by comparing the lineage field and ensuring they match.

The `serial` field is a bit more straightforward. Every time Terraform saves a new iteration of the state it increases the value of the serial field by 1. If your backend supports versioning, or if you ever have to restore from a backend, you can use this field to make sure you've got the latest possible version. Some backends, such as the `cloud` block-based ones, will even use the field to ensure they don't accidentally overwrite a newer version of state with an older one.

6.3.4   *Resources, outputs, and checks*

The final portion that we're going to look at are the resources, outputs, and checks that are saved in the state. These are the fields that state exists for, as they map back real-world infrastructure to the code that generated it.

The resources section of the state contains both resources and data sources. The first thing you'll notice is the metadata about the object. This includes the fields that uniquely identify the object: module, type, and name. These combined fields should always be unique for each resource. Each item in the resources section also includes the provider, which is how Terraform notices if a resource was generated with a different provider. The final piece is the `attributes` block, which saves every attribute for the resource.

Listing 6.4   Resources in Terraform state

```
{
  "resources": [
    {
      "module": "module.my_password",      ◀── This field, combined with the name field below, form the resource address.
      "mode": "managed",      ◀── This field has the value of managed for resources and data for data sources.
```

This field, combined with the name field below, form the resource address.

This field has the value of managed for resources and data for data sources.

This always maps to a type
of resource or data source.

This is the user-provided name
for the resource or data source.

```
"type": "random_password",
"name": "new_password",
"provider": "provider[\"registry.terraform.io/hashicorp/random\"]",
"instances": [
  {
    "schema_version": 3,
    "attributes": {
      "bcrypt_hash": "$2a$10$DxQHHtRQY9.I.vGpLGLjV..
c9pbvfh2vFDax0OFRag1TN4Om44t0.",
      "id": "none",
      "keepers": null,
      "length": 12,
      "lower": true,
      "min_lower": 0,
      "min_numeric": 0,
      "min_special": 0,
      "min_upper": 0,
      "number": true,
      "numeric": true,
      "override_special": null,
      "result": "[-Cz\u003em@XQnZc",
      "special": true,
      "upper": true
    },
    "sensitive_attributes": []
  }
]
}
]
}
```

The state
tracks which
provider is in
charge of every
resource.

Attributes are resource
specific, and include both
computed attributes and
user parameters.

The schema
version is
controlled by the
provider used to
manage the
resource.

Note that sensitive data
is stored in the state.

This field is no longer used, as the
sensitive data fields are stored in
the providers themselves.

The `outputs` field is used by Terraform to save any of the root-level module outputs. This is what allows the `terraform show` command to work, as it can read from the state file and display the various outputs. It is also what allows the `terraform_remote_state` data source to work, which we'll discuss later in the chapter.

One thing to pay attention to is what isn't here: the outputs from our module. This is because our module is not at the top level. Terraform does not save any of the module outputs except for the top level, which means the only way those outputs get saved in state is as the attribute of any resource that uses them.

Listing 6.5 Outputs in Terraform state

```
{
  "outputs": {
    "password": {
      "value": "[-Cz\u003em@XQnZc",
```

Unlike other fields the Outputs
field is an object, not an array.

Note that the sensitive
value is here in plain text.

```
        "type": "string",
        "sensitive": true
      }
    }
}
```

◄─── The type of the output is stored here so that other projects can access it without needing the underlying code that generated it.

◄─── This output is marked as sensitive so Terraform won't display it by mistake.

The final section of the state that we're going to review is the checks section. Checks are a relatively new feature of Terraform that allow you to validate your resource was created as expected by writing assertions directly in your Terraform configuration. As they're a more advanced feature, we discuss them in detail in chapter 10. Terraform saves all of the results of checks in state, including the checks from child modules. Terraform also saves the results of every assertion defined in the check block.

Listing 6.6   Checks in Terraform state

```
{
  "check_results": [
    {
      "object_kind": "check",
      "config_addr": "module.my_password.check.health_check",
      "status": "pass",
      "objects": [
        {
          "object_addr": "module.my_password.check.health_check",
          "status": "pass"
        }
      ]
    }
  ]
}
```

If there are no checks this value will be null instead of an empty array.

This is the address to the block that generated this check.

Each individual assertion will also have its results saved.

The status of the check is preserved.

6.4   Storing state

By default, Terraform stores the state in a `tfstate` file on the system that it is run on using what it calls the local backend. This is meant purely for development purposes. Local state files are not resilient, as a single hardware failure can make them disappear. They may not be secure, depending on what protections are on the machine running it. They're certainly not available to anyone beyond the users of that individual machine.

As you can see, the local backend fails at every one of the important considerations from the previous section. This is okay though, as it isn't meant for production use. Having the local backend makes it easy to get started with Terraform and makes local development easier, but for any production environment you're going to want to use something other than the local backend.

The good news is that, as of Terraform v1.3, all of the built-in backends can meet the other requirements. For some, this may require some extra configuration on the vendor side though, so it's still important to think through those requirements during setup. If you use the s3 provider without setting up state locking, for instance, your backend state can easily end up corrupted. This is why it's absolutely critical that you review the documentation for your backend to learn about any of these backend-specific requirements that may exist.

6.4.1 Possible backends

Terraform backends are built directly into Terraform and cannot be added using extensions. This means you can mostly expect the different backends to have the same core functionality, although how they implement that functionality can be different.

Since backends offer a standard set of functionality to Terraform, the primary difference between backends is where they store state. Each backend has a different location for storage, with their own access requirements and authentication methods. The main deciding factor in what backend to use is typically what technology is already being used by the team running Terraform. If you're using AWS, then chances are you're going to use the S3 backend, while someone on Azure will likely use the AzureRM backend, which uses the Azure Storage platform.

There are also specialized systems for running Terraform. These are often referred to as TACOS (Terraform Automation and Collaboration Software). These systems provide state management and some continuous integration/continuous delivery (CI/CD) tools (which will be a topic we get into in depth in the next chapter). If you happen to use one of these, you'll end up using the remote or cloud backend instead.

The point is that choosing a backend isn't something you really spend a lot of time doing. It's generally best to stick with the technology you're already using, and if you aren't using any of these technologies already, you should pick the one your team is most familiar with (see table 6.1).

Table 6.1   Terraform backends

Backend	System	Workspaces	Notes
local	Local Filesystem	Yes	Should never be used in production.
azurerm	Azure	Yes	A good option if you're already using Azure.
consul	Consul	Yes	A good option for self-hosting, especially if Consul is configured for high availability.
cos	Tencent	Yes	A good option if you're already using Tencent.
gcs	Google Cloud Storage	Yes	A good option if you're already using GCP.
http	Custom HTTP API	No	Allows developers to build their own backend with a simple HTTP-based API.
kubernetes	Kubernetes Secrets	Yes	Avoid using before the Terraform release v1.6 due to limits in how large the state can become in those earlier versions.

Table 6.1   Terraform backends (*continued*)

Backend	System	Workspaces	Notes
oss	Alibaba Cloud	Yes	Uses the Alibaba Cloud Table Store for locking.
pg	PostgreSQL	Yes	Allows users to store state in a SQL database.
s3	AWS S3	Yes	Requires DynamoDB for locking, which makes it unsuitable for Wasabi or other S3 emulation systems.
remote	Terraform Enterprise	Yes	Originally created for Terraform Enterprise, this backend is being replaced by the `cloud` block.
cloud	TACOS	No	The `cloud` block is more than just a backend, as it allows for controlling operations as well.

Regardless of what backend you use, you should make sure you review the official up-to-date documentation. When new versions of Terraform come out, you should also read the changelogs to confirm that your backend won't need any changes. The backend system in Terraform does tend to have regular changes that aren't backward compatible, so when performing an upgrade on Terraform, you should absolutely confirm that your backend configuration is still valid.

6.4.2   *Configuring the backend Itself*

We are not going to go into detail on how to configure each specific backend. They change fairly regularly and are all very well documented. There are, however, some important themes to consider when setting up your backend, before you actually have Terraform use it (see figure 6.1):

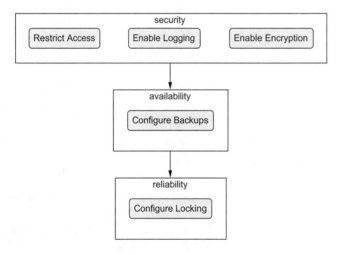

Figure 6.1   Basic backend configuration requirements

- Restrict access so your backend is only accessible by the people who need it. If you're using CI/CD pipelines to run production jobs, then there's no reason that developers should need state access.

- Enable logging of all access to the state so you can track any problems that come up.

- Create backups of your state, and make sure those backups are reliable. In the event of an emergency, you will be absolutely grateful for it.

- Enable encryption if the backend has it as an option. Many of them encrypt automatically, but others require it to be enabled explicitly.

- Enable locking if your backend requires explicit config for it. For many backends, this is automatic, but some (such as S3) require additional configuration. Never use a backend without locking or you'll risk corrupting your state.

How exactly you do this depends on the backend you're using. For some, such as the cloud backends, everything except the backups are built right in. With the backends you're managing yourself, whether that be a cloud backend (S3, GCP, AzureRM) or an even lower-level backend such as Consul where you're managing all the infrastructure yourself, it's important to read through their design and security documentation to make sure you're hitting all of the key points mentioned earlier.

> **NOTE** It's also very important to remember the golden rule of backups: if you haven't tested it recently, your backups are worthless. This is not a Terraform-specific lesson but one that you should take into account with every system you work on. Always test your backups, ideally on a regular basis, so you know they're available when you need them.

Without regular testing, you can never be sure that your backups work. Even if they worked last month, it's possible that something has broken between then and now. At the same time, it's important that your team knows what to do if backups are needed, and testing backups is a great opportunity to test your general disaster recovery posture.

6.4.3 Backend block

The configuration for backends starts with the Terraform `backend` block. This is a block inside of the Terraform settings block that should only be defined in your root-level module. This block is where the configuration for your backend goes.

Each backend has its own distinct parameters. Depending on which one you're using, you'll need to review the documentation and pick out the best parameters for you. In most cases, the parameters include something to identify your project, and for many you need some sort of authentication values. Just like providers, backends can normally use a variety of authentication methods that are specific to the backend. If you're using a cloud provider, such as GCP, Azure, or AWS, then their default environment variables and file system configuration will also apply to the backends.

Rather than use one of the cloud vendors, we're going to start by using Consul. Consul is another application made by HashiCorp that includes a service mesh (which isn't needed here) and a key/value store. The key/value store is used to store and manage configuration values, and Terraform can use it as a backend to store state. Consul is one of the backends that you manage yourself, and you can even run it locally to test your backend storage.

To run Consul locally, we're going to use `docker compose`. This is a really popular tool that lets you create reusable environments. We're going to use this along with the HashiCorp Consul image to launch Consul locally. First we need to create our docker compose file.

Listing 6.7   Terraform `backend` block with Consul

```
services:
  consul:
    image: hashicorp/consul:latest
    volumes:
      - consul-data:/consul/data
    environment:
      - CONSUL_HTTP_TOKEN="01a56e2d-a96a-4ca5-9d39-d5152015f533"
    ports:
      - 8500:8500/tcp

volumes:
  consul-data:
```

We want to pull the latest version of the Hashicorp Consul image.

A volume allows us to upgrade the container without losing our state.

This token was created with the uuidgen shell utility.

In the same directory as that file, we need to run a command to launch our services. If you haven't installed Docker yet, you should do so. The Docker website (https://docs.docker.com/engine/install/) has installation instructions for most systems. Once installed, run this command:

```
docker compose up -d
```

Now you will have a copy of Consul running locally that you can use for testing. Our next step is to configure our backend. To do this, we create a `terraform` block with a `backend` block inside of it. The `backend` block needs to be labeled `consul` to tell Terraform that's the backend we want to use. Inside the `backend` block we need to put our Consul-specific configuration, which includes the host address for Consul and the access token we used in our docker compose file.

Listing 6.8   Terraform `backend` block with Consul

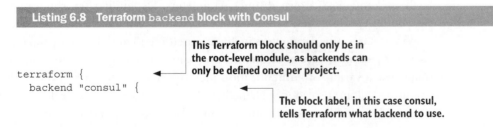

This Terraform block should only be in the root-level module, as backends can only be defined once per project.

```
terraform {
  backend "consul" {
```

The block label, in this case consul, tells Terraform what backend to use.

All of these options are Consul specific, and other backends use their own parameters.

```
address      = "localhost:8500"
scheme       = "http"
path         = "path/to/save/state"
access_token = "01a56e2d-a96a-4ca5-9d39-d5152015f533"
  }
}
```

This should normally be https for security reasons, but we're running Consul locally.

Hardcoding credentials is a very bad practice. We'll discuss how to avoid this in the next example.

You may have noticed that there are parameters for backends that don't make sense to hardcode. It's bad practice to commit credentials into your code repositories, and you often want your parameters to be flexible so your code can power multiple environments. Terraform supports that by allowing you to define partial configurations in your code, with the expectation that you'll fill in the rest of the parameters using another method.

Since there are very few parameters that should actually be hardcoded, it's extremely common for the `backend` block to be completely empty. Terraform still needs that block to exist so it knows what backend to use, so it can't be excluded.

Listing 6.9   Terraform partial configuration

```
terraform {
  backend "consul" {
    scheme = "https"
  }
}
```

In this case, we've removed the address, path, and access_token so we can define them for each project.

If we wanted to enforce https we could hard code it here.

When using a partial configuration, Terraform needs to pull the data in from another source. By default, it will directly ask you for the data using an interactive prompt, but this behavior is rarely desired. Instead, you can specify Terraform variable files to load into the backend using the `-backend-config` flag. The command takes a path to a `tfvars` file as a required argument:

```
terraform init -backend-config=PATH
```

Listing 6.10   Terraform backend configuration file

Moving the address to our backend config file makes it easier to deploy in test environments.

```
address      = "localhost:8500"
path         = "path/to/save/state"
access_token = "01a56e2d-a96a-4ca5-9d39-d5152015f533"
```

Each project will end up with a different path to specify a unique state file.

Sensitive data in tfvars files is still dangerous, but there's an alternative in 6.4.4.

It is also possible to pass parameters to Terraform using command-line flags. This method is not as secure though, as commands are often saved in your shell history or presented in logs. This is less of a concern if you're only passing in identifying information but should be remembered for things like passwords and authentication tokens.

Listing 6.11   Terraform backend command-line configuration

```
terraform init \
  -backend-config="address=localhost:8500" \          Each project needs its
  -backend-config="path=path/to/save/state" \         own unique path.
  -backend-config="access_token=01a56e2d-a96a-4ca5-9d39-d5152015f533"
```

Sensitive values in CLI flags can be dangerous as commands are often logged.

These methods are all interchangeable. If you use multiple methods, Terraform will prioritize the command-line flags over the configuration file. If, for some reason, you use the same configuration value in the command line more than once, then Terraform will use the last one defined in the command.

Regardless of what method you use, these parameters do get saved on disk in the `.terraform` directory. This allows them to be used between runs of `terraform plan` and `terraform apply` without having to be set each time. It also allows Terraform to notice when the backend changes, which will allow it to help you migrate your state (which we'll discuss in section 6.4.6 of this chapter). This also means that if you're using this method to pass authentication data to the backend, your credentials are now saved in that directory. In chapter 7, we'll discuss a few ways to keep that more secure.

6.4.4   *Alternative authentication methods*

All of the backends, with the exception of the local backend, expect some level of authentication. The problem is that every backend tends to do this a bit differently, as every backend is accessing the systems and APIs of a different vendor. As we've seen in the previous section, it is possible for many backends to hardcode your authentication methods, but that is hardly a secure way to handle things.

The good news is that for most backends there are other ways to pass authentication along. The bad news is that it's different for every backend. In general, though, you have three choices:

- Hardcode your authentication into your `backend` block or configuration files
- Utilize a configuration file (controlled outside of Terraform)
- Use environment variables to configure authentication

In general, you should avoid the first option, as hardcoding configuration makes your code less portable and can be insecure. The second option is very common when working alongside cloud providers. Azure, GCP, and AWS can all use local configuration files, and if those configuration files are in the default location, then Terraform will pick them up and use them. The third option, environment variables, tends to be used more in CI/CD settings (as we'll get into in the next chapter). Most CI/CD systems expose secrets using environment variables, which makes them a natural place to store authentication data. Since every backend handles this a bit differently, you should make sure to review the documentation for the backend you choose.

6.4.5 *Cloud block*

The Terraform `cloud` block is used for a special kind of backend. Unlike other backends, which are designed to allow Terraform to access other standard storage methods, the cloud backend defines a standard that other services can use to create a backend. This lets third parties build out systems that Terraform can integrate with without having to reprogram Terraform itself.

In that regard, it is very similar to the HTTP backend, which lets developers build out their own REST-based backend. The `cloud` block allows for much more complex behavior beyond just state storage though, such as enabling command-line interface (CLI)-driven runs that take place on third-party systems. To put it that another way, when running Terraform using the normal backends, all of the work is still done on the machine running Terraform. The `cloud` block not only configures a backend for state storage but also overrides the `plan` and `apply` operations (but not others like `import` or the various `state` commands) so that they are run remotely.

This is a fairly powerful feature, as it allows people to develop locally while sharing a centrally managed configuration. It also lets people test their code in the same systems they'd use to deploy them. This is a discussion we'll get into in the next chapter, which is focused on CI/CD systems.

When configuring the `cloud` block, you should specify the cloud service you want to connect to. This is one of the few areas where HashiCorp Terraform and OpenTofu differ slightly. With HashiCorp Terraform, this defaults to Terraform Cloud, while OpenTofu does not specify a specific vendor as the default. You also need to tell Terraform how to pick up your workspaces, which can be done either by specifying tags or a name.

Using tags opens up a lot of extra features for you, most of which are centered around the `terraform workspace` command. If you specify tags, then you can switch between workspaces using the `terraform workspace` command. This can be helpful if you're managing a lot of infrastructure with the exact same Terraform project.

> **NOTE** The `terraform workspace` command works differently when you're using the cloud backend than otherwise. When you aren't using the `cloud` block, Terraform treats workspaces as separate pieces of state based on the same code, but the `cloud` block links workspaces to distinct environments inside of HashiCorp Cloud. This is a constant source of confusion for developers. The use of the cloud backend tends to be very entwined with the HashiCorp Terraform product.

Listing 6.12   Terraform `cloud` block with tags

```
terraform {
  cloud {
    organization = "acme-org"
    hostname     = "app.terraform.io"

    workspaces {
      tags = ["acme_application", "development"]
    }
  }
}
    hostname     = "app.terraform.io"

    workspaces {
      tags = ["acme_application", "development"]
    }
  }
}
```

This field is required with OpenTofu but with Hashicorp Terraform it defaults to app.terraform.io.

When Tags are used the terraform workspace command can be used to switch between matching workspaces.

This field is required with OpenTofu but with Hashicorp Terraform it defaults to app.terraform.io.

When tags are used the terraform workspace command can be used to switch between matching workspaces.

It is also possible to specify a specific workspace when you use the name field to specify a single specific workspace. This disables the `terraform workspace` command and locks you into the single workspace you've configured.

Listing 6.13   Terraform `cloud` block with named project

```
terraform {
  cloud {
    organization = "acme-org"
    hostname     = "acme.scalr.io"

    workspaces {
      name = "acme_development_workspace"
    }
  }
}
```

The cloud block works with vendors like Scalr, not just with Hashicorp.

When a name is provided then only that workspace can be managed and the terraform workspace command will not function.

You may have noticed that there are no credentials in this block. Once you've configured this block, you should run the `terraform login` command. Just like the `cloud` block itself, you should specify the hostname to log into. This should be the same hostname that you configured your `cloud` block for:

```
terraform login acme.scalr.io
```

Once run, this command will force you to log in through the cloud service, after which it will save an authentication token to disk. Terraform will automatically read that token when it runs, allowing you to run Terraform commands locally against your cloud service without having to hardcode credentials.

The first vendor to support the `cloud` block was HashiCorp with its Terraform Cloud product. Since then, other groups such as Scalr and Env0 have adopted it for their own services. The next chapter will talk about these different systems, as well as other speciality Terraform systems.

6.4.6 *Migrating backends*

One thing you may be wondering is what happens if you want to change your backend. You might start a project using S3 and decide you want to move to a more Terraform-specific environment, or you may even want to migrate your state from one S3 bucket to a different one. There are a lot of reasons why you might decide to move from one backend to another, most of which will be driven by team and organization concerns more than technical ones.

The good news is that Terraform makes it extremely easy to migrate state from one backend to another. When you run `terraform init` (with or without a backend configuration file), Terraform saves the information for your backend in the `.terraform` directory. If you change your backend configuration, either with small configuration changes or a complete change to a different backend, Terraform will notice it the next time you run `terraform init` and will fail with an error and a helpful message to use the `-migrate-state` flag if you want to migrate your state or use the `-reconfigure` flag if you want to discard state and start fresh with the new backend.

It's important to note that Terraform will only migrate the current version of the state. If you happen to use a system that saves multiple versions, you will have to migrate them yourself, and how you do that will depend on the backend systems you are using. Since in most cases these older state versions primarily exist as a backup in case of corruption, you may find that you don't need to migrate those older versions at all, although I do recommend at least backing them up in case you find you need them later.

6.4.7 *Workspaces*

Workspaces are instances of your configuration that utilize the same code, plugins, and modules but have a different set of state. Workspaces can be managed with the `terraform workspace` subcommand. That command has four commands of its own:

- `terraform workspace list` presents a list of available workspaces.
- `terraform workspace new` allows you to create a new workspace.
- `terraform workspace delete` deletes an existing workspace.
- `terraform workspace select` switches to the specified workspace.

When using workspaces, Terraform defines a special global variable that you can access in your code, `terraform.workspace`. This variable is available during plan, which means it can be used with `count` and `for_each` parameters. This allows you to make decisions based on the workspace name, such as reducing the number of resources if your workspace begins with `dev-`.

Listing 6.14 Terraform workspace interpolation

```
locals {
  networks = {
```
◄─── **Sometimes people put settings directly in code instead of using variables.**

```
    "production" : {
      "vpc" : "vpc-e32ffed2c1e50a63",
      "subnets" : [
        "subnet-567da47a5d96d615",
        "subnet-cdb086048b5390d3",
        "subnet-2929ff68ae6bd378",
        "subnet-b16fa52dc74c5f01"
      ]
    },
    "staging" : {
      "vpc" : "vpc-82504ae9e1ecc804",
      "subnets" : [
        "subnet-ebefe1990b376f42",
        "subnet-02634d1bfd9aa148"
      ]
    },
    "default" : {
      "vpc" : "vpc-a19de3767f7478f4",
      "subnets" : [
        "subnet-7d68bda996b35683",
        "subnet-fd9e97e6e0bbe4ff"
      ]
    }
  }

  current_network = local.networks[terraform.workspace]
}
```

Each key should correspond to a workspace.

Different environments tend to use different networks.

It's a good idea to set a default, since this is what local development will use.

We populate our current settings from our big list using the workspace variable.

NOTE   One of the most confusing decisions that HashiCorp has made when creating Terraform and Terraform Cloud was the use of the word "workspaces" to discuss what are essentially two different systems. The original workspaces that we've been discussing so far share a lot of resources, including the code to actually run. In Terraform Cloud, workspaces are all completely independent of each other.

When you switch workspaces on one of the cloud-block-based backends, you are not keeping the same code or modules that you might expect. When you use the cloud block, the terraform workspace command changes. Instead of referring to the standard workspace feature, they start to work with the cloud version of the workspaces. If you're looking to use workspaces for local development but are also using Terraform Cloud, you may want to develop with the local backend instead.

6.4.8   *Upgrading backends*

Terraform backends do have differences between versions, and it's one of the areas where backward compatibility is not guaranteed. Terraform v1.3 removed several legacy backends that didn't support state locking.

Since Terraform backends are built directly into Terraform itself, you are always upgrading backends whenever you upgrade Terraform. The vast majority of the time there are no changes to be made. Sometimes, however, parameters change or get added. When this occurs, you may need to change some of your backend settings. This is why it is always important to read the upgrade notes when switching between versions of Terraform, as some of the changes in the backend could require you to make some changes on your own side.

6.5 *Manipulating state*

There are many reasons why you may want to change state. You may find that resources would be better with different names but don't want Terraform to destroy and re-create the resource under the new name. You might want to remove something from Terraform's control without destroying it or add a new resource into the state that Terraform didn't previously control. The important distinguishing part of these actions is the goal to change state without changing infrastructure itself.

Terraform offers several ways to change state without changing the controlled infra-structure. With Terraform, you can manipulate state directly from Terraform code, or you can do it using the CLI. If you're particularly brave (and desperate), you can even manipulate the state directly, although this is really a last resort.

6.5.1 *Backup and restore*

Before you even consider making changes to your state, you should make sure you back up the existing state. This is absolutely critical, as manipulating state is a poten-tially destructive action and you want the safety net of a backup in place.

The good news is that Terraform makes this very easy with the `terraform state pull` command. This command will grab the latest version of the state from your backend and dump it directly to `stdout`. This allows you to view the state yourself, or more com-monly it allows you to save the state to your own file. For example, if you wanted to pull the state down from the backend and save it to the file `my_backup.tfstate`, you'd run the following command:

```
terraform state pull > my_backup.tfstate
```

With this file, you can revert any change you've made to the state by using the `terraform state push` command. As the name implies, this allows you to take a local state file and push it up to the backend. This command can work either by specifying a file as an argument or by piping the command in through `stdin`. To restore our backup from the file we saved earlier, we can run either of the following commands, as they both do the same thing:

```
cat my_backup.tfstate | terraform state push
terraform state push my_backup.tfstate
```

One thing to note is that `terraform state push` has some protections in it. If you attempt to push a state that has a different lineage or that has a lower serial than the one in the backend, the command will fail. If you're trying to restore a backup as a way to revert the state file after having made changes, you'll need to use the `-force` flag to bypass those projects:

```
terraform state push -force my_backup.tfstate
```

6.5.2   *Code-driven changes*

The best way to make state changes is to do it right in your code. One of the most common reasons to edit state is because you want to refactor a module and relocate resources from one place to another. This might mean changing the name of a resource, or it could include taking a resource from the root-level module and placing it inside of a new module. When this occurs, you have to migrate the already-existing resources to the new location or Terraform will destroy and re-create them. The other common reason to edit state is to remove something from state without destroying it, which is what would happen if you simply deleted the resource from your code. Terraform introduced the `moved` block, and later the `removed` block, to address these problems.

The `moved` block is a special block that lets Terraform know that a resource has changed from one location to another. The block has two parameters, `to` and `from`, which tell Terraform where it should update resources. The block will only be processed when the `from` resource exists in state, so after the first migration occurs, the block stops doing anything.

The `removed` block also takes the `from` parameter—only this time it just removes the resource from state instead of relocating it. You are also required to define the `lifecycle` block to specify whether to `destroy` the resource or not.

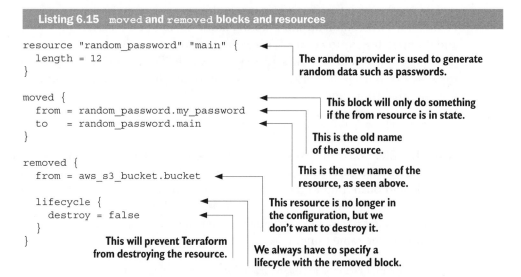

Listing 6.15   `moved` and `removed` blocks and resources

```
resource "random_password" "main" {
  length = 12
}
```
The random provider is used to generate random data such as passwords.

```
moved {
  from = random_password.my_password
  to   = random_password.main
}
```
This block will only do something if the from resource is in state.

This is the old name of the resource.

This is the new name of the resource, as seen above.

```
removed {
  from = aws_s3_bucket.bucket

  lifecycle {
    destroy = false
  }
}
```
This resource is no longer in the configuration, but we don't want to destroy it.

This will prevent Terraform from destroying the resource.

We always have to specify a lifecycle with the removed block.

The `moved` block works the same for modules as it does for resources. This makes it possible for you to move resources out of your main module and into child modules, which can be useful as your projects evolve.

Listing 6.16   `moved` block and modules

```
module "password" {
  source = "./modules/password"
}
```
Our resource now lives inside of the module.

This block will only do something if the from resource is in state.

```
moved {
  from = random_password.my_password
  to   = module.password.random_password.main
}
```

This is the old name of the resource.

This is where the resource now lives.

The `moved` block is useful because it will automatically work for every environment using your modules. When you're developing shared modules, the `moved` block is critical as it allows you to freely modify the internals of your module without forcing your module users into painful upgrade situations.

6.5.3 CLI-driven changes

Terraform has a variety of commands you can use to manipulate state. This is the second-best way to manage state changes: if possible, you should use code, rather than the CLI, to make changes. That being said, there are a few things that can't easily be done in code, and the CLI is much better than attempting to manually edit the state.

Before Terraform introduced the `removed` block, we used to have to use a special command to remove things from state without destroying them. If you attempt to remove a resource from your code, Terraform will see that and attempt to remove the infrastructure itself, and while that does remove it from state, you may not want to actually destroy the infrastructure itself.

There are a few times when this can come up. Later in this chapter, we're going to talk about how to access resources from the state of other projects, so that you can split your resources into multiple Terraform projects that work together instead of one large project. If you were migrating from a single Terraform project to multiple, there may be resources, such as databases, that you don't want to destroy.

The `terraform state rm` command lets you remove resources from Terraform state without making any real-world changes to infrastructure. Running this command keeps the corresponding infrastructure intact while removing the corresponding resource from state. It's important to note, though, that if you don't also make a change in your code, Terraform will attempt to create the resource again in the next run.

Listing 6.17 Removing resource from state

The terraform state list command is useful for finding the addresses of resources.

```
$ terraform state list
module.my_password.data.null_data_source.values
module.my_password.random_password.main

$ terraform state rm module.my_password.random_password.new_password
Removed module.my_password.random_password.new_password
Successfully removed 1 resource instance(s).
```

Using the address above we remove this resource from our state file.

Another case for using the CLI is if you ever need to migrate from one provider to another to control the same resources. As we saw earlier in this chapter, Terraform records the provider used when a resource is created in state. If you change providers, you may find that Terraform throws an error.

A big question you might be asking is: When would I ever change providers? It is honestly something that is extremely rare. The most common example is if you're ever testing development versions of a provider. This may be a provider your team is developing or a development version of a third-party provider. Either way, you may find yourself wanting to switch to that other provider and back again once done testing, but to do that you need to update your resources in state.

The `terraform state replace-provider` command makes this really easy. The command takes two arguments: the provider you are currently using and the provider you want to replace it with. Terraform will then update your state for you, giving you the option to approve the changes before they're applied:

```
terraform state replace-provider hashicorp/random registry.custom_registry.
io/hashicorp/random
```

Terraform also has commands for moving an item in state and another for importing items, `terraform import` and `terraform state mv`. However, there really isn't any good reason for using them now that the `moved` and `import` blocks exist. These commands have existed for almost as long as Terraform has, so they are unlikely to be removed any time soon, but, as a rule, if you find yourself about to use either of these commands, you should strongly consider going back a section and looking at the `moved` block or skipping ahead to chapter 8 for the `import` block.

6.5.4   *Manually editing*

The final way of manipulating state is by manually editing a state file. This should be considered the method of last resort, and it should only be done if you can't accomplish your goals with the other tools. For example, if you find that your state has been corrupted for some reason, you may revert to editing it manually in an attempt to recover. To do this you need to run the `terraform state pull` command to pull the state down locally, modify your state, and then save the state with the `terraform state push` command.

Editing your state manually is a very bad idea. With the Terraform CLI and code-driven changes, Terraform does most of the work. It ensures that your state matches the expected data structure and formatting while also being easily repeatable (if you're using the CLI, you can share the commands, and if you're using the `moved` block, the changes are stored right in your code). When you manually edit state, you introduce a lot more uncertainty and potential errors while losing that repeatability. It's possible that you could misformat your state so that it can't be read at all, as the JSON format is not very forgiving. You could also accidentally remove a resource or relationship that's important, causing Terraform to attempt to re-create an already-existing resource.

If you decide to ignore this advice and move forward anyway, be careful. Make sure you have a backup, run your changes through a JSON validator, and compare the differences between your backup and your changed files to see if you missed anything. You should also consider incrementing the serial field by 1 so you don't have to use the `force` option. This way, other error checking in the command will still occur.

6.6 State drift

State drift occurs when changes to your infrastructure occur outside of Terraform and thus aren't saved in the state. State drift is typically detected when Terraform runs a refresh, either at the start of a plan or with the `terraform refresh` command (which, if you remember, should be avoided for the newer `terraform plan --refresh-only` command). When state drift occurs, Terraform will create a plan that brings the system back in line with the Terraform configuration.

State drift is often a symptom of another problem though. Infrastructure rarely changes by itself, and when it does it should be in a predictable way that can be accounted for in code. When state drift is detected, it is important to identify why it occurred so you can correct the underlying problem at the source.

The first question you should ask yourself when state drift is detected is: What changed and why? The answers are going to change how you respond. Discovering the actual source of the drift can be a bit of a challenge and will require understanding the underlying system itself, reviewing logs to see when the change occurred and what it was triggered by, and communicating with the rest of your team to understand what recent changes were made that may have caused it.

Once you've identified the problem, you can begin to resolve it. In general, there are four categories of state drift errors, shown in figure 6.2.

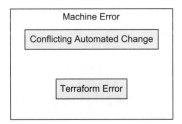
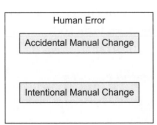

Figure 6.2
Types of state drift

These are categories of errors, not specific errors, and they can each have their own variety of sources. When you've identified the specific error that caused the drift, you can identify what category it fits into and use that to put a solution together.

6.6.1 Accidental manual changes

One of the more common error types is simple human error. A developer could log into the wrong account, run the wrong command, or do any number of things to accidentally change infrastructure when they didn't mean to.

When this occurs, it's important to remember that this isn't the fault of the individual who made the mistake but instead is a problem with the systems around them. Humans are not perfect, and they make mistakes, so it's important to bake that fact into all of your designs and systems. Restricting access to production accounts, enforcing the use of CI/CD, and putting in policies around manual changes will reduce the likelihood of these errors occurring.

When they do occur, it's important not to freak out, as these are often the easiest errors to fix. The vast majority of the time, a `terraform plan` will figure out exactly how to fix the infrastructure.

6.6.2 *Intentional manual changes*

A similar but more complicated problem is when someone manually changes the infrastructure outside of Terraform. What makes this more complicated is that someone wanted the change to happen. Generally speaking, people only make manual changes if it's important, such as when an on-call engineer gets a call that something is down. Their goal is to resolve things quickly, but their fixes could be reverted once Terraform runs again.

One way to avoid this problem is with a policy that all changes need to occur using Terraform, regardless of the reason the change is being made. Depending on the team, this may get a lot of resistance, but with a team that has a solid deployment pipeline (which we'll discuss more in the next chapter), it's often easier to change systems with Terraform than it is to do so manually.

Even with that policy, there may be cases where someone makes a manual change, or a team may be in a place where their pipelines aren't stable enough to rely on. When this happens, it's important to get the infrastructure changes represented in Terraform as quickly as possible. Until that is done, any Terraform run will revert those changes to match what is in the Terraform code. As a result, it's not safe to run Terraform until the changes are back in the code.

6.6.3 *Conflicting automated changes*

Another common problem occurs when the state of managed resources changes in a way that's actually expected:

- New artifacts, such as machine images or container images, could be published and detected by data sources.
- External systems could add their own tags or annotations to resources, which can be common when using virtual machines with other orchestration systems.
- Autoscaling systems could be at a different task or machine level than when originally launched.
- Versions could have changed due to automatic updates, such as when AWS Relational Database Service (RDS) upgrades minor database versions during maintenance windows.

All of these are expected and can't really by themselves be considered errors. They should be handled properly though. In general, you have two options for these types of state drift: apply them or ignore them. When it comes to new artifacts, for instance, you might decide that the best thing to do is have all of the relevant resources (virtual machines, container runs, functions as a service, etc.) get redeployed with the latest resource. It's also perfectly valid to say that once a resource is launched, it should not be updated if specific attributes change.

This is the primary reason that the `ignore_changes` lifecycle rule was created for, as it lets you ignore changes to specific attributes so that they aren't updated. It is extremely common to use this for attributes that point at artifacts and for the desired count that is typically present in auto-scaling groups.

Listing 6.18 Ignoring changes

```
resource "aws_instance" "main" {
  tags = {
    Name        = var.name
    Application = var.application
  }

  lifecycle {
    ignore_changes = [tags]
  }
}
```

Tags are regularly used to attach metadata to instances.

The name tag is special in AWS, as it makes the name visible in the console.

A lot of teams use application tags to track expenses.

If the tags change outside of Terraform we will ignore that change.

For some attributes that change automatically, there isn't anything that needs to be done at all. Thinking about the RDS example from earlier, there really isn't a problem that comes from the state drift. A refresh-only plan will bring the state up to date again.

6.6.4 Terraform errors

By far the biggest and most annoying case that can occur is when Terraform itself has an error or fails. There are several ways this can occur:

- Terraform crashes before it can save the state.
- The machine or container running Terraform has an error.
- Terraform saves a corrupted version of state.
- Terraform authentication to the backend expires.

Most of the time these errors result in an outdated state, as Terraform makes changes but those changes aren't persisted to the backend. When this happens, you have to review your logs to see if Terraform created any resources. Terraform is pretty smart, but it cannot automatically associate resources with state unless it created them. If Terraform creates a resource and then fails to save that resource to state, then it won't know that resource exists in future runs. When this occurs, Terraform will attempt to create a brand-new resource. When this happens, your best-case scenario is that it simply wastes money as you pay for a resource that you aren't using, while the worst-case scenario is that it blocks you from deploying or causes your existing system to fail.

To solve this, you need to review the logs, identify the resources that were created, and then mediate them. This can mean either running `terraform import` to bring the resource into your state or manually deleting the resource so that Terraform can safely create a new one.

Although it is rare, it is also possible for the state to get corrupted. When this occurs, Terraform will not be able to function at all, as it won't be able to read the existing state. When this happens, your only option is to restore to a backup. This is one reason why most backends support some method for versioning, although even with versioning it's important to take external backups as well in case your overall system goes down.

6.7   *Accessing state across projects*

As projects end up managing more and more resources, there is a performance hit that comes into play. Every time you run a plan, Terraform has to go through a refresh and then compare the results to your configuration. For small projects, this can happen pretty quickly, but when projects get into the hundreds or even thousands of resources, this can really add up. Splitting a project up into multiple smaller projects can let developers iterate faster, at the cost of having to manage more projects and coordinate data between them.

Even outside of large projects, there are times when splitting up a project can improve performance. Although many cloud resources are very rapidly deployed, there are some that take an extremely long time and force developers to wait. Cloud databases are fairly notorious for this, and this can drive a team to split out their database needs into a separate project from the rest of their application.

More often than performance, however, is Conway's law: the idea that "The structure of any system designed by an organization is isomorphic to the structure of the organization." As companies grow and evolve, they tend to split into more teams and more realms of responsibility. In a small company or startup, one team may be responsible for everything, but as companies grow, it's more common to see groups take responsibility in certain areas. It's pretty common for large companies to have network, security, DNS, and database teams (as well as many others) that are responsible for those respective areas. In companies with this structure, it's common for teams to not directly manage their own network infrastructure, so they need a way to retrieve values like their virtual private cloud ID to use in their own systems (see figure 6.3).

6.7.1   *terraform_remote_state*

Accessing remote state is most commonly done with the `terraform_remote_state` data source. This data source is built directly into Terraform itself and does not come from a separate provider. It allows you to read the outputs of another Terraform state and bring them into your code. It is a read-only operation that does not change the other state in any way.

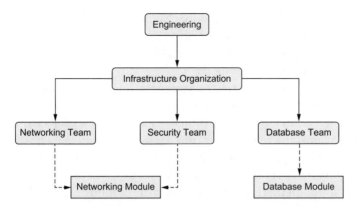

Figure 6.3   An example of how organization structure can mirror module ownership

When using `terraform_remote_state`, you have to configure a backend. This takes a different format than the generic `backend` block. There are two parameters, `backend` and `config`, that control the backend settings. The `backend` expects a string specifying which backend to use. The `config` parameter expects an object with the settings for the backend. In theory, the `config` parameter is optional, but you'll need to use it in pretty much any case where it would actually be useful to you. The exact keys for the configuration depends on the specific backend you're using.

Listing 6.19   Reading an RDS instance from another state

```
data "terraform_remote_state" "rds" {       ◀──        This resource reads from the
  backend = "s3"                        ◀──             state of other projects.

  config = {                                    ◀──     The backend can be any
    bucket = var.state_bucket_name                      Terraform backend.
    key    = var.rds_state_path
    region = var.state_region                           Each backend will have its own
  }                                                     configuration requirements.
}
                                                        This example module is a child
                                                        module that runs locally.
module "service" {
  source = "./modules/service"           ◀──            In our mock example we pass an image
  image  = "my_example_image"         ◀──               name that points to a container.
  env = {
    rds_uri : data.terraform_remote_state.rds.outputs.rds_uri  ◀──
  }                                             We pass the output from the
}                                               other project in to our service.

                                                Services usually get information
                                                from environment variables.
```

An extremely important thing to remember is that the state you are reading has to come from a project that exposes outputs from the top-level module that you can use.

If you need to access the RDS Amazon Resource Name (ARN), like we did earlier, the state file that generated the RDS instance needs to return the ARN as an output, as we see in listing 6.19 where the output of `data.terraform_remote_state.rds` is passed to the `module.service` environment parameter..

If possible, you should use the `defaults` parameter of `terraform_remote_state`. This parameter allows you to set values for if the remote state you're accessing is either missing the outputs or is completely empty (which occurs with new projects). This turns a hard dependency against the remote state, where you can't even launch your project until the remote project is up, into a soft dependency where you can set up resources and then later update when the other project is ready. This gives you a bit more robustness and flexibility, although there may be cases where it simply isn't possible.

Listing 6.20   Defaults

```
data "terraform_remote_state" "rds" {
  backend = "s3"

  config = {
    bucket = var.state_bucket_name
    key    = var.rds_state_path
    region = var.state_region
  }

  defaults = {
    rds_uri : null
  }
}
```

By setting these values we make sure it is present even if the remote state does not have it.

A null value makes it so the output will exist, although it will be null.

6.7.2   *Structuring for remote state*

Although `terraform_remote_state` is powerful, it is possible to use it in a way that makes your code less maintainable over time. When values come from other projects, it can sometimes be difficult to trace back where these values are coming from, especially during an error. The additional dependency on another project's state also makes your code less portable. There are some practices you can follow to avoid these pitfalls.

One method you can use is to treat your `terraform_remote_state` calls as another set of variables for your top-level module. In general, your top-level module is used to compose other modules together and has a more limited amount of direct logic in it. If you put your `terraform_remote_state` blocks in this top-level module, you can then feed the values into the modules with your actual logic. This keeps the `terraform_remote_state` out of those modules, which in turn makes them more reusable.

Listing 6.21   Remote state on the top-level module

```
data "terraform_remote_state" "network" {
  backend = "gcs"
```

The GCS backend is used by teams on Google Cloud Platform.

```
  config = {
    bucket = var.state_bucket_name
    prefix = var.network_prefix
  }
}
```

The configuration is similar, but slightly different, than the S3 configuration.

```
module "service" {
  source     = "./modules/service"
  image      = "my_example_image"
  vpc_id     = terraform_remote_state.network.outputs.vpc_id
  subnet_ids = terraform_remote_state.network.outputs.private_subnet_ids
}
```

Since we didn't use any defaults, Terraform will fail if these values aren't present.

Another option that can work nicely is playing all of your `terraform_remote_state` calls into dedicated modules. This can be tricky because of the backend configuration requirements, and it doesn't work well at all for modules you may want to open source. However, for modules that are only meant to be distributed inside of a single organization, these kinds of modules make more sense. If you have a team that generates networks separately from the rest of their infrastructure, for instance, they may create a module that makes it easier to read the state from those network projects.

Listing 6.22 Remote state with a shared module

```
variable "network_name" {
  type        = string
  description = "Name of the network to pull data in from."
}
```

This reusable module only needs a single variable instead of the full config.

```
data "terraform_remote_state" "network" {
  backend = "consul"

  config = {
    address = "consul.internal"
    scheme  = "https"
    path    = "terraform/state/networks/${var.network_name}"
  }
}
```

The team maintaining this can hardcode the server.

Since there is only one server the scheme can also be hardcoded.

The network name is added to complete the path to the state.

```
output "vpc_id" {
  value = data.terraform_remote_state.network.outputs.vpc_id
}
```

To make this available outside the module it has to be put in an output block.

```
output "private_subnet_ids" {
  value = data.terraform_remote_state.network.outputs.private_subnet_ids
}

output "public_subnet_ids" {
  value = data.terraform_remote_state.network.outputs.public_subnet_ids
}
```

6.7.3   *Alternatives to terraform_remote_state*

Before using remote state lookups, you should consider whether it really is the best approach. Allowing systems to access remote state brings up all of the problems that have been discussed in the security section: anyone with access to the state also has access to the attributes, including the sensitive values, that are in that state.

In general, people should first see if there are data sources that can be used to look up the resources instead of pulling the data from the remote state. For example, if you're pulling in the IP address of a database using state, you could do a lookup of that database instance using data sources. This allows your code to be a bit more standalone while still allowing you to offload the creation and management of the resource from the module you're working on.

The downside to this method is that it isn't always easy to look up the resources you want to. In some cases there aren't data sources you can use, or they don't allow lookups that are as precise as you'd like. In chapter 10, we discuss some tagging strategies you can use when creating resources to make it easier for lookups to occur, but in the event that this isn't an option, you'll need to consider other options or fall back to accessing remote state.

Another alternative is to use input variables to fill in the values that you were considering looking up. This method is more secure than granting access to the remote state, but it also requires a bit more work and maintenance to keep all the values up to date. In general, I recommend minimizing the number of variables you're pulling in this way and instead see if you can use data sources to pull the needed values in automatically for you.

6.8   *State-only resources*

In chapter 5, we made a certificate authority using the TLS provider. For this we created keys, signing requests, and certificates. The interesting thing about all of this is that we didn't connect to a third-party service: we didn't have to use external APIs and the resources weren't saved in files or on another system. Instead, everything for these resources was stored directly in state.

The TLS provider is an example of a state-only provider. State-only providers do not directly interact with other systems. Instead, they calculate their values programmatically and persist them in state.

6.8.1   *Random provider*

The `random` provider is probably the most-used state provider in the Terraform ecosystem. It is used to generate random data without having to regenerate that data every single time Terraform runs.

To understand why this is important, consider how most languages generate random data: via a function. Most languages have at least one function to generate randomness and often include entire libraries for it. The problem that Terraform would run into with this goes back to section 4.3.3 where we discussed pure versus impure functions.

Random functions are impure functions, in that they will return different results every time they run. That means that every Terraform plan would generate a change, essentially causing state drift every run.

The random resources instead persist their randomness between runs. They will create their random data the first time they are called and then will only change that data if a parameter named `keepers` changes. The `keepers` parameter is an object that can have any values you want, and if any of those values change, it will trigger the random resource to create new data.

Listing 6.23   Some random resources

```
resource "random_uuid" "example" {                    Create a UUID.

  keepers = {                                         Keepers are optional, but when provided they
    "name" = var.name                                 allow the random values to be regenerated.
  }
}                                                     If the input variable name ever changes
                                                      the number will be regenerated.
```

There are a lot of resources in the `random` provider. It can be used to generate bytes, integers, names (using the pets resource), or UUIDs. It can also be used to randomly shuffle lists of items.

Listing 6.24   More random resources

```
resource "random_integer" "number" {                 Create a number between 0 and 10,
  min = 0                                             based on our passed parameters.
  max = 10
}

output "number" {                                     The generated number is
  value = random_integer.number.result               saved in the result attribute.
}
                                                      This UUID will be generated
resource "random_uuid" "uuid" {                       once and then persisted.

}

output "uuid" {                                       The UUID Is In the
  value = random_uuid.uuid.result                     result attribute.
}
                                                      Creates human-readable
resource "random_pet" "uniqueish-suffix" {            names like "sage-longhorn"
  length = 2
}                                                     We are stating that our name
                                                      should include at least two words.
output "suffix" {
  value = random_pet.uniqueish-suffix.id              Unlike the other resources, random_pet
}                                                     saves the results in the id attribute.
```

There is also a special random resource called `random_password`. The `random_password` resource is the only resource in the provider that is guaranteed to use a cryptographic random number generator, which means that it can be used to create passwords. The attribute for the password is marked as `sensitive`, so it should not show up in logs and will present a warning if it is used as a root-level module output.

Listing 6.25   Random password

```
resource "random_password" "password" {      │  The length field is the
  length = 16                              ◄──┘  only required field.

  lower   = true
  numeric = true         These parameters allow you to
  special = true         disable certain types of characters.
  upper   = true

  min_lower   = 0
  min_numeric = 0        These parameters allow you to set
  min_special = 0        requirements for the generated password.
  min_upper   = 0

  override_special = "!@#$%&*()-_=+[]{}<>:?"  ◄──┐  You can also specify
}                                                │  which specific special
                                                 │  characters to include.
```

As a reminder, sensitive values do still get stored in state, so when you use the `random_password` resource to create actual credentials, you need to be extra careful about how you're storing your state and who can access it.

6.8.2   *Time provider*

The `time` provider allows you to record the time of events without causing state drift. Back in chapter 4, when we introduced functions, we discussed how using the `timestamp` function creates problems because it returns a different value each time. The `time` provider avoids this problem by only generating a timestamp on creation or if the `triggers` parameter changes (similar to how the random resources re-create their values if their `keepers` parameter changes).

The `time` provider has four resources, three of which are used to record times. The `time_offset`, `time_rotating`, and `time_static` resources all record times but work slightly differently. The `time_static` resource is the simplest, as it just records its creation time (and regenerates it when `triggers` changes).

The `time_rotating` resource takes parameters that tell it how long to keep its value. When Terraform runs, the resource checks to see if the time has expired, and if so it generates a new value. The `time_offset` value works similarly to `time_static` except it lets you specify a time: for example, you can tell it to set a time that's seven hours in the future and it will do so.

Listing 6.26 Time stamps with the `time` provider

```
resource "time_offset" "two_hours_after_now" {
  offset_hours = 2
}

resource "time_rotating" "every_two_days" {
  rotation_days = 2
}

resource "aws_instance" "rotating_machine" {

  lifecycle {
    replace_triggered_by = [time_rotating.every_two_days.id]
  }
}

resource "time_static" "on_creation" {
  triggers = {
    "name" = aws_instance.dependent.arn
  }
}

output "instance_last_update" {
  value = time_static.on_creation.rfc3339
}
```

This resource will record the current time plus any provided offsets.

The saved time will be two hours after the resource is created.

This resource will get updated by Terraform if more than two days has passed.

Truncating aws_instance attributes.

When the time_rotating resource is updated it will trigger a replacement of this resource.

This resource always stores the current timestamp.

The triggers parameter forces the timestamp to update if it ever changes. Lifecycle rules can also be used.

When the ARN of the instance changes, update this resource.

RFC3339 is a standard for saving dates as strings.

The `time` provider has a fourth resource, `time_sleep`, that can be used to delay execution in Terraform. As an example, let's say you have two AWS instances that you want to launch. The first one has to run some provisioning scripts, and you do not want the second machine to launch until those scripts have run. You can use a sleep resource between the first and second machine to add a delay.

Listing 6.27 Delaying resource creation with `time_sleep`

```
resource "aws_instance" "main" {
}

resource "time_sleep" "delay" {
  create_duration = "2m"

  depends_on = [aws_instance.main]
}

resource "aws_instance" "dependent" {
```

Truncating attributes for this example.

We want there to be a two-minute delay between aws_instance.main finishing and aws_instance.dependent starting.

This resource will not be created until aws_instance.main is created.

Truncating attributes for this example.

```
    depends_on = [time_sleep.delay]
}
```

◀———— **This dependency means that this resource won't be created until after time_sleep.delay finishes creation.**

6.8.3   *Null provider*

The `null` provider is one of my personal favorite providers, particularly when I'm try-ing to test out new automation or tools built on top of Terraform. It is a provider with a single resource, `null resource`, which creates resources that do absolutely noth-ing at all. They follow the complete resource lifecycle, in that they can be created, deleted, and updated, but they don't do anything outside of that. Unlike other state-only resources, the `null resource` doesn't even generate data. Although this seems fairly useless at first glance, the ability to do nothing (often called a "no op" in different languages, as in "no operation") gives developers a great tool for testing and allows for the use of some Terraform features without attaching them to a specific real resource.

Listing 6.28   `null resource`

```
resource "null_resource" "nothing" {
  triggers = {
    "rebuild" = timestamp()
  }
}
```

◀———— **This resource has a full lifecycle, but does absolutely nothing.**

◀———— **By setting the trigger to be the timestamp function we ensure this specific null_resource will get re-created every run.**

Up until Terraform v1.4, the `null resource` was primarily used to run custom provi-sioners. This is a feature of Terraform that allows you to run custom programs and scripts on machines; we go over that in chapter 8. The use of provisioners for the `null_resource` is an older practice though, and there are more modern ways to handle that. This means that the `null_resource` really does nothing.

This makes it a fantastic tool for testing generic flows that aren't tied to a specific project. When setting up CI/CD pipelines, generating code automatically, or building your own interfaces with Terraform, you need to have something to test with. Using real systems introduces another level of complexity that is not needed while testing these systems and generally makes the apply phase run longer. We talk about this more in chapters 10 and 11.

Utilizing the `null_resource` to build test workspaces allows you to run real Terra-form code quickly, which should make it easier for you to test your systems. You can take the previous example and use it as a root-level module without any need to configure providers since the default configuration just works. You can then use that to test your pipelines (whether they're in GitHub Actions or CircleCI or one of the TACOS like Terraform Cloud, Spacelift, or Env0) and state backend configuration independently of your actual infrastructure.

In the next chapter, we discuss CI/CD in detail. Keep the `null` provider in mind when you start building out the processes and workflows for your CI/CD platforms.

6.8.4 *terraform_data*

The `terraform_data` resource is a built-in resource that comes with Terraform itself, without the need for another provider. It was added in Terraform v1.4 and is meant as a replacement for the `null` provider. Just like the `null_resource`, the `terraform_data` resource implements the lifecycle of a resource without actually doing anything. Also just like the `null resource`, it can be used for testing and to run custom provisioners (which we discuss in chapter 8).

Listing 6.29 Replacing the `null resource` with `terraform_data`

```
resource "terraform_data" "nothing" {
  triggers_replace = {
    "rebuild" = timestamp()
  }
}
```

This resource uses triggers_replace instead of triggers, but otherwise functions just like the null resource.

Just like in the null example, we're using a timestamp to force a re-creation each time.

The `terraform_data` resource can also be used to trigger replacements that would otherwise not be possible. The `replace_triggered_by lifecycle` parameter cannot take local or input variables as a value, which means that you're limited in the logic you can apply inside of a local.

Listing 6.30 Triggering resource replaced with `terraform_data`

```
variable "user_input" {
  type = number
}

locals {
  is_even = var.user_input % 2 == 0
}

resource "terraform_data" "local_replacement" {
  triggers_replace = {
    "is_even" = local.is_even
  }
}

resource "aws_instance" "myinstance" {
  lifecycle {
    replace_triggered_by = [terraform_data.local_replacement]
  }
}
```

If the local.is_even value changes then this resource is replaced.

If the terraform_data resource is replaced then replace this resource.

Even though we can't use locals directly we were able to use a local to trigger this replacement through terraform_data.

The final use of `terraform_data` is to manage provisioners. Provisioners are a feature of Terraform that allow you to write custom code that can run either locally or on a separate machine. They're often used, as the name suggests, to provision infrastructure after launching. We talk about these more in chapter 10.

Listing 6.31   Triggering provisioners with `terraform_data`

```
resource "aws_instance" "main" {
}

resource "time_sleep" "delay" {
  create_duration = "1m"
  depends_on      = [aws_instance.main]
}

resource "terraform_data" "provision" {
  depends_on = [time_sleep.delay]

  triggers_replace = {
    "ami" = aws_instance.main.arn
  }

  provisioner "run_script" {
    command = "provisioning_script.sh"
  }
}
```

◄— Like other examples we're truncating parameters here.

◄— Delay for one minute to make sure the instance has finished launching.

◄— This resource will not be created until the delay resource is finished.

◄— If the instance is replaced we want to rerun this script.

◄— The provisioner block lets us specify a script to run.

Although `terraform_data` can replace just about everything `null_resource` can, you are still likely to encounter `null_resource`. The `terraform_data` resource was added fairly recently, and the `null` provider has been installed over 9 million times in the first week of 2025.

Just like the `null` provider, the `terraform_data` source can also be used for testing CI/CD pipelines. In the next chapter, we explore how to apply CI/CD principles to our use of Terraform to increase the quality and security of the infrastructure it manages. This will build off our discussion of state storage to allow automated systems to access state so they can run Terraform in a centralized way.

Summary

- Terraform uses state to reduce complexity, improve performance, and provide functionality such as remote state viewing and state-only resources.
- When working with teams, a centralized state storage solution is essential, and this is provided by Terraform backends.
- Terraform backends are generally chosen from technology teams already using or through the use of specialized Terraform CI/CD tools.
- State drift occurs when the Terraform state does not match the real-world infrastructure.
- State can be accessed across projects, allowing the outputs from one project to be used in another project.
- State-only resources enable the use of data, such as the time or even random numbers, to be generated in a Terraform-centric way.

Code quality and continuous integration

Infrastructure as code (IaC) provides a number of benefits, but one of the biggest is that it allows the industry to apply the lessons learned from decades of software development to managing infrastructure. Software development has been around since the 1950s, and it's an understatement to say that it has evolved quite a bit since then. Not only have the languages software developers used grown to take on new complexity and functionality, but the tools they use have also grown to make tackling that complexity feasible.

When developing using the Terraform and OpenTofu languages, you are developing software. Developing high-quality software is not a trivial task though. To make

207

it easier, developers rely on tools, such as code linters (tools that look through your code for problems), formatters, and security scanners. Terraform is no exception to this. When working with Terraform, you have a number of tools at your disposal to help you create better software.

What exactly is high-quality software? Although this is by itself a huge topic, high-quality software has a few common features that make the project more pleasant to work with:

- Maintenance is low effort as the software follows standards and best practices.
- Adding new features is easy because the software is well structured.
- Introducing errors is harder because safety nets exist.
- Running common tasks, like linting or testing, is simple for developers.
- Documentation is accurate, complete, and up to date.

Building and maintaining high-quality software requires a bit of initial effort (which we'll discuss quite a bit in this chapter), but that effort is returned by making it easy to develop, expand, and use that software. In other words, or at least in words that product managers will appreciate, you can add features and fix problems faster in high-quality software than you can in lower-quality software, which makes your team go faster.

To put this in perspective, imagine yourself joining a new team. It's your first week on the job, and you're asked to add a new feature to a module. You're excited but nervous, as most people are when joining a new team.

Now imagine the worst-case scenario, where the team hasn't integrated the tools and safeguards needed. Without documentation, you have to read through all of the code to understand it. You know there are quality control tools out there that could help you, but you don't remember their commands and find yourself constantly looking them up. It's much easier for errors to get missed, and when that happens, it may break someone else's system. When you make a pull request (PR), the people reviewing it have no idea if the code works or not, and are giving you feedback on formatting while ignoring the actual functionality behind it. Developing features is stressful, and you don't have confidence or safeguards in place.

The good news is your new team put some effort into making it easy for developers to work on their projects. They have extensive documentation about their module. They used a tool called Make to save common commands so you didn't need to look them all up. They have several quality control tools to help you catch any errors and even use a tool that integrates into Git to make sure you don't forget to run those tools before you commit your code. Getting started is easy, and you have safeguards in place that give you confidence in the work you build. When you make a PR, all of these quality controls are run automatically and their status reported back to the team, blocking the PR immediately if a test happens to fail.

In this chapter, we go through the practices, systems, and tools to take your team to that high-performing level. We discuss how you can use software development tools such as Make to standardize commands across systems, while using built-in Terraform commands and third-party quality control systems to enforce standards and best practices. Then we're going to wrap it all up by automatically running and validating our PR to ensure our modules always have the highest quality.

7.1 Continuous integration practices

Continuous integration (CI) is one of the important lessons that comes out of the software development world, and it's one that comes up in almost every training session and conversation that I've had with people who are new to Terraform. CI is a software development practice where teams are easily able to merge their work into the mainline of a project regularly and thus do it very regularly. To do this, teams use tools that help test the quality of their code and often run those tools as a gate to merging code.

As a real-world example, there are millions of open source projects on GitHub. Many of them have built-in test suites and utilize GitHub Actions to automatically run those test suites whenever someone makes a PR. If the tests don't pass, then the code isn't merged. We can bring those same practices into our development with Terraform to improve our code quality and make it easier for others to work with our modules (see figure 7.1).

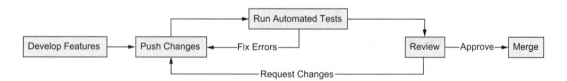

Figure 7.1   CI workflow

As important as CI is, it is not the entire story. In fact, CI is the end result of a larger journey. Systems such as Jenkins, GitHub Actions, GitLab Pipelines, CircleCI, and the huge number of other CI systems can't really do much by themselves. They primarily work by running the tests that teams build into their projects, as well as other third-party tools designed to help maintain software quality.

To put this another way, teams can't use CI until they build a proper code quality system into their projects. It isn't possible to automate tests until those tests are written, and even off-the-shelf code quality software has to be configured. That's why this chapter discusses both the code quality tools themselves as well as how to run them automatically. We talk about how we can enforce best practices and what tools are needed, and then close out the chapter by discussing how to run those tools automatically using CI systems.

In this chapter, we not only focus on CI systems themselves but also review the practices and tools that make it possible to develop high-quality code, culminating in using CI systems to enforce that code quality.

CI does not mean "we run tests before merging code." The goal of CI, regardless of what language you use, is to regularly integrate new features into the main build of the project. While the end result tends to differ among teams, the higher-performing teams will generally integrate multiple changes into their project every day.

NOTE   Software developers are likely familiar with the concepts in section 7.1, while those coming from a more systems background may be encountering these concepts for the first time. If you're comfortable with Git, source control management, PRs, and software reviews, you can skip ahead to section 7.2 or consider this section a review.

7.1.1   *SCM*

Probably one of the biggest things that most teams will likely take for granted is their SCM system, which is likely going to be either GitHub or GitLab for most people. At their core, these systems store the source code for projects, but these days they also do much more than that. Many SCMs have their own action runner, which is used for things like automating testing, and they often include additional features like issue trackers and security scanning.

Terraform was created well after SCMs became commonplace. We're also living in a world where the version control system `git` has become the de facto standard for source control. As a result, many systems for Terraform, such as module registries, operate under the assumption that you're using one of the popular SCMs.

7.1.2   *Branching and PRs*

Branching is supported by every major version control system, and it's a critical component of CI. Back in chapter 1, we introduced the concept of forks to explain how OpenTofu and Terraform relate to each other. In many ways, branches can be considered miniforks: they are temporary copies of the main branch of development that exist so developers can work on changes in isolation. Unlike a fork, developers typically merge their code back into the main line of code.

In an active code project, this can happen dozens of times a day. Branches get created, developed in, and then either merged or destroyed as a general practice. The act of merging code from one branch into another is done through a process known as a PR. It's called that because it's a request by the developer for the main project to pull the developers proposed changes in (see figure 7.2).

For the branching model to work, there needs to be a main branch that people agree to work off. This branch is often stored on the SCM itself. For example, when using OpenTofu, they keep their main branch in the OpenTofu repository, which itself exists on the GitHub OpenTofu organization. The main branch of that repository has all of the features that are complete and ready for the next release. When developers make new features, they open a pull request, and, if approved, those changes are merged into the main branch (see figure 7.3).

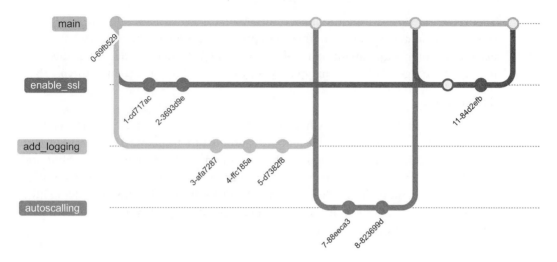

Figure 7.2 Git branching

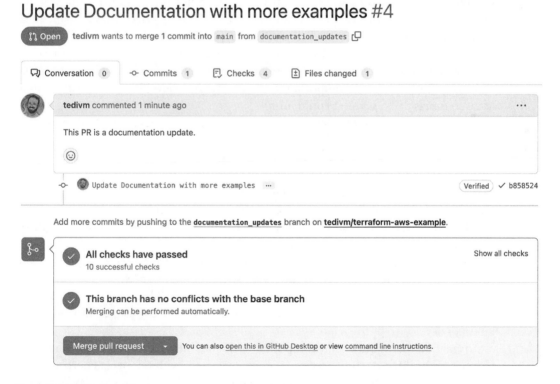

Figure 7.3 Pull request

This model gives us a unique opportunity. When a PR is made, developers have to review the changes to make sure they are appropriate. One of the things we can do to make that easier is add quality control tests into the PR itself. By the end of this chapter, we'll have a good idea of what quality controls to add and how to add them.

7.1.3   Code reviews

Once a PR is made, developers have to make the decision to pull the new code in, request changes, or outright reject the proposed functionality. This is where code reviews come in. SCMs have systems built into them to allow code reviews inline with the PR itself. This allows people to accept or reject the PR. It's also possible to highlight code and comment on it to help guide the PR author into making an acceptable PR.

Code reviews are common for every language. When reviewing Terraform code, there are a few things to pay attention to:

- Security
- Best practices and consistency
- Comments and documentation

Security is an important thing to review for all software projects, but it takes on a particular level of urgency when working with Terraform. Since the Terraform code is going to literally control infrastructure, it can have drastic consequences if it was maliciously altered. Even beyond direct maliciousness, it's possible someone could accidentally misconfigure a resource in such a way that your system isn't secure. Although there are automated ways to test for some of these misconfigurations (and these will be coming up later in the chapter), it's important that developers review PR with security in mind to catch things that a scanner could miss.

For this reason, a code review is also a review of how the controlled infrastructure is configured, which means it may require reviewing the documentation yourself to identify the weaknesses in the system that you need to look out for. As a very simple example, when working with AWS Relational Database Service, you may put something in the wrong subnet or forget to configure backups. These types of misconfigurations are unlikely to get caught by automated systems and depend on the reviewer understanding the capabilities and requirements of the infrastructure being configured programming.

A less serious but still important consideration is reviewing for best practices and consistency. Every team builds up their own style, naming conventions, and internal language over time. Regardless of what that exact style looks like, it should remain both internally consistent to the module being worked on and consistent with the other modules developed by the team.

A final but no less important component is documentation. It's an unfortunate fact in our industry that documentation is often neglected by developers. There are a lot of tools in the Terraform system that make documentation easier to generate from variable descriptions and other Terraform components (as we'll discuss later), but someone still has to write those descriptions. Although it may seem tedious, writing good documentation makes your modules significantly more valuable to your users. In addition, writing good comments makes it easier for you and your teammates to make future changes to your code. If you're ever reviewing code and need the author to explain something, that's a good sign that there needs to be a comment with that explanation right in the code itself.

So that's what you should look at. Let's take a minute to talk about what you *shouldn't* be reviewing.If you can automate the testing of something, then you should do that, and then rely on your CI systems to test that for you. By the end of this chapter, you'll have a good grasp on how to do that, and once you do, it'll enable developers to focus on the things that can't be automated.

The exact formatting of a document can be tested, as can whether the code runs or tests pass. A large part of this chapter discusses how we can implement this automation. This is a key part of reducing the cognitive load of reviewers so that reviewing code is a faster and simpler process.

> **TIP** If something can be reviewed automatically, such as the formatting of code or analysis of code for security vulnerabilities, you should rely on automation to review it and free up your developers to focus on what matters.

Time spent on creating new tests and automating quality checks is time that is ultimately saved during code reviews and even later on by reduced outages and incidents that take up team time to resolve.

7.2 Local development

Before a feature can be integrated with the codebase, it has to be written. If we truly want to practice CI, where teams are pulling multiple features into their codebase each and every day, we need to make development and testing as easy as possible for developers to do locally. In an ideal world, running tests and quality control would be so simple that it becomes second nature.

In this section, we focus on that local development. Although the initial focus is around that local development, it will also be the foundation for our automated work later in the chapter. It really is important that your testing and development environments match as much as possible, as divergence between your development and testing environments can allow errors to sneak through. That's why we start with the developer and their perspective. In this section, we talk about how we can make it easier for all of our modules to have those safety nets without taking a lot of additional work.

7.2.1 Standardizing and bootstrapping with software templates

The first thing we can do to make development easier is to give our projects structure and to configure all of our quality-control tools right from the start. By reducing the burden around configuring quality-control tools, we increase the likelihood of those tools actually being used.

There is a lot of work that goes into understanding and configuring tools, and then more work that goes into building out the CI pipelines around those tools. For this reason, it's not uncommon to see teams skip out on some of these tools even though they bring a lot of value. However, the vast majority of the configuration and even the pipelines don't change between projects. Teams do not need to start from scratch every time but can instead use templates to start their projects.

Bootstrapping new projects from a template is not a new concept. Many software frameworks ship with tools to start projects with the boilerplate already set up. Developers who have experimented with the React framework are likely familiar with the `create-react-app` utility, and that's just one of many examples out there. Although creating a project from scratch is a great learning experience, it can be absolutely tedious the third, fourth, and fifth time you've done it. It's also easy to forget an important step or misconfigure a tool if you're doing it manually each time, and over time your projects can diverge significantly between teams, which makes collaboration more difficult.

The simplest way to create a shared template is to create a repository with all of the boilerplate code in it and then copy that content into a new repository as a starting point. Popular SCMs even have features to support this, such as GitHub Template Repositories, which allow you to create your own repository from an existing template. This is an absolutely great first step.

Eventually, your templates may get more complex though. You may want to add options in or include dynamically generated strings. When copying a repository, developers are also expected to go in and manually update certain fields, such as the project name. Once you've reached this point, it's probably time to explore more powerful template tools.

One of the most popular ones is Cookiecutter (https://www.cookiecutter.io/). Cookiecutter is an open source project that's easy to install on most systems and can be used to create new projects from templates. What makes it powerful is that template developers can incorporate logic into their templates. For example, template developers can ask users of Cookiecutter what they want for a project name and license, and the generated project will have that filled in.

Another way to use it is to generate project-specific configuration files. Later on in this chapter we discuss a tool called TFLint, and that tool requires different plugins depending on the provider used. With Cookiecutter, you can ask a user what their provider is and then create configuration files based on their responses. The tools in this chapter can be used for Terraform modules, including Terraform root modules and workspaces.

Listing 7.1   Cookiecutter template example

```
plugin "terraform" {
  enabled = true
  preset  = "all"
}

{% if cookiecutter.__short_primary_provider == "aws" %}
plugin "aws" {
    enabled = true
```

> Since we always want this enabled it is listed without any conditional statements.

> This block only shows up if we're using the AWS provider.

```
    version = "0.29.0"
    source  = "github.com/terraform-linters/tflint-ruleset-aws"
}
{% endif %}

{% if cookiecutter.__short_primary_provider == "gcp" %}
plugin "google" {
    enabled = true
    version = "0.27.0"
    source  = "github.com/terraform-linters/tflint-ruleset-google"
}
{% endif %}

{% if cookiecutter.__short_primary_provider == "azurerm" %}
plugin "azurerm" {
    enabled = true
    version = "0.25.1"
    source  = "github.com/terraform-linters/tflint-ruleset-azurerm"
}
{% endif %}
```

This block only shows up if we're using the GCP provider.

This block only shows up if we're using the AzureRM provider.

As part of building out this chapter, we explore the configuration of a lot of tools. To make it easier to see the end result, and to give you a starting point for your own template, we've created a Cookiecutter template and open sourced it in the TerraformInDepth (https://github.com/TerraformInDepth/) GitHub organization. This template is in the https://mng.bz/OBMn repository and can be called directly by Cookiecutter. You can also fork this repository into your own organization to customize as needed for your own use.

> **NOTE** The terraform-module-cookiecutter project is an active open source project that includes features that we discuss in chapters 8 and 9 as well. The actual questions and output you'll see running the next command may differ slightly from what we display. However, the purpose of this chapter is to show how we build this template, not just to demonstrate an existing project, so follow along to build your own starting template.

Listing 7.2   Calling Cookiecutter with `terraform-module-cookiecutter`

```
$ cookiecutter gh:TerraformInDepth/terraform-module-cookiecutter
  [1/6] name (): terraform-aws-test-module
  [2/6] Select license
    1 - All Rights Reserved
    2 - MIT license
    3 - BSD license
    4 - Apache Software License 2.0
    5 - GNU General Public License v3
    Choose from [1/2/3/4/5] (1):
  [3/6] author (): Robert Hafner
  [4/6] primary_provider (hashicorp/aws):
  [5/6] provider_min_version (5.0):
  [6/6] private_registry_url ():
```

Here we call the cookiecutter command pointing at the template on GitHub.

Cookiecutter asks us questions to fill in for the template.

Since we're not using a private registry this is left blank.

```
$ ls -la terraform-aws-test-module
.
..
.checkov.yml
.github
.gitignore
.opentofu-version
.pre-commit-config.yml
.terraform-docs.yml
.terraform-version
.tflint.hcl
LICENSE
README.md
main.tf
makefile
outputs.tf
providers.tf
variables.tf
```

◄——— Now we run "ls" to list
all the generated files.

Although the examples in this chapter and the Cookiecutter template are great starting points, they are also fairly generic. As you develop with Terraform, you and your team are going to form your own opinions. You also have to consider the requirements and systems your team uses. If you know everyone on your team is going to publish modules to Artifactory as your module registry, for instance, you may want to incorporate that pipeline directly into your own templates.

7.2.2   *Repeatable tasks with makefiles*

Another burden that keeps teams from adopting more quality-control tools is the huge number of them that exist. In this chapter alone, we're introducing well over a dozen new commands. That's a lot of commands, and it's unreasonable to expect anyone to memorize them all. Instead, we use a tool called Make to record these commands so they can be accessed easily.

> **NOTE**   This `makefile` is going to be built and expanded on throughout the chapter. By the end of the chapter you should have a single large makefile that contains all of our commands. This `makefile` is also available on GitHub in our Cookiecutter template from the previous section if you want to see it in full.

Make is a rather old tool, first created in 1976, but has been seeing a resurgence lately. The `make` command is available for pretty much every system architecture ever built and is often already installed on people's development machines. The language is also extremely simple, at least for our use cases: like most languages, there are advanced features and complexities, but you can spend years using `make` without encountering them. This combination of portability and simplicity mean it's an ideal tool for sharing reusable workflows.

As a result, Make tends to be really popular with people who are working with system-level languages (such as Go or C) and has been really popular with the DevOps and platform engineering crowd. There are certainly other options out there, but they tend to be more language specific. For example, the package.json spec for Javascript/ Node packages has a scripts field that can serve a similar purpose, but it is only usable for people in the Javascript ecosystem.

To use Make, you start by creating a makefile (literally a text file with the name "makefile," no extension) in your project root directory. From there you define targets that run commands. For example, if you had a target named test, you would call make test to run the commands for that target. You can also define variables in makefiles that can be overridden in the command line.

> **WARNING** Be careful with spaces and tabs! The Make utility is very specific about its formatting. When adding commands to a target, like in our next example, you have to use tabs and not spaces for your indent. If you use spaces to indent, you will get an error.

Listing 7.3 makefile **syntax**

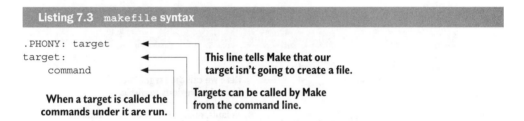

As is tradition, we can see this in action with a Hello World example. Here, we define our message using a variable so that it can be overridden. Note the use of the PHONY keyword. This just tells Make that we don't expect our command to create a new file and that it will be present for all of our targets. Make was originally created to make it easier to compile languages such as C, so a lot of the syntax assumes you'll be creating a file. The PHONY line lets Make know that this target doesn't have "real" output, so Make will run it every time it is invoked.

Listing 7.4 makefile **Hello World**

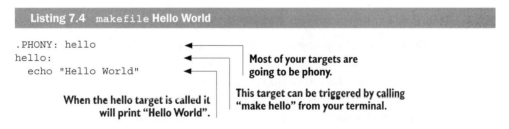

Now that we've created the file, we can see it in action. If we call the make hello target directly, it uses our predefined variable, but we can override that by passing in our own.

Listing 7.5 **Using the** makefile

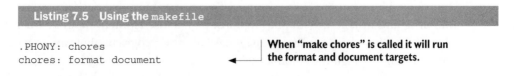

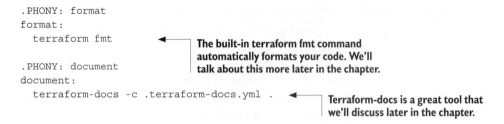

```
.PHONY: format
format:
  terraform fmt
```
The built-in terraform fmt command automatically formats your code. We'll talk about this more later in the chapter.

```
.PHONY: document
document:
  terraform-docs -c .terraform-docs.yml .
```
Terraform-docs is a great tool that we'll discuss later in the chapter.

Another useful feature of Make is the ability to group commands together. Make allows you to specify dependencies for targets, so one target can require that another target be completed before it can be run. This feature can be used with an empty target to act as a group so that running a single command calls all of the targets. This is commonly used to create groups such as `tests`, which allow all tests to be run by calling `make tests`.

Listing 7.6   Target grouping with makefiles

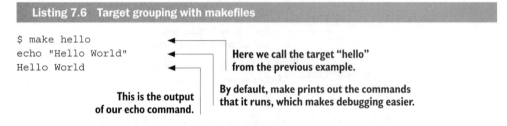

```
$ make hello
echo "Hello World"
Hello World
```
Here we call the target "hello" from the previous example.

This is the output of our echo command.

By default, make prints out the commands that it runs, which makes debugging easier.

Make is a very powerful utility, and we've really just scratched the surface of what we can do with it. In the next section, we show a little more of that power. For our use cases, however, we really only need to focus on the very core features that make it easy for teams to repeatedly run commands without having to resort to documentation or memorization. Throughout this chapter, we'll be expanding our `makefile` definitions to incorporate the new tools we introduce.

7.2.3   *Installing applications with makefiles*

In this chapter, we're going to install a lot of tools. We have tools for validating, testing, formatting, and securing your code. We even have a tool to manage different versions of Terraform and OpenTofu on the same machine. This can make working with our projects more difficult, as it adds an additional burden onto developers who are trying to jump in and make changes.

The good news is that there are solutions to this problem. The bad news is that there are *a lot* of solutions to this problem, and they tend to be specific to the type of computer someone is using. These days every modern operating system has a package manager for it. Linux systems have programs like `apt`, `yum`, and `apk` that are used to manage the programs installed. With MacOS, most people use Homebrew, while on Windows there's the Chocolatey package manager. All of these programs allow you to install programs locally through the command line.

To make it easier for developers, we can put the installation commands for our packages in the makefile for the project. This way, people can run a simple command, such as make install, and have the appropriate tools installed. Since makefiles can also contain basic logic, we can take this a step further by detecting the appropriate package manager to use when the command is run. This is useful for teams or organizations where the developers aren't all using the same system.

Once the logic is set up to detect the package managers, the actual installation packages can be listed out in a variable. This makes adding and removing packages really simple, even for people who don't necessarily understand the logic in the makefile itself.

NOTE This example focuses on Windows and MacOS, which have some pretty standard tools for installation. When expanding this for Linux, you have to take into account your specific package installer (apt, yum, apk, snap, etc.) for the flavor of Linux you're supporting.

Listing 7.7 Package installation with makefiles

> This line checks package managers until it finds one installed and then saves the path.

> This is the list of packages we install if choco is present.

> This is the list of packages we want to install if brew is present.

```
BREW_PACKAGES := cosign tenv terraform-docs tflint checkov trivy
CHOCOLATEY_PACKAGES := cosign tenv terraform-docs tflint trivy

INSTALLER_PATH := $(shell { command -v brew || command -v choco; }
  2>/dev/null)
INSTALLER := $(shell { basename $(INSTALLER_PATH) ; } 2>/dev/null)
```

> Here we get the name of the package manager from the path.

```
.PHONY: install
install: install_$(INSTALLER)
```

> The install command calls the target, which is generated from the INSTALLER variable.

```
.PHONY: install_brew
install_brew:
    brew tap tofuutils/tap
    brew install $(BREW_PACKAGES)
```

> This will get called if $(INSTALLER) is brew.

> This brew-specific command installs an extra registry that contains tenv.

```
.PHONY: install_choco
install_choco:
    choco install $(CHOCOLATEY_PACKAGES)
```

> We call brew, passing in our list of packages above.

```
.PHONY: install_
install_:
    echo "No package manager found."
```

> This will get called if $(INSTALLER) is choco.

> If no package manager is found, $(INSTALLER) will be an empty string and this will be the mapped target.

> We call choco, passing in our list of packages above.

If that looks complicated, don't worry: it's the kind of boilerplate code that should live in your software template to get reused between projects. What you really need to know right now is that if you ever need to add additional packages, you can update the variables at the top. You can get more advanced than that: one of the benefits of Make being so established is that there are a lot of resources out there you can learn from.

7.2.4   *Terraform and OpenTofu*

The current schism in the Terraform world between OpenTofu and HashiCorp Terraform introduces some complications for developers: What program should you support, what do you do if you're supporting modules used by multiple teams who each have different opens on that question, and what can you do to keep your options open?

At the moment, it turns out this question isn't nearly as difficult as it first appears. OpenTofu and Terraform are remarkably compatible with each other and share the vast majority of commands. By taking advantage of some features of Make, we can update our `makefile` so it's easy to switch between the two. This can be done by replacing all direct calls to `terraform` with a variable. If the variable is set by users on the command line, it'll keep their definition; otherwise, it will take our default.

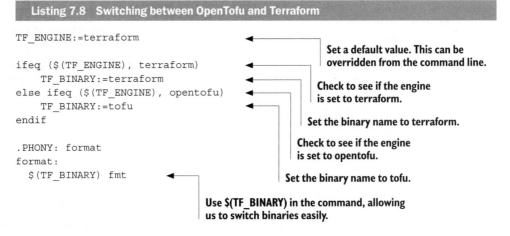

Listing 7.8 Switching between OpenTofu and Terraform

```
TF_ENGINE:=terraform                          ◄──────  Set a default value. This can be
                                                        overridden from the command line.
ifeq ($(TF_ENGINE), terraform)                ◄──────
    TF_BINARY:=terraform                      ◄──────  Check to see if the engine
else ifeq ($(TF_ENGINE), opentofu)            ◄──────  is set to terraform.
    TF_BINARY:=tofu                           ◄──────
endif                                                   Set the binary name to terraform.

.PHONY: format                                          Check to see if the engine
format:                                                 is set to opentofu.
    $(TF_BINARY) fmt           ◄──────
                                                        Set the binary name to tofu.

                         Use $(TF_BINARY) in the command, allowing
                         us to switch binaries easily.
```

With this in place, teams are able to switch between versions easily. If at any point a team wants to change their default engine, all it takes is changing the `TF_ENGINE` variable in the file. It's also possible to override the version when running a `make` command, so even if the default is `terraform` it's possible to use `tofu`:

```
make format TF_ENGINE=opentofu
```

This method gives us the best of all options. We can easily set a default that works for our team, but we can override that default when testing. Switching the default is as easy as changing a single string. When we automate testing on a CI system, we can use this to test against both OpenTofu and Terraform without having to change any code.

7.2.5   *Terraform and OpenTofu versions*

In an ideal world, you would always use the latest version of Terraform or Open-Tofu, but the world is far from ideal. As new versions of Terraform and OpenTofu are released, they come with changes, and sometimes those changes are breaking. When these new versions are released, you have to test your projects, and that doesn't happen instantly. As a result, it's not uncommon for teams to support slightly older versions of their preferred Terraform runner.

For teams just starting out with Terraform, this isn't an immediately noticeable problem. Over time, as teams build up stable modules and pipelines, they find themselves with more maintenance work. Once this occurs, developers may find that they need to switch between versions. Even outside of that maintenance work, developers may simply want to test out the new alpha release. Having to uninstall one version and install another every time someone wants to switch versions is a pretty tedious task, so it's no surprise that there are tools to manage this.

Originally, there were two popular options for managing versions of Terraform: `tfswitch` and `tfenv`. Over time, people seemed to settle on `tfenv` as the standard, in part because it followed the same patterns as tools like `rbenv` and `pyenv` (version managers for Ruby and Python, respectively). Up until very recently, `tfenv` was the most obvious choice.

The release of OpenTofu changed this. There was discussion about potentially incorporating OpenTofu into `tfenv`, and there was even a short-lived `tofuenv` tool. Ultimately, a new tool that worked with Terraform, OpenTofu, and even Terragrunt (a tool we discuss in chapter 11) named `tenv` was created. This allows teams that are looking to support both tools (such as module developers who support multiple teams or companies looking to avoid vendor lock-in) to easily switch between the programs and manage versions for both.

The `tenv` website (https://github.com/tofuutils/tenv) has installation instructions for every major operating system, and we've already placed the installation into our `makefile`. Once installed, `tenv` takes over the `terraform`, `tofu`, and `terragrunt` commands and routes the commands to the appropriate version. It picks the version based either off configuration files or by using the system default. This means that if you have three different projects, all of them could be using different versions of Terraform and OpenTofu, and this would be handled transparently for you.

When you call either `terraform` or `tofu` from a shell, the `tenv` command hijacks that call and silently routes it to a `terraform` or `tofu` binary of the appropriate version for the project. From a user perspective, this is transparent. This makes it really easy to let each project specify the expected version of its respective Terraform engine to work with.

To select an appropriate version, `tenv` looks for `.terraform-version` or `.opentofu-version` files (depending on the program you're using). It first looks in your current directory, and then recursively looks through parent directories until it finds one. If none are found, it will check your home directory before finally using your default value. There are a few options for the version you can specify:

- An exact version (1.5.7)
- A version constraint (~>1.5)
- `latest`, `latest-stable`, or `latest-pre` (prelease)
- `latest-allowed` or `min-required`

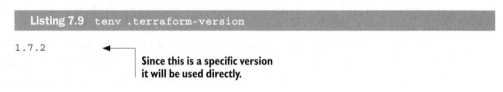

Listing 7.9 `tenv .terraform-version`

```
1.7.2
```

Since this is a specific version it will be used directly.

The OpenTofu configuration file uses the exact same version syntax.

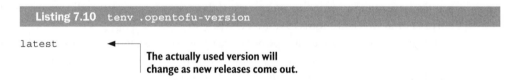

Listing 7.10 `tenv .opentofu-version`

```
latest
```

The actually used version will change as new releases come out.

You can also override the version file to test new versions using `tenv tf use VERSION` and `tenv tofu use VERSION` commands.

Even if a version file is present, it can be overridden by using the `tenv tf use VERSION` and `tenv tofu use VERSION` commands. These allow developers to switch between versions on a specific project. This is really powerful when combined with the special versions `latest-allowed` and `min-required`. When creating modules and specifying version ranges, you're telling users which ranges should be expected to work. These special flags allow you to switch between the minimum and maximum supported versions for testing so you can confirm that these ranges are accurate.

7.2.6 *Pre-commit hooks*

The final feature we want to enable for our local environments is a feature of Git known as a pre-commit hook. These are scripts that get run whenever you make a Git commit, and if the scripts fail, they don't allow the commit to happen. This can act as a safety net for developers and allows them to catch and fix problems quickly instead of having to wait for an external process to discover them.

Imagine a scenario where you've spent hours debugging a problem and writing updates. You've finally resolved the problem and triumphantly push your change up to your company SCM. Instead of success, however, your PR gets a big red X, signifying failure. It turns out you didn't properly format a file.

These kinds of frustrations happen all the time. Although the fix is pretty easy, the delay in getting your feature merged can breach you out of your zone. These are the kind of problems that can be checked as part of a pre-commit hook so you notice and correct the problem earlier in the cycle.

To manage our pre-commit hooks, we use the pre-commit framework (https://pre-commit.com/). This is a simple tool that lets us define our pre-commit hooks in a config file. This allows other people to install the same hooks in their local development environment easily. We can use this to add our makefile targets in as checks that get called during every commit, and if any of them fail, this will block the commit until we fix the problem.

Listing 7.11 `.pre-commit-config.yaml` to `makefile`

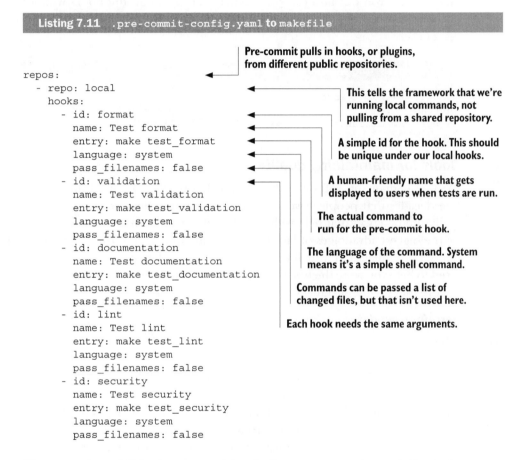

```yaml
repos:
  - repo: local
    hooks:
      - id: format
        name: Test format
        entry: make test_format
        language: system
        pass_filenames: false
      - id: validation
        name: Test validation
        entry: make test_validation
        language: system
        pass_filenames: false
      - id: documentation
        name: Test documentation
        entry: make test_documentation
        language: system
        pass_filenames: false
      - id: lint
        name: Test lint
        entry: make test_lint
        language: system
        pass_filenames: false
      - id: security
        name: Test security
        entry: make test_security
        language: system
        pass_filenames: false
```

Pre-commit pulls in hooks, or plugins, from different public repositories.

This tells the framework that we're running local commands, not pulling from a shared repository.

A simple id for the hook. This should be unique under our local hooks.

A human-friendly name that gets displayed to users when tests are run.

The actual command to run for the pre-commit hook.

The language of the command. System means it's a simple shell command.

Commands can be passed a list of changed files, but that isn't used here.

Each hook needs the same arguments.

There are also published pre-commit hooks that you can use instead of mapping to our `makefile`. The most relevant one for us is the `pre-commit-terraform` plugin made by Anton Babenko and maintained by Maksym Vlasov and George Yermulnik. This plugin has hooks available for most, if not all, of the tools we discuss in this chapter.

Listing 7.12 `.pre-commit-config.yaml` with plugins

```yaml
repos:
  - repo: https://github.com/antonbabenko/pre-commit-terraform
    rev: v1.88.0
    hooks:
```

Check the repo url above for the latest release version.

```
    - id: terraform_fmt
    - id: terraform_validate
    - id: terraform_docs
    - id: terraform_tflint
    - id: terraform_checkov
```

These hooks are run directly, not through our makefile.

From here, developers only have to run `pre-commit install` and it will run on every `git commit`. You can also call `pre-commit run` to run all the hooks without making a commit. As we've done with other tools, we can add this command right into our `makefile`.

> **Listing 7.13   Pre-commit makefile targets**

```
.PHONY: precommit_install
precommit_install:
    pre-commit install
```

This command installs the pre-commit hooks into the Git repository.

7.3   *Tools for maintaining quality*

Writing high-quality software is hard regardless of what language you are using. Over the decades that people have been writing software, developers have come up with tools and practices that help with this. The ability to learn from these practices is one of the biggest advantages of IaC. When working with Terraform, there are a variety of tools, both integrated into Terraform and developed as standalone tools, that can be used to help you write the best possible code and detect any problems that may happen before they go into production.

7.3.1   *terraform validate*

The absolute simplest test that you can perform is to use the `terraform validate` command against your project. The `validate` command runs a few different checks on your code. The most obvious type of error it will identify is syntax errors. It will also check that for naming errors, so if a developer happens to make a mistake on a function or attribute name, it'll get caught here. These are the types of errors that would prevent Terraform code from even running.

Since this command only considers your code, it does not need to have a backend configured and it does not need to have any variables set. It does, however, need to have an initialized workspace. When you're using `terraform validate` in an automated setting, you may not have a backend configured (and you may not want one), in which case you can run the `init` command with the backend explicitly disabled to create a workspace:

```
terraform init -backend=false
```

Once your workspace is initialized, you can run `validate`. When things go well, the command returns the message "Success! The configuration is valid." Otherwise, it gives you an error message similar to what you'd receive at the start of running a plan.

Listing 7.14 `terraform validate` **output**

```
terraform validate
```
This line is Make showing us the command that it is running.

```
|
| Error: Duplicate resource "terraform_data" configuration
|
|   on main.tf line 6:
|    6: resource "terraform_data" "this" {
|
| A terraform_data resource named "this" was already declared at
| main.tf:2,1-33. Resource names must be unique per type in each module.
|
make: *** [test_validation] Error 1
```

Since the command returns a failure, Make also returns an error.

This is the same error you'd see during a plan, only without the need to generate a plan.

As with all of our commands, we want to add this to our `makefile` so it will be easier for other developers to use and so we can incorporate it into our CI pipelines later in the chapter. One thing to think about is our `terraform init` command. We want developers to test and run their code locally, but we don't want to erase their backend configuration if they happen to be working with a developer workspace. The good news is that the `-backend=false` command will leave any previously configured backend. This will allow us to keep the command in our `makefile`.

Another neat trick we can use to speed up our development cycle is to split the `terraform init` into its own target. It was mentioned earlier that Make is often used to generate files. If it has a target that isn't PHONY, and that target already exists, Make will skip running the command again. On the other hand, if the target doesn't exist and another target depends on it, the command will be run to generate it. So this time we won't use the PHONY keyword: we want to point to a real file on disk for our target, the `.terraform` directory created by `terraform init`. If Make sees that the target is a file or directory that already exists, it won't run the command again, speeding up our testing slightly.

Listing 7.15 `terraform validate` **makefile**

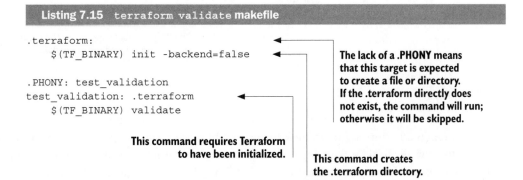

```
.terraform:
    $(TF_BINARY) init -backend=false

.PHONY: test_validation
test_validation: .terraform
    $(TF_BINARY) validate
```

The lack of a .PHONY means that this target is expected to create a file or directory. If the .terraform directly does not exist, the command will run; otherwise it will be skipped.

This command requires Terraform to have been initialized.

This command creates the .terraform directory.

You may have noticed that we didn't call Terraform directly but used the `TF_BINARY` variable we created in section 7.2.4. This allows us to easily switch between OpenTofu and Terraform and, as we'll see later in the chapter, lets us automatically run our validation steps against both once we integrate with a CI system.

7.3.2   *Terratest and Terraform testing*

Testing your code is a critical part of every software project. Every language out there has at least one testing framework, and popular languages tend to have multiple options. At the moment, there are two primary options for this in the Terraform ecosystem: Terratest and the new Terraform testing framework.

Terratest, developed by Gruntwork, has been the de facto standard of testing with Terraform since it was released in 2016. It's built in Go and uses the built-in testing framework as a base. This means tests are expected to be written in Go, which for many teams is a bit of a blocker. That said, it is extremely powerful, as any test that can be defined in a traditional imperative programming language such as Go can be written with Terratest.

The Terraform testing framework is a new feature of Terraform, released with version 1.6.0, that tries to resolve the problem of needing another programming language for testing. It provides the ability to define test suites using Terraform itself. It is a fairly new feature of Terraform, and as such it changes quickly. This is also an area where OpenTofu may lag behind in features as new functionality is released in the HashiCorp Terraform.

Unlike most of the topics in this chapter, where we're able to create standard configurations that can be reused throughout different projects, testing tends to be very specific to the module being developed. Testing, the software development lifecycle, and CI are also very intertwined topics, but attempting to cover all of these things in one chapter would make for an extremely dense chapter. There is an entire chapter (chapter 9) dedicated to testing, so for now we're going to update our `makefile` with the stubs for testing and then we will update them in the next chapter with the specifics.

Listing 7.16   **Terraform test** `makefile` **stubs**

```
.PHONY: terratest
terratest:
    @echo "Not yet implemented."          ◀──┐  We'll fill this section out in chapter 9.

.PHONY: terraform_test
terraform_test:                               ┌  The "@" symbol suppresses the command
    @echo "Not yet implemented."          ◀──┘  from being printed to the console.
```

7.3.3   *TFlint*

Linters are tools that do static analysis of software (evaluation of the code itself without actually running it) to look for errors, bugs, and stylistic policies. In general, they don't really look at your logic but instead try to enforce certain levels of quality and standards. Linters are available for pretty much every language and are a big part of how software teams maintain quality. The most commonly used linter for Terraform is a program called TFLint.

TFLint is designed around plugins, where each individual plugin provides a set of rules that TFLint will enforce. The most commonly used plugin is the Terraform plugin. This plugin contains some generic rules, such as enforcing that all outputs and variables have descriptions or that every variable contains a type. Despite being installed alongside TFLint, this plugin is not enabled by default. Instead, it has to be declared in a `.tflint.hcl` file in the project root.

Listing 7.17   TFLint Terraform plugin

```
plugin "terraform" {
  enabled = true          ◄────
  preset  = "recommended" ◄────
}                                  This plugin contains
                                   generic Terraform rules.

                                   Although it seems silly to run TFLint without
           The default preset is   this plugin it is not enabled by default.
        "recommended", although the
           "all" option is also available.
```

By default, the TFLint Terraform plugin uses a subset of all of its rules. The `recommended` preset rules are pretty good, but in my opinion there are some rules that it doesn't enable that are useful. In particular, the rules that enforce adding descriptions to variables and outputs are extremely useful. By switching to the `all` preset, you can take advantage of these extra rules. You can also add additional rules after selecting "recommended" or exclude rules after selecting "all."

Listing 7.18   TFLint customizing rules

```
plugin "terraform" {
  enabled = true
  preset  = "recommended" ◄──── The "recommended" list only contains
}                                some of the Terraform generic rules.

rule "terraform_comment_syntax" { ◄──── This rule requires all comments
  enabled = enable                       start with # instead of //.
}                                 ◄──── This rule is not part of the "recommended"
                                        preset, so we enable it now.
```

The TFLint team also maintains plugins for AWS, GCP, Azure, and the Open Policy Agent (OPA). The first three of these provide rules specifically for their equivalent providers and contain hundreds of rules (700+, 200+, and 100+ rules, respectively). The OPA plugin is a special case, as it allows developers to write their own rules using the OPA specification.

Listing 7.19   TFLint cloud plugins

```
plugin "aws" {
    enabled = true          ◄──── This plugin is used alongside the AWS provider.
```

```
                                    ┌─ This is the latest version at the time this book
                                    │  was published, but there are likely new releases.
    version = "0.30.0"         ◄────┘
    source  = "github.com/terraform-linters/tflint-ruleset-aws"
}
                                    ┌─ This plugin is used alongside the Azure provider.
plugin "azurerm" {             ◄────┘
    enabled = true                  ┌─ This is the latest version at the time this book was
    version = "0.25.1"         ◄────┘  published, but there are likely new releases.
    source  = "github.com/terraform-linters/tflint-ruleset-azurerm"
}
                                    ┌─ This plugin is used alongside
plugin "google" {              ◄────┘  the Google provider.
    enabled = false
    version = "0.27.0"                                          ◄───┐
    source  = "github.com/terraform-linters/tflint-ruleset-google" ◄┐│
}                                                                   ││
```

This is the latest version at the time this book was │
published, but there are likely new releases. ────────┘

It's possible to install and then disable a
plugin, although there's no real reason to. ──────────┘

It is also possible to build your own plugin. The TFLint project has a template for creating plugins (https://mng.bz/YDrN) as well as documentation (https://mng.bz/GeVq). However, doing so requires using Go and is not something teams typically take on their own. An easier way to write custom policies is to use the OPA plugin, which we discuss in section 7.5 of this chapter.

Once you have TFLint configured, you need to run `tflint --init` to install your plugins. Just like the `terraform init` call, this will download and store the plugins locally for your use. We can put this directly in our `Makefile`, so people won't need to explicitly remember each time.

Listing 7.20   TFLint `makefile`

```
.PHONY: test_tflint
test_tflint:                       ┌─ It's easier to run the init each time, and
    tflint --init             ◄────┘  doesn't take long if it has already run.
    tflint                    ◄────┐  We don't need any arguments as our settings
                                   └─ can be read from the configuration file.
```

After that, you are free to call `tflint` to validate that your code is following all rules and policies. Let's go ahead and trigger an error by removing the `required_version` attribute from our generated project. The `required_version` attribute is considered important since it prevents people from running your module on versions that aren't supported, so TFLint has a rule to detect its usage. Since we haven't started writing any actual Terraform code yet, we'll also see a warning that we've defined AWS in `required_providers` but haven't used it.

Listing 7.21 TFLint usage

```
$ make test_tflint
tflint --init
tflint
2 issue(s) found:
```

Call out to the Make
target to run tflint.

Since this command is really
fast we run it every time.

Now Make runs tflint.

```
Warning: terraform "required_version" attribute is required (
  terraform_required_version)

  on  line 0:
   (source code not available)
```

I never set a minimum Terraform
version in my module.

```
Reference: https://github.com/terraform-linters/tflint-ruleset-terraform/
  blob/v0.5.0/docs/rules/terraform_required_version.md

Warning: provider 'aws' is declared in required_providers but not used by
  the module (terraform_unused_required_providers)

  on providers.tf line 3:
   3:      aws = {
   4:        source  = "hashicorp/aws"
   5:        version = "~> 5.0"
   6:      }
```

Since this was a
brand-new module with
no resources, TFLint
detected that the AWS
provider was declared
but not used.

```
Reference: https://github.com/terraform-linters/tflint-ruleset-terraform/
  blob/v0.5.0/docs/rules/terraform_unused_required_providers.md

make: *** [test_lint] Error 2
```

Make exited with an error after
TFLint returned its own failure.

Linting isn't perfect, and there may be places where you simply do not agree with TFLint. There are a lot of reasons this could occur, such as TFLlint not yet having an update available after features have changed on one of the clouds (new instance families being released, for example). If this happens, you can either disable the rule altogether or add specially formatted comments above the line you want `tflint` to ignore. Let's go over each, starting with disabling a rule completely.

Let's say, for instance, that you want to enable all of the rules in the Terraform plugin except one. Maybe your team has really strong opinions on comments and wants to support both # and // as comment styles. This breaks the `terraform_comment_syntax` rule, which enforces only # as comment markers. You can disable this one rule while still leaving the rest available.

Listing 7.22 TFLint disable rules

```
plugin "terraform" {
  enabled = true
  preset  = "all"
```

This time we are enabling
every rule of the plugin.

```
}

rule "terraform_comment_syntax" {
  enabled = false
}
```

This rule requires all comments start with # instead of //.

This rule was enabled by the all preset but is now disabled.

It's also possible to ignore specific instances of problems, rather than disabling a rule altogether. This is done using inline comments. One of the TFLint rules, `terraform_module_pinned_source`, doesn't allow you to reference Git repositories without pinning it to a specific version. During development, you might find yourself working on a few modules that also haven't had a real release yet, so you may want to disable that rule when calling those modules.

Another example might occur when you are testing out new values that TFLint isn't aware of. As an example, AWS regularly releases new instance types. When this happens, there may be some lag before that type is in the ruleset, which can cause the `aws_instance_invalid_type` rule to be triggered. If your team is part of a beta program, you may even have access to instance types that aren't available to the public yet. In that case, you can disable the rule right in your code.

Listing 7.23   TFLint inline exceptions

```
resource "aws_instance" "this" {
  ami = "ami-867166b8518f055af"
  # tflint-ignore: aws_instance_invalid_type
  instance_type = "p8.48xlarge"
}
```

This comment tells TFLint to ignore the rule aws_instance_invalid_type on the next line.

If you were part of an AWS beta, you might have access to instances that aren't publicly known.

7.4   *Validating security*

Defining infrastructure using code provides a very unique opportunity to be proactive with regards to security. When you're manually creating and configuring infrastructure, you can only review security after the fact. With IaC, and Terraform specifically, you get the ability to analyze the code itself before it's actually deployed. This can allow you to catch security problems before they become actual vulnerabilities.

A huge part of this is humans doing PR reviews, but there are several tools that allow some checks to be run automatically. Two of those, Checkov and Trivy, are open source tools that you can incorporate into your regular testing without cost. While this does not replace the human review, it does provide another safeguard for developers.

You may be asking yourself whether you should run either Trivy or Checkov, but since both of these tools are free to use, there is no harm in using both. There's also always a chance that one system will catch a problem that the other would have missed: Trivy covers more providers than Checkov, but Checkov does have rules that Trivy doesn't detect. When it comes to security, there is nothing wrong with a little redundancy.

7.4.1 *Checkov*

Checkov is an open source security scanner that can be used to review not only Terraform code but also Terraform plans and even other IaC tools such as Helm and CloudFormation. Unlike many other tools, Checkov can run completely locally and does not require a central service. This essentially makes it free, both in the open source sense of the word and in the sense that it costs you almost nothing in resources to run it.

When using Checkov, you generally don't have configuration files. Instead, everything is managed by the command line. This makes having a standardized way of saving and running these commands even more important since changes you make (such as adding in custom policies, which we explore in section 7.5) are made to the commands themselves. For that resource, we can start by adding some new targets to our `makefile`.

Listing 7.24 Checkov `makefile` targets

```
.PHONY: security
security: test_checkov          ◄──── A generic security target can be
                                       expanded as more tools are added.

.PHONY: test_checkov
test_checkov:
    checkov --directory .       ◄──── Checkov is pretty simple to
                                       run, just requiring a location.
```

Once a problem has been found, it needs to be either corrected or explained. Most of the time, the problems found will be pretty straightforward: either a feature needs to be enabled (or disabled) to keep things secure or a certain option should be changed. For instance, forgetting to enable encryption on a storage device will likely trigger an error. For those things, simply fixing the problem is your best bet.

There are times, though, when the result is actually intentional. You may purposefully disable encryption because you're building a public dataset, for example, or you may need to pick a slightly less security encryption protocol because you have to support older clients. When that happens, you need to create an exception to the rule and document it.

> **TIP** Listing 7.25 will trigger multiple rules from Checkov, but we only add an exception for one of them. Every finding should be reviewed, and exceptions should only be added for expected behavior. For everything else, you should solve the problem that Checkov points out, not just tell Checkov to ignore it.

Listing 7.25 Checkov adding exceptions

```
resource "aws_instance" "this" {
  ami           = "ami-867166b8518f055af"
  instance_type = "t3.large"
```

```
    #checkov:skip=CKV_AWS_88:This instance is meant to be publicly
↩️ accessible.
    associate_public_ip_address = true
}
```
◄── **Checkov exceptions should always include a reason.**

The documentation portion of this is absolutely critical. It lets your code reviewers understand why you are making the exception, and it makes it easier for that exception to be audited in the future.

7.4.2   *Trivy (formally TFSec)*

Trivy is another open source security scanner. It is very similar to Checkov in that it works with Terraform and many other tools as well. One of the interesting things about Trivy is that their IaC scanning is built by the team that created the (now deprecated) TFSec tool. TFSec was a pretty popular tool, and Trivy has become rather well liked as well.

As with Checkov, there isn't a lot of configuration that goes into running Trivy. In general, you want to run it with as many rules as you can and then review what it finds. To that end, we can go ahead and add it to our `makefile`.

Listing 7.26   Trivy `makefile` targets

```
.PHONY: security
security: test_checkov test_trivy

.PHONY: test_trivy
test_trivy:
    trivy config .
```
◄── **The security target is more useful now that we have two scanners in use.**

◄── **Trivy, like Checkov, is pretty easy to run.**

Once a problem has been found, it needs to be either corrected or explained, just like with Checkov. Trivy has a few different options for how to do this. The `.trivyignore` file can be used to list any rule that you want to disable. This disables the rule for the entire project though, so this method should be used with care. The file also takes comments that should be used to justify those exceptions.

Listing 7.27   Disabling rules with `.trivyignore`

```
# Allow public IP addresses to be used in this module.

AVD-AWS-0009
```
◄── **Do not forget to add comments above the rules so people know what they are.**

Trivy also supports inline exceptions using comments, similar to TFLint and Checkov. This method allows you to apply more granularity to the exceptions, rather than issuing blanket exceptions over the whole project.

Listing 7.28   Trivy inline exceptions

```
resource "aws_instance" "this" {
  ami          = "ami-867166b8518f055af"
```

```
    instance_type = "t3.large"

    #checkov:skip=CKV_AWS_88:This instance is meant to be publicly
    accessible.
    # Trivy: Ignore Public IP address rule.
    #trivy:ignore:AVD-AWS-0009
    associate_public_ip_address = true
}
```

Checkov and Trivy exceptions can be side by side.

Finally, we can place the exception above the line.

Trivy exceptions do not take a description, so a description should be placed above it.

7.4.3 Snyk, Checkmarx, and Mend

In addition to the open source options, there are many commercial solutions. Three of the more common solutions are Snyk, Checkmarx, and Mend. These solutions don't just provide scanning; they also have central platforms and dashboards that can be used to review the problems across multiple projects. Some even offer advanced features like Software Bill of Materials, which are becoming more popular among security teams.

In general, if you aren't already using one of these tools, you are likely fine using just Checkov and Trivy. If your company already has licenses for these, then you should absolutely take advantage of them. I would still recommend using Checkov alongside any of these paid solutions though, as it never hurts to have an extra layer of protection and in this case it literally costs you nothing after the initial setup.

7.5 Custom policy enforcement

Beyond code quality rules, you may also want to enforce policy decisions. It's pretty common for teams to have policies they have to abide by. Sometimes these are technical decisions, sometimes they're compliance related, and other times they might be financial or contractual. One of the great things about IaC is that it allows some of these policies to be enforced using code. The Terraform ecosystem has two great tools that we've already discussed, Checkov and Trivy, that we can use to enforce policies in our code.

As an example, in 2021 AWS announced an upgrade to their general-purpose storage devices. They introduced the GP3 Volume to replace their GP2 Volume, and there was literally no reason not to migrate it. It was faster and cheaper, which meant that not using it would cost more money for worse performance. Although this is not a code error, it is the kind of mistake you can use code to prevent.

Writing your own custom rules for enforcement is possible but not trivial. There are also different places where rules can be enforced. In this chapter, we focus on enforcing rules in your code itself, but in the next chapter we talk about enforcing policies on the planning side of things.

7.5.1 OPA with TFLint

OPA is a declarative framework that lets developers define policies (such as requiring specific formats for resource names attributes, restricting the use of specific features, or even requiring that specific tags are set on resources that allow tags) using a standard language called Rego. As a framework, it is often integrated into other projects when adding support for policies is desired. TFLint has a plugin that allows you to define policies using the Rego language that OPA uses for configuration.

> **NOTE**   Learning Rego is hard. Using OPA with TFLint should mostly be considered if your team is already using OPA somewhere else. Otherwise, your best bet is to skip this section and go to section 7.5.2, as it is much easier to write custom policies with Checkov.

To get started, you should create a directory `.tflint.d/policies` in your project, as this is where the plugin expects policy files to exist. You will also need to add the OPA plugin to the `.tflint.hcl` configuration file.

Listing 7.29   Enabling OPA plugin

```
plugin "opa" {
  enabled = true
  version = "0.6.0"
  source  = "github.com/terraform-linters/tflint-ruleset-opa"
}
```

This version may have changed since this book was published. Make sure to use the latest versions.

The OPA plugin, like the others, lives on GitHub.

From there, you can start creating policies. The Rego language is very rich, and it has the TFLint packages on top of it. The TFLint plugin is also still experimental, which means some things may change between versions. Your best bet is to read the current plugin documentation (https://mng.bz/zZja), which has a fantastic walk-through of the different components of building a policy. The TFLint project has an example on their website (https://mng.bz/0Q4x) of using the OPA Rego language to enforce the name of S3 buckets.

Listing 7.30   OPA example policy

```
package tflint

import rego.v1

deny_invalid_s3_bucket_name contains issue if {
    buckets := terraform.resources("aws_s3_bucket", {"bucket": "string"},
{})
    name := buckets[_].config.bucket
    not startswith(name.value, "example-com-")

    issue := tflint.issue(`Bucket names should always start with
"example-com-"`, name.range)
}
```

This is where the policy name comes from.

This call looks through resources for S3 buckets.

If the name starts with "example-com-" then the policy ends here and the issue isn't created.

This last step saves the generated issue so it gets raised by TFLint.

7.5.2 Custom Checkov rules

Checkov also has the ability to enforce custom policies, and in many ways it's much easier to work with than OPA and Rego. While TFLint requires you to learn either OPA or Go to create custom policies, Checkov has the ability to read custom policies from a simple YAML file.

YAML was designed to be a more human-friendly language for defining data. It's a superset of JSON, which means that it can read JSON but also has additional functionality. As a simple example, let's look at what it would take to prevent teams from using certain AWS Instance Families. Some of these instance families can be expensive, such as the P and G lines, which contain GPUs. Accidentally launching one of these can really break the budget, so we can use Checkov with a custom policy to prevent that.

Listing 7.31 Checkov YAML example policy

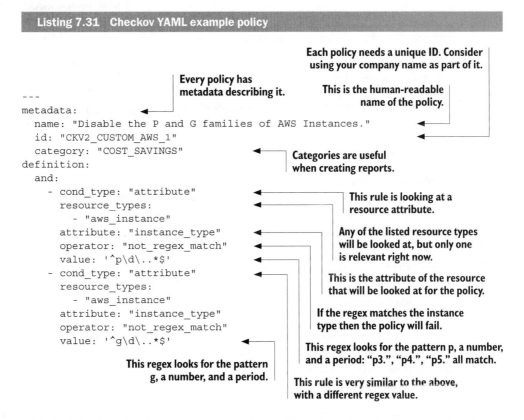

Checkov also has the ability to define policies with Python. For the vast majority of uses, you should simply use the YAML option. Introducing Python adds an additional layer of complexity that tends not to be needed in the vast majority of cases. The only place where Python really makes sense is if you need to incorporate an API call into your policy.

Although you could place your custom policies in every project you make, this can be a bit of a maintenance nightmare. Checkov has the ability to load policies directly from a Git repository, including remote ones located on an SCM. Rather than maintaining a bunch of independent policies, you could create a shared repository with the policies that apply to all of your modules. As the policies get updated in the single repository, every repository will end up using them.

Once we've put these policies into a repository, we need to tell Checkov where to get them from. Unlike TFLint, Checkov does not use a standard configuration file that we could define this in. Instead, we need to update our `makefile` to include a new command-line flag that tells Checkov to pull down the policies. This way, anyone using the makefile will automatically call the proper command.

Listing 7.32   Checkov `makefile` with remote policies

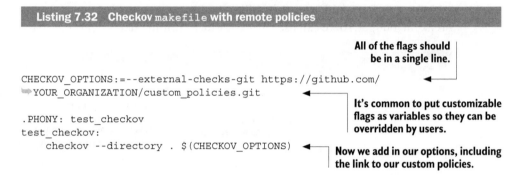

```
CHECKOV_OPTIONS:=--external-checks-git https://github.com/
➡YOUR_ORGANIZATION/custom_policies.git

.PHONY: test_checkov
test_checkov:
    checkov --directory . $(CHECKOV_OPTIONS)
```

All of the flags should be in a single line.

It's common to put customizable flags as variables so they can be overridden by users.

Now we add in our options, including the link to our custom policies.

7.6   *Automating chores*

No one likes doing chores, and unfortunately programming has a lot of chores. From little things like maintaining standard formatting to larger tasks like building documentation, programming comes with a lot of busy work. Programmers love their automation though, and there are a lot of tools that allow us to automate the common chores of programming. Terraform has several built-in commands that help us automate chores, and the Terraform ecosystem as a whole includes many tools that we go over in this section.

Just like with our previous sections, we're going to continue building on our `makefile` to add our automated chores in. For this, we're going to make a new high-level target named, appropriately enough, `chores` so that we can use that to run all of our chore automation with a single comment. Although this is a small thing, it's pretty powerful, as developers will simply need to run `make chores` to update documentation and formatting.

> **TIP** Some of the targets we're going to create were previewed in listing 7.6, so make sure when you review these that you don't create duplicate targets. Make will return a warning if you do.

Listing 7.33   Makefile `chore` target

```
.PHONY: chores
chores: documentation format
```

As new automations are added this target can be expanded.

7.6.1 *terraform-docs*

Writing good documentation is one of the most important parts of creating reusable modules. If you want people to use the modules, they need to be able to see how to use the modules. One aspect of this is writing detailed descriptions of your inputs and outputs, which is absolutely critical. The problem is that reading through source code is not exactly a great user experience, and manually copying descriptions into documentation is tedious and error-prone.

The `terraform-docs` utility resolves this problem beautifully. It will read through Terraform code and automatically generate documentation in a variety of formats (the most popular being markdown tables). You can even tell `terraform-docs` to inject the generated documentation into other documentation. This is commonly used to inject all of the inputs, outputs, modules, and created resources into the `README.md` file of a repository alongside a description of the project, instructions for installation, and any other documentation the authors feel is relevant.

This isn't a one-off operation either. `terraform-docs` can be called over and over again as modules change to update existing documentation in place without altering the customizations outside of the `terraform-docs` section. `terraform-docs` also provides a flag, `--output-check`, which can be used to test that documentation is up to date and does not need to be generated.

Listing 7.34 Makefile targets for `terraform-docs`

```
.PHONY: documentation
documentation:
    terraform-docs -c .terraform-docs.yml .
```
◀── **This target updates our documentation for us.**

```
.PHONY: test_documentation
test_documentation:
    terraform-docs -c .terraform-docs.yml --output-check .
```
◀── **This target only tests that our documentation is up to date, but does not change anything.**

`terraform-docs` has many other features that can be customized using a `.terraform-docs.yml` file. While most of the options that are found in the configuration file can also be passed using the command-line interface, it's good practice to use a configuration to keep the generated documentation consistent between users. The most common changes to the default settings are to set a format (which is required) and an output file.

Listing 7.35 `terraform-docs` basic settings

```
formatter: "markdown table"

output:
```
◀── **There are a lot of options available, but "markdown table" is the most commonly used.**

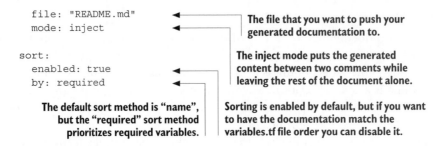

```
    file: "README.md"
    mode: inject

sort:
    enabled: true
    by: required
```

The file that you want to push your generated documentation to.

The inject mode puts the generated content between two comments while leaving the rest of the document alone.

The default sort method is "name", but the "required" sort method prioritizes required variables.

Sorting is enabled by default, but if you want to have the documentation match the variables.tf file order you can disable it.

With that done, developers can now run either `make documentation` or `make chores` to automatically update the `readme` file. With our settings, and specifically the inject mode, we need to format our `readme` file document correctly by adding in placeholder comments so `terraform-docs` knows where to put the generated content.

Listing 7.36 `terraform-docs readme` **example**

```
# My Module

This is where you'd put a description of the module.

## Usage

<!-- BEGIN_TF_DOCS -->

<!-- END_TF_DOCS -->
```

From here to "END_TF_DOCS" is generated and controlled by terraform-docs.

From "BEGIN_TF_DOCS" to here is generated and controlled by terraform-docs.

7.6.2   *terraform fmt*

Maintaining coding format standards is not a requirement to run Terraform, but it is a good practice. Consistent formatting and spacing make code more pleasant to work with and easier to read. One of the nice things about Terraform is that it has a simple style guide that can be automatically applied and enforced with the built-in `terraform fmt` tool.

It's important to note that `terraform fmt` won't be able to enforce every best practice or coding standard as it is a fairly rudimentary tool (by design). Other tools, such as `tflint` or any of the security scanners we've discussed, provide feedback not just on the format of your code but on the actual content. That said, it does catch some low-hanging-fruit errors, and it makes your code more consistent between projects.

Listing 7.37 Makefile targets for `terraform fmt`

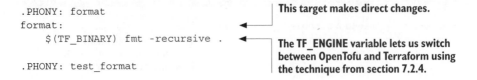

```
.PHONY: format
format:
    $(TF_BINARY) fmt -recursive .

.PHONY: test_format
```

This target makes direct changes.

The TF_ENGINE variable lets us switch between OpenTofu and Terraform using the technique from section 7.2.4.

```
test_format:
    $(TF_BINARY) fmt -check -recursive .
```

◄──── **This target only tests that the formatting is right, and returns an error if it would have made changes.**

7.6.3 *tflint autofix*

Although we discussed tflint already, we skipped over one of its best features: the ability to automatically fix many of the problems that it discovers. Telling tflint to fix problems is as easy as passing the --fix flag. Not every rule that tflint has can be automatically fixed, but many of them can. The simpler a rule, the more likely it can be automatically fixed: for instance, the rule requiring specific comment styles can be automatically fixed once it is enabled. It's important to note that when fixes do occur, the file also gets reformatted, so unrelated things may change (but this is the same as running terraform fmt anyway, so it shouldn't be a huge problem).

Listing 7.38 Makefile targets for tflint

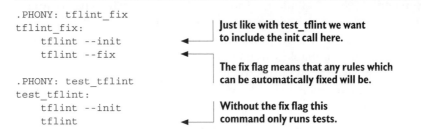

```
.PHONY: tflint_fix
tflint_fix:
    tflint --init
    tflint --fix

.PHONY: test_tflint
test_tflint:
    tflint --init
    tflint
```

Just like with test_tflint we want to include the init call here.

The fix flag means that any rules which can be automatically fixed will be.

Without the fix flag this command only runs tests.

One important difference between this chore and the others is that we are not adding it to our chore alias. We don't want to automatically apply changes without giving them some scrutiny, so it's better to run tflint first to see what violations might exist and then make a decision on how to resolve them (which can, and often will, include running autofix).

> **WARNING** tflint is powerful and has a lot of rules that it can apply, but it isn't always right. While it does push best practices, there are cases where the best practices may not be the right decision. Always review your autofixes.

For instance, you may have an application that's using some deprecated features of AWS that tflint is catching as an error. Although this is something that you want to watch for, it is not unexpected for your specific application. If you had run the tflint autofix utility without reviewing it first, then you would have made a change you really didn't want to make, potentially breaking a system. What you should do instead is run tflint, review the results, add any exceptions to your code so tflint will ignore them, and then run autofix on whatever is left.

7.7 *Enforcing quality with CI systems*

Now we have a solid foundation for CI. We have a variety of tools running locally that teams can use to create high-quality software, as well as run basic chores to keep code clean and understandable. Although we haven't created in-depth tests yet, we have the placeholders to add those later, and with the tools we have now, we can already increase our quality. Now we're ready to take it a step further by enforcing the use of these tools and incorporating our tests into the PR process.

7.7.1   Selecting a CI system

The first thing we need is a decision on what CI system to use. There are a lot of options to look at, as CI has been around for a long time and there have been many open source and proprietary systems created over time.

Since CI is such a core practice of software developers, there's a good chance your team or organization already has a CI solution, in which case you should probably go ahead and use it. To be blunt, there's nothing on the CI side of things that makes Terraform all that unique among programming languages (on the delivery side of things, this is a different story, as we'll see in the next chapter) so there's no harm in just going with the system that is already available.

If you don't have a CI solution already available, you have to make some choices. The first thing you should do is check to see if your SCM has support for CI operations. Both GitHub and GitLab have their own built-in CI solutions that are perfectly reasonable tools, and if they are available, this is absolutely where you should start. Utilizing a tool already built into your SCM means you have a fairly easy onboarding process and don't need to worry about linking your SCM and CI systems. Quite frankly, this is where I would personally end the search, as both GitLab Pipelines and GitHub Actions handle every CI use case we've discussed in a very easy-to-use way.

You also have the option of running your own system. There are dozens of options out there that allow for self-hosting. That said, for small teams, the cost of running your own solution may outweigh the cost of simply purchasing a software as a service-based product, so really evaluate if it's worth the effort. This is one of those cases where small teams should just use the cloud versions (GitHub.com, GitLab.com), and any organization that's large enough to need something more bespoke is going to have a separate team managing it. In other words, try not to distract yourself and just use the easiest-to-use system you have available.

7.7.2   Building the basic workflows

These days, most CI systems operate in a very similar way. Developers define the different jobs they want to run, and each job consists of triggers and steps to run. For example, a job may be triggered by someone pushing a commit to their SCM and then running steps that include installing the test suite and then running it. A job is typically a three-step process, as shown in figure 7.4.

Figure 7.4   Basic CI workflow

We focus on GitHub Actions for the time being, as it's the most popular SCM and CI combination out there, but the concepts we're discussing translate to all of the other services. For instance, every CI solution has its own version of sharable actions or scripts. What GitHub calls a marketplace action, GitLab calls a component and CircleCI calls an orb. Although the language they use to describe things is different, the concepts are the same.

Listing 7.39　Simple GitHub action

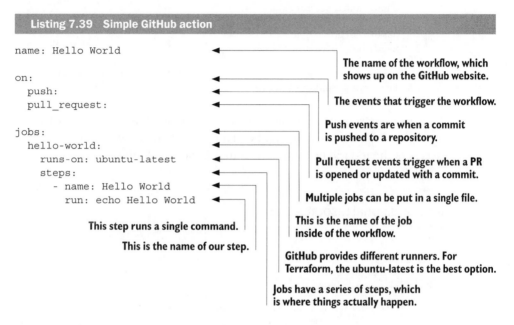

Of course, a simple Hello World isn't all that helpful. What we really want to do is download our code, install our test utility, and run our tests against it to confirm that they pass. To do this, we're going to take advantage of GitHub marketplace actions, which are shared actions that users can add to their pipeline. In our first example, we're going to do three things:

- Download our code
- Install TFLint
- Run TFLint using our `makefile`

Let's apply this to TFLint. We want to create a workflow that runs every time someone makes a commit to our repository or makes a PR. Inside of our project, we're going to create the file `.github/workflows/tflint.yml`, and we will define our workflow there.

Listing 7.40　TFLint on GitHub Actions

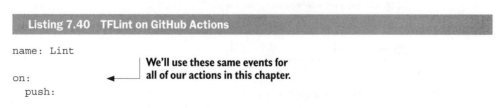

```
    pull_request:

jobs:
  tflint:
    runs-on: ubuntu-latest

    steps:
      - name: Checkout source code
        uses: actions/checkout@v4

      - name: Setup TFLint
        uses: terraform-linters/setup-tflint@v4

      - name: Run TFLint
        run: make test_tflint
```

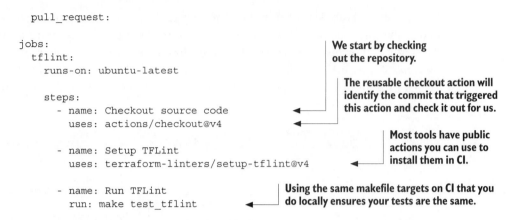

We start by checking out the repository.

The reusable checkout action will identify the commit that triggered this action and check it out for us.

Most tools have public actions you can use to install them in CI.

Using the same makefile targets on CI that you do locally ensures your tests are the same.

If any of these steps fail for any reason, then the workflow will be marked as a failure (see figure 7.5). Since GitHub and GitHub Actions are tightly integrated, the failure or success of the test will be associated with the specific PR that triggered it.

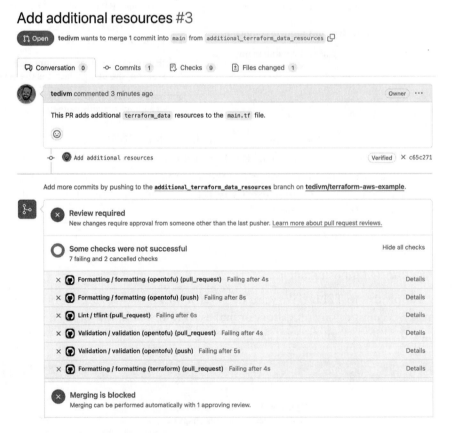

Figure 7.5 A PR with failing tests

This same pattern can be used to run all of the tests that we've created. If any of them fail, then the PR will be blocked. The status of the tests is also available for anyone on the team to see, so it's easier to identify what went wrong and what needs to be corrected.

You may have also noticed that there is nothing in these tests that are unique for a specific project. These workflows can be used for any Terraform module that has the same makefile that we do. This is why you want to create and add all of these workflows to your software template, so that teams can start new projects that immediately take advantage of CI before they write a single line of code.

7.7.3 *Validating both OpenTofu and Terraform*

Many of the quality control checks that we are running don't actually depend on Terraform itself. Checkov, TFLint, and Terraform-Docs don't actually do anything with the Terraform binary itself and don't depend on Terraform to build their results. They are independent programs that scan your code by themselves. However, there are at least three cases where we do expect to use Terraform as part of our quality control:

- Formatting
- Validation
- Testing

Both the formatting and validation tests directly rely on running a Terraform binary and reviewing the results. In theory, the results from each of these should be the same, but reality has a habit of getting in the way of these theories. While the expectation is that OpenTofu and Terraform are compatible, it is always good to confirm this expectation. This is even more important when testing the functionality of our code itself, and even though we are waiting until chapter 9 to tackle that, the methods here will still apply.

Going back to the start of this chapter, we added a variable to our `makefile` to allow us to easily switch between `tofu` and `terraform`. This variable can be changed with an argument when we call `make`. This can be combined with a feature of GitHub Actions called a matrix strategy that lets us run the same pipeline multiple times with different options. We can even tweak our workflow to only install either OpenTofu or Terraform depending on which one is needed.

> **WARNING** Confirm your versions! If you set your Terraform required versions to start at v1.7, you're going to want to remove v1.6 from the versions you test against. Since this is a book, there's also a good chance new versions that you do want to test against have been released. For reusable modules, you often want to maintain wide compatibility with different Terraform versions, while stuff that isn't shared may be locked to a specific version. We'll talk more about this in the next chapter.

Listing 7.41 OpenTofu and Terraform in one workflow

```
name: Validation

on:
```

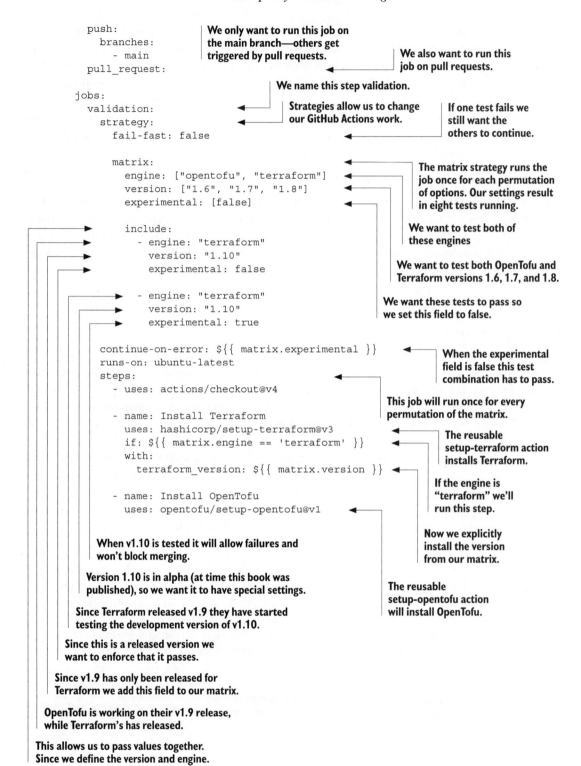

```
push:
  branches:
    - main
  pull_request:

jobs:
  validation:
    strategy:
      fail-fast: false

      matrix:
        engine: ["opentofu", "terraform"]
        version: ["1.6", "1.7", "1.8"]
        experimental: [false]

        include:
          - engine: "terraform"
            version: "1.10"
            experimental: false

          - engine: "terraform"
            version: "1.10"
            experimental: true

      continue-on-error: ${{ matrix.experimental }}
      runs-on: ubuntu-latest
      steps:
        - uses: actions/checkout@v4

        - name: Install Terraform
          uses: hashicorp/setup-terraform@v3
          if: ${{ matrix.engine == 'terraform' }}
          with:
            terraform_version: ${{ matrix.version }}

        - name: Install OpenTofu
          uses: opentofu/setup-opentofu@v1
```

We only want to run this job on the main branch—others get triggered by pull requests.

We also want to run this job on pull requests.

We name this step validation.

Strategies allow us to change our GitHub Actions work.

If one test fails we still want the others to continue.

The matrix strategy runs the job once for each permutation of options. Our settings result in eight tests running.

We want to test both of these engines

We want to test both OpenTofu and Terraform versions 1.6, 1.7, and 1.8.

We want these tests to pass so we set this field to false.

When the experimental field is false this test combination has to pass.

This job will run once for every permutation of the matrix.

The reusable setup-terraform action installs Terraform.

If the engine is "terraform" we'll run this step.

Now we explicitly install the version from our matrix.

The reusable setup-opentofu action will install OpenTofu.

When v1.10 is tested it will allow failures and won't block merging.

Version 1.10 is in alpha (at time this book was published), so we want it to have special settings.

Since Terraform released v1.9 they have started testing the development version of v1.10.

Since this is a released version we want to enforce that it passes.

Since v1.9 has only been released for Terraform we add this field to our matrix.

OpenTofu is working on their v1.9 release, while Terraform's has released.

This allows us to pass values together. Since we define the version and engine.

If the engine is "opentofu" we'll run this step.

Now we explicitly install the version from our matrix.

```
if: ${{ matrix.engine == 'opentofu' }}
with:
   tofu_version: ${{ matrix.version }}

- name: Test Validation
  run: make test_validation TF_ENGINE=${{matrix.engine}}
```

Now we pass the engine in to the **TF_ENGINE** variable of our makefile, switching our binaries around.

As long as we continue to support the `makefile` parameter, this same logic can be applied to the tests we will be writing in chapter 9. This relatively simple change to our workflows, combined with our earlier decision to utilize makefiles, has made it much easier to maintain compatibility between the two different flavors of Terraform. This in turn makes it easier for us to avoid locking ourselves into a specific vendor or having to enforce use of OpenTofu or Terraform for the users of any modules you develop.

7.7.4 Branch protection and required pipelines

If your tests fail, you shouldn't merge code in. This seems like common sense, but it's pretty easy to merge things (all it takes is a button), and people can sometimes be tempted to move quickly and hold off on fixing errors until later. This is, as you can probably guess, a bad idea. That's why every SCM out there has the ability to block merges unless some conditions are met.

The two most common conditions are that tests are passing and that the code has been reviewed by someone other than the author. The tests passing is pretty obvious: if tests fail, then merging into main would break the main branch and prevent any other developers from getting much done. Requiring at least one (and many teams require two) approvals before merging the code acts as both a quality control and a security check to confirm that no one is adding any functionality that they shouldn't be.

Exactly how you create branch protections depends on your SCM, but in general it's as simple as going to the settings for the repository and looking for something that says "branch protection" (see figure 7.6). Once a repository is in production, enabling branch protection should be one of the first things you do.

One thing you're probably wondering is: What happens in an emergency? What if there's an outage and no one around to review your test or something in the test suite itself breaks? These are reasonable concerns. GitHub and GitLab both have the ability to override any of these blocks with a simple checkbox on the PR page. Our CI tools are meant to help, not hinder, teams and can be bypassed when they get in the way.

7.7.5 Automated updates with Dependabot

If you're using GitHub, you also have an option to use the Dependabot tool. This automated tool is extremely useful for keeping your dependencies up to date. When it

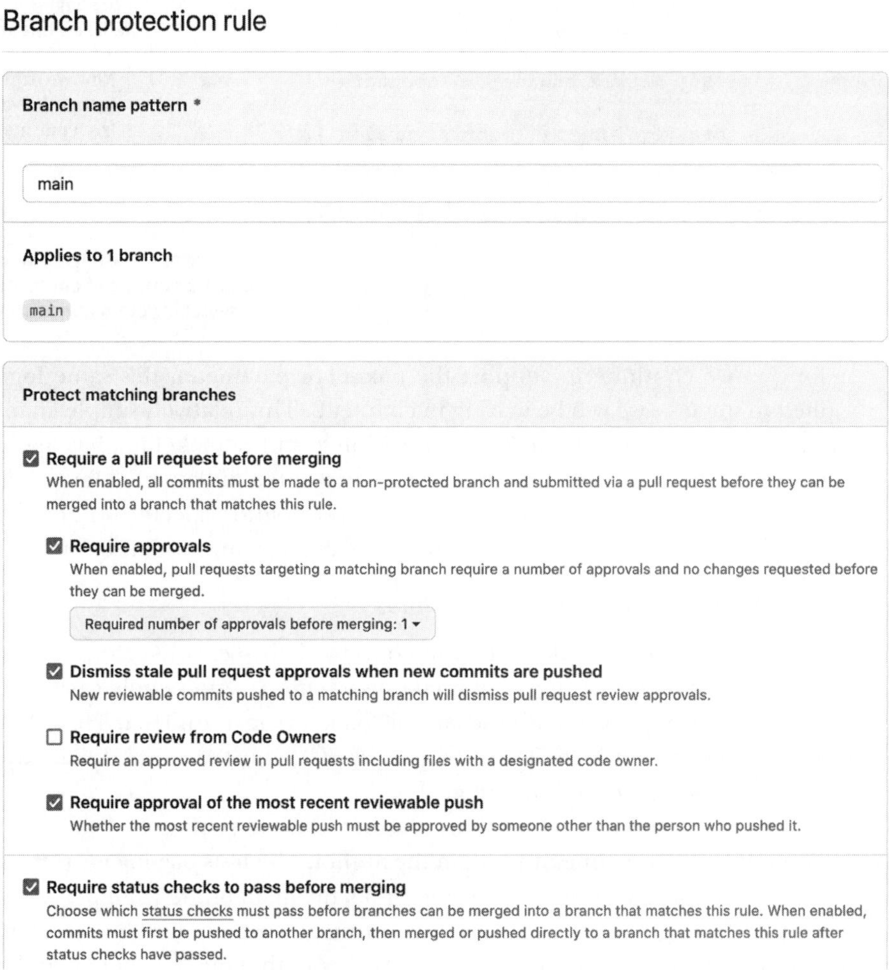

Branch protection rule

Branch name pattern *

```
main
```

Applies to 1 branch

`main`

Protect matching branches

☑ **Require a pull request before merging**
When enabled, all commits must be made to a non-protected branch and submitted via a pull request before they can be merged into a branch that matches this rule.

☑ **Require approvals**
When enabled, pull requests targeting a matching branch require a number of approvals and no changes requested before they can be merged.

Required number of approvals before merging: 1 ▾

☑ **Dismiss stale pull request approvals when new commits are pushed**
New reviewable commits pushed to a matching branch will dismiss pull request review approvals.

☐ **Require review from Code Owners**
Require an approved review in pull requests including files with a designated code owner.

☑ **Require approval of the most recent reviewable push**
Whether the most recent reviewable push must be approved by someone other than the person who pushed it.

☑ **Require status checks to pass before merging**
Choose which status checks must pass before branches can be merged into a branch that matches this rule. When enabled, commits must first be pushed to another branch, then merged or pushed directly to a branch that matches this rule after status checks have passed.

Figure 7.6   Branch protection on GitHub

notices that a dependency is out of date, it creates a PR to update it, which allows tests to run and developers to review the changes just like any other PR.

This can be used for our GitHub Actions themselves. We've used actions such as the checkout and setup actions, and in each case we've set a high-level version to run. When new versions come out, we can have Dependabot create a PR to update our workflow files with the new versions. All we need to do to enable this is to create and populate `.github/dependabot.yml` with our Dependabot configuration.

Listing 7.42   Dependabot configuration for actions

```
version: 2
updates:
```

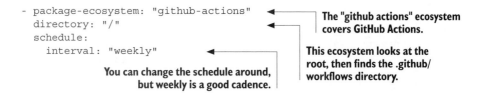

```
- package-ecosystem: "github-actions"
  directory: "/"
  schedule:
    interval: "weekly"
```

The "github actions" ecosystem covers GitHub Actions.

This ecosystem looks at the root, then finds the .github/workflows directory.

You can change the schedule around, but weekly is a good cadence.

GitHub Actions is just the starting point though. Our Terraform code uses versions for modules and providers, and as projects get more complex, it can be difficult to keep track of the different versions being used. Fortunately, Dependabot has support for Terraform and can create PRs to update versions for us.

Listing 7.43 Dependabot configuration for modules

```
version: 2
updates:
  - package-ecosystem: "github-actions"
    directory: "/"
    schedule:
      interval: "weekly"

  - package-ecosystem: "terraform"
    directory: "/"
    schedule:
      interval: "weekly"
```

Multiple ecosystems can be configured at once, so we can leave this here.

The Terraform ecosystem will look at modules and providers for updates.

Once done, Dependabot will start running. If you have any actions or modules that are not using the latest versions, you should expect a PR to be opened to update them (see figure 7.7). The PR will even trigger tests so you can see if any additional changes need to be made. We'll talk more about versioning strategies in chapter 11.

If you're using a private module registry, you can specify that in the registry section of the Dependabot configuration. You will have to save the login token for this as a secret in your GitHub repository, which can be done through the repository's settings tab. One important thing to note is that the registry has to be accessible to GitHub itself, which means that registries locked behind a firewall or private network might not be able to use this feature. It's possible to use self-hosted runners (https://mng.bz/KG2K) to solve this problem.

Listing 7.44 Dependabot configuration for private registries

```
version: 2
updates:
  - package-ecosystem: "github-actions"
    directory: "/"
    schedule:
      interval: "weekly"

  - package-ecosystem: "terraform"
    directory: "/"
```

The problem with updating Terraform is that most teams use private registries for their modules.

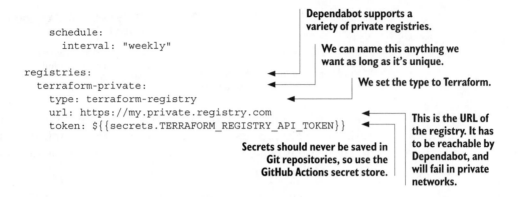

```
    schedule:
      interval: "weekly"

registries:
  terraform-private:
    type: terraform-registry
    url: https://my.private.registry.com
    token: ${{secrets.TERRAFORM_REGISTRY_API_TOKEN}}
```

Dependabot supports a variety of private registries.

We can name this anything we want as long as it's unique.

We set the type to Terraform.

This is the URL of the registry. It has to be reachable by Dependabot, and will fail in private networks.

Secrets should never be saved in Git repositories, so use the GitHub Actions secret store.

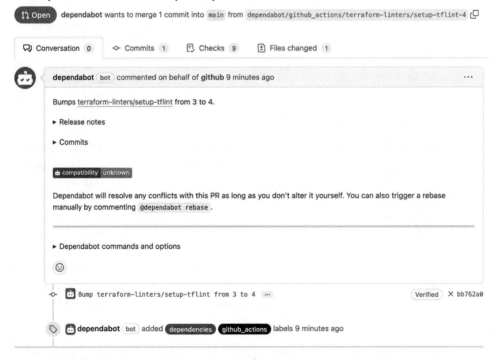

Figure 7.7   Dependabot PR

Although Dependabot is owned by GitHub, it is an open source project. There is a community fork with support for GitLab that users of that platform can use, although it does take a little more effort to manage the initial setup.

We've gone over a lot of tools in this chapter, and it can easily seem overwhelming. Don't forget, though, that you are not expected to memorize how all of these tools work. It's very common to refer back to documentation, but even more importantly your common configurations and commands should all be placed in reusable files and templates. The bulk of this chapter can be applied, with minimal changes, to all of your projects. That's why we started off with a Cookiecutter template and `makefile`.

One important note that you may be wondering is where the continuous delivery (CD) went. CI and CD are often discussed hand in hand (so much so that the systems that run them are normally referred to as CI/CD systems). The reality is these are both rather large topics, and with Terraform in particular there is a lot of nuance that goes into delivery. In our next chapter, we focus purely on the delivery aspects of Terraform.

Summary

- IaC is powerful because of the lessons we can learn from software development.
- Automated quality-control tools such as linters and security scanners can greatly improve code quality with minimal effort.
- The use of automation to enforce policy and test code allows developers to move faster by giving them safety nets.
- Automation reduces the cognitive load of code reviews, allowing developers to focus on the proposed changes themselves.
- Automation should be easy and repeatable, which is why tools like Make and Cookiecutter should be used to create standards between projects.
- CI systems work alongside source control management systems to allow teams to move quickly while ensuring high-quality code.

Continuous delivery
and deployment

This chapter covers

- Publishing modules to private registries
- Reducing maintenance burdens with semantic versioning
- Deploying infrastructure
- Continuous delivery platforms
- GitOps
- Terragrunt
- Secret management

As the software industry has evolved, so have the tools that we use for it. Continuous integration (CI) and continuous delivery (CD) have been so entwined that most people refer to them together as CI/CD, and until recently it was common to use CI systems as delivery and deployment tools. If this book was written 10 years ago, it's very likely that CI/CD would be a single chapter.

The industry has moved on to the point where it's recognized that CI is not CD (see figure 8.1). CI systems are focused around source code and making sure there is always a workable copy of the program available. This is why so many source control management (SCM) tools have CI features built right into them. In the last chapter, we discussed why this is important: it increases security, reduces errors, and makes developing new features easier. All of this is vital to make CI possible, but it doesn't actually build our infrastructure.

CD, on the other hand, is focused on regularly deploying changes into environments. Teams that practice CD principles are able to rapidly deploy new features and bug fixes. According to DORA (the DevOps Research Agency, a group that creates a yearly report on how the industry functions), high-performing teams deploy multiple times a day, with a low failure rate and a fast recovery time. By adopting the tools and practices around CD, teams can improve their own performance while also introducing safety around their deployments.

Over the last decade there has been a rise in the number and popularity of dedicated CD platforms and a move away from using tools designed for CI for CD. Although it is possible to use CI systems as CD systems, the fact that they weren't designed for it introduces a lot of inefficiencies. Terraform and Kubernetes are two tools that have really adopted the GitOps and CD methodology almost from the start, and as a result they both have a lot of tools in this space. Although our focus is on Terraform, it should be noted that many of the tools and principles we discuss in this chapter can apply well beyond just Terraform.

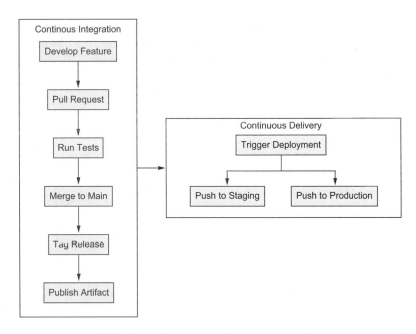

Figure 8.1 CI and CD boundaries

In this chapter, we look at delivery from two perspectives. The first, and much simpler side of things, is delivering modules to other teams so they can use them in their own code. Next, we tackle a much more complex topic: delivering your infrastructure changes to their production environments. This includes going over the high-level topics as well as a review of the more popular delivery tools available.

8.1 Delivering modules

Developing reusable modules is one of the major benefits of organizations adopting Terraform, but it's only useful if the modules are easily usable. This goes beyond just quality control, as our last chapter focused on, to include versioning and the use of registries. Just like with CI practices, there is a lot we can learn here from how other languages handle dependency management and software delivery.

8.1.1 Semantic versioning and constraints

Every method for delivering modules that we go through in this chapter has one thing in common: they are all triggered via Git tags with a specific format: `vX.Y.Z` (where X, Y, and Z are numbers). This requirement is baked right into the Terraform Module Registry Protocol itself. The reason for this is because Terraform assumes that published modules are following the Semantic Versioning 2.0 (https://semver.org/) conventions.

Maintaining software dependencies is a bit of a chore. If you had to upgrade each module you used manually every time there was an update, it would get obnoxious pretty quickly and would encourage teams to use fewer modules. Not every module upgrade requires the same level of inspection though. Semantic versioning allows software developers to version their software in a way that signals what level of change developers can expect (see figure 8.2).

Semantic versioning breaks changes into three categories:

- Patch changes are simple bug fixes that should be safe for developers to upgrade to without review.
- Minor changes introduce new features without breaking anything that currently exists. In theory, developers should be able to upgrade to these versions without needing to make changes to their own code, but these changes do tend to be more complex, so there is a higher chance of new bugs being introduced.
- Major changes signify that the changes are large enough that upgrading will require some effort.

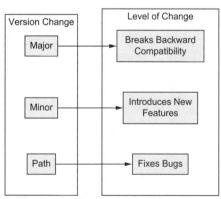

Figure 8.2   Semantic version fields to change level

This is expressed in the version string itself. Each of the fields (`Major`, `Minor`, and `Patch`) are represented by a number and are expressed by the pattern `vMajor.Minor.Patch`. For example, the first stable version of a module will be v1.0.0 and, as bug fixes are added, the last digit increments (`v1.0.1`, `v1.0.2`, etc.). If a new feature is added then the `Minor` version is incremented and the `Patch` is reset to zero, resulting in `v1.1.0`. Finally, if anything breaks backward compatibility, the `Major` version is incremented and the others are reset, leading to `v2.0.0`. (See table 8.1.)

Table 8.1 Example changelog and semantic versions

Change	Field to increment	Version
First stable release		v1.0.0
Fix error in variable validation	Patch	v1.0.1
Improve documentation	Patch	v1.0.2
Expose additional resource parameters as variables	Minor	v1.1.0
Fix TFLint rule violation	Patch	v1.1.1
Refactor input variable names	Major	v2.0.0

By itself, this is pretty cool, as it signifies to the people using modules what amount of effort will be needed to upgrade. What makes this even more powerful is the Terraform version constraint features. When you define a version in Terraform, whether it's a provider, module, or even Terraform itself, you can define a range of versions that are acceptable rather than a single version (see table 8.2).

Table 8.2 Example constraints with their allowed versions

Constraint	Allowed versions
= 1.1.1	Only `v1.1.1` is allowed.
>= 1.1.0, < 2.0.0	The minimum version is `v1.1.0`, and any `Minor` or `Patch` versions are allowed. Upgrading the `Major` version is not allowed.
>= 1.1.0, < 2.0.0, != 1.3.2	The same as above, except we're also forbidding version `v1.3.2` from being used. Excluding specific versions is useful when bugs are introduced to a specific version and then fixed.
~> 1.1.0	The pessimistic constraint operator allows only the rightmost field to be upgraded. In this case, that means `v1.1` and any bug fixes are allowed, but `Minor` and `Major` upgrades are excluded.
~> 1.1	This sets the floor at `v1.1`, but since the rightmost value is the `Minor` field it allows `Minor` and `Patch` upgrades. It is the exact same as `>= 1.1.0, <2.0.0` but is more concise.

When developing modules for reuse by other teams or developers, you should attempt to support the widest range of versions possible so your users aren't locked into a tight set of versions. This is because many developers will use multiple modules in their project, and the tighter your version constraints, the more likely your module will have conflicts with other modules. To make life easier for your users, you should restrict your version constraint to the lowest version that will work for your modules and then allow anything except `Major` upgrades (which will always have some sort of backward compatibility breaking changes). The best way to accomplish this is by using the pessimistic constraint while defining a `Major` and `Minor` version (e.g., `~> 1.1`).

Listing 8.1   Using version constraints

```
module "specific_example" {
  source  = "registry.example.com/example/provider/feature»
  version = "1.1.1"                                    ◄──────┐
}                                                             │  Only this specific version
                                                              │  will be installed.

module "update_except_major" {
  source  = "registry.example.com/example/provider/feature"
  version = ">= 1.1.0, < 2.0.0"                        ◄──────┐
}                                                             │  The minimum version is 1.1.0,
                                                              │  and upgrades can occur up to,
module "update_except_major_excluding" {                     │  but not including, 2.0.0.
  source  = "registry.example.com/example/provider/feature"
  version = ">= 1.1.0, < 2.0.0, != 1.3.2"   ◄──────┐
}                                                   │  The same as "update_except_
                                                    │  major" but excluding 1.3.2.
module "pessimistic_constraint_bugfix" {
  source  = "registry.example.com/example/provider/feature"
  version = "~> 1.1.0"                                ◄──────┐
}                                                             │  Will update any bug release:
                                                              │  equal to ">=1.1.0 , < 1.2.0"
module "pessimistic_constraint_minor" {
  source  = "registry.example.com/example/provider/feature"
  version = "~> 1.1"                                  ◄──────┐
}                                                             │  Will update any minor or bug release:
                                                              │  equal to ">=1.1.0 , < 2.0.0"
```

This is why Terraform forces modules to use a specific format for versioning, as it makes it easier to specify safe ranges of versions. Of course, this also means that developers releasing modules have a responsibility to use semantic versioning properly. There aren't any good ways to enforce this programmatically, so it is up to developer teams to enforce this with culture. When creating new releases, you should review all of the changes, identify any that break backward compatibility, and then either fix them to maintain compatibility or increment the `Major` version field.

8.1.2   *SCM-based module delivery*

One thing you may ask yourself is: Why not just load your modules directly from your SCM? After all, Terraform does support loading modules directly from Git and even has some shortcuts for pulling them down from GitHub. Since you're already using

SCM, it requires very little extra work, especially if you're simply pulling from the default branch.

Listing 8.2 Defining a module source with Git

```
module "github_example" {
  source = "github.com/tedivm/terraform-aws-lambda"     ◀──── Terraform has special
}                                                              handling for GitHub.

module "generic_git_example" {
  source = "git@github.com:tedivm/terraform-aws-lambda.git"   ◀────
}
                              Terraform can also handle generic Git
                              sources. This module points to the
                              same module as the above example.
```

The biggest flaw with this approach is that the Git sources do not support the version field. If you want to lock down to a specific version of a module, you can do so using the `ref` field to refer to a specific Git reference (such as `commit` or `tag`) when defining the module source, but that locks you down to a very specific version.

Listing 8.3 Defining a module source with Git reference

```
module "generic_git_example" {
  source = "git@github.com:tedivm/terraform-aws-lambda.git?ref=v1.0.1"   ◀────
}
                              To use the ref field you have to use the generic
                              Git format, not the GitHub-specific format.
```

Although this may seem like a minor thing, being able to fully take advantage of version constraints really reduces the burden on teams using your modules. Without it, you end up dealing with a tradeoff: reducing your own stability or increasing your maintenance burden:

- If users install from the default branch, they don't have any chance to review backward incompatible changes, which could result in their code breaking randomly.
- If users pin to specific commits or versions, then they won't be able to automatically pull in bug fixes or enhancements that don't break backward compatibility and instead have to manually run all of those upgrades. This can be an absolute maintenance nightmare, especially as teams use more and more modules. As a result, a lot of teams who go this route rarely update their module versions.

This doesn't mean you should never pull your modules directly from the SCM. Smaller teams may be able to manage these tradeoffs. It's also a very common practice to pull directly from SCM when working with development branches as a way to test changes to modules before they are finished. For example, if you're using a network module and find a bug, you may temporarily use a bugfix branch of that module locally while waiting for it to be merged and released.

From a scalability perspective though, it makes sense to adopt a registry quickly to take advantage of version constraints.

8.1.3   Public software registries

Software registries have been around since at least 1995 with the launch of Perl's CPAN package registry. Every modern language at this point has a public registry for the open source project: Javascript has NPM, Python has PyPI, PHP has Packagist, and so on.

With the Terraform license change, the state of public registries has gotten a little complicated. HashiCorp has maintained a registry for modules and providers for long enough that I honestly couldn't tell you when it launched (my wonderful technical editor says 2017). That registry does not actually host any software but instead acts as an index that points to other packages (which is a pretty common method for package managers). After HashiCorp changed the license to Terraform, they also came out with a change to their Terms of Service that added some pretty severe limitations to how their index could be used. As a result, the OpenTofu team has launched their own registry.

Although this is unfortunate, the good news is that it really only affects you if you are releasing your modules on an open source registry. The reality for most developers is that their code is meant to be used internally to their company, not as a general-purpose tool released out to the world. This means you are most likely going to use a private registry.

Let's say you do want to release your module publicly though. To do this, you first have to make sure your repository is public and published on GitHub (yes, it has to be GitHub right now: other SCMs such as GitLabs aren't supported). Then you have to submit a link to that repository to each registry. This only has to be done once, since the registries are just indexes to your project.

So submit your module to the OpenTofu registry first; go to the OpenTofu.org site and follow the link to the registry. From there, you will find a link to a form to submit your module. At the moment, submission of new modules is done through a form on GitHub, but it's very likely that this will change in the future as the OpenTofu registry is built out (see figure 8.3).

Registering a module on the Hashicorp Terraform registry is very similar. Start by going to the registry.terraform.io website and log in. Once logged in, click Publish and then Module. You'll be given a dropdown to select a GitHub repository (see figure 8.4).

That's it! Both of the registries will now monitor the public repository for your module, and whenever you create a new Git tag with a proper semantic version (which we'll discuss later in this section), it will be added to the registry. That means that after the initial registration, all you have to do is create a tag or release in GitHub for it to be picked up on the registry.

8.1.4   Private registries

Of course, the vast majority of people aren't developing open source modules but are generally being paid to develop modules as part of their day job. In this case, publishing your code publicly probably isn't appropriate. At this point, you need a private registry.

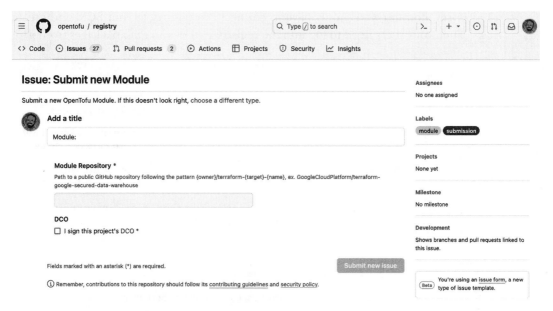

Figure 8.3   Registering a module for the OpenTofu module registry

**Figure 8.4
Registering a module
for the HashiCorp
Terraform module
registry**

Just like with CI systems, registries are becoming more and more of a commodity. Most of the Terraform deployment tools we discuss later in this chapter come with their own module registry, and the vast majority of those integrate with your SCM in the same way that the public registry does. This means that for most registries that support

Terraform modules, you simply have to connect the registry to your SCM and create tags. Then your users need to log into the registry so they can grab packages from it.

Listing 8.4   Logging into a private registry

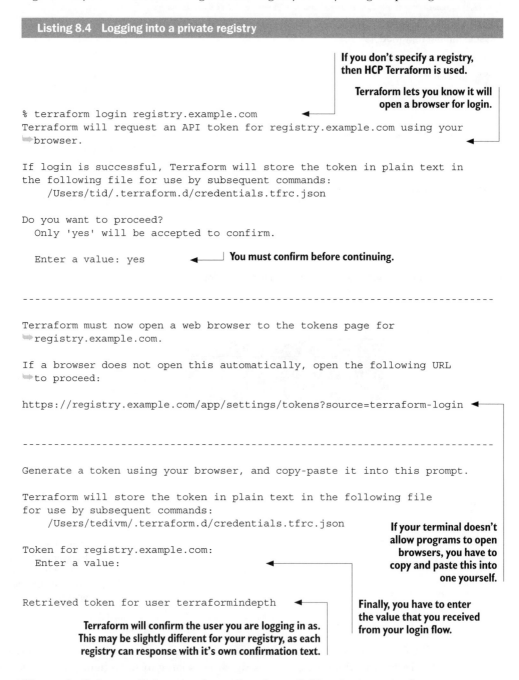

```
% terraform login registry.example.com
Terraform will request an API token for registry.example.com using your
  browser.

If login is successful, Terraform will store the token in plain text in
the following file for use by subsequent commands:
    /Users/tid/.terraform.d/credentials.tfrc.json

Do you want to proceed?
  Only 'yes' will be accepted to confirm.

  Enter a value: yes



----------------------------------------------------------------------------

Terraform must now open a web browser to the tokens page for
  registry.example.com.

If a browser does not open this automatically, open the following URL
  to proceed:

https://registry.example.com/app/settings/tokens?source=terraform-login


----------------------------------------------------------------------------

Generate a token using your browser, and copy-paste it into this prompt.

Terraform will store the token in plain text in the following file
for use by subsequent commands:
    /Users/tedivm/.terraform.d/credentials.tfrc.json

Token for registry.example.com:
  Enter a value:


Retrieved token for user terraformindepth
```

If you don't specify a registry, then HCP Terraform is used.

Terraform lets you know it will open a browser for login.

You must confirm before continuing.

If your terminal doesn't allow programs to open browsers, you have to copy and paste this into one yourself.

Finally, you have to enter the value that you received from your login flow.

Terraform will confirm the user you are logging in as. This may be slightly different for your registry, as each registry can response with it's own confirmation text.

If you don't have a private registry already available, there are a few open source options available. The most popular and well maintained of these is a program called

Terrareg (https://matthewjohn.github.io/terrareg/). Running something like Terrareg is a lot more work than using a commercial tool, but it will avoid the license fees associated with commercial products.

Software registries are also a feature of many Terraform CD platforms. If you don't have a private registry already, this may be a factor to consider when deciding whether to use an orchestrator that comes with a registry or not. Later in this chapter we discuss the different options available in this direction.

8.1.5 Artifactory

One of the most popular commercial software registries is a program called Artifactory, developed by JFrog. This application is remarkable in that it supports the package managers for pretty much every programming language (and even some things that are not programming languages). For companies that reach a certain size, it's almost a guarantee that they have an Artifactory installation somewhere.

Unfortunately, publishing Terraform modules to Artifactory isn't as simple as the other registries. While other registries typically integrate with your SCM and watch for new tags to be published, Artifactory requires that you push new module releases to it. The JFrog command-line interface (CLI), `jf`, can be used to log in and publish modules. Before the `jf` command will work, you have to login to Artifactory with it.

Listing 8.5 Creating registry configuration on system

```
jfrog config add --artifactory-url=https://registry.example.com/
```
You have to point the Artifactory url to your private registry.

Once you're logged in, you can push your module to Artifactory. Since this is a repeated action, it should be defined in your `makefile` (and, if you have a lot of Artifactory use, to your project Cookiecutter template too).

Listing 8.6 Pushing to Artifactory `makefile` target

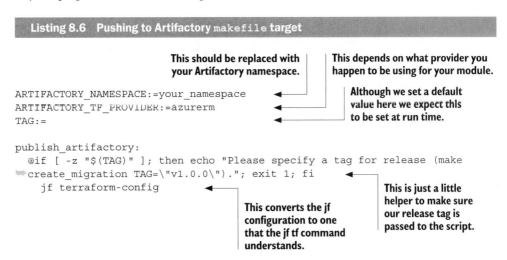

This should be replaced with your Artifactory namespace.

This depends on what provider you happen to be using for your module.

Although we set a default value here we expect this to be set at run time.

```
ARTIFACTORY_NAMESPACE:=your_namespace
ARTIFACTORY_TF_PROVIDER:=azurerm
TAG:=

publish_artifactory:
  @if [ -z "$(TAG)" ]; then echo "Please specify a tag for release (make
create_migration TAG=\"v1.0.0\")."; exit 1; fi
    jf terraform-config
```

This is just a little helper to make sure our release tag is passed to the script.

This converts the jf configuration to one that the jf tf command understands.

```
jf tf p --namespace=$(ARTIFACTORY_NAMESPACE) --provider=$(
ARTIFACTORY_TF_PROVIDER) --tag=$(TAG)
```

This final step pushes the package up to Artifactory.

Once your `makefile` has been updated, you can then add a new pipeline to your GitHub workflows to publish the module. The big difference here between other workflows is going to be the trigger, as we want this flow to only run when a new release has been created in GitHub.

Unlike your local installation, you aren't going to run the authentication command on GitHub. Instead, we're going to use OpenID Connect (OIDC) to grant permission to our workflow to publish to Artifactory. We discuss OIDC later in this chapter, but for now just know that it allows connections between services without the need for a service user or password. The JFrog GitHub action (https://mng.bz/9Y0l) has support for OIDC and instructions on how to enable it, so you should give those a very quick review for the most up-to-date instructions on setting it up.

After enabling OIDC, you can go ahead and create your pipeline. This is similar to our other GitHub Actions workflows from the previous chapter, except we're going to trigger it on tags instead of on every commit. This is because we only want to publish specific tagged releases.

Listing 8.7 Pushing to Artifactory GitHub action

```
name: Publish to Artifactory

on:
  push:
    tags:
      - "v[0-9]+.[0-9]+.[0-9]+"

jobs:
  artifactory:
    runs-on: ubuntu-latest

    permissions:
      id-token: write

    steps:
      - uses: actions/checkout@v4

      - uses: jfrog/setup-jfrog-cli@v4
        env:
          JF_URL: https://registry.example.com
        with:
          oidc-provider-name: github-action-workflow
```

Select the event that triggers a run.

We want to run on pushes that have tags with a very specific format.

This field tells GitHub that it can share an OIDC token with the workflow.

We check out our code.

This should be the URL to the private registry you want to use.

The OIDC provider name will match the one you considered in the jfrog action instructions.

```
- name: Publish Module
  run: make publish_artifactory TAG=${{ github.ref_name }}
```

In our final step, we pass the tag used to trigger the workflow to our makefile for publishing.

8.2 Deploying infrastructure

Terraform is an infrastructure management tool, and that means developers using Terraform also need to consider how that infrastructure is delivered. This is a much more complex topic than module delivery. When delivering modules, we are, at the end of the day, simply delivering a bundle of text files. Infrastructure, on the other hand, consists of complex systems that are often in use at the time they're being upgraded.

There's a common aphorism in the industry that deploying changes to software infrastructure is like rebuilding a plane while it's flying: in general, the systems being changed are actually in use, which adds a level of risk to every deployment. Terraform helps by limiting the changes to just what is needed and making those changes directly, but Terraform is only part of the deployment process (a key part, but not the only one). To understand why we use tools like CD platforms, we need to understand what goes into a deployment.

8.2.1 What is a deployment?

Every time you run `terraform apply`, whether locally or through an automated system, you are running a deployment. Unlike simple software packages, your deployment isn't a simple artifact but is the entire set of infrastructure that you've defined using Terraform and a new version of the state of your project (see figure 8.5).

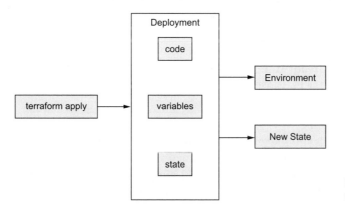

Figure 8.5 Deployment components

Deployments can be done locally, but it's a really bad practice to do it this way unless you're explicitly developing in a temporary environment only meant to be used by a single developer. If an environment is meant to stay up for a long time or is being used by more than a single developer, then deployments should be centralized.

If deployments aren't centralized, you end up with a mess very quickly. Although backend state locking does prevent two jobs from running at the same time, it doesn't prevent two different team members from overwriting each other's work because neither of them have the changes the other wrote (see figure 8.6).

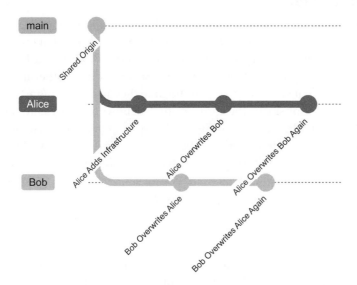

Figure 8.6   Local deployment chaos

The alternative is to deploy using a centralized system with a single source of truth. To put it another way, instead of Alice and Bob each deploying from their laptops, they should push their code to a shared location, and when new code is pushed to that location, it should automatically be deployed. Since Alice and Bob (and most software teams out there) are already using an SCM, they can use their Git repositories as the source of truth, a practice known as GitOps that we'll discuss more later in this chapter.

8.2.2 Environments

Let's say you work for a company that makes a software project that records analytics from sensors inside of factories, creatively named Factory Analytics. A system such as this has a lot of components: data streams, API endpoints, data storage, and alerting systems, just to name a few. The whole system is defined in Terraform.

You're being tasked with adding a new feature. The first thing you do after checking out the latest changes to your local system is to run `terraform apply` to launch a new developer instance of the system with a local backend. This allows you to test your changes in isolation from systems that may be in use by your customers, so you can comfortably and safely experiment with your changes. Once you are happy with what you've developed, you run `terraform destroy` and open a pull request.

While developing those changes, you were using what's known as a feature environment. The ability to launch and destroy entire instances of a system is one of the more powerful abilities of Terraform, and applying it to the development lifecycle with feature environments allows developers to move quickly in a way that does not compromise safety.

Environments are not just used for development. Any time an isolated instance of a system is needed, a new environment can be created. Besides development environments, companies often have staging environments that are used for testing and production environments that are in use by customers. The exact number and structure of environments depends a lot on the needs of the business.

A common pattern, especially among startups and smaller companies, is to have a staging and production environment (see figure 8.7). The staging environment is used for testing. In general, automated testing should be used and incorporated into the CI process, so staging environments are often used for manual testing.

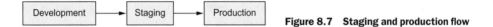

Figure 8.7   Staging and production flow

Another common pattern is to split deployments into regions. This is often done for legal reasons, as different companies have different laws about how data can be stored and transferred. It can also be done to put systems closer to their users, which in general can reduce latency and improve the user experience. Factory Analytics, for instance, may want to put separate installations in Asia, Europe, and North America for performance and legal reasons (see figure 8.8).

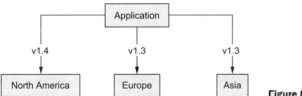

Figure 8.8   Region-based environments

Yet another use case for multiple environments is when companies need to have completely isolated instances of an application. Factory Analytics may have contracts with companies that have strict security requirements that don't allow them to use an environment shared with other customers. Since environments are all controlled individually, this means that each customer can run different versions and have their own upgrade schedule (see figure 8.9).

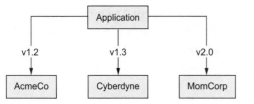

Figure 8.9   Customer-specific environments

Environments should be isolated from each other as much as possible. From an infrastructure viewpoint, this means that they should have their own accounts, networks, subdomains, databases, and other components. The goal is that one environment should not be able to access the data in other environments, and one environment should not depend on another environment of the same application to function. From the Terraform viewpoint, this means that each environment should have its own variables and state.

8.2.3   CD

The last chapter on CI focused on the idea that everything that gets merged into the main branch should always work and be usable. CD, on the other hand, is focused on getting features and functionality deployed and used by users in a quick and safe manner. Teams that practice CD regularly deploy changes to their systems multiple times a day and do so with minimal errors.

This is possible due to a few important practices. The first is CI. Everything we discussed in the last chapter acts as a foundation for this one: the more quality controls you put in place during the software development process, the more safety you have when deploying software. This is where the effort of CI really pays off, by giving you the safety net to deploy changes with the confidence that those changes will work.

Automating your deployments is another key practice to follow. Between a deployment starting and ending, developers should not have to take any manual actions. When you introduce humans into a process, you make room for human error and create unnecessary work for those humans. When you add safety and reduce work, you remove two major barriers to deployments.

The final point is one that comes naturally once the other two have been adopted: keep the deployments small. Rather than having one big deployment once a week, have three tiny deployments every day. Smaller deployments tend to be faster, and they often have much less risk. When there is a problem related to a change, it tends to be more obvious what caused it when your deployments only push out a single feature at a time.

8.2.4   *Deployment requirements and limitations*

Your deployment system needs to have access to the platforms it is working with. If you're deploying to a cloud provider, that typically means credentials. Terraform isn't just for the cloud, though, and can control a huge variety of platforms. Access isn't just about credentials but the network access to reach the machines being managed. If you're deploying into private clouds, you need to consider how that access will work.

Another consideration is time. Some systems are notorious for taking a long time to launch or modify. Databases in particular can have creation times that last as long as an hour for a single instance.

The final point is consistency. You do not want to run more than one deployment at a time to the same environment, as individual changes from one deployment can overwrite or influence the other deployment.

With this in mind, using a centralized system for running deployments has become a requirement for most teams. Managing network access can be used with deployment runners in a linked environment, while those same tools can manage job queuing to make sure changes run in the order they were created (and not on top of each other). Having a highly available deployment tool means that longer running jobs are less of a concern, and you don't have to worry about your laptop going to sleep and causing a deployment to fail.

8.3 GitOps

Working with Terraform is easier when there is a single source of truth for infrastructure and when deployments are driven from this single source of truth. This keeps people from overwriting each other's changes while also making it very easy for people to find the code that was used to create the existing infrastructure.

This need to have a single source of truth for infrastructure, combined with the desire for centralized deployments, has grown into the practice known as GitOps. To avoid the confusion that has come from other "ops" (e.g., what is DevOps? Ask any two people and you'll get three answers!), the Cloud Native Computing Foundation created a set of principles for GitOps. The four principles (https://mng.bz/jpgx) of GitOps-managed systems are defined as

- *Declarative*—A system managed by GitOps must have its desired state expressed declaratively.
- *Versioned and immutable*—The desired state is stored in a way that enforces immutability and versioning and retains a complete version history.
- *Pulled automatically*—Software agents automatically pull the desired state declarations from the source.
- *Continuously reconciled*—Software agents continuously observe the actual system state and attempt to apply the desired state.

WARNING Be careful when reading the word "continuously," as, to quote the Cloud Native Computing Foundation (https://mng.bz/W2P0), "Continuous is intended to match the industry standard term: reconciliation continues to happen, not that it must be instantaneous."

These principles may sound very familiar. Terraform is a declarative language used to express the desired state of a system, with each version of state being unique and immutable, and is used to continuously reconcile the desired state with the real state. Using a tool like Terraform is essentially a requirement of GitOps.

GitOps adds two additional components that Terraform by itself lacks. First is the use of an SCM as the source of truth for your infrastructure. What that means in practice is that developers should be able to go to a shared Git repository to see the exact configuration used to launch the infrastructure that is currently running. By making your Git repositories the source of truth and then integrating with a system that deploys from that source, you make it possible for anyone to analyze the intended system just by reviewing the repository. This also creates a changelog (or an audit log, depending on how you look at it) for the system. Once things are in Git, it allows CD systems to meet that third requirement and pull that desired state from that source.

The second is the idea that GitOps-based deployment systems will pull the configuration directly from the source. What this means in the GitOp world is that whatever system is calling Terraform will pull the source code that represents the desired state of the system in and hand it off to Terraform. Terraform by itself doesn't really care about how you pull that configuration in; it just needs to be called from inside the directory with that code. The actual fetching of the source code is handled by the orchestration tool that you select.

8.3.1 GitOps development workflows

Now that you know why GitOps is important, I'm going to let you in on a little secret: everything about GitOps is shockingly simple:

1. A developer checks out the current changes from the Git repository for the project and creates a new branch.
2. That developer does their normal local development, including spinning up any temporary environments from their local machine for testing.
3. When ready, the developer opens a pull request:
   a. Automated tests run, and the developer pushes up any needed fixes.
   b. A speculative plan is run to tell everyone what changes are going to be made.
   c. Reviewers add feedback and approve the pull request once everything is addressed.
4. The developer merges their changes into the main branch.
5. The project is deployed from the main branch.

What's interesting about this flow is that, for the vast majority of developers, it's already what they're doing. With the exception of the automatic deployment at the end of this process, it is the same as any other type of software development, whether that's a Terraform module or a Python library (see figure 8.10).

One thing you may notice is that there's a heavy emphasis on the pull request process itself. This is one of the areas where CD is really enabled by CI. The better your tests are (and we'll discuss how to make good tests in the next chapter), the easier it will be for developers to review pull requests. The tools we mentioned in the last chapter (our linters, security scanners, and validation workflows) also provide another safety net that brings confidence to your deployments.

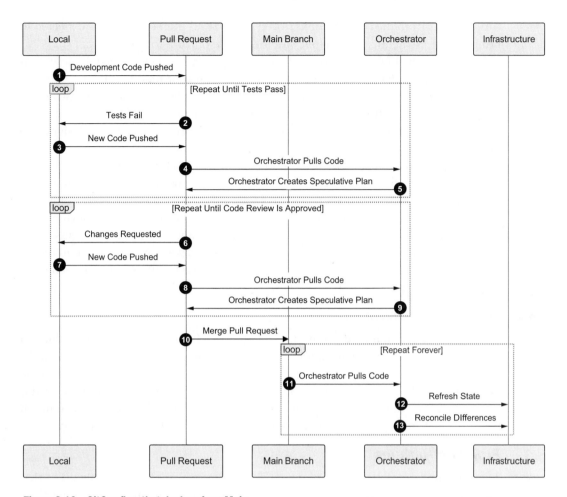

Figure 8.10 GitOps flow that deploys from Main

Without proper tests and CI tools, GitOps can be a lot more dangerous. At best, you have to rely on your developers catching any mistakes in their reviews, which is both unreliable in the long term and a major time commitment for your developers. At worst, teams merge low-quality code, create errors and outages, and increase the amount of time it takes to deploy new features. By using the CI tools, you can take advantage of automation to build safety nets around your systems that make CD possible. Automated deployments without CI is like driving without a seatbelt: you may get away with it for a while, but eventually you're going to have a lot of regrets.

8.3.2 *Continuous reconciliation*

An incredibly important part of GitOps that is easy to miss is the need for continuous reconciliation. What this means is that if something in the infrastructure changes (or "drifts") away from the configuration stored in the SCM, then the system is expected to bring the infrastructure back in line with the source of truth for the system.

You may be feeling a sense of déjà vu at this point: Haven't we talked about drift before? In section 6.6, we devoted a significant amount of time to talking about the different types of drift that can occur and how Terraform handles them. Infrastructure as code (IaC) and GitOps have both developed as practices together and have heavy influence on each other, so it's no surprise that Terraform seems almost designed to work with the GitOps practices.

Terraform can detect and fix drift, so we have the capabilities of reconciliation. Terraform by itself is not continuous though, so it can only be used as part of a larger system to give continuous reconciliation and thus follow GitOps practices. If we're only running the reconciliation process on pull requests, then we can easily miss all sorts of state drift. This idea of continuous reconciliation is perhaps one of the biggest drivers of the split between CI and CD systems. With most CD systems, you have the option to reconcile state, and even run Terraform automatically to correct drift, on a regular schedule instead of just on pull requests or merges.

8.3.3   *GitOps and CD platforms*

It is possible to deploy directly from CI systems like GitHub Actions, but the introduction of CD (and the automatic remediation of state drift) is much more complicated to implement using CI systems. Dedicated CD platforms have risen in popularity at the same time as GitOps, and both the philosophy and the tools have influenced each other. At this point, any CD platform worth considering (see section 8.6 for a breakdown of common features and various platforms) already has deep support for the GitOps philosophy.

8.4   *Project structures*

The root module is the entry point to a Terraform project. It is the only place that variables can be injected by the users running a plan or apply, and it is the only place where providers can be configured. So far, in this book, we've mostly focused on reusable modules, which we have used as root modules for development but that aren't part of a larger application. This works because root modules are modules, so everything we've learned about them still applies. That said, when it comes to delivery, we need to revisit things.

Let's start with a simple three-tier application (a common architecture with separate presentation, application, and data layers). Although these applications are simple, they have quite a few components to them (see figure 8.11).

To build this in Terraform, you're likely going to use a separate module for the content delivery network, load balancer, container service, database, and cache. All of this will get put into a single module that calls out to these reusable modules to build the full application, wiring the outputs of some modules to the inputs of others. You're also going to have a few input variables that allow developers to change settings based on the environment. For example, your development environment may use a small database to save money and is likely to be hosted on a different network (see figure 8.12).

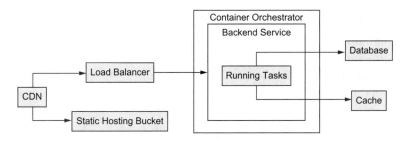

Figure 8.11   Three-tier web application architecture

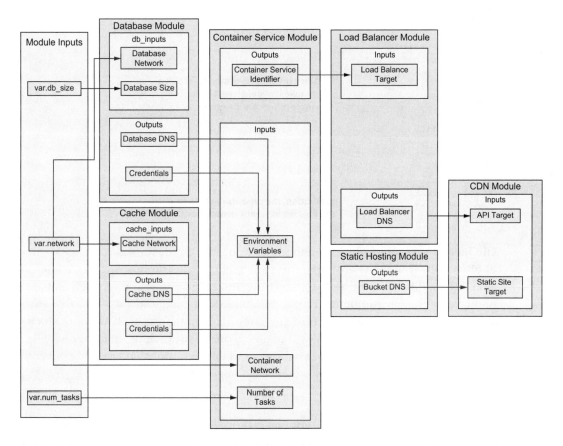

Figure 8.12   Module usage for the three-tier application module

This module defines the system we want to build, but is it a root module? Every module in Terraform has the capability of being called at the top level, so it absolutely can be your root module: it just doesn't *have* to be. Let's explore the options.

8.4.1 *Application as root module*

It isn't uncommon to use the application module as your root module. For one thing, it's the module most people are developing anyway, which should include launching it as a root module for local development. Since Terraform allows state backends to be configured on the fly, there's nothing stopping people from using a single codebase as their entry point, and variables can be used to configure the individual providers.

When this method is used, developers will place the configuration for each environment they deploy to into their own `tfvars` files: `staging.tfvars`, `prod.tfvars`, etc.

Listing 8.8   Root module with variable files

```
.checkov.yml
.github
.gitignore
.opentofu-version
.pre-commit-config.yml
.terraform-docs.yml
.terraform-version
.tflint.hcl
README.md
main.tf
makefile
outputs.tf
providers.tf
variables.tf
.staging.tfvars
.production.tfvars
.future.tfvars
```

Since the root-level module is still a module it should have all the support files you'd expect.

In addition, the repository contains a settings file for every environment.

The biggest problem with this method, and possibly the dealbreaker for me, is that all of your environments are using the same code for their infrastructure. While the variables are different, the actual underlying Terraform configuration itself is shared among all of the environments. To put this another way, you lose any ability to control which version of your infrastructure any given environment uses. If you introduce a new variable or feature, you deploy it to all of your environments, not just one. Sure, you may be able to gate the feature behind a variable, but you're still pushing out code to every environment without the benefits of a staged rollout.

8.4.2 *Environment as root module*

Another way to look at your root modules is through the lens of environments. Rather than attempting to use a single root module to support multiple environments, you can create a single module for every environment.

Listing 8.9   Environment root modules

```
staging/main.tf
production/main.tf
future/main.tf
```

Each environment gets its own folder with a main.tf file.

At first this might seem like a lot of work, but when working this way the root-level module is really just a thin wrapper around your application module. In fact, for most cases, the only thing that is defined here is a `module` block to your application module.

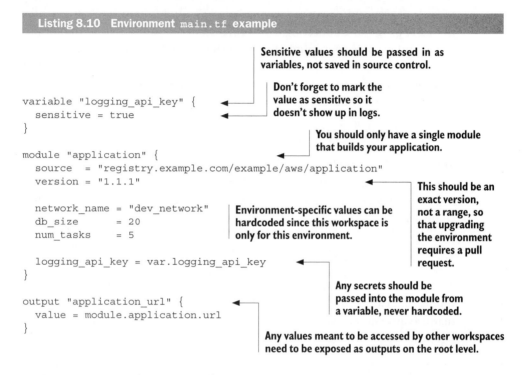

Listing 8.10 Environment `main.tf` example

Sensitive values should be passed in as variables, not saved in source control.

Don't forget to mark the value as sensitive so it doesn't show up in logs.

You should only have a single module that builds your application.

```
variable "logging_api_key" {
  sensitive = true
}
module "application" {
  source  = "registry.example.com/example/aws/application"
  version = "1.1.1"

  network_name = "dev_network"
  db_size      = 20
  num_tasks    = 5

  logging_api_key = var.logging_api_key
}
output "application_url" {
  value = module.application.url
}
```

This should be an exact version, not a range, so that upgrading the environment requires a pull request.

Environment-specific values can be hardcoded since this workspace is only for this environment.

Any secrets should be passed into the module from a variable, never hardcoded.

Any values meant to be accessed by other workspaces need to be exposed as outputs on the root level.

The most immediate and obvious benefit to this method is the ability to declare specific versions of your application module for each environment. This makes each environment truly independent in a way that doesn't happen if you're sharing a root module between all of them.

A smaller benefit is that you can skip managing most input variables. Since each environment has its own module, you know that the root `module` is only being used once, so you can simply define the parameters you want on the `module` block itself with the values you want for that environment. The exception to this is for any sensitive value that you would not want to save in SCM, but we'll discuss how to handle that later in this chapter.

A common question that comes up with managing environments in this way is whether teams should use a single repository for their top-level modules or if they should split them into multiple repositories. My personal preference is to keep all of the environments for a single application in the same repository unless there is a compelling reason to split them up. Since most of the time a single team is managing all of the environments, it makes it easier to maintain if they're all working out of one shared repository. On the other hand, if multiple teams are managing different installations of the same module, then each team should have their own repository maintaining their environments.

8.4.3 *Terragrunt*

Terragrunt is a thin wrapper over Terraform that takes the environment as a root module to the next level. Rather than create a literal Terraform module as your root module, Terragrunt lets you create a simple configuration file that essentially serves the same purpose. By pointing this configuration at your application module, you can install and manage your infrastructure across a number of environments.

If you've followed along from chapter 7, there's a good chance you have a version manager for Terragrunt on your system, as the `tenv` tool supports OpenTofu, Terraform, and Terragrunt. You do need to install it though:

```
tenv terragrunt install
```

Terragrunt has a built-in command named `scaffold`, which will generate a configuration file from a module that you have published in a registry or SCM. You could hypothetically generate a configuration for our example module with the following command:

```
terragrunt scaffold github.com/TerraformInDepth/three_tier_example
```

This will create a `terragrunt.hcl` file containing placeholders for your required inputs that can be filled out to configure your environment. You can point the command at any Git repository or module in a registry and Terragrunt will create your configuration using the latest version of the module.

Listing 8.11   Terragrunt configuration

> **This points to a specific version of a module. Terragrunt doesn't even support version constraints since they should not be used at the top level.**

```
# This is a Terragrunt module generated by boilerplate.
terraform {
  source = "git::https://github.com/TerraformInDepth/three_teir_example?
ref=v1.0.2"
}
```

> **The Terragrunt config generator will create boilerplates for required variables, but you can also add optional ones.**

```
inputs = {
  # -----------------------------------------------------------------------
  # Required input variables
  # -----------------------------------------------------------------------

  # Type: number
  # Description: The number of tasks to launch for the container service.
  num_tasks = "" # TODO: fill in value

  # Type: string
  # Description: The size of the DB instance to use.
  db_size = "" # TODO: fill in value
```

```
# Type: string
# Description: The network to launch the services into.
network = "" # TODO: fill in value

}
```

The makers of Terragrunt wanted it to be simple to use so they mirrored the command structure of Terraform. Instead of running `terraform plan` or `terraform apply`, you instead run `terragrunt plan` and `terragrunt apply`. Behind the scenes, Terragrunt will essentially generate the root module for you.

Terragrunt also allows you to run commands on multiple configurations at once with the `run-all` command, which also supports the same command structure (e.g., `terragrunt run-all plan`). This makes Terragrunt especially powerful for teams that run a lot of environments.

Listing 8.12 Terragrunt repository structure

```
staging/terragrunt.hcl
staging/main.tf
production/terragrunt.hcl
future/terragrunt.hcl
```

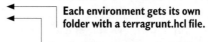

Each environment gets its own folder with a terragrunt.hcl file.

A main.tf file can be used to define the provider, but there are features of Terragrunt that will automatically generate those for you.

NOTE Terragrunt configuration does not support Terraform version constraints. Instead, you always refer to a specific module version. As a result, you need to update your configuration every time there is an upgrade to the module that you want to deploy. Since each environment has a single module that it refers to, this tends to not be a big deal from a maintenance perspective. If you keep your configuration in an SCM (which you absolutely should do), it also has the benefit of creating an audit trail since each version change will have a corresponding commit.

Terragrunt is an amazing tool with a lot of great features beyond just the simple deployments we've gone over here. It should be noted, though, that using Terragrunt is certainly not a requirement for using Terraform, and many teams never touch it at all. It is definitely worth considering for teams that are managing a lot of environments.

8.5 *Managing secrets*

As much as it would be desirable to throw all of our variables into Git so we can track their changes using the GitOps practices, we run into a very big problem: secrets. There are a lot of values that we simply do not want to put into source control. Sensitive values, such as provider authentication or service API keys, cannot be placed into an SCM without becoming available to all of the people who can access the repository. I cannot stress this enough: even if you trust everyone on your team, you should absolutely not store credentials in Git. You have no way to track where that repository goes after it is cloned, and, generally speaking, teams grant more access to their Git repositories than they realize (GitHub applications, for instance, often have source code access).

8.5.1   OpenID Connect

The best way to store a secret is to eliminate the need for the secret in the first place. There is a growing movement in the industry to use secure protocols to authenticate machine to machine workflows, and one of the best examples of that is the OIDC standard. This standard was created by the OpenID Foundation and is built on top of OAuth 2.0. It has a lot of use well beyond IaC, but for IaC developers it is absolutely a game changer as it completely eliminates the need for service users and API sharing for a huge number of services.

You don't really need to know the details of the standard (although it is fascinating on its own, diving into it could take up an entire book; if you want to learn more, head over to http://openid.net/). What's really important to know is that every major cloud provider and platform supports OIDC; the vendors that don't likely have it in their roadmaps very soon as the industry continues to adopt it, and security experts are very confident that it works well. Outside of that, all you need to worry about is how to use it, and the good news there is that using it is far easier than understanding it.

Although each vendor you work with is going to be different, and you will need to read their unique documentation, the general process for setting up OIDC tends to remain the same:

1 The platform you want to grant access to (such as GitHub Actions or one of our CD platforms) will have a provider URL in their documentation. For GitHhub Actions, this is `https://token.actions.githubusercontent.com`, but other platforms will have their own unique URL.

2 On the side of the vendor you want to connect to, you have to then add that URL as a new provider. Each vendor will have a slightly different way to do it, but it's generally a simple web form or API. If it is an API-driven process, you can likely manage it with Terraform.

Listing 8.13   Registering an OIDC provider with AWS

This is the URL for the GitHub Actions OIDC token service.

```
locals {
  gh_actions_token_url = "https://token.actions.githubusercontent.com"  ◄
}

data "tls_certificate" "gh_actions" {
  url = local.gh_actions_token_url                                      ◄
}

resource "aws_iam_openid_connect_provider" "github" {                   ◄
  url            = local.gh_actions_token_url  ◄
```

OIDC uses the TLS certificate to verify the identity of the service.

This resource should only be called once per account per url.

These values comes from the GitHub Actions documentation.

```
thumbprint_list = data.tls_certificate.gh_actions.certificates[*].
shal_fingerprint
client_id_list  = ["sts.amazonaws.com"]
}
```

For AWS, you will almost always use the security token service as the client.

This is the SHAI fingerprint of the certificates attached to the GitHub OIDC service.

In general, this type of configuration only has to occur once, as it is done to allow the identity provider (IdP) to authenticate to the vendor. At this point, it's important to point out the distinction between authentication and authorization. Authentication is how a system maps a request to a specific identity (typically a user or a machine), while authorization is how a system grants an identity permission to do something.

What we've done so far is authentication only. We're telling our vendor that any identity provided by our IdP should be treated as valid. This is what allows GitHub Actions to say, "this repository is running this workflow" or Spacelift to say, "this is the running stack" and for AWS or Azure to believe it.

To actually authorize an identity, we need to take another step. This part of the process is very specific to the vendor you are working with, but for the major cloud vendors it's typically part of their identity and access management system. For AWS, this means creating an identity and access management role that can be assumed by the identity being provided, while Azure requires you to map the identity to a service principal (see figure 8.13).

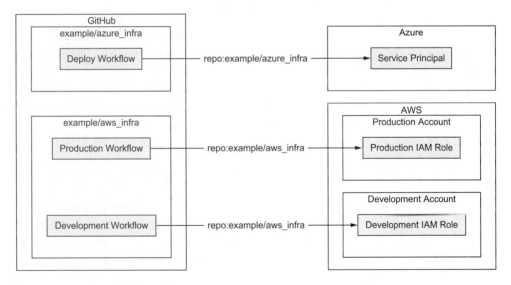

Figure 8.13   OIDC IdP to identity mapping

Regardless of which system you're using, you are going to want to restrict the relationship between your third-party IdP and the cloud identity it maps to. When using AWS, for instance, you have to create a role with a principal that allows your IdP to be used and conditions to limit the role to only being assumed by the specific repository and workflows that you specify. This last bit is extremely important: without the conditions, you open up your role to be assumed by any of the other users of your IdP service.

Listing 8.14   Allowing a GitHub Actions workflow to assume a role

```
jobs:
  terraform:
    name: Run Terraform against AWS
    runs-on: ubuntu-latest

    permissions:
      id-token: write
      contents: read

    steps:
      - name: Checkout
        uses: actions/checkout@v4

      - name: Configure AWS credentials
        uses: aws-actions/configure-aws-credentials@v4
        with:
          role-to-assume: arn:aws:iam::999999999999:role/github-actions-${{
github.repository }}
          region: us-west-2
```

The AWS action needs the OIDC token to be accessible.

Checkout our repository.

This action is published by AWS and converts the OIDC token into AWS credentials.

When using OIDC you have to tell AWS what role you want to assume.

AWS requires a region when logging in.

GitHub Actions is not the only IdP out there. For example, you might use Spacelift (a vendor we'll talk about later in this chapter); you can go through the same process to configure Spacelift as a provider, and then you can allow it to assume roles as well. The thing to note here is that every vendor defines the subject field using its own structure and additional fields (like the GitHub Actions workflow field we used earlier). This is why you have to read the specific documentation for both your IdP and the platform you're connecting with. When working with Spacelift, we'll want to make sure we set conditions that utilize the Spacelift-specific tokens to limit our access to the specific stack.

With Spacelift (and many of the CD platforms we'll discuss in this chapter), you may need to explicitly configure your provider to use OIDC, rather than relying on a built-in action. How you do this is specific to the platform you're using, but when using Spacelift you can point your provider to an OIDC file it automatically creates for each run.

Listing 8.15   Allowing a Spacelift stack to assume a role

```
variable "aws_role_arn" {
  type        = string
  description = "The AWS Role to assume."
}
```

```
provider "aws" {
  assume_role_with_web_identity {
    role_arn                 = var.aws_role_arn
    web_identity_token_file = "/mnt/workspace/spacelift.oidc"
  }
}
```
This file is created by Spacelift when run on their system.

Once this is done, you are ready to log into your cloud vendor (or other infrastructure provider) without needing to use any credentials. Instead, you'll use the OIDC flow to exchange your OIDC token for temporary credentials that you can use instead (see figure 8.14).

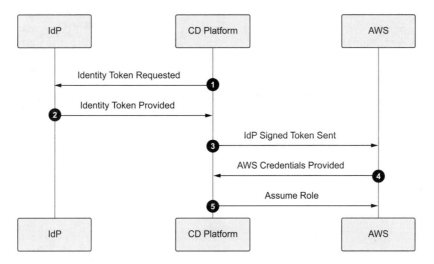

Figure 8.14   OIDC and AWS workflow

Although that looks complicated, it is pretty easy in practice. Most vendors publish easy-to-use repeatable actions that can be used to handle authentication with a few easy steps. This should allow you to eliminate the use of credentials for the vast majority of the providers you may use, not only solving the problem of how to store sensitive information but also eliminating the work that comes with credential rotation and managing service user accounts.

8.5.2   Secret managers

Unfortunately, OIDC is not an option for every secret you may need to save. You may have API keys to specific services that don't support OIDC, as just one of many possible examples. Instead of storing these secrets in text, you can instead use a secret manager.

Secret managers are basically password managers for automated processes. Every major cloud has its own, from the Azure Key Vault to AWS Secret Manager, and there are even options like HashiCorp's Vault that you can host yourself. With a secret manager in place, your team can securely store your sensitive data in a centralized place that has the full benefits of role-based access controls.

Once a secret is created in a secret manager, it will have a unique identifier that you can use to look up the value of the secret. Instead of saving the secret value itself in a variable, you save the path to the secret and then use a `data source` to retrieve the value.

Listing 8.16   Examples of different secret managers

```
#
# AWS
#

data "aws_secretsmanager_secret" "example" {          ◄───┐  With AWS you        Once you have
  arn = var.secret_arn                                     │  have to look up     the secret you
}                                                             the secret first.    can get the
                                                                                  version, which
                                                                                  is the latest
data "aws_secretsmanager_secret_version" "secret-version" {  ◄──┐                 version by
  secret_id = data.aws_secretsmanager_secret.example.id         │                 default.
}

                                                                          The version
output "aws_secret_value" {                                               contains the
  value    = data.aws_secretsmanager_secret-version.value  ◄───┐          secret value.
  sensitive = true                                    ◄──┐
}                                                         │  You have to make your output
                                                            as sensitive to prevent
#                                                           Terraform from raising an error.
# Vault
#

data "vault_generic_secret" "example" {       ◄───┐  Vault only has one resource to look up
  path = var.vault_path                            │  instead of two. That said, Vault also has
}                                                     more secret types than just generic.

output "vault_secret" {
  value    = data.vault_generic_secret.example.data[var.vault_key]  ◄───┐
  sensitive = true
}                                               All Vault secrets are objects,
                                                so we need to pass in a key to
#                                               get a specific value.
# Azure
#
                                                Azure allows multiple vaults per
                                                account so you need to specify
data "azurerm_key_vault" "example" {      ◄───  which one you are referring to.
  name                = var.azure_vault_id
  resource_group_name = var.azure_resource_group
}

data "azurerm_key_vault_secret" "example" {     ◄───┐  Now you can specify
  name         = var.azure_secret_name               │  the secret to retrieve.
  key_vault_id = data.azurerm_key_vault.example.id
}
```

```
output "secret_value" {
  value    = data.azurerm_key_vault_secret.example.value
  sensitive = true
}
```

The secret contains the value directly.

Using a secret manager does present one problem though: If you are storing your secrets in your secret manager, how do you securely store the credentials to the secret manager itself? The good news is that every secret manager worth using supports OIDC, which removes the need to store any credentials for them.

> **WARNING** One warning about using data sources to pull in sensitive values is that those values may still be present in your state file, so even if you utilize a centralized secrets manager, you may still expose your sensitive data to developers if you are giving them access to state. If your resources support it, you should consider using a machine-to-machine method to retrieve secrets. For example, AWS EC2 Container Service allows you to supply an Amazon Resource Name to a secrets manager secret directly, and it will load the secret for you.

8.5.3 Orchestrator Settings

If OIDC is not an option and you do not have a secrets manager available, then your last option is to store your sensitive values inside of the orchestrator you are using. CD platforms, whether Terraform specific or not, all have ways to store sensitive values inside of their systems. Most of them work by allowing you to write the secrets but not directly read them, so you can only replace them once used.

The problem with this method is typically one of scale and maintenance. Imagine you have to update an API key across all of your projects. If you have five projects you're maintaining, this isn't a huge burden. If you have 500, then managing secrets across projects becomes more of a hassle, and at that point you should consider a secrets manager that allows you to manage credentials in a single place.

Regardless of where you store your secrets (in your CD orchestrator itself or in a dedicated secrets manager), your CD orchestrator will have access to them. In 2021, a company called Travis CI revealed that a security vulnerability meant that secrets stored on their platform for open source projects could be revealed to users pretty trivially. If you can, try to avoid the need for secrets in the first place (such as by using OIDC to connect to systems), and if that isn't possible then consider additional measures such as auditing the use of your credentials for suspicious behavior.

8.6 CD platform features

Selecting a CD platform can appear complicated, but if you understand the features that they each offer and know what is important to you, then it's easy to narrow the list down. Before looking at the platforms themselves, we walk through the features that you will need to think about and break down regarding why they're important to you and your team.

8.6.1 Common features

Pretty much every orchestrator you should consider will have a standard set of features:

- GitOps-based workflows
- Role-based access control
- OIDC support
- Secret management
- Speculative plan support

Some of the tools get these features by their tight integration with GitHub, while others build it into their systems. As a general rule, though, you can expect every platform we look at to primarily use one variety of the GitOps flow or another and to have a robust user authentication system. Tools that support Terraform as a first-party provider will also be capable of generating speculative plans when changes are suggested via a pull request and will generally support OIDC and have a way to manage secrets.

8.6.2 Terraform vs. OpenTofu

By far one of the biggest differences between Terraform and OpenTofu is around delivery systems. HashiCorp has a delivery orchestration system called HCP Terraform, and that is the primary way HashiCorp has made money off of Terraform. The problem that HashiCorp ran into is that other companies came out with their own delivery orchestration systems that also supported Terraform, and a lot of them were really popular.

This seems to be one of the biggest drivers in the HashiCorp license change, as the new Business Source License for Terraform explicitly does not allow Terraform to be used by competitors to create their own product. As a result, those competitors responded by creating OpenTofu, which continues to be an open source tool.

What this means is that if you are a team that wants to use newer versions of HashiCorp Terraform, then you are locking yourself into using HCP Terraform or self-hosting your CD systems. If you want to take advantage of the larger ecosystem of CD platforms or prefer using completely open source code, then you have to use OpenTofu to do so.

8.6.3 State management and private registry

Systems that offer delivery, state management, and private registries are often referred to as Terraform Automation and Collaboration Software (colloquially referred to as TACOS). These all-in-one packages attempt to make running Terraform straightforward for developers.

Tools that offer state management generally do so transparently. Since they are running delivery directly on their own instances, they have full control to manage the backend on your behalf. They will have a way for you to inspect and review previous versions of state using their own web interface. Although these are great as a primary state storage solution, you should still remember to take external backups.

Private registries are pretty straightforward and were discussed a bit at the start of this chapter, and there isn't a huge amount of differentiation to look for in vendors that provide them—either they're provided or they aren't, for the most part—but at the end of the day they're really just a directory of modules.

8.6.4 Drift detection and correction

One of the requirements of GitOps is the idea of continuous reconciliation: when the infrastructure drifts away from the system as defined in code, then this needs to be detected and corrected. Terraform makes this fairly simple: drift can be detected by creating a new plan and looking for changes, and it can be corrected by running that plan.

The idea of automatically making changes to running systems, particularly without a human review, is frightening to a lot of people. For this reason, many teams enable drift detection but not automatic correction. A lot of platforms make this easy and build it directly into their systems, with connections to chat platforms like Slack for when drift occurs.

8.6.5 IaC frameworks

As much as I'd like to pretend otherwise, Terraform is not the only IaC tool out there. There are times when it may not make sense to use Terraform: for example, if your company has a Kubernetes platform available, it probably makes more sense to use something like Helm (a tool similar to Terraform in many ways but designed specifically around Kubernetes). Even teams that aren't using tools like Kubernetes today may want to use them in the future, and having two separate deployment systems can be a frustrating developer experience.

Many of the CD platforms we discuss only support Terraform and OpenTofu. This can be a severe limitation as companies grow and may even be a dealbreaker at the enterprise level. This is another area where business needs to intersect with technical choices: having to negotiate a contract for every IaC or orchestration tool the company uses can limit the willingness of a company to use new tools, which in turn can harm the ability of the company to evolve with the industry.

So if you're comparing two different CD platforms and they are both identical but one has support for tools beyond just Terraform, then pick that one even if you don't have a need for those tools today.

8.6.6 Policy enforcement

In the last chapter, we talked about policy enforcement on the CI side, but it's also possible (and often desirable) to enforce policy on the delivery side as well. Policy enforcement on the module side is somewhat limited, as it can't take into account the variables that a user could pass in.

For example, in chapter 7, we attempted to enforce a policy that users could not use specific machine types. The idea there was to save money by preventing teams from accidentally launching GPUs. The problem with this is that most modules don't hardcode this type of data into the module but instead expose these parameters as input variables. That means that there isn't a way for tools like Checkov to scan the modules themselves, since it's the users of the modules themselves that set the instance type.

This makes policy enforcement at the deployment level much more robust, so it's natural that many delivery systems include some sort of policy tool. What's interesting is that most of them chose the same tool: Open Policy Agent (OPA). You may remember OPA from the last chapter: it's an open source framework that uses its own language, Rego, to define policy documents. The fact that so many tools are using it is great for users, as it means the policy documents they write for one tool should translate over to others. The downside is that it does require learning yet another language.

For a while, HCP Terraform was the odd system out. The company created a new policy agent tool called Sentinel, with another language altogether, to define policies with. However, in 2023 HashiCorp announced native support for OPA in HCP Terraform, meaning the vast majority of the ecosystem is using OPA. Since OPA is used by so many tools (not just inside of the Terraform ecosystem but in any place where a policy engine is needed), it makes the most sense for teams to learn and standardize around OPA over a tool such as Sentinel.

8.6.7 *Infrastructure cost estimates*

One of the more interesting things that IaC gives us is the ability to analyze our infrastructure programmatically, and one of the ways that companies have benefitted from this is by automating their cost estimates. Giving developers the ability to see the financial effect of their changes, especially in an automated and hard-to-ignore way, encourages better use of financial resources and reminds developers that when you work in a cloud world, all of your resources have a price tag attached to them.

HCP Terraform includes cost estimation as part of its service. The other orchestrators we discuss here offer cost estimation through integration with another service called Infracost, which means you do need to purchase an Infracost account if you use one of these vendors and want price estimation.

Regardless of which engine is used, there are some limitations that should be considered. The first is that all of these tools are extremely limited in the number of vendors they support: Google, Azure, and AWS are pretty much the only systems that you can get cost estimation for. As a result, if you aren't using one of these vendors, these features are basically useless. Even teams that are hosting on one of these clouds are likely using other vendors as well (maybe Domain Main System is controlled by a different vendor, or a third-party content delivery network is in use as well), meaning that these estimates are likely to be incomplete.

The other limitation is that these estimates are just that: estimates. They are never going to be completely accurate, especially when so much of the cloud experience is charged based on consumption. Although Infracost does make an attempt to estimate how much a consumption-based resource might cost, it doesn't have any real way of accurately knowing. An application may add a new feature that greatly increases the amount of bandwidth used, for instance, and that isn't something that these automated services can guess.

If you can live with these limitations, then cost estimation is a fantastic tool that really does help teams consider the cost-benefit analysis around their system designs. Tools like Infracost are pretty new though, which means you should expect to see improvements over time (and, hopefully, the addition of other vendors).

8.7 CD platform overview

Not every platform supports every feature, so it's important to understand what features are important to you. Do you want an open source option that you host yourself, or do you want a software as a service that you can just jump into without worrying about managing yourself? Do you want built-in cost estimates and a private registry? Note that the providers listed in table 8.3 can't be broken up into just a list of features, and each has its focus and appeal.

Table 8.3 CD platform feature matrix

System	Open source	State backend	Registry	Terraform only	Policy enforcement	Cost estimates
HCP Terraform	No	Yes	Yes	Yes	Sentinel and OPA	Yes
Spacelift	No	Yes	Yes	No	OPA	Infracost
EnvO	No	Yes	Yes	No	OPA	Infracost
Scalr	No	Yes	Yes	Yes	OPA	Infracost
Digger	Yes	No	No	Yes	OPA	No
Terrateam	No	No	No	Yes	Checkov and OPA	Infracost
Atlantis	Yes	No	No	Yes	None	No
Terrakube	Yes	Yes	Yes	Yes	OPA	Infracost
Harness	No	No	No	No	OPA	Infracost
Octopus Deploy	No	No	No	No	None	Infracost

8.7.1 HCP Terraform

NOTE HCP Terraform is the only service that offers the closed source versions of Terraform, and it does not support OpenTofu or Terragrunt. All other commercial vendors switch to OpenTofu for v1.6 and beyond.

HCP Terraform (previously called Terraform Cloud) is the original Terraform automation and collaboration software, and like other TACOS, it includes state management, module registries, and infrastructure delivery in a single package. HCP Terraform (and its self-hosted variant, Terraform Enterprise) was created by HashiCorp, the makers of Terraform.

For years HCP Terraform was the de facto standard tool for teams that wanted a TACOS. It is heavily tied into GitHub in a way that makes it easy for teams to use. Being attached to HashiCorp also gave it some very amazing name recognition.

There are two major problems that prevent me from recommending that teams use HCP Terraform. The first is that it only supports Terraform, and as discussed in the previous section, I feel that teams should consider using delivery tools that support more than one language. I would never recommend a CI tool that only supports Java, and recommending a CD tool that only supports Terraform seems like a similar prospect.

The second problem is the pricing model that HashiCorp has switched to for HCP Terraform. Most tools in this space charge based on the number of projects, the amount of concurrency, the number of minutes that nodes are processing jobs for, or the number of people using the tool. Recently, HashiCorp changed its pricing model to charge hourly for the number of resources that exist in your state file.

To put this in perspective, creating a virtual private cloud (VPC) that follows best practices (separate public and private subnets, spread across three availability zones, with a network address translation instance) uses roughly 72 resources. The vast majority of these sources are free: AWS does not charge for a route inside of a routing table, for instance. HCP Terraform will charge an hourly fee for each of these resources. The VPC example, with 72 resources, amounts to a monthly fee of $7.25 for every VPC that developers launch.

$$\text{Resources} \times \text{Hourly Fee} \times \text{Hours per Day} \times \text{Days per Month} = \text{HCP Terraform Fee}$$

This model is hard to justify. It encourages developers to reduce the number of resources they use, even if using more resources reduces application complexity and increases security. It adds costs to resources that even the cloud providers themselves don't charge for. It also seems disconnected from the actual costs HashiCorp faces, as developers aren't charged for the number of runs (which ties back to CPU and network resources HashiCorp has to pay for) but are instead charged for what is essentially a database entry.

That being said, despite the negatives, HCP Terraform has some interesting standout features. Unlike many other tools, it has its own cost estimation built in. HCP Terraform is also heavily integrated into the Terraform CLI program. When the cloud backend is configured, developers can trigger runs on HCP Terraform right from their CLI. This is very useful when running plans for changes, as it'll run directly from HCP Terraform and include any configured secrets.

8.7.2 *Env0 and Spacelift*

Env0 and Spacelift are official sponsors of OpenTofu, with each of them providing five full-time developers to the OpenTofu project.

Env0 and Spacelift are TACOS plus more. Both of these tools are leaders in the IaC space. They provide excellent documentation, have polished user interfaces, and support the GitOps workflows we've come to expect.

One of the biggest distinguishing features for both of these products is that they support more than just Terraform. Both of these platforms support Terragrunt, Helm, Ansible, Cloudformation, Pulumi, and even custom systems. Both products have also regularly expanded their offerings, so you can expect feature sets to grow.

For teams that want the full IaC experience, including a private module registry and state management, this is the best option. The biggest drawback, unfortunately, is that with the new Terraform licensing you should not expect any new versions of Terraform to be supported by either of these platforms. The good news is that they are both sponsors of OpenTofu, so teams can bring their Terraform code over and expect it to work.

One of the big questions you might be asking yourself is: How do these companies differ? To be honest, they both have very similar products and solid support, and they are even working together on OpenTofu. Although there are small differences that come up, most of the compelling features make their way to both platforms.

8.7.3 Scalr

Scalr is an official sponsor of OpenTofu and is providing three full-time developers to the OpenTofu project. Like Spacelift and Env0, Scalr offers the full Terraform suite.

Scalr as a company has an interesting background. It was building tools for IT teams as far back as 2011, but at some point it pivoted and released its Terraform platform. Unlike Spacelift and Env0, Scalr focused purely on the Terraform ecosystem (including, of course, OpenTofu). This means that other tools, such as Kubernetes-based deployment tools, are not supported.

On the other hand, Scalr supports the Terraform CLI-driven workflows in a way that Spacelift and Env0 do not. Scalr is extremely similar to HCP Terraform and supports many of the CLI-driven integrations that it does. This makes Scalr a great choice for teams that are used to the HCP Terraform workflow or have built their own automation around it but have a desire to migrate to a different platform.

8.7.4 Digger and Terrateam

Digger and Terrateam are part of a new generation of tools for running Terraform. Unlike the other TACOS, these tools focus completely on the deployment aspect of things and do not have private registries or state backends (although Terrateam does have this on their roadmap).

What makes these systems really interesting is that they integrate heavily with GitHub, well beyond what other tools do. Both of these tools take GitOps to another level by using GitHub Issues and pull requests as a user interface. Developers can reply to comments in pull requests with Terraform commands, and the systems will run them (and don't worry, both have robust role-based access controls so only comments from specific people will work).

This is a very different workflow than the other orchestration systems, but it is one that seems to be getting more popular. It's definitely worth having a conversation with your team about whether this particular style of work is appealing. That being said, the flow might not be for everyone; there's really a lot of personal preference that plays into whether you want to use one of these tools with their tight reliance on GitHub for much of their interaction or if you want a more traditional delivery application.

8.7.5   *Harness and Octopus Deploy*

Harness is an official sponsor of OpenTofu and is providing five full-time developers to the OpenTofu project.

Both Harness and Octopus Deploy bill themselves as CD platforms. They are not focused on IaC but instead on creating extensible systems, in the same way that GitHub Actions expands its CI functionality through the action marketplace. While Octopus Deploy is focused purely on the deployment space, Harness also has other products in the developer platform space such as feature flags, internal development platforms, and even its own SCM.

The biggest benefit around using Harness or Octopus Deploy is that they can go well beyond the use cases that the typical IaC tool can. This is more than just supporting Helm charts or other Kubernetes workflows (although that is part of it). These tools can support releasing individual containers, pushing software to physical hardware nodes, and integration with advanced observability systems. This makes them both ideal for environments that have a mixture of legacy and modern deployment practices.

At the same time, because they weren't designed for Terraform specifically, they are missing a few features other products are. They do not have a private module registry, which means teams will need to bring their own. They also do not have any state management systems. That said, they tend to target the enterprise market, where it's likely that teams are already using something like Artifactory to solve these problems.

8.7.6   *Atlantis and Terrakube*

Atlantis and Terrakube are open source systems that developers host themselves. They both integrate with your SCM and support the full GitOps flow. The biggest difference between the two is that Atlantis follows the GitOps Plus model that Digger and Terrateam do, while Terrakube is more of a traditional TACOS-style system (complete with a module registry and state backend).

The big question that comes up here is whether your team wants to use an open source product or a commercial product. If you want to use an open source project, then you should use Terrakube if you want the full feature set and Atlantis if you want that extremely tight integration with your SCM.

When choosing to host your own solution, you're making a tradeoff. You will potentially save money by skipping the commercial products, and for smaller companies and startups that is a very important consideration. There's also another benefit that has recently come up, which is that these tools are allowed to keep using the newer versions of Terraform. When HashiCorp changed its license, it explicitly disallowed commercial services while still allowing self-hosting, so these tools are legally able to run both Terraform and OpenTofu.

At the same time, self-hosting your own product also has its own risks, as the system becomes another point of failure that your team is responsible for managing. If you do decide to host your own deployment tool, you should make sure it isn't dependent on your other systems to run. An absolute worst-case scenario during an outage is to have your deployment system also fail, as it limits your ability to respond to that outage. This means you want your deployment system in its own cloud account, on its own network, and possibly even in a completely different region than the rest of your infrastructure is hosted in.

This is not to say you shouldn't do this. Hosting your own solution can make some compliance factors easier, and it allows you to bridge your isolated networks to your system easier. Of course it also does save some money. In the end, this is another business decision that has to be weighed, but if you do go with a self-hosted solution, these two open source projects are where you should start.

Regardless of what platform you decide to use, the combination of CI and CD practices are going to allow you to develop in a faster and safer way. In the next chapter, we'll continue that journey with automated testing of Terraform modules themselves.

Summary

- Module delivery is similar to publishing other software libraries.
- Semantic versioning makes it easier for developers to use shared modules by making dangerous upgrades obvious.
- Delivering infrastructure is very different from delivering modules.
- Practices such as GitOps and CD make delivering infrastructure changes safer.
- CD platforms can be an important tool to enable CD.
- Different teams have different needs and will need to match those needs to the right CD platform.

Testing and refactoring

The ability to run automated tests is by far one of the most powerful benefits of using infrastructure as code (IaC). While writing tests does require some level of upfront effort, the payout is more than worth it. Automated testing grants three immediate benefits that will exist for the life of the project:

- Modules that have automated testing tend to be of higher quality, as errors and bugs tend to be found faster. When bugs are found, test suites are typically updated to take that bug into account, which reduces the changes of

288

regression (a type of error class where previously resolved bugs are introduced back into the codebase or where features that previously worked stop working).

- Automated testing helps reduce the amount of effort for developers to properly review pull requests. Without automated tests, developers would have to pull down the changes, run the code themselves, and then evaluate the response. That level of effort will result in developers either ignoring pull requests or skipping any sort of testing at all.
- Projects with test suites tend to do a better job maintaining backward compatibility. If someone introduces a breaking change, that should also break the tests. This helps developers identify when their changes break compatibility, which helps them better manage those changes or redesign their changes to maintain compatibility.

All of these things increase resiliency of your infrastructure while ultimately saving your developers time. As important as this all is, there is a fourth even more important reason testing is vital to a team: a well-developed test suite increases the psychological safety of your team. It may seem weird that we're talking about something like psychological safety in a software book, but at the end of the day most development teams are looking to build software and systems productively, and study after study has shown that one of the best ways to improve productivity for teams is by making sure those teams feel safe.

Incidents, outages, breaches, bugs—all of these can be stressful. Deploying software into production and then having it break is demoralizing. Trying to debug systems while people are actively trying to use them can be frustrating. By increasing our system resiliency, we also provide a better environment for teams to function in. While there is certainly a lot more to psychological safety than simply having a test suite, having automated testing can definitely contribute. Test suites help teams build confidence in their ability to make changes and remove the tension or anxiety that build up with a fragile code base.

A proper test suite also makes it easier to make large changes to your code. By providing the safety net of tests, you make refactoring, both small scale and large, easier for your team. This in turn helps your modules mature and evolve as your team and the industry as a whole evolve. Terraform has the benefit of having two separate, and powerful, testing frameworks that you can work with (and that we'll discuss in this chapter). Since it is decoupled from any specific cloud vendor, it also tends to be easier to integrate with third-party continuous integration (CI) systems.

9.1 The theory of IaC testing

Testing IaC has a lot of similarities with testing software in general, but as its own specialized subset of software development, IaC also introduces its own complexities and challenges. The lessons that apply to software testing apply to infrastructure testing as well, but there are additional complexities that come from working with real infrastructure. Understanding the nuances that come with IaC can help developers build better tests suites, so before we get into the practical aspects of testing, we explore some of the theory around testing IaC.

9.1.1 What to test (and what not to test)

Now that we've discussed why testing is important, we need to talk a bit about what you should test. As much as we'd like the answer to be "everything," the reality is that developers have a limited amount of time to work on any given project and need to prioritize what is important. In the case of IaC, you want to focus on your specific systems and configurations and how they interact.

What do I mean by your specific systems? With Terraform, you can generally assume that the providers you are using are well tested and function, so you want to test your code rather than test the providers themselves. Passing a variable to a resource, creating that resource, and then testing that the attribute matches the input is not a useful test. Instead, you should look at your actual logic:

- If you transform data, you should test that those transforms work as expected.
- When creating strings from data sources and other attributes, you should confirm those strings match.
- Anything involving regular expressions should be tested with multiple patterns.
- Dynamic blocks should be tested to confirm they work with zero, one, or many different blocks depending on the use cases.
- The system functionality, such as whether HTTP endpoints are available, generated credentials function, or other system-specific functionality should be tested.

This list is not meant to be comprehensive but to give an idea of the type of things you should cover in your test suite.

Let's take the simple example of setting a Domain Name System (DNS) record from a variable. In this case, we have a single simple resource that takes in a variable to create the record.

Listing 9.1   Simple DNS record

```
variable "zone_id" {
  type = string
}

variable "records" {
  type = list(string)
}

variable "name" {
  type = string
}

resource "aws_route53_record" "main" {        ◄─── This resource creates a record
  zone_id = var.zone_id                              but doesn't have any logic.
  name    = var.name          ◄─── The name is passed in directly.
```

```
    records = var.records
    type    = "A"                          ◄────┐   Records are passed
    ttl     = "300"                             │   in without change.
}
```

Other than the fact that the resource is created (which is testing your specific variables more than the actual code), there isn't much to test here. You can check that each parameter that you pass in is also what you get out, but that doesn't provide much value on top of what the AWS provider already tests for.

On the other hand, what if our system is instead calculating a domain instead of just passing a value through? Once you start introducing logic into your code, the value of testing increases.

Listing 9.2 DNS record with dynamic name

```
variable "zone_id" {
  type = string
}

variable "records" {
  type = list(string)
}

variable "name" {
  type = string
}

variable "domain" {
  type = string
}                                                We're looking up the
                                                 region to use in the name.

data "aws_region" "current" {}        ◄────┘
                                                 Unlike our previous example,
                                                            we're dynamically
resource "aws_route53_record" "main" {                  generating the name.
  zone_id = var.zone_id
  name    = "${var.name}.${data.aws_region.current.name}.${var.domain}"  ◄──┘
  records = var.records
  type    = "A"
  ttl     = "300"
}
```

For this code, you can test not only that the resource was created but also that your logic made sense. When you transform data (such as variables or resource attributes) and use that data, you want to confirm the transformation worked. With the previous code this would include confirming that the string constructed inside of the module and passed to the `aws_route53_record` matches your expectations.

Another thing you want to test is that your system actually functions the way you expect it to. Imagine that the DNS record we set was part of a large system and that the record created pointed toward a web service. In that case, you would not only test that the name of the record was what you expect but that the web service itself is actually reachable at that address. If you're creating a module for managing a database that saves the credentials in a secret manager, you'll want to confirm those credentials work.

9.1.2   *How IaC testing differs from software testing*

As much as I wish that IaC was just as simple to test as a simple Python library, there are unfortunately some pretty major differences that come up when testing with tools like Terraform. These differences are all centered around one core concept: IaC launches infrastructure. While that may seem obvious, it's important to understand the implications.

The first and biggest factor is time. Although a lot of infrastructure can be created quickly (things like DNS records are practically instantaneous), many components can take quite a bit of time. Launching a virtual machine instance can easily take a couple of minutes, while launching a full-fledged database can extend beyond the 30-minute mark. To be honest, this really sucks. With standard software development, you can often make changes, run tests, read errors, and make new changes all within a minute or two. With Terraform you have to launch and destroy your infrastructure, which can mean that cycle time is significantly longer.

The other factor is money. With your average unit test for a standard software project, you generally don't have to think about money. When you run your tests locally, there is no extra charge, and while you may have to pay for minutes on your CI platform, it tends to be a small enough charge that no one thinks about it. Launching infrastructure is rarely free. Virtual machines and databases cost money while they're running. This makes it absolutely critical that any resources that are created are destroyed once the tests are finished. Done properly, these costs can often be reduced down to the point where they are a rounding error on your infrastructure bill, but safeguards should be put in place. We'll discuss how to remedy both of these problems throughout this chapter.

> **NOTE**   Although testing can take both time and money, it's really important to consider the costs of not testing as well. Testing provides a very important safety net and reduces the chances of an outage, and outages can have their own financial effects.

9.1.3   *Terraform testing frameworks*

Up until 2023, there was only a single option for running tests against Terraform, and that was Terratest. Terratest is written by Gruntwork, the same folks who write Terragrunt, and it is built on top of the Go testing package. Terratest is an extremely mature piece of software that includes a lot of helper functions for validating your code.

The biggest drawback to Terratest is that developers have to write their tests in Go. Although Go is a popular language, knowledge of it isn't universal. For teams who are learning Terraform for the first time, it can be pretty daunting to have to learn a second language at the same time. For this reason, it's not uncommon to see people writing only very simple tests with Terratest or not writing tests at all.

Recently, the HashiCorp and OpenTofu projects have released a native Terraform testing framework. This allows developers to write their tests using native HashiCorp Configuration Language (HCL), which removes the need to learn another language. For many teams, this will make it significantly easier to build a test suite for their modules and infrastructure (see table 9.1).

Table 9.1 **Terratest and Terraform testing framework comparison**

	Terratest	**Terraform testing framework**
Language	Go	HCL
Release year	2018	2023
Native	No	Yes
Flexible versions	Yes	No
Copilot support	No	Yes
Community contributions	Yes	No
Third-party libraries	Yes	No

NOTE Copilot, a product by GitHub, is a large-language-model-based tool that provides code examples and other advanced functionality to developers. In many ways, it can be considered the most advanced autocomplete ever made.

The Terraform Testing Suite was first released in version v1.6 of Terraform and Open-Tofu and has been extended with new functionality in every release since then. As a result, it is the first major piece of functionality written after the license change and is one of the areas where both Terraform and OpenTofu have their biggest implementation differences. So far this hasn't been a huge deal, as those details tend to be hidden from the average developer using Terraform, but it does mean that there's a possibility of subtle differences between them.

The other problem with the Terraform testing framework is that, because it is so new, it cannot be used to test versions of Terraform that are older. In other words, if you have a module that is being used by teams running older versions of Terraform, you can't use the testing framework with those older versions. This is one area where Terragrunt, which is built to interface with Terraform but is a completely separate program, has an advantage.

Despite those downsides, the Terraform testing framework is going to continue to mature and is very likely going to be the future of testing with Terraform. For teams that are just starting their journey into testing, I would generally recommend that they use the Terraform testing framework over Terratest. Since people developing with Terraform are expected to know Terraform, having all of the project code (both infrastructure and testing) in the same language reduces the barriers to entry for bringing people into the projects.

That being said, Terratest is not going away any time soon. For teams already using Terratest, or teams that have to support a wide range of Terraform versions, it likely makes sense to stick with Terratest. Terratest also has a huge "first to market" advantage, as it existed for seven years before the Terraform testing framework was released. The vast majority of tests written for Terraform so far are with Terratest. Even if you ultimately decide to never use Terratest for your projects, it's good to have some familiarity with it as you're very likely to encounter it at some point in your career.

9.1.4   *Unit testing vs. integration testing*

Even among functional testing, there are a lot of different types of tests. Among software developers, the two most common types of tests are unit testing and integration testing.

Unit testing is the practice of testing isolated pieces of code to ensure they work as expected. For a typical language, you would likely create individual unit tests for each individual function in your program. With unit tests, you attempt to remove or write "mocks" (code that pretends to be an external service while returning consistent predictable results) for any external dependencies on the code so you can test it specifically, with the idea being that if each component in your system works as expected, the systems built on top of those components is more likely to work.

Integration testing, on the other hand, tests how the different components work together. It tests the overall system to ensure that it works, without necessarily isolating the individual systems. Rather than using mocks, integration tests rely on the real systems they interact with.

In the real world, most test suites are a combination of both types of tests, with the difference between "fully isolated" and "completely integrated" being more of a spectrum than a binary. Sometimes developers of unit tests have no choice but to utilize an external system or their tests would be incomplete. The important thing about writing tests is that they meet the goal of providing your team a safety net.

Terraform, and other IaC platforms, are difficult to unit test. By definition, you are configuring external systems, as that is the entire point of Terraform. While there are tools that make it easier to emulate external systems for testing, these tools are often different enough from the original system that they aren't useful for testing Terraform modules against.

This doesn't mean unit tests don't exist for Terraform, but, in general, it's not the Terraform developer who is writing them. Terraform providers are written in Go and, as we alluded to earlier in this chapter, often have extensive unit testing (although they are often not "pure" unit tests, as they do tend to interact with real systems). If you consider every resource and data source to be the equivalent of a function, you can certainly consider them to be well tested on their own.

The majority of tests that developers are going to have to worry about with Terraform are integration tests: ensuring all of their resources (both direct and via modules) are working together properly and for a variety of configurations. While this will include some functionality that is closer to unit testing, such as testing that data transformations (like our DNS record example) work the way they are supposed to, even that functionality will typically depend on resources being created.

9.2 Testing IaC in practice

Theory is one thing, and practice is another. While we had to build a solid grounding in the theory behind testing with IaC, there's also a lot of IaC-specific practices to adopt that will make our testing easier to build, run, and maintain.

9.2.1 Simple testing flow

Testing IaC has a very simple flow (see figure 9.1). First you select the configuration options you want to test. Then you launch the resources with those options. Once they are launched, you can run tests against that infrastructure. Finally, you tear all of the resources down again, ideally leaving you with a clean slate.

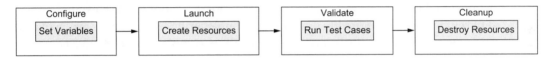

Figure 9.1 IaC testing flow

A single test will have a unique configuration and a variety of test cases inside of it. A single test for a web service may check that the service is responding at specific endpoints (possibly with different responses expected for each endpoint), redirecting from port 80 to port 443, for example, and sending logs to an external logging service. Each of those checks can be run on the same configuration, so they can be grouped together in a single test.

There's a lot of value in grouping test cases together like this. Since infrastructure can take a long time to launch, we don't want to create and destroy our system for every one of those tests. It's also very common for there to be a lot of little things that can be tested with a single configuration, so it can keep your tests simpler when grouping them together.

> **TIP** Don't forget that tests are also code and have to be maintained and expanded just like other software projects. Keeping things simple and well commented will help you and your team build great test suites.

Oftentimes, particularly with more complex modules, you will have test cases that require different configurations and can't be grouped in a single test. For example, a Simple Storage Solution (S3) module might have a group of test cases focused on a configuration that is completely private and meant for logging, with another group of test cases using S3 as a public-facing static web host. Since both of these groups have specific needs that contradict each other, it requires a separate set of configuration values and tests to confirm they work. In the next section, we talk about how to organize these configurations.

9.2.2   *Starting with examples*

What if I told you that with one simple practice you could

- Simplify the process of testing
- Make it easier for developers to expand your code
- Provide working examples that users of your module could learn from

One of the most important lessons I've learned in my years of development is that you should always make it easy for your developers to work locally. If you're the maintainer of a module, it should be easy for you to launch that module and iterate on it. If the module is complex, then you should be able to easily launch different variations of that module without having to jump through hoops or write boilerplate code every time.

To do this, I adopted a pattern that has worked remarkably well. For every module I create, I build fully working examples of how to use that module. Each example shows different features and functionality. For very simple modules (a DNS record manager, for instance) there may be just one example, while complex modules (like container orchestrators) will typically have a lot more.

Examples should be more than just simple demonstrations of the module and should include examples of your module integrating with other systems. As an example, AWS Application Load Balancers (ALBs) can integrate with EC2 Container Service (ECS; containers), Lambda functions, and direct IP addresses. If I was maintaining a module to manage an ALB, I would include an example of each of these integrations. This would make it faster for users of the module to learn about and use the module.

Listing 9.3   ALB examples structure

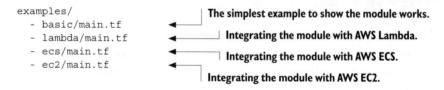

```
examples/
  - basic/main.tf
  - lambda/main.tf
  - ecs/main.tf
  - ec2/main.tf
```

The simplest example to show the module works.

Integrating the module with AWS Lambda.

Integrating the module with AWS ECS.

Integrating the module with AWS EC2.

It also makes it easier for maintainers of the module to extend it. If you make it so your examples are fully functioning and actually run, then module developers can simply change their directory to the example they want to work with and launch it.

The final benefit of this model (and the one that makes it relevant to this chapter) is that these examples can be used as the basis for your tests. When writing tests for Terraform, you often have to create custom Terraform code outside of your module. If you want to test how an ALB works with Lambda, then you're going to need an ALB that's connected to a Lambda. It isn't enough to simply change your variables around (as you would with a unit test); to properly test a Terraform module, you generally have to test the module with connections to resources that are external to that module.

Creating working examples alongside your module means your users have something to learn from, your developers have something to work with, and your tests have multiple configurations to validate. As new features get added to your module, you can either extend your existing examples or add new ones, and by tying them directly into your tests, you know your examples always work.

9.2.3 Concurrency and automated testing

Due to the length of time it takes for tests to run, they are often run concurrently with each other. This means that more than one test environment (with its own configuration) is likely to be created at the same time. This is true even if your test suite only has a single configuration that it tests, as it is always possible for multiple people to open different pull requests at the same time.

With typical software, this isn't a big deal. Tests are typically run in memory on a dedicated node (such as a GitHub Actions runner) and aren't capable of interfering with each other. When we're testing IaC projects, we're literally launching infrastructure. Real resources are created and destroyed as part of testing. Since the tests are working with outside systems and are making real changes, some thought has to be put into making sure tests are actually capable of running at the same time.

The biggest way this shows itself is with resources that require unique names. If two tests run at the same time and attempt to create a resource with the same name, then one of those tests will likely fail. There are even some resources (such as the AWS Secrets Manager's `aws_secretsmanager_secret` resource) where you have to wait for a long time (a full week by default) after deleting before you can create a new one with the same name.

Fortunately, this problem has a very simple solution: add some randomness to your names. By utilizing the `random` provider with your tests, you can make it so that test runs each get their own unique name (or, at least, statistically very likely to have their own name). This will make it so you can easily run tests concurrently.

Listing 9.4 Adding randomness to names for testing

```
resource "random_string" "random" {
  length  = 8
  special = false
  upper   = false
}

module "alb_example" {
  source = "../"
  name   = "testing_${random_string.random.result}"
  ...
}
```

The length of the random string should be high enough to reduce the chance of collision.

Lots of systems will get upset if you use special characters in names.

Since names may be case insensitive it's easier to just stick with lowercase.

The name is now random, reducing the chance of collision.

The rest of your parameters would go here.

For resources that can't have duplicated names even after deletion (such as our AWS Secrets Manager example), you may want to add randomness to the name inside of your module itself. This can prevent problems when you purposefully bring an environment down and back up again with the same name outside of testing.

9.2.4   *Timeouts*

Another big annoyance that can occur with IaC testing is hitting timeouts. Outside of the IaC world, you tend not to run into timeouts in tests nearly as often, as tests tend to run very quickly. Unfortunately, that is not the case when launching infrastructure.

When dealing with timeouts, there are two places you need to look: your test system itself (such as Terratest, which uses the Go testing package and inherits its timeouts) and your CI system (GitHub Actions, Jenkins, etc.). For both of these, you want to make sure your timeouts are high enough to give your tests time to complete, including time to tear down resources.

Hitting a timeout is remarkably annoying. When you hit a timeout, your tests are immediately stopped. This can result in orphaned resources remaining in your account (costing money). Since tests generally aren't configured with a state backend, it also means you have a lot of manual cleanup to do (something we'll address in the next section), and even if you do configure a state backend for your tests, a timeout often means that the state file isn't saved anyways.

We'll review how to configure timeouts for the testing systems we go over in sections 9.3 and 9.4, as it does tend to be specific to the testing framework. For your CI systems, just make sure to look up the defaults and make sure they meet your requirements. GitHub Actions, for instance, has a default timeout of 360 minutes, which is way more than you should need. For other systems, especially self-managed ones like Jenkins, you should always confirm the default or preemptively set a high value in your job.

9.2.5   *Automatic cleanup*

Sometimes tests fail in a way that doesn't allow the test suite to properly clean up. This can happen for a number of reasons: Terraform can crash before saving state, a logic error prevents `terraform destroy` from running, or the CI system itself can have an error that causes the job to stop before it finishes executing. Regardless of the cause, these types of errors can leave resources running inside of accounts. In the cloud world we live in, that means money being spent until those resources are cleaned up.

For this reason, I find it helpful to have a way to easily reset an account back to its original settings with all resources deleted. Better yet, I like to run these resets on a schedule using automation.

> **WARNING** Automatically erasing resources can be dangerous. To reduce the risk, you should always run your tests in an isolated account and only run account reset scripts against those test accounts. Never run tests in your production accounts!

Since Terraform has thousands of providers, there is not a single straightforward way to automate this cleanup that works for all of them. Instead, you have to research the tools for your system. The good news is that this is a very common need, so a lot of tools exist.

In general, the first thing I do when looking for a reset tool is search for "Vendor Nuke." For example, if you search for "AWS Nuke," the first thing that will show up is a GitHub `repository` `rebuy-de/aws-nuke` (https://github.com/rebuy-de/aws-nuke). If you run the same search for Azure, you'll find `ekristen/azure-nuke` (https://github .com/ekristen/azure-nuke). If that doesn't work, searches along a similar theme ("vendor cleanup," "vendor account reset") will often find things.

Listing 9.5   GitHub Actions for account cleanup

```
name: AWS Nuke Job

on:
  schedule:
    - cron: "0 0 * * *" # Runs every day at midnight

env:
  AWS_ROLE_ARN: arn:aws:iam::ACCOUNT_ID:role/ROLE_NAME
  AWS_DEFAULT_REGION: us-east-1
  AWS_NUKE_VERSION: 2.25.0

jobs:
  aws-nuke:
    runs-on: ubuntu-latest

    permissions:
      id-token: write
      contents: read

    steps:
      - name: Checkout code
        uses: actions/checkout@v4

      - name: Setup AWS credentials
        uses: aws-actions/configure-aws-credentials@v4
        with:
          role-to-assume: ${{ env.AWS_ROLE_ARN }}
          aws-region: ${{ env.AWS_DEFAULT_REGION }}

      - name: Install AWS Nuke
        run: |
          curl -L https://github.com/rebuy-de/aws-nuke/releases/download/
  v${AWS_NUKE_VERSION}/aws-nuke-v${AWS_NUKE_VERSION}-linux-amd64.tar.gz
  --output aws_nuke.tar.gz
          tar -xvf aws_nuke.tar.gz
          sudo mv aws-nuke-v${AWS_NUKE_VERSION}-linux-amd64
  /usr/local/bin/aws-nuke

      - name: Run AWS Nuke
        run: aws-nuke --config nuke-config.yml
```

This should be the role with permission to delete everything.

AWS requires a region to be set.

The version of AWS Nuke to use. You generally want to manually upgrade this after testing.

We use this to enable OIDC from GitHub to AWS.

This will log us in using OIDC.

Download and install AWS Nuke.

Run AWS Nuke with the configuration file.

This configuration file should be crafted with care to only delete what you want.

Some vendors, such as Azure and GCP, make it easier to clean up infrastructure by allowing you to easily group resources together under projects or resource groups. For those, you can typically erase the entire project or resource group to clean up all the resources launched there.

Unfortunately, not every vendor has a simple way to reset your account. If you are in a position where automatically resetting your test accounts isn't possible, then you should make sure you examine any test failures to ensure all resources are cleaned up. It's also always a good idea to set up alerts on your accounts when they go over the expected budget (how to do this will depend on your vendor).

9.2.6   *Authentication and secrets*

Although your tests are not creating long-term infrastructure, they are interacting with your various vendors, and this will include needing to actually authenticate. You should review section 8.5 for how to properly manage secrets. In particular, you should strongly consider using OpenID Connect as your authentication method of choice for your tests if they are supported by the systems you're managing.

9.2.7   *Testing as code*

As a final thought before we jump into the specific frameworks available for testing with Terraform, always remember that your test suites are also code themselves. That means you want to apply the same level of quality that you would to any software to your tests themselves.

Use variables that have easy-to-understand names. Add comments to the different steps and configurations in your tests, including descriptions of what you're hoping to accomplish with that test. When reviewing pull requests, give as much attention to the tests as you do to the code. Don't be afraid to refactor tests when needed, especially if it makes writing more tests easier. Investing in your test suites is one of the best ways to build high-quality projects.

9.3   *Terratest*

Terratest, as discussed earlier in the chapter, is a testing framework for Terraform built on top of the Go testing package. It is an open source project written by the folks at Gruntwork, and is pretty much the de facto testing tool for Terraform.

Terratest is the first testing suite written for Terraform to get major adoption. The vast majority of existing tests written for Terraform are written using Terratest, and the odds are every developer using Terraform is going to encounter Terratest at some point. If you don't currently know Go, it may be tempting to skip this section and jump ahead to the Terraform testing framework, but I promise you it's not nearly as complicated as it looks at first, and even if you don't use Terratest, it's important to understand how the industry works and the tools that are in use.

9.3.1   *Getting started with Go*

Terratest is written using the Go testing package. Depending on who you ask, this is either its greatest strength or its biggest weakness. On the one hand, it means that you have the power of the entire Go language at your fingertips, including third-party libraries that may help you better test your modules. On the other hand, it's an entirely new language for your team to learn.

That being said, the task of learning Go may be somewhat overstated. In this case, we're talking about a rather limited subset of the language, the Test framework. With this limited scope in mind, it makes it easier for developers to get started with the language and pick up things as they expand their tests. In other words, to use Terratest, you aren't building full-scale applications with Go but are instead writing the equivalent of small scripts, so it's a bit easier to approach.

> **TIP** Having trouble searching for Go? When running searches, to learn more you may want to try Golang, as the word "go" is so generic and commonly used that it may be hard to find what you're looking for.

When writing tests with Go testing always follows the same pattern. First, you create a file in the `tests` directory of a project with a name that ends with `_test.go` (such as `module_test.go`). At the top of your file, you put your package name (almost always `tests` when we're creating tests). Then you import any packages you may need, including the testing package, before creating a test function.

Listing 9.6   Example test in Go

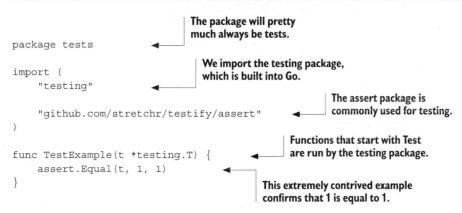

```
package tests            ◀——  The package will pretty
                               much always be tests.

import (                 ◀——  We import the testing package,
    "testing"                 which is built into Go.

    "github.com/stretchr/testify/assert"   ◀——  The assert package is
)                                                commonly used for testing.

func TestExample(t *testing.T) {   ◀——  Functions that start with Test
    assert.Equal(t, 1, 1)                are run by the testing package.
}                        ◀——  This extremely contrived example
                               confirms that 1 is equal to 1.
```

Before we can run our tests, we have to initialize our Go package and download any dependencies. This is similar to the `terraform init` command for Terraform and is run for similar purposes. Inside of the `tests` directory you'll want to run two commands:

1 First we run `go mod init`. This command takes a single argument: the name of your module. Most of the time, this is a path to your repository on GitHub, for instance, `go mod init github.com/TerraformInDepth/terraform-module -example`. Once you run this command, a file named `go.mod` will be created that contains metadata about your Go package.

2 Next, we run `go mod tidy`. This command downloads any needed packages and creates a file named `go.sum` with a list of all dependencies and a checksum of their version. It also updates the `go.mod` file to add or remove any direct dependencies.

Any time you change the packages you're importing, you'll want to run `go mod tidy` again, but outside of that you only need to run these commands once before you can run tests.

To run tests, you just need to run the command `go test` from inside of your tests directory.

Listing 9.7   `go test` **output**

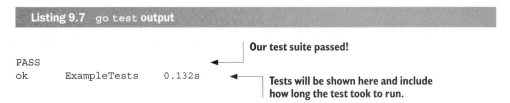

```
PASS
ok      ExampleTests    0.132s
```

Our test suite passed!

Tests will be shown here and include how long the test took to run.

That's it! We've written our first Go "program" (although, as mentioned, it resembled a simple script) and have run it. Although there were a few steps there, they don't really change, so later in this chapter we'll update our `makefile` so we don't have to memorize these commands.

You might be wondering what it looks like when tests fail. Let's change our test to assert that `1=2`, something that is obviously wrong, and run our tests again. We don't have to run `go mod init` or `go mod tidy` again, just `go test`.

Listing 9.8   `go test` **failed test**

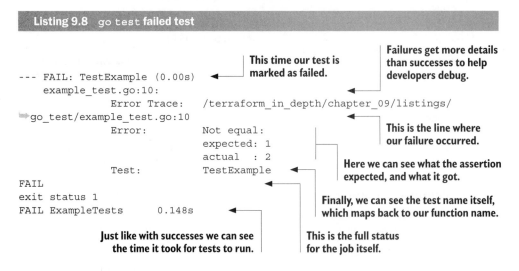

```
--- FAIL: TestExample (0.00s)
    example_test.go:10:
                Error Trace:    /terraform_in_depth/chapter_09/listings/
go_test/example_test.go:10
                Error:          Not equal:
                                expected: 1
                                actual  : 2
                Test:           TestExample
FAIL
exit status 1
FAIL ExampleTests    0.148s
```

This time our test is marked as failed.

Failures get more details than successes to help developers debug.

This is the line where our failure occurred.

Here we can see what the assertion expected, and what it got.

Finally, we can see the test name itself, which maps back to our function name.

Just like with successes we can see the time it took for tests to run.

This is the full status for the job itself.

9.3.2   *Terratest Hello World*

Now that you've seen the generic Go testing package we can dive into Terratest itself. Terratest is basically a set of helper functions designed to work with the Go testing package so that it can be used for testing.

Before we get into the test suite itself, let's build the simplest possible Terraform module: an input variable that passes an attribute to a single resource that then returns an attribute as an output.

Listing 9.9 Simple project for testing

```
variable "test_input" {
  type = string          ◀──────┐  We have a single simple input.
}

resource "terraform_data" "this" {    ◀───┘  For this test we have a single
  input = var.test_input    ◀──────         state-only resource.
}                                      Our input is passed to the
                                       terraform_data resource.
output "test_output" {
  value = terraform_data.this.output    ◀──────  We return the output of the
}                                               terraform_data resource.
```

With this simple module, we can put together a basic test case. Our test script is going to follow the same pattern we saw in the last section: a package declaration, a list of imports, and then our first test function. This time we're going to import the `terraform` module from Terratest and add some Terraform-specific tests to our test function.

The test functions created with Terratest all follow the same basic pattern:

1 Create your `terraformOptions` object. This is used to pass options to Terraform just like you would in the command-line interface. We use it to set the directory where Terraform should run, pass input variables to Terraform, and switch between Terraform and OpenTofu.

2 Call `terraform.Destroy` with `defer` so that it's called after our test has finished running. This is important to ensure that your resources are cleaned up when the test completes, even if the test itself fails.

3 Call `terraform.InitAndApply` to initialize and apply Terraform in the directory we specified.

4 Call module-specific validations of the launched environment. This can be as simple as validating outputs to more complex tasks like ensuring an HTTP endpoint is responding.

An example test would be to see if our module is actually returning the input we provide as an output. This will follow the same pattern we outlined earlier.

NOTE The first difference from our Go testing example you'll notice in the next example is that we're importing the `os` module and using it to load an environment variable that we then pass into the `TerraformBinary` field of our `terraform.Options` object. This allows us to set an environment variable to switch between the `terraform` and `tofu` binaries, so our single test suite can be used with both programs.

Listing 9.10   Basic structure of a Terratest test

```
package tests
                        ◄————  We import our packages.
import (
    "os"
    "testing"           ◄————  This is the same testing
                               package as before.
                                                    Now we also pull
    "github.com/gruntwork-io/terratest/modules/terraform"  ◄——  in Terratest.
    "github.com/stretchr/testify/assert"
)                                          This allows multiple tests to
                                           run at the same time.
func TestExample(t *testing.T) {
    t.Parallel()        ◄————  This is what we'll pass to the input
                               and will expect from the output.
    testInput := "test"  ◄————
                                         We use this to switch
                                         between Terraform
    terraformBinary := os.Getenv("TERRATEST_BINARY")  ◄——  and OpenTofu.
    if len(terraformBinary) <= 0 {
        terraformBinary = "terraform"
    }                               ◄——  If the environment variable is not
                                         set, we default to Terraform.

    terraformOptions := terraform.WithDefaultRetryableErrors(t,
  &terraform.Options{

        TerraformDir:     "../",          We use the binary
        TerraformBinary: terraformBinary,  ◄——  we set above.

        Vars: map[string]interface{}{      We pass the test input to
            "test_input": testInput,   ◄——  the Terraform module.
        },
    })                              We defer the destroy to ensure the resources
                                    are cleaned up after tests are run.
    defer terraform.Destroy(t, terraformOptions)  ◄——

    terraform.InitAndApply(t, terraformOptions)  ◄——  We run the Terraform
                                                       init and apply.
    testOutput := terraform.Output(t, terraformOptions, "test_output")  ◄——

    assert.Equal(t, testInput, testOutput)  ◄——  We get the output from
}                                                 the Terraform module.
        Finally, we test that the
        output is equal to the input.
```

Now we can run our test! For this, we run through the same process as any Go testing project: cd testing; go mod init PACKAGENAME; go mod tidy; go test -v. As previously, we can run the tests again without needing to run the init or tidy commands.

Listing 9.11   Go testing output

```
=== RUN    TestExample
=== PAUSE TestExample
=== CONT  TestExample
TestExample retry.go:91: terraform [init -upgrade=false]
```

Terratest runs the plan and applies it automatically.

Terraform init output skipped for conciseness.

```
TestExample logger.go:66: Running command terraform with args
➡[init -upgrade=false]
TestExample retry.go:91: terraform [apply -input=false -auto-approve
➡-var test_input=test -lock=false]
TestExample logger.go:66: Running command terraform with args [apply
➡-input=false -auto-approve -var test_input=test -lock=false]
TestExample logger.go:66:
TestExample logger.go:66: Terraform used the selected providers to generate
➡the following execution
TestExample logger.go:66: plan. Resource actions are indicated with the
➡following symbols:
TestExample logger.go:66:   + create
TestExample logger.go:66:
TestExample logger.go:66: Terraform will perform the following actions:
TestExample logger.go:66:
TestExample logger.go:66:   # terraform_data.this will be created
TestExample logger.go:66:   + resource "terraform_data" "this" {
TestExample logger.go:66:       + id     = (known after apply)
TestExample logger.go:66:       + input  = "test"
TestExample logger.go:66:       + output = (known after apply)
TestExample logger.go:66:     }
TestExample logger.go:66:
TestExample logger.go:66: Plan: 1 to add, 0 to change, 0 to destroy.
TestExample logger.go:66:
TestExample logger.go:66: Changes to Outputs:
TestExample logger.go:66:   + test_output = (known after apply)
TestExample logger.go:66: terraform_data.this: Creating...
TestExample logger.go:66: terraform_data.this: Creation complete after 0s
➡[id=37c58929-ea6e-2a46-41ad-3609b78ec857]
TestExample logger.go:66:
TestExample logger.go:66: Apply complete! Resources: 1 added, 0 changed,
➡0 destroyed.
TestExample logger.go:66:
TestExample logger.go:66: Outputs:
TestExample logger.go:66:
TestExample logger.go:66: test_output = "test"
TestExample retry.go:91: terraform [output -no-color -json test_output]
TestExample logger.go:66: Running command terraform with args [output
➡-no-color -json test_output]
TestExample logger.go:66: "test"
TestExample retry.go:91: terraform [destroy -auto-approve -input=false
➡-var test_input=test -lock=false]
TestExample logger.go:66: Running command terraform with args [destroy
➡-auto-approve -input=false -var test_input=test -lock=false]
TestExample logger.go:66: terraform_data.this: Refreshing state...
➡[id=37c58929-ea6e-2a46-41ad-3609b78ec857]
```

Terratest grabs the outputs with the output command.

Terratest only runs the destroy after checking your assertions.

```
TestExample logger.go:66:
TestExample logger.go:66: Terraform used the selected providers to generate
➥the following execution
TestExample logger.go:66: plan. Resource actions are indicated with the
➥following symbols:
TestExample logger.go:66:     - destroy
TestExample logger.go:66:
TestExample logger.go:66: Terraform will perform the following actions:
TestExample logger.go:66:
TestExample logger.go:66:   # terraform_data.this will be destroyed
TestExample logger.go:66:   - resource "terraform_data" "this" {
TestExample logger.go:66:       - id      = "37c58929-ea6e-2a46-41ad-
➥3609b78ec857" -> null
TestExample logger.go:66:       - input  = "test" -> null
TestExample logger.go:66:       - output = "test" -> null
TestExample logger.go:66:     }
TestExample logger.go:66:
TestExample logger.go:66: Plan: 0 to add, 0 to change, 1 to destroy.
TestExample logger.go:66:
TestExample logger.go:66: Changes to Outputs:
TestExample logger.go:66:   - test_output = "test" -> null
TestExample logger.go:66: terraform_data.this: Destroying...
➥[id=37c58929-ea6e-2a46-41ad-3609b78ec857]
TestExample logger.go:66: terraform_data.this: Destruction complete after 0s
TestExample logger.go:66:
TestExample logger.go:66: Destroy complete! Resources: 1 destroyed.
TestExample logger.go:66:
--- PASS: TestExample (0.16s)                    ◄──────┐ Terratest
PASS                                                    │ shows the
ok    github.com/TerraformInDepth/terraform-null-test 0.690s ◄─┐ │ results of
                                                          │ │ the test.
                              Each individual test gets ──┘ │
                                its own output as well. ────┘
```

The nice thing about our simple example is that it runs quickly. This is not the case for most IaC projects though, as launching a resource as a database (and then tearing them down again) can easily take as long as an hour. Go testing will time out when tests take longer than 10 minutes by default, so you should make sure to use the `timeout` flag to increase the time-out for tests that will take longer (e.g., `go tests -timeout 60m`).

> **WARNING** If you forget the `timeout` flag, there's a chance your test will be killed before resources are destroyed. This can cost you time and money, so you do not want to forget to set this flag.

9.3.3   *Building on examples*

When writing tests, you often want to test your module in a variety of scenarios, including testing how those modules interact with other systems and modules. While it is possible to use your module directly as a workspace to launch and create infrastructure, this often limits your ability to do full integration testing.

This is where the `examples` folder we talked about earlier really begins to shine. When writing your tests, you not only have the option of using your module itself as your entry point but also all of the examples you've written. In general, this is as easy as switching the directory you're pointing to and adjusting your input variables.

The Cookiecutter template we've been building for the last few chapters is a perfect place to put your boilerplate for testing examples. The one hosted (https://mng.bz/ OBMn) on the TerraformInDepth (https://github.com/TerraformInDepth/) GitHub organization has already been updated to include this.

Listing 9.12   Testing examples with Terratest

```
package tests

import (
    "os"
    "testing"

    "github.com/gruntwork-io/terratest/modules/terraform"
    "github.com/stretchr/testify/assert"    ◀── We will use this package to
)                                                build out our assertions.
func TestExample(t *testing.T) {
    t.Parallel()

    terraformBinary := os.Getenv("TERRATEST_BINARY")
    if len(terraformBinary) <= 0 {
        terraformBinary = "terraform"
    }

    terraformOptions := terraform.WithDefaultRetryableErrors(t,
  &terraform.Options{

        TerraformDir:    "../examples/basic",    ◀── To utilize one of our examples
        TerraformBinary: terraformBinary,            we just need to point
                                                     Terratest to the directory.
        Vars: map[string]interface{}{
            "test_input": "test",    ◀── The variables passed here will
        },                              be specific to the example,
    })                                  not the root module.

    defer terraform.Destroy(t, terraformOptions)

    terraform.InitAndApply(t, terraformOptions)


}            ◀── Now we can build out assertions here.
                 If you don't use the assert package we
                 imported above you will get an error.
```

By utilizing your examples for tests, you provide extra incentive to write examples for the different use cases your module supports, and as an added bonus, you will immediately know if any new code breaks your existing examples. This gives your module users a great starting point for their own development, as well as confidence that your modules will function as expected.

Using these examples as a source for your tests also tends to simplify the tests themselves. Since these examples are full Terraform code, you can create any resources you need for testing right in the examples themselves. You can reduce the number of required inputs by utilizing data sources or creating custom outputs specific to your test without polluting the main module.

9.3.4   *Terratest helpers*

Perhaps one of the biggest advantages that Terratest has over the Terraform testing framework is the giant collection of helper functions that ship with Terratest. These helpers are all organized into Go packages inside of Terratest itself and can be imported into your tests as needed.

There are over 20 separate helper packages, including provider-specific packages (such as the modules for AWS, Azure, Oracle Cloud, and GCP), protocol-level packages like the http-helper and dns-helpers, and packages that are just useful for testing.

The best way to review the available helpers is to dig into the Terratest repository itself (https://github.com/gruntwork-io/terratest). The modules directory of the Git repository contains all of the helpers organized by provider or service type. The Git repository tends to be more up to date than the Terratest website itself, so you might find some interesting modules in there that you wouldn't have found otherwise.

Also remember that Go is a very mature language with a huge variety of third-party libraries. You are not limited to just the helpers provided by Terratest but have the entire Go ecosystem to build off of.

9.3.5   *Updating our makefile and template*

Before we go any further in our testing, let's make our lives a little easier. When using Terratests, you are often going to run the same commands over and over again, and there are important flags (such as the `timeout` flag) that are easy to forget and that will make a mess if you forget. We can use the solution we built in chapter 7, our `makefile`, to save these commands and speed up our development.

Our main goal is to call Terratest and have it run all of the tests. We do not want our developers to have to think about `go mod init` or `go mod tidy`, but we want tests to work when that command runs. This is one of those areas where Make really shines, as we can set it up so our `terratest` target depends on having our `go.mod` and `go.sum`, but we can also make it so those files are only generated when needed.

Another goal is to make it easy for people using our `makefile` to change the behavior of the tests. A user may want to only run a single test rather than the whole test suite, or they may want to switch between OpenTofu and Terraform. To make this simple, we're going to add a variable they can override, `GO_TEST_OPTS`, that will default to an empty string. We're also going to take advantage of the `TF_BINARY` variable we created in section 7.2.4 by passing it into our tests as an environment variable, where it will then be passed to our `terraform.Options` object.

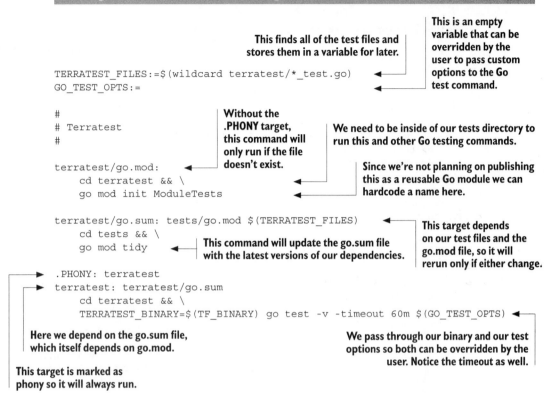

Listing 9.13 Terratest `makefile` changes

This finds all of the test files and stores them in a variable for later.

This is an empty variable that can be overridden by the user to pass custom options to the Go test command.

```
TERRATEST_FILES:=$(wildcard terratest/*_test.go)
GO_TEST_OPTS:=
```

```
#
# Terratest
#
```

Without the .PHONY target, this command will only run if the file doesn't exist.

We need to be inside of our tests directory to run this and other Go testing commands.

```
terratest/go.mod:
    cd terratest && \
    go mod init ModuleTests
```

Since we're not planning on publishing this as a reusable Go module we can hardcode a name here.

```
terratest/go.sum: tests/go.mod $(TERRATEST_FILES)
    cd tests && \
    go mod tidy
```

This command will update the go.sum file with the latest versions of our dependencies.

This target depends on our test files and the go.mod file, so it will rerun only if either change.

```
.PHONY: terratest
terratest: terratest/go.sum
    cd terratest && \
    TERRATEST_BINARY=$(TF_BINARY) go test -v -timeout 60m $(GO_TEST_OPTS)
```

Here we depend on the go.sum file, which itself depends on go.mod.

We pass through our binary and our test options so both can be overridden by the user. Notice the timeout as well.

This target is marked as phony so it will always run.

Now anyone can run `make terratest` and have the tests get run with all of our preferred options. If the test files get updated, `go mod tidy` will automatically be run, and we can switch between OpenTofu and Terratest using the same methods we have throughout the rest of the book. For example, if a user wanted to only run a specific test, they could run the following command:

```
make terratest GO_TEST_OPTS="-run TestExample"
```

We can take this even further and add the basic test structure from earlier in this section to our template. This way, we give developers of a new module a basic skeleton for tests. I've found that doing this really lowers the barrier for writing tests, especially for those who aren't as familiar with Go or Terratest, as they can see they only need to make a few small changes to add real value. This is also a great time to add some comments to really help get people started.

Listing 9.14 Terratest basic test template

```
package test

import (
```

```
    "os"
    "testing"

    "github.com/gruntwork-io/terratest/modules/terraform"
)

func TestTerraformBasicExample(t *testing.T) {
    t.Parallel()

    // Allow the TerraformBinary option to be changed by users.
    // This makes it possible to switch to tofu easily.
    terraformBinary := os.Getenv("TERRATEST_BINARY")
    if len(terraformBinary) <= 0 {
        terraformBinary = "terraform"
    }

    terraformOptions := terraform.WithDefaultRetryableErrors(t,
&terraform.Options{

        // Point this at the specific module or example to test.
        TerraformDir: "../examples/basic",

        // Switch between Terraform binaries.
        TerraformBinary: terraformBinary,

        Vars: map[string]interface{}{
            // Input Variables go here.
            // "test_input": testInput,
        },
    })

    // Run terraform destroy after all other test code has run,
even with errors.
    defer terraform.Destroy(t, terraformOptions)

    // Run terraform apply immediately.
    terraform.InitAndApply(t, terraformOptions)

    // Get any outputs from Terraform.
    // testOutput := terraform.Output(t, terraformOptions, "test_output")

    // Run assertions to confirm that outputs are what you expect.
    //assert.Equal(t, testInput, testOutput)
}
```

Notice how there are a lot of comments here: this will make it easier for new developers to create tests.

By putting this switch in our test template we make sure it's always present.

We're pointing to the basic example here.

We don't just have a comment, we also have an example to help developers get started.

Note that this won't work, it's just an example of how to pass a variable.

Even though our example doesn't have an output or assertion yet, we provide the structure for the developer to fill in.

The example template in the TerraformInDepth GitHub organization already has these changes.

9.3.6 *Testing with CI*

Now that our tests are written, we need to make sure they are always run. The easiest way to do that is to add our tests to our CI system.

Listing 9.15 Terratest with GitHub Actions

```
name: Terratest

on:
  push:
  pull_request:

jobs:
  terratest:
    strategy:
      matrix:
        engine: ["opentofu", "terraform"]
        version: ["1.6", "1.7", "1.9"]
        experimental: [false]
        include:
          - version: "1.9"
            engine: "opentofu"
            experimental: true
          - version: "1.9"
            engine: "terraform"
            experimental: false

    continue-on-error: ${{ matrix.experimental }}
    runs-on: ubuntu-latest
    steps:
      - uses: actions/checkout@v4

      - name: Install Terraform
        uses: hashicorp/setup-terraform@v3
        if: ${{ matrix.engine == 'terraform' }}
        with:
          terraform_version: ${{ matrix.version }}

      - name: Install OpenTofu
        uses: opentofu/setup-opentofu@v1
        if: ${{ matrix.engine == 'opentofu' }}
        with:
          tofu_version: ${{ matrix.version }}

      - name: Run Terratest
        run: make terratest TF_ENGINE=${{matrix.engine}}
```

> We want to test both Terraform and OpenTofu, and we want to test multiple versions of each.

> Since our makefile and test uses the same **TF_ENGINE** variable to switch between engines we can include it here.

This example is great for projects that only have a single test function that they are running. Even if that test function has a lot of assertions, it's only a single function and can run pretty easily. If you have multiple test functions though, you run into a problem with the previous workflow:

1 Either you allow all the tests to run at the same time with all of their console logs being mixed together

2 Or you set the concurrency to 1 so only one test runs at a time, causing your tests to take significantly longer to run.

Imagine you're building a module for AWS Relational Database Service (RDS; the poster child of resources that take entirely too long to launch and destroy, with a total cycle time of about 45 minutes). If you have four separate examples that you're testing, then you're either going to have four separate jobs sending out messages at the same time (making it very difficult to debug) or you're going to have a 3-hour test cycle. It's really not ideal.

Fortunately, we have other options. The Go testing package's command-line interface tool has an option to specify a specific test to run. We can use that with the GO_ TEST_OPTS variable in our `makefile` to run only one test, and we can combine that with the GitHub Actions matrix strategy we're already using to switch between the different versions and Terraform engines we want to test. We can create a new field that lists all of our test functions, and GitHub Actions will run each of them independently.

Listing 9.16   Terratest with GitHub Actions strategy matrix

```
name: Terratest

on:
  push:
  pull_request:

jobs:
  terratest:
    strategy:
      matrix:
        engine: ["opentofu", "terraform"]
        version: ["1.6", "1.7", "1.8"]
        experimental: [false]
        test: [BasicTest, LambdaTest, ECSTest, Ec2Test]    ◀──┐  Add our test cases as
                                                              │  another matrix item.

        include:
          - version: "1.9"
            engine: "opentofu"
            experimental: true
            test: [BasicTest, LambdaTest, ECSTest, Ec2Test]  ◀──┐ Unfortunately,
          - version: "1.9"                                      │ we have to
            engine: "terraform"                                 │ duplicate the
            experimental: false                                 │ test cases in our
            test: [BasicTest, LambdaTest, ECSTest, Ec2Test]  ◀──┘ include section.

    continue-on-error: ${{ matrix.experimental }}         ◀──┐ This means
    runs-on: ubuntu-latest                                   │ duplicating it
    steps:                                                   │ here as well.
      - uses: actions/checkout@v4

      - name: Install Terraform
        uses: hashicorp/setup-terraform@v3
        if: ${{ matrix.engine == 'terraform' }}
        with:
          terraform_version: ${{ matrix.version }}

      - name: Install OpenTofu
```

```
     uses: opentofu/setup-opentofu@v1
     if: ${{ matrix.engine == 'opentofu' }}
     with:
       tofu_version: ${{ matrix.version }}

   - name: Run Terratest
     run: make terratest TF_ENGINE=${{matrix.engine}}
➡ GO_TEST_OPTIONS="-run ${{matrix.test}}"
```

> Now we pass the test cases through to our make command.

That's it! Now for every pull request that comes in, you'll have every one of your tests run, using every version of Terraform that you want to support for your module across both Terraform and OpenTofu. In the event that something breaks, you'll see that directly in your pull request, just like with the other tests we introduced in chapter 7.

9.3.7 Terratest and Copilot

GitHub Copilot is part of a new wave of large-language-model-based products that utilize AI to give developers suggestions for their code. It can basically be considered one of the most advanced autocomplete tools ever created. Copilot can be enabled on GitHub (https://github.com/features/copilot), and has integrations with most common IDEs.

Large language models (LLMs) are created by combining extremely large datasets with advanced algorithms and model training. They are designed to take in data (often called prompts) and return their best guess at the desired response. Although they can do a decent job at generalizing, they do better at tasks that are present in their training data. At the moment, Copilot isn't that great with Terraform (although it can write some fantastic comments), but it has a lot more Go examples available in its datasets and performs much better there.

Copilot can be an amazing tool for teams and developers that are still trying to learn Go. It is also really powerful when combined with our method of using examples as the basis for our tests. When using Copilot Chat, your prompt will be passed to Copilot along with any open windows you have to their model and return a response.

Let's take our extremely simple example from the start of the section. With that code in our window, we pass a simple prompt to Copilot Chat.

 Write a test for this Terraform code using Terratest. As part of the test make sure the input variable and output variable match.

That prompt should trigger a response from Copilot with a generated test suite. It's important to note that LLMs are being updated all the time, so your results may not be exactly the same as the response that I got. It should be fairly close though.

Listing 9.17 Copilot-generated test

```
package test

import (
```

```
    "testing"

    "github.com/gruntwork-io/terratest/modules/terraform"
    "github.com/stretchr/testify/assert"
)

func TestTerraformModule(t *testing.T) {
    // Define the input variable
    testInput := "example_input"

    terraformOptions := &terraform.Options{
        // The path to where your Terraform code is located
        TerraformDir: "../",

        // Variables to pass to our Terraform code using -var options
        Vars: map[string]interface{}{
            "test_input": testInput,
        },
    }

    // This will run `terraform init` and `terraform apply` and fail the
    test if there are any errors
    defer terraform.Destroy(t, terraformOptions)
    terraform.InitAndApply(t, terraformOptions)

    // Check if the output variable "test_output" matches the input
    variable "test_input"
    testOutput := terraform.Output(t, terraformOptions, "test_output")
    assert.Equal(t, testInput, testOutput)
}
```

Copilot is using the base Options, rather than the WithDefaultRetryableErrors options.

Copilot did figure out our test_input name.

Just like in our examples, Copilot is using defer to destroy the resources after the test.

Copilot also figured out our output name.

The results are pretty remarkable. It was able to identify the names of the input variables and outputs, and it followed the same structure we've seen elsewhere. There are a couple of problems though:

- Our code to switch between OpenTofu and Terraform isn't present. This is because Copilot isn't aware of our quality-of-life improvement and likely hasn't seen it elsewhere.
- Instead of using the recommended `terraform.WithDefaultRetryableErrors`, Copilot is using the plain `terraform.Options` object.

Both of these problems may be correctable with a different prompt, but then you have to remember to include it in all of your prompts. Instead, you should use Copilot as an inspiration, look inside of the test function for things you may have missed, and then adjust your own tests with those suggestions. This will allow you to keep the skeleton with improvements you know while supplementing your code with improvements from the LLM.

Even with that downside, this is a powerful tool. To see why, let's look at our example from earlier where we used Terratest helpers to check that an HTTP endpoint was available. First, we have to open that file in our editor so that Copilot gets the context:

Write a test for this Terraform code using Terratest. As part of this test ensure that the http endpoint is reachable. Utilize Terratest helpers to automatically retry.

With this prompt, Copilot will return a test that does exactly what we've asked, with the same limitations as we've seen earlier. You'll still want to copy the assertions and related code into our structure if you want to support switching between OpenTofu and Terraform or take advantage of the recommended default options.

Listing 9.18 Copilot-generated endpoint test

```
package test

import (
    "testing"
    "time"

    "github.com/gruntwork-io/terratest/modules/http-helper"
    "github.com/gruntwork-io/terratest/modules/retry"
    "github.com/gruntwork-io/terratest/modules/terraform"
    "github.com/stretchr/testify/require"
)

func TestHttpEndpoint(t *testing.T) {
    // Define the terraform options
    terraformOptions := &terraform.Options{
        TerraformDir: "../",
    }

    // Init and apply
    terraform.InitAndApply(t, terraformOptions)

    // Get output
    endpointUrl := terraform.Output(t, terraformOptions, "endpoint_url")

    // Define a maximum of 10 retries with a time between retries of
30 seconds
    maxRetries := 10
    timeBetweenRetries := 30 * time.Second

    // Define the expected status code
    expectedStatusCode := 200

    // Verify that we get back a 200 OK with the expected text
    http_helper.HttpGetWithRetry(t, endpointUrl, nil, expectedStatusCode,
"", maxRetries, timeBetweenRetries)
}
```

Note that this module is not actually used in the code.

This module is also not used.

When looking at this function note how similar it is to our test structure.

Copilot is nice enough to leave a lot of comments.

Here we lose our code to switch between OpenTofu and Terraform.

Users might want to change these values to something more appropriate for their use case.

Copilot made an assumption that our endpoint would be in an output with this name.

This can be really helpful for a developer who didn't know how to check endpoints in Go.

NOTE It's worth mentioning that there is an error in this code, although it's a minor one that can be resolved automatically for most users. The retry package is imported by Copilot but is not actually used anywhere. Go is rather strict about this and will throw an error, but most editors will automatically detect and resolve the problem when the developer saves the file.

As you can see, this can be very helpful. A developer can ask Copilot to generate different assertions and copy them into their test function to build up a pretty robust test suite, even if they aren't super familiar with Go. That said, it isn't perfect, so it's always useful if you can have a member of your team who is familiar with Go review pull requests for any problems.

9.4   Terraform testing framework

The Terraform testing framework was introduced in Terraform and OpenTofu version v1.6, with new features being introduced in every release after that. While certainly newer than Terratest, it has the advantages of being integrated directly into Terraform and using pure HCL as the language of choice for writing tests.

The benefits of using HCL are probably obvious. For teams that are just learning Terraform for the first time, it can be pretty daunting to tell them they also need to learn Go in order to write tests. While the testing framework does introduce new HCL blocks, this isn't a far leap from what developers are already learning.

The direct integration with Terraform itself has its own subtle benefits. Terratest relies on outputs to really understand what happened in a project. The Terraform testing framework has the benefit of being able to directly access the attributes of any values (such as resource attributes and even local variables) by Terraform without the need to pass it back as an output.

9.4.1   Hello World

For our first test using the native Terraform tests command, we're going to use the same starting module as section 9.3.1: a simple module that takes in a variable, passes it to the `terraform_data` resource, and then defines an output using an attribute of that resource.

Terraform tests are a little bit different than our Go tests. For our tests, we're going to define a new file that ends in `.tftest.hcl` right in our main directory. Inside of this file, we utilize the new `run` and `variables` blocks to define our test. Inside of our `run` block, we define our assertions with the `assert` block.

> **Listing 9.19   Hello World test**

```
variables {
  test_input = "test"
}

run "input_and_output_match" {
```

The variables block takes the module input variables in as parameters. It applies to all tests in the file.

This is our input variable, which we expect to match the output.

Each run block is a test.

> **Run blocks can have multiple assert blocks.**

```
  assert {
    condition     = output.test_output == "test"
    error_message = "The output does not match the input."
  }
}
```

> **This is the condition we are testing.**

> **This is the error message we will get if the condition is not met.**

Each `run` block represents an action with Terraform. By default, this action is an apply, but the `command` parameter can be used to change this to a `plan` instead.

Listing 9.20 Hello World test plan

```
variables {
  test_input = "test"
}

run "input_and_output_match" {

  command = plan

  assert {
    condition     = output.test_output == "test"
    error_message = "The output does not match the input."
  }
}
```

> **The default command is "apply". We can change it to "plan" to test the plan output.**

> **This will fail because the plan can not create the resource to get the output from.**

When working with plans, it's important to remember that you can only access things that are available during the plan. If you try to read the output of a module during a plan, you may end up getting an error.

Listing 9.21 Plan "unknown condition" output

```
% terraform test
tests/example.tftest.hcl... in progress
  run "input_and_output_match"... fail
|
| Error: Unknown condition value
|
|   on tests/example.tftest.hcl line 9, in run "input_and_output_match":
|    9:      condition     = output.test_output == "test"
|
| Condition expression could not be evaluated at this time. This means you
have executed a `run` block with `command = plan` and one of the values your
condition depended on is not known until
| after the plan has been applied. Either remove this value from your
condition, or execute an `apply` command from this `run` block.
|
tests/example.tftest.hcl... tearing down
tests/example.tftest.hcl... fail

Failure! 0 passed, 1 failed.
```

> **You can see here that the test failed.**

> **This error means that there was a problem with your test, not the module itself.**

> **You will always get a list of the passes and failures at the end.**

This can make working with plans somewhat limited, as a lot of values simply won't be available. However, there are a lot of cases where it can be helpful, especially if you're testing the values that you're passing to resources rather than their attributes.

9.4.2   Accessing named values

One of the really cool features of the testing framework is that it can access all of the values inside of your module, not just what you output. By providing a full resource path, you can pull any value you need for your tests out of your module after it's run. This isn't limited to resources and data sources either: you can use it to validate your local variables too!

Listing 9.22   Accessing named values

```
variables {
  test_input = "test"
}

run "input_passed_to_resource" {
  assert {
    condition     = terraform_data.this.input == "test"
    error_message = "The resource parameter does not match the input."
  }
}
```

> We are able to test the resource directly, not just through an output.

With this functionality, you can test the internal state of your modules in a way that isn't possible with tools like Terratest, which work by wrapping Terraform instead of integrating with Terraform.

9.4.3   Mocks

Mocks are a new feature that was introduced in Terraform v1.7 and is still considered beta (at least at the time of writing). Mocks work by replacing the real provider used by your modules with a fake version of that provider, which returns fake computed values but does not actually create any real infrastructure. Since real infrastructure isn't being created, you can avoid a lot of the drawbacks of IaC testing: time and money. While it may take half an hour to launch a real RDS instance, it only takes a fraction of a second to launch a fake one. Mocks are useful for testing logic, and with them you can get as close as possible to creating unit tests.

Listing 9.23   Mocks

```
mock_provider "aws" {}
```

> Enabling mocks is as simple as adding a mock_provider block. Now all AWS resources will be mocked.

Since mocks do return fake data, they typically cannot be used as a simple swap in replacement. The data that comes out of mocks rarely matches what you'd expect from the real infrastructure. The types will be the same, but the values themselves will be set to a specific default based on the type (see table 9.2).

Table 9.2 Mock value defaults

Type	Mock value
Numbers	0
Booleans	False
Maps	{}
Lists and Sets	[]
Objects	Attributes are created using the above defaults

This can be pretty limiting, but the good news is that you can override that default inside of your test with any value you need. In fact, Terraform provides two separate ways to override those values: by setting a resource-type default value (for instance, providing a default value for every `aws_subnet.id`) or by overriding the value of a specific resource in your module.

Creating mocks for tests is pretty simple. Inside of the `mock_provider` block, you can use the `mock_resource` and `mock_data` blocks to create new defaults for any resource or data type you want. This will affect all of the resources in this test. Let's see what it would look like to mock our DNS example from earlier in the chapter.

Listing 9.24 Mock resources and data sources

```
mock_provider "aws" {
  mock_data "aws_region" {          ◄──  Here we provide mock data
    defaults = {                          for all of the tests in this file.
      name = "us-east-1"
    }
  }
}

run "dns_record_name" {

  command = plan                    ◄──  Since we are testing what a
                                         parameter is going to be set to we
  variables {                            can run a plan instead of an apply.
    zone_id = "Z1234567890"
    records = ["127.0.0.1"]
    domain  = "example.com"
    name    = "my_test"
  }

  assert {                                            Now our domain will be
    condition       = aws_route53_record.main.name == generated with the region
 ➥ "my_test.us-east-1.example.com"                    we set in our mock.
```

```
    error_message = "Domain name not properly generated from region."
  }
}
```

It's also possible to reuse mocks between testing by defining your mocks in `tfmock.hcl` files. In this case, you define the `mock_resource` and `mock_data` blocks on the top level and then import them into your individual tests.

Listing 9.25   Mock files

```
mock_data "aws_region" {
  defaults = {
    name = "us-east-1"
  }
}
```
◄——— **All mocks in this file will be loaded when imported. It's possible to build up a library of mocks this way.**

Now that our file has been created, we can include it. One interesting note is that Terraform does not allow you to import a single mock file but instead expects the source to be a directory. It will then load all mock files in that directory.

Listing 9.26   Importing mock files

```
mock_provider "aws" {
  source = "./tests/aws/"
}
```
◄——— **The source has to be a directory, not a file, and all files in the directory will be loaded as mocks.**

The final way to change data is with the `override_resource`, `override_data`, and `override_module` blocks. These blocks can be defined inside of the `mock_provider` block, on the top level of the file, or in the `run` blocks themselves. When put in the `mock_provider` block, they are only used if that `mock` provider happens to create the resource. When put on the top level of the file, they'll affect every `run` block, and when put inside of a specific `run` block, they will only affect that block.

Listing 9.27   Overrides and scope

```
mock_provider "aws" {}


run "dns_record_name" {

  command = plan

  override_data {
    target = data.aws_region.current
    values = {
      name = "us-east-1"
    }
  }
}
```
◄——— **Rather than changing the default for every data source we can target a specific one.**

◄——— **This is the path to the exact resource we want to override.**

```
variables {
  zone_id = "Z1234567890"
  records = ["127.0.0.1"]
  domain  = "example.com"
  name    = "my_test"
}

assert {                                                    Now our domain
  condition      = aws_route53_record.main.name ==          uses our region.
"my_test.us-east-1.example.com"
  error_message = "Domain name not properly generated from region."
}
}
```

Mocks are a great way to test your logic, but they have their own drawbacks. The more complicated your modules are, the more difficult it becomes to manage the mock data needed to properly test your code. This can easily reach a point where you're defining so much that your tests become detached from real-world circumstances. You might assume that a value can only have a specific format, for instance, but if the provider changes that and you don't update your mocks, then your tests will miss it. When upgrading major versions of a provider you've built mocks for, you should make sure to review them to ensure they match the provider as expected.

You should primarily use mocks not to completely replace your integration tests but to supplement them with unit tests. You should always make sure to run your full integration tests against real infrastructure, but mocks can be used to test edge cases or smaller pieces of your code in a way that may not be trivial when launching a lot of infrastructure.

9.4.4 Building on examples

As we discussed in the Terratest section, there are a lot of benefits to using real examples as test cases for your project. Regardless of whether you're using the Terraform testing framework or Terratest, these benefits remain the same, with the main difference being how you implement it.

Unfortunately, Terraform doesn't make this as easy as Terratest does. When using the Terraform testing framework, there's an assumption that your tests are always running against the module in the folder you're running the `terraform test` command from. This means that if you want to run tests against your examples, you have to put those tests alongside the examples themselves. On the one hand, this is kind of nice, in that you can see which tests are associated with which examples. On the other hand, calling your tests is no longer as simple as running `terraform tests` in your root directory: you have to go to each folder, initialize the module, and run the tests from there.

Listing 9.28 The `module` block

```
TERRAFORM_EXAMPLES:=$(wildcard examples/*)        Collect a list of all directories in
TF_TEST_OPTS:=                                     the examples directory.
```

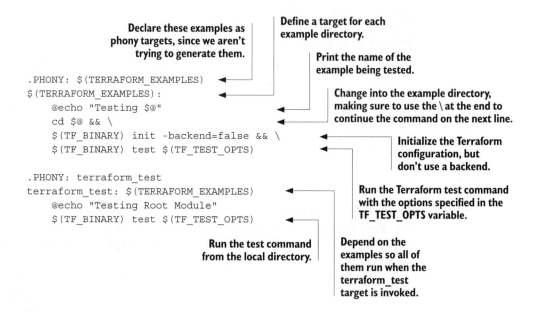

Now when you run `make terraform_test`, it will run every test. You can also call the different examples directly, such as `make examples/basic` to run the tests in the `examples/basic/tests` folder.

9.4.5   *Managing versions*

The Terraform testing framework and Terraform itself are very tightly coupled, as they are both run using the exact same binary. This means that the version of Terraform you are testing is also the version of the Terraform testing framework that you are using.

The positive of this is that switching between different versions is as simple as changing your Terraform version. If you are using `tenv`, as recommended in chapter 7, this is as easy as updating your relevant configuration file (`.terraform-version` or `.opentofu-version`). If you want to switch between OpenTofu and Terraform, you can take advantage of the makefile features we've already made.

What if you want to switch your version while testing though? Just like we want to use different versions of our tools with Terratest, we may want to do the same with Terraform or OpenTofu. One way to do this is to keep editing your version files, but that can be tedious. We're going to upgrade our `makefile` to allow us to specify the version we want to run as another option we pass to Make, just like we do with the `TF_ENGINE` option, by allowing a new `TF_VERSION` option.

> **NOTE** We need to remember that this makefile is also used in our CI platform, where we already have code for switching between versions using the various install actions. Most CI platforms define an environment variable CI to let code know that it's running inside of a CI system, so we can switch the command we use when we detect that.

Listing 9.29 `makefile` **support**

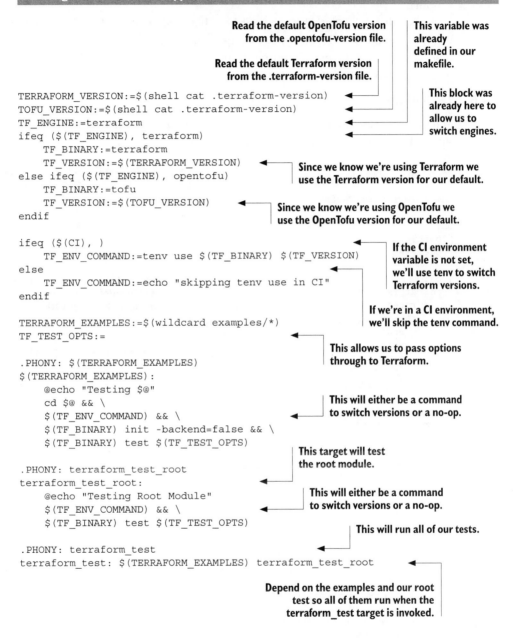

Read the default OpenTofu version
from the .opentofu-version file.

This variable was
already
defined in our
makefile.

Read the default Terraform version
from the .terraform-version file.

```
TERRAFORM_VERSION:=$(shell cat .terraform-version)
TOFU_VERSION:=$(shell cat .terraform-version)
TF_ENGINE:=terraform
ifeq ($(TF_ENGINE), terraform)
    TF_BINARY:=terraform
    TF_VERSION:=$(TERRAFORM_VERSION)
else ifeq ($(TF_ENGINE), opentofu)
    TF_BINARY:=tofu
    TF_VERSION:=$(TOFU_VERSION)
endif

ifeq ($(CI), )
    TF_ENV_COMMAND:=tenv use $(TF_BINARY) $(TF_VERSION)
else
    TF_ENV_COMMAND:=echo "skipping tenv use in CI"
endif

TERRAFORM_EXAMPLES:=$(wildcard examples/*)
TF_TEST_OPTS:=

.PHONY: $(TERRAFORM_EXAMPLES)
$(TERRAFORM_EXAMPLES):
    @echo "Testing $@"
    cd $@ && \
    $(TF_ENV_COMMAND) && \
    $(TF_BINARY) init -backend=false && \
    $(TF_BINARY) test $(TF_TEST_OPTS)

.PHONY: terraform_test_root
terraform_test_root:
    @echo "Testing Root Module"
    $(TF_ENV_COMMAND) && \
    $(TF_BINARY) test $(TF_TEST_OPTS)

.PHONY: terraform_test
terraform_test: $(TERRAFORM_EXAMPLES) terraform_test_root
```

This block was
already here to
allow us to
switch engines.

Since we know we're using Terraform we
use the Terraform version for our default.

Since we know we're using OpenTofu we
use the OpenTofu version for our default.

If the CI environment
variable is not set,
we'll use tenv to switch
Terraform versions.

If we're in a CI environment,
we'll skip the tenv command.

This allows us to pass options
through to Terraform.

This will either be a command
to switch versions or a no-op.

This target will test
the root module.

This will either be a command
to switch versions or a no-op.

This will run all of our tests.

Depend on the examples and our root
test so all of them run when the
terraform_test target is invoked.

When using the built-in testing framework, we do run into a problem—one that we don't have with Terratest. Although this tight coupling between Terraform and the testing framework does make using the testing framework easier, it has its drawbacks. It is impossible to use the framework to test Terraform v1.5, and if you're using the mock features that were introduced in v1.7 then you can no longer test v1.6. You are always locked into only using the features of the lowest version of Terraform that you have to support.

For small companies, this may not be a big deal, as it tends to be easier to always use later versions of Terraform. For larger companies that take advantage of shared modules, this may be more limiting though, as you can't always rely on other teams to upgrade on the schedule you'd prefer.

9.4.6 Testing with CI

Making our tests run on CI is very similar to what we did with Terratest, and even more similar to how we configured the validation step in chapter 7.

Listing 9.30 Terraform testing with GitHub Actions

```
name: Terraform Tests

on:
  push:
  pull_request:

jobs:
  terraform_test:
    strategy:
      matrix:
        engine: ["opentofu", "terraform"]        ◄── We want to test both Terraform and OpenTofu, and we want to test multiple versions of each.
        version: ["1.7"]
        experimental: [false]        ◄── Mocks were introduced in v1.7 so we can't test earlier versions and use them.
        include:
          - version: "1.8"
            engine: "opentofu"
            experimental: true
          - version: "1.8"
            engine: "terraform"
            experimental: false

    continue-on-error: ${{ matrix.experimental }}
    runs-on: ubuntu-latest
    steps:
      - uses: actions/checkout@v4

      - name: Install Terraform
        uses: hashicorp/setup-terraform@v3
        if: ${{ matrix.engine == 'terraform' }}
        with:
          terraform_version: ${{ matrix.version }}

      - name: Install OpenTofu
        uses: opentofu/setup-opentofu@v1
        if: ${{ matrix.engine == 'opentofu' }}        
        with:
          tofu_version: ${{ matrix.version }}        Just like in our other make commands, we pass the engine through to switch between OpenTofu and Terratest.

      - name: Run Terraform Test Framework
        run: make terraform_test TF_ENGINE=${{matrix.engine}}    ◄──
```

Just like in the Terratest section on CI, we will occasionally want to run tests in parallel with each other rather than back to back. This is even more important with the Terraform testing framework as this framework only runs one test at a time. To do this, we can utilize the same method as we did with Terratest: use a strategy matrix to pass through custom flags (in this case the -filter flag) to our terraform test command.

Listing 9.31 Terraform testing with GitHub Actions strategy matrix

```
name: Terraform Tests

on:
  push:
  pull_request:

jobs:
  terraform_test:
    strategy:
      matrix:
        engine: ["opentofu", "terraform"]
        version: ["1.7", "1.8"]
        experimental: [false]
        test:
          - "examples/basic"
          - "terraform_test_root"

        include:
          - version: "1.9"
            engine: "terraform"
            experimental: false
            test:
              - "examples/basic"
              - "terraform_test_root"

          - version: "1.10"
            engine: "terraform"
            experimental: true
            test:
              - "examples/basic"
              - "terraform_test_root"

    continue-on-error: ${{ matrix.experimental }}
    runs on: ubuntu-latest
    steps:
      - uses: actions/checkout@v4

      - name: Install Terraform
        uses: hashicorp/setup-terraform@v3
        if: ${{ matrix.engine == 'terraform' }}
        with:
          terraform_version: ${{ matrix.version }}

      - name: Install OpenTofu
        uses: opentofu/setup-opentofu@v1
```

> Terratest uses the files themselves for filtering, so we add them here.

> Since our example folders are targets in our makefile that run our tests we can include that here.

> We don't want to forget any root-level tests.

> We have a bit of duplication here.

> This one we allow to fail.

> We have a bit of duplication here.

```
      if: ${{ matrix.engine == 'opentofu' }}
      with:
        tofu_version: ${{ matrix.version }}

    - name: Run Terraform Test Framework
      run: make ${{matrix.test}} TF_ENGINE=${{matrix.engine}}"
```

> Now we pass the test cases through to our make command.

We do have a limitation here that is not seen with Terratest. We have to limit the versions of the tests we're using much more than with Terratest due to that tight coupling between the testing framework and Terraform itself. As the framework stabilizes and support for older versions drops, this should be less of a concern.

9.4.7   *Terraform testing framework and Copilot*

The Terraform testing framework is very new. This means that most AI models will not have been trained on any Terraform testing framework code, or if they have, it doesn't include a lot of examples. At the same time, the framework is still evolving with new features coming out in every release.

At the time of writing, Copilot is completely unaware of the Terraform testing framework. If you ask it to write a test, it will respond telling you to use Terratest:

> Terraform doesn't support traditional unit tests like other programming languages. However, you can use a tool like terratest to write tests.

While this is likely to change, for the near future, tools like Copilot will not do the best job at generating tests using the Terraform testing framework. At this point, you are better off writing them yourself or relying on Terratest if you really want to generate your tests automatically. This technology is rapidly evolving though, and this advice will probably change in the not too distant future, but, for now at least, LLM-based systems like Copilot have a weakness around new features and functionality.

9.5   *Refactoring*

Testing provides stability and safety nets for your modules. With testing, you can be sure that any changes you make to your modules don't break existing functionality. That safety gives you freedom. It allows you to make changes to your code with less risk that you'll introduce a breaking change. Once you have a test suite in place, you gain the ability to refactor your code without nearly as much risk.

If someone, regardless of whether they were a beginner or an expert, wrote the absolute best module they possibly could today, there's a good chance that if they looked at it a year from now, they'd want to rewrite half of it. This is for a combination of reasons: people learn over time, so they find better ways to do things; software standards themselves change and evolve; upstream dependencies (such as providers) change; and even Terraform itself gains new features that make it easier or cleaner to do some tasks.

There was a time when Terraform didn't support validation blocks in variables, for instance, so every module made in that period wouldn't have them. Skip ahead to after validation blocks have been standard and that code looks sloppy, even if it was an absolutely perfect module for its time. Even though the code hasn't changed at all, its quality has dropped.

As you build modules, you're going to find that your opinion about how they should function will change, for any of the reasons that we've discussed earlier. When that happens, you may want to refactor your code.

9.5.1 Refactoring vs. development

Refactoring is the process of restructuring or rewriting code to make it easier to maintain and extend. Unlike feature development, which is typically centered around the users of a project (even if those users are other developers, such as with Terraform modules), refactoring is primarily focused on making it easier for developers of a project to actually develop that project.

For many organizations, refactoring is often delayed or pushed back in favor of feature development. After all, it's new features that get users excited and allow products to get built and sold. Not only can this mentality push off refactoring, it can also encourage taking shortcuts (such as reducing testing, not adding validation, or simply not putting as much thought into a feature) that will ultimately lead to more work in the future.

Developers often refer to important functionality getting skipped or needed changes being delayed as "technical debt." Over time, this debt can accumulate and turn into a larger problem. At its best, this debt slows teams down; at its worst, it can lead to bugs or even outages.

Although there is no hard rule on how much time you should spend on refactoring, for a mature but active code base you can expect to spend around 20% of your time on refactoring and code quality. For a project that has accrued a lot of technical debt, you may have to pay down a lot of it, which means spending a larger amount of time on refactoring (or allowing your codebase to continue to decay).

9.5.2 Internal vs. external refactoring

In the strictest meaning of the word, refactoring means to change the structure of code without changing the external behavior of the project. By that definition, all refactoring should be internal: that is, refactoring should happen inside of the program or module without affecting the external interfaces or usage of the system.

Language tends to be pretty fickle though. If you were to run a search for "API refactoring," you'd find thousands of results, despite the fact that APIs are by their very purpose an external interface. It's not uncommon to hear programmers talk about refactoring their applications with breaking changes.

For this reason, I distinguish between two types of refactoring: internal refactoring and external refactoring. The major difference between the two is that internal refactoring should be mostly invisible to your users, while external refactoring makes changes that your users will notice.

An easy way to look at this is to examine the inputs and outputs of modules themselves, as these are the external interfaces to your module. If you change an existing input variable or an existing output, then you've made an external change. If you make changes that don't modify either of those, then you've most likely made an internal change.

> **NOTE** Your test suite should help you avoid accidentally making external changes when you are intending to make internal ones. Internal refactoring should never break your tests, and if they do, it's a sign that there are unintended consequences to your changes. This is why having a solid test suite can make refactoring a lot easier.

Since internal refactoring does not affect the user directly, you can feel free to refactor whenever you feel a need to. When it comes to external refactoring there are more things to consider. We're going to focus on internal refactoring for the rest of this section, and in the next section we'll talk about how to manage your external refactoring and breaking changes.

9.5.3   *Reorganizing your project*

One of the easiest things you can do to refactor your project is to reorganize your resources and modules to make things easier to find. This is one area where Terraform makes things very easy, as it doesn't care about the order or even which file you define resources in, since it defines the order it creates or modifies resources based using a graph that it generates (for a refresher on graphs, head back to chapter 5). If all you're doing is moving resources around, even if you're creating and deleting files in the process, then Terraform should not detect any changes when creating a plan.

Most modules start off following the standard module structure and have three files for their logic: `outputs.tf`, `variables.tf`, and `main.tf`. As a general rule, you should leave your outputs and inputs in the `outputs.tf` and `variables.tf` files, but you might want to reorder them to group-related variables together and possibly add header comments about the different groups.

Listing 9.32   Variable file with group headers

```
#########################
# Networking
#########################

variable "vpc_id" {
  type        = string
  description = "The ID of the VPC to deploy the resources into."
}

variable "subnet_ids" {
  type        = list(string)
  description = "A list of subnet IDs to deploy the resources into."
}

#########################
# Load Balancing
#########################
```

```
variable "acm_certificate_arn" {
  type        = string
  description = "The ARN of the ACM certificate to use for the
➡load balancer."
}


##########################
# Logging
##########################

variable "cloudwatch_log_group_name" {
  type        = string
  description = "The name of the CloudWatch log group to send logs to."
}
```

Over time, though, your `main.tf` file can grow to considerable size, making it difficult for developers to find what they're looking for. When this happens, you have two options: organize the resources and use headers like we did for the variables or split resources into multiple files. Which of these two options you take is 100% up to you, and from a logic standpoint it makes absolutely no difference to how Terraform functions. I've found that teams that do a lot of work inside the terminal tend to prefer a single well-organized `main.tf` file, while those who work with IDEs (such as VSCode) tend to prefer multiple files.

> **TIP** Consistency is key. Regardless of whether you prefer one `main.tf` or a collection of different files, you should remain consistent between your modules. Pick one of these standards as a team and stick to it so it's easier for you to switch between projects.

How you organize your modules is up to you. A common way to do it is based on functionality. If you have a module for creating web services, you might break it up into separate files for load balancing, networking, logging, and the container orchestrator. For a module that controls a larger application, you might break it up by the different services inside that application.

9.5.4 *Renaming resources and modules*

The name of a resource is important. It tells other developers the purpose of that resource and can help distinguish it from other resources or modules of the same type. A common but pretty straightforward way to improve your code is to give it a better name.

In chapter 6, we introduced the `moved` block, which is the Terraform-specific method for changing a name. This block tells Terraform that a resource that existed with one name now has a new name. Without this block, Terraform would destroy the old resource and create a new one under the same name.

While adding a `moved` block is a great way to make changes without disrupting your users, removing an existing `moved` block would break backward compatibility with your module. Once it is removed, Terraform will no longer be able to recognize that rename when users on an older version of your module migrate to a new one. Once a block is created, you can only delete it when releasing a major upgrade, and even then you should consider leaving them in place as they don't cause any harm.

9.5.5   *Renaming variables*

Renaming an input variable is tricky. At first glance, it seems like this would automatically break compatibility, but there is a trick (known as "parallel change" or "expand and contract") you can use to rename your variable without disrupting your users.

When you want to rename an input variable, first copy it and create a duplicate version with the new name. You'll now have two separate inputs with the same description and validation rules. Now update the description of your original variable to describe it as deprecated and replace the default value with `null`. As the last step, create a local variable and assign it the old variable if it's set; otherwise, use the new one.

Listing 9.33   Renaming variables

```
variable "my_old_variable" {
  type    = string
  default = null                        Set the old variable to null so you
}                                        can detect when it isn't used.

variable "my_new_variable" {
  type    = string
  default = "my_fancy_default"          Set your new variable
}                                        to the real default value.

locals {
  use_this_variable = var.my_old_variable != null ? var.my_old_variable :
  var.my_new_variable
}                                        Use the old variable if it's not null,
                                         otherwise use the new variable.
output "my_output" {
  value = local.use_this_variable       Instead of referring to the input
}                                        variable refer to the local variable.
```

While this method does result in some duplication of code, it allows your users to switch over to the new variable name over time without blocking them from updating your module. When there's a real benefit to the variable name change, such as standardizing on a name across multiple modules, this method can let you bring value to your users without causing disruption. Then in your next major release, you can delete all of the deprecated variables.

9.6   *External refactoring*

The idea of external refactoring is a bit of an oxymoron. Since refactoring means making changes inside of a module without changing how it functions externally, then the idea of external refactoring should be impossible.

At the same time, the benefits of refactoring aren't limited to the inside of your project. As you and other developers actually use the modules you create, you are likely to learn about the systems and how they're used. This in turn is going to suggest ways that you could have designed your interfaces differently to make them easier to use.

As a simple example, when teams build a lot of modules, they may not pay a huge amount of attention to their variable names. An org with two different modules that contain a parameter looking for a list of subnet IDs may use the variable name `subnets` in one and `subnet_ids` in another. Although that seems like a small usability problem, these things add up, and having to constantly check documentation for variable names can break a developer's flow.

9.6.1 *When to break compatibility*

Breaking backward compatibility is probably one of the most annoying things that a developer can do. It requires the users of their modules to have to make changes to their code with minimal, if any, immediate benefit for them. Developers hate maintenance (which is why we've discussed so many tools to automate chores in this book), so it's important to minimize the extra work we create for them.

Unfortunately, there are times when you have no choice but to break backward compatibility. Just a few reasons backward compatibility may need to be broken include:

- Discovery of insecure settings that require new behavior or default values
- Developer usability changes, such as variable renaming for clarity or consistency
- Provider releases that themselves break backward compatibility
- New functionality that requires changes to properly function

These are not the only reasons developers may find themselves breaking with older versions of their modules, but they are some of the most common ones.

Once you discover a need to break backward compatibility, you have to decide how to handle it. As a general rule, you want to reduce the number of breaking changes you introduce. Having a lot of releases with breaking changes in them, even if those changes are small, can be frustrating for users. It requires users to make changes where they may not see immediate benefit, and it prevents them from upgrading until they do make those changes.

If you can help it, you should try to push your backward compatibility changes forward and release them all together at once. A great time to do this is when upstream providers come out with a new version that itself breaks compatibility. Changing the major version (e.g., v3 to v4) of a provider means inheriting backward compatibility breaking changes that the provider themselves have. This can cascade down from the provider to the module in a way that requires the module to change the interface to their user. A provider may require more information than it previously did, or it may have removed a deprecated feature that was used in the module.

Since provider changes are out of your control but have to be addressed, a new major provider version can be a great opportunity to also manage other refactoring that you've been pushing off. Of course, not all breaking changes can wait. If you have an instance that is a legitimate security concern, you should not sit on it and wait for a convenient time to fix it but should push out an update as soon as is feasible for your team.

9.6.2   Planning your next major version

We now have two goals that are in conflict with each other. On the one hand, we want to always have the best possible code: we want our modules to be easy for our users to utilize and for our developers to maintain and build on. At the same time, we want to minimize any backward compatibility breaks. Managing that can be a bit of a challenge.

One method that can help is to maintain a wishlist of refactoring ideas. This can be managed as tickets in your tracking system (Jira, GitHub Issues) or even just a shared document like a markdown file that lives in your repository. As new ideas or thoughts come in, your team should consider if there is any way to accomplish the idea without breaking compatibility, and if not they should get added to the list.

The size of the items on the list can vary quite a bit. You might have some small items like changing the name of a variable, or it might see something bigger like removing a feature altogether. What these problems have in common is that changing them would disrupt your users.

9.6.3   Building your next major version

Eventually, you'll want to consider a new major version. Maybe your provider has had an upgrade, or maybe it's just been a long time (try to avoid more than one major upgrade a year) since your last major upgrade and you have a wishlist full of changes that will benefit the project.

Once your team has selected the features for this release, it's time to actually build them. If your wishlist has more than a single feature (such as a provider version upgrade), you should create a separate branch for development on it. This will allow your team to all contribute with their own features and pull requests while still keeping your main branch working and official (see figure 9.2).

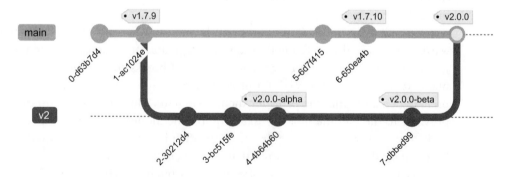

Figure 9.2   Major release Git branching

Although not required, you should consider writing upgrade notes as well. This is traditionally kept in either an UPGRADE.md or CHANGELOG.md file in the repository itself. As your developers add breaking changes, they should update this file with instructions for your users. For instance, if you renamed a variable, you should document it there so developers can see that change and update their usage of the module accordingly.

Once you're happy and features are complete, you can merge this back into your main branch and tag a new release.

9.6.4 *Maintaining your previous major version*

Once you're released your new major version, you can't quite wash your hands of the previous one just yet. Although it's common to refuse to add any new features to your old module versions, there are going to be times when bug fixes are needed. Teams are not likely to adopt the major release all at once, and part of the benefit of using semantic versioning with your releases is that they don't have to. This is especially true if your module takes a lot of effort to upgrade or if it requires a new provider version.

If your users come to you with a bug in your old version, it's up to you whether or not to fix it, although doing so is a great way to earn trust from your users. The process for upgrading an older version can vary depending on exactly how you've structured your Git repository, but, in general, you should be able to create a new branch off of the tag of the version you want to upgrade and use that as the basis for your next release.

Now that we've tackled testing and refactoring, we are ready to close out the second part of this book. You have the knowledge to write Terraform, the ability to maintain high-quality modules, and the skills needed to put that all into production. The rest of this book focuses on advanced Terraform topics, starting with design patterns for a variety of problems you may run into and leading into the development of your own provider.

Summary

- Testing your modules provides a safety net for your systems and psychological safety for your users.
- Automated test suites make it easier for developers to review pull requests and identify breaking changes.
- IaC has many challenges when it comes to testing, such as longer run time and orphaned resources.
- Terratest is the most mature and capable testing framework for Terraform but is written in Go.
- The Terraform testing framework is new but promises developers a fully Terraform-centric experience.
- As projects mature, they often need to be refactored to reduce tech debt and improve feature development.
- Changes that break backward compatibility should be carefully managed.

Part 3

Advanced Terraform topics

The final section of the book focuses on advanced topics:

- In chapter 10, we introduced design patterns and advanced features of Terraform, with each section of the chapter focusing on a different concept. Here, we'll break down patterns for resource naming, discuss how to create dynamic networks, and explain what to do when you encounter problems that Terraform can't easily manage.
- Chapter 11 is all about alternative ways to interact with Terraform, including writing Terraform with the cloud development framework or controlling it with the machine-readable UI.
- Chapter 12 teaches you how to develop and maintain custom providers, which allow you to expand Terraform with new functions, data sources, and resources.

Once you complete this section, you'll not only be able to use Terraform but you'll have the knowledge to expand Terraform itself or embed it into your own larger applications and tools.

10

Advanced
Terraform topics

This chapter covers

- Domain Name System and resource naming strategies
- Network creation with dynamic subnetting
- Using provisioners to break out of Terraform
- Local and external providers
- Validation with checks and conditions
- When not to use Terraform (and what to do instead)

The first two parts of the book covered the Terraform language itself and how to use Terraform in production. This knowledge should be more than enough to get you through most of the problems that you're going to encounter. That being said, there are topics you may encounter that require some additional tools to work through.

This chapter is a bit different from previous ones. Rather than dive into a single topic, we explore a variety of useful patterns, niche providers, and advanced features of Terraform. Some of what we discuss, such as how to name your resources or the use of conditions and checks, may end up being tools that you use every day. Other parts of this chapter, such as the use of the external provider, will offer you tools that you likely won't use every day but you will be grateful to have when you encounter a particularly thorny problem.

10.1 Names and domains

When working with any infrastructure, you are going to encounter times when you need to name resources or create domains. With Terraform, you have the ability to create and enforce naming patterns using code, which can make organization of your resources much easier and consistent. Although this seems like a small thing, it has some pretty enormous effects when you have hundreds or even thousands of resources across multiple applications and systems.

10.1.1 Naming considerations

Names are used to find resources and metadata about those resources. This can mean digging through your cloud provider's web interface, running commands through a command-line interface, or searching through your logs and metrics provider to understand what a resource is doing. A good naming scheme should result in names that are

- Unique
- Human readable
- Identifiable
- Sortable

The *unique* constraint is the only one that is enforced for technology reasons. Many systems will refuse to let you create two resources with the same name, so if your naming scheme does not enforce uniqueness, then it won't work for those systems. That being said, this is still a good idea even without the technical constraints. If you have two resources with the same name, it's easy to confuse the two, which can lead to human errors where changes are made to the wrong system.

Making sure names are *human readable* isn't a technical requirement, but since humans are the ones maintaining the system, the naming scheme should work for them. If someone is switching between multiple browser tabs trying to trace down a problem, it's much easier for them to remember names like `prod-api-lb` and `dev-backend-db` than `abd236a` and `6d8a900`.

Resources should be *identifiable* by their name. In the last example, it's easy to tell that one resource is a production API load balancer, while the other is a development back-end database. Had we given them names like `large-finch` or `current-walrus` [from the petname library (https://github.com/dustinkirkland/golang-petname), used by the `random_pet` resource in the `random` provider], the names would have been human readable but not identifiable.

The final constraint to consider is making names *sortable*. It is very common to list resources out, and if you are using a sortable naming scheme, you can cluster common resources together. With the `prod-` and `dev-` prefixes in our previous example, it meant that all of our production and development resources would naturally sort together. This has the additional benefit of making it easy to filter resources based on name.

10.1.2 *Hierarchical naming schemes*

All of our constraints lead us to a hierarchical naming scheme. These schemes are pretty common in the computer science field. With a hierarchical naming scheme, you start with the primary component and then extend that component's name for use with subcomponents. This can happen recursively, as each subcomponent has subsystems of its own (see table 10.1).

Table 10.1 Examples of hierarchical naming schemes

System	Description	Examples
Domain Name System	Domains are split into subdomains.	example.com auth.example.com db.auth.example.com

Terraform	Resource names in modules inherit the module path.	`module.service.aws_ecs_cluster.main`
		
		`module.lb.module.logs.aws_s3_bucket.main`

As you can see from the example systems, Terraform itself already uses a hierarchical naming scheme to address its own resources. These names are used in command outputs and inside of the Terraform state itself. The depth in the code of a resource (that is, whether it's called inside a module, submodule, or many layers of submodules deep) defines the name of the resource. We can mirror the structure when building our own systems.

Let's say we're building a simple software as a service application with an API. This system will use a module to create the database and another module to create the API service. Each of these modules has its own module that it calls.

Figure 10.1 shows the module definitions and their relationships but ignores dependencies between the modules in order to highlight the creation graph itself.

At the top-level module, we need to define our root name. For this I like to have a name that is unique to the top-level module, such as the name of the application that it builds, and a variable for the environment. For example, our Acme project could simply be named "acme," and each environment that gets launched from the module will have a unique name passed in through the environment variable.

When the top-level module defines the submodules it plans on calling, it should give them each a unique name prefixed with its own name. For example, the API module can get a name such as `acme-${var.environment}-api` and the database module `acme-${var.environment}-db`.

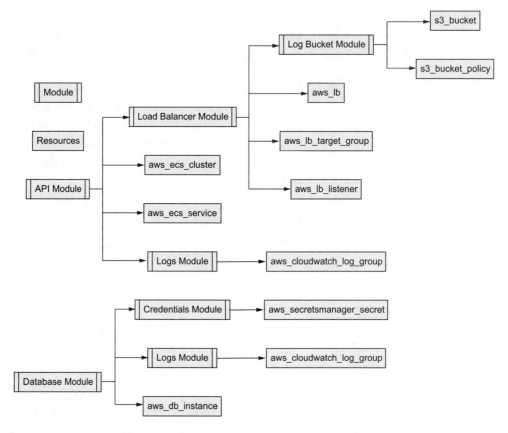

Figure 10.1   Acme API module structure

Listing 10.1   Top-level module

```
variable "environment" {
  description = "The name of the environment the application is being
launched in."
  type        = string
}

locals {
  application = "acme"
  base_name   = "${local.application}-${var.environment}"
}

module "api" {
  source = "./service"
  name   = "${local.base_name}-api"
}

module "database" {
```

The application name is hardcoded in the module since it is consistent across all environments.

We are going to use the environment variable to create a unique name.

We pass the base name plus a suffix to the service module to create a unique name.

```
    source = "./db"
    name   = "${local.base_name}-db"
}
```
◄— **Each usage of our name should have a unique suffix to prevent naming conflicts.**

When you're building your own service-specific modules, you should continue this pattern. Unlike top-level modules, these service modules will get their full-name prefix as an input variable, rather than just the environment. If the module has a single resource that can be considered the primary resource (a database module might consider the database instance itself the primary resource), it can use the name passed in directly, but for all other resources and submodules, you should use the name as a prefix and add a descriptor to the end.

Listing 10.2 Service module names

```
variable "name" {
  description = "The name of the service."
  type        = string
}
```
◄— **For our service or submodules we use the name passed in and don't think about environments.**

```
module "laad_balancer" {
  source = "./alb"
  name   = "${var.name}-lb"
}
```
Any modules used inside of the load balancer will continue to build on the name we pass in. ◄—

```
module "log_bucket" {
  source = "./bucket"
  name   = "${var.name}-logs"
}
```
This builds on our name from the top-level module. For a dev environment this would be acme-dev-logs. ◄—

```
resource "aws_ecs_cluster" "main" {
  name = "${var.name}-cluster"
}
```
Resources should also build on the name. ◄—

```
resource "aws_ecs_service" "main" {
  name            = "${var.name}-service"
  cluster         = aws_ecs_cluster.main.id
  task_definition = file("${path.module}/task_definition.json")
  desired_count   = 1
}
```
In theory, we could just name this var.name since it is the primary resource. ◄—

Depending on the system itself, you may want to add some randomness to the name. We discussed in the last chapter that some resources, such as `aws_secretsmanager_secret`, can't be easily destroyed and re-created unless randomness is added to the name. The `aws_s3_bucket` resource also needs randomness to avoid a security problem called S3 namespace squatting (https://mng.bz/EadJ). When you encounter resource-specific naming constraints, you should manage those in your module itself so users of your modules don't need to think about it.

TIP While Terraform recommends using the `random_id` or `random_password` resource over the `random_string` resource, in this particular case `random_string` makes more sense. It can fit more randomness into fewer characters than the `random_id` resource can, while it avoids marking our names as sensitive like the `random_password` one does.

Listing 10.3   Resource-specific naming constraints

Although the aws_secretsmanager_secret resource has a name_prefix parameter, it uses a large random string that might make custom names difficult to squeeze in.

We only need a small random string to make our name unique.

```
variable "name" {
  description = "The prefix used in the name of the secret."
  type        = string
}

resource "random_string" "suffix" {
  length  = 6
  special = false
  upper   = false
}

resource "aws_secretsmanager_secret" "main" {
  name = "${var.name}-${random_string.suffix.result}"
}
```

We do have to be careful to only use characters that are allowed in the name of the secret.

Sticking to just lowercase letters in the name will make it easier to refer to and find resources.

We use the name variable and a random string to create a unique name.

With this method in place, your names should mostly generate themselves. With our Acme example, we get a naming structure that matches our system (see figure 10.2). This lets us easily drill down on resources by filtering on the name, it is extremely human readable and identifiable, and it always results in unique names.

The one caveat to this system is that it can result in some longer names if you happen to have a lot of nested modules. In general, you want to avoid nesting your modules too deep anyway, but you can minimize this problem by using short but descriptive names (e.g., `db` instead of `database`). You should also avoid adding the resource type to the name itself: for instance, there's no need to name an S3 bucket `logging_bucket` when it can just be `logging` or even just `logs`, since the fact that it is a bucket is inherent to what it is.

Another problem that can come up is that your team may not manage all of the modules it uses. If you are using third-party modules, or modules from other teams, you may have little choice over the naming patterns used. If possible, you should attempt to establish best practices and shared patterns among the teams you work with, but if that isn't possible or you're using modules from outside of your organization, then you might have to be flexible with your naming structure.

10.1.3   Domains

When it comes to constraints and goals, domains are very similar to names. The Domain Name System itself, as discussed in the previous section, already uses a hierarchical

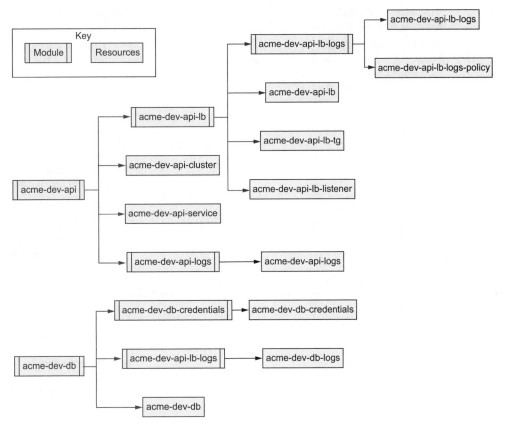

Figure 10.2 Acme API resource names

naming scheme. The big things to consider are related to implementation and formatting more than any philosophical difference.

Just like with a naming scheme, you'll want to create a base domain to use in your top-level module that consists of a unique module or application name and then the environment itself. However, unlike our previous discussion with names, you're also going to need to allow your developers to pass through their own top-level domain. This is because domains don't exist in a vacuum, and your application is going to need to attach to a domain that you own.

If you're using the top-level domain `example.net`, your system is named `Acme`, and you're deploying it to the development environment, then you want to start with `dev .acme.example.net` as your base domain. As the domain is passed through to other modules, such as your load balancer, they'll append their own subdomains onto the passed-through domain.

Listing 10.4   Base domain

```
variable "environment" {
  description = "The name of the environment the application is being
launched in."
  type        = string
}

variable "domain" {
  description = "The base domain to build resources off of."
  type        = string
}

variable "dns_zone" {
  description = "The Route 53 zone to create records in."
  type        = string
}

locals {
  application = "acme"
  base_name   = "${local.application}-${var.environment}"
  base_domain = "${var.environment}.${local.application}.${var.domain}"
}

module "api" {
  source = "./service"
  name   = "${local.base_name}-api"
  domain = "api.${local.base_domain}"
}
```

> The zone and the base domain are often, but not always, the same.

> The domain name is similar to the base name, but in the opposite order.

> We build on the base domain in the same way we build on the name.

Although these domains are very useful inside of your application, they aren't very pretty. In general, your main website and any other domains used for external customers should have a name geared toward their usage. I tend to use .com domains for public facing uses and .net domains for internal use to help segment those two areas.

10.2   Network management

Working with cloud service providers typically requires a bit of networking. Whether it's AWS, Azure, GCP, or one of the many other providers out there, you are often in control of your software-defined network. This normally starts with a virtual private cloud (VPC) where you define your high-level network and then a series of subnets to break that network into different segments.

Most of the time when you're writing modules, you are consuming the network, not creating it. On the consumer side, things tend to be pretty easy: you accept a VPC ID or a list of subnet IDs and then pass those to your resources. Things get a bit more complicated when you're trying to create those networks, especially if you're trying to create a reusable module to do so. The good news is Terraform has a set of network functions that we can use to create flexible networking modules.

10.2.1 Subnetting with Classless Inter-Domain Routing

Networking is a rather large topic, and before building any networking module you are going to have to research the specific resources that are needed for the cloud system you're interacting with. Having to do some research before designing a module is common (as we talked about in chapter 4), especially since different cloud service providers can handle the same concepts in different ways.

That being said, Terraform has some built-in networking features that can be used regardless of the service provider you're using. In particular, Terraform makes the concept of subnetting significantly easier with the `cidrsubnet` function and the other IP network functions.

Classless Inter-Domain Routing (CIDR; pronounced "cider") is a way to divide networks into subnetworks. One of the things this standard created was CIDR notation, a way to describe a network with a simple string. This notation combines the base IP address of the network itself with a prefix that defines how much of that address is the network and which parts are reserved for hosts in that network.

Take, for instance, the CIDR notation `192.168.0.0/16`. IPv4 addresses are 32 bits, and the `/16` in our network means that this network reserves 16 bits for the network identifier. The remaining bits are reserved either for hosts or to build smaller networks (see table 10.2).

Table 10.2 CIDR main network

CIDR	192.168.0.0/16
CIDR subnet mask	255.255.0.0
CIDR wildcard mask	0.0.255.255
Binary network mask	11111111.11111111.00000000.00000000
Binary wildcard mask	00000000.00000000.11111111.11111111
Network range	192.168.0.0 - 192.168.255.255
Maximum addresses	65,534

That is a pretty big network. We can divide that network up by taking more bits from our hosts and adding them to the network mask instead. Each bit we take raises the number of networks we can use by a power of 2 (1 bit would give us two networks, 2 bits gives us four networks, 3 bits gives eight networks, etc.). Let's split our network up by taking two additional bits. (See table 10.3.)

Table 10.3 CIDR subnetting

CIDRs	192.168.0.0/18
	192.168.64.0/18
	192.168.128.0/18
	192.168.192.0/18

Table 10.3   CIDR subnetting (*continued*)

CIDR subnet mask	255.255.192.0
CIDR wildcard mask	0.0.63.255
Binary network mask	11111111.11111111.11000000.00000000
Binary wildcard mask	00000000.00000000.00111111.11111111
Network ranges	192.168.0.0 - 192.168.63.255
	192.168.64.0 - 192.168.127.255
	192.168.128.0 - 192.168.191.255
	192.168.192.0 - 192.168.255.255
Maximum addresses per network	16,382

By taking those 2 bits, we were able to make four smaller networks for use. Each of those networks can be individually divided up as well, allowing for smaller and smaller networks.

The `cidrsubnet` function makes this very easy. It takes three arguments: the CIDR notation for your original network, the number of bits you want to take for your subnets, and the network number you want to return. It will then return the new network address in CIDR notation. If we need to, we can also use the `cidrnetmask` function to get the subnet mask for our network.

Listing 10.5   Terraform Console `cidrsubnet` usage

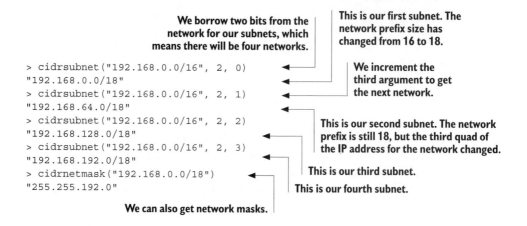

We borrow two bits from the network for our subnets, which means there will be four networks.

This is our first subnet. The network prefix size has changed from 16 to 18.

We increment the third argument to get the next network.

```
> cidrsubnet("192.168.0.0/16", 2, 0)
"192.168.0.0/18"
> cidrsubnet("192.168.0.0/16", 2, 1)
"192.168.64.0/18"
> cidrsubnet("192.168.0.0/16", 2, 2)
"192.168.128.0/18"
> cidrsubnet("192.168.0.0/16", 2, 3)
"192.168.192.0/18"
> cidrnetmask("192.168.0.0/18")
"255.255.192.0"
```

This is our second subnet. The network prefix is still 18, but the third quad of the IP address for the network changed.

This is our third subnet.

This is our fourth subnet.

We can also get network masks.

10.2.2   *Common topologies*

Before you can create your network module, you have to make some decisions around what your network topology is going to look like. Once you've defined your standard network, you can codify that into a Terraform module so that you can easily share that standard across your users.

Most of the time when defining a network, there are three considerations to keep in mind:

- *Segmentation of services*—By segmenting your services and data using separate networks, you make it more difficult for a potential hacker to move from one resource to another.
- *High availability needs of the application*—By spreading your network out to more physical locations (Availability Zones in AWS and Azure, Regions in GCP), you make your application more resilient to errors in any one location.
- *Size of the network*—When deploying your applications, you want to have enough space to grow your application, but you don't want to waste IP addresses.

The first thing to think about is segmentation. The goal of segmentation is mostly around security. The most common pattern for segmenting a network is to split out the services that are allowed to be accessed directly from the internet from the ones that should remain private. This requires one subnet that lives on the internet side, where services are given both a public and private IP address and a second subnet that only has private IP addresses. These two subnets will be allowed to route to each other on the private network, and if the private network needs to access anything on the internet, it has to travel through a service on the public network.

NOTE Network segmentation is just one layer of security protection. In addition to network segmentation, you should also use security groups or firewalls on each of your services, rather than relying on network segmentation alone.

Let's use a standard three-tier application with a container running the API, database, cache, and load balancer. In this case, the API container, database, and cache would exist on the private network, because none of those services should be directly accessible from the internet. The load balancer, on the other hand, would live in the public subnet so that they could be reached from the internet. If the software running in the API container needed to reach out to the internet, it would do so through a Network Address Translation (NAT) service on the public network (see figure 10.3).

Three-segment networks are also an option (see figure 10.4). In this case, you still have the public and private subnets but also introduce a third subnet that is completely isolated from the other two. This isolated network generally doesn't have any direct connection to the internet but instead uses very explicitly created bridges (either network or service) to move data in and out of the protected network. The primary reason for this level of isolation is for dealing with extremely sensitive data.

The next challenges are around high availability. Although not common, cloud vendors do have outages. The best way to avoid being caught up in one is to split your services among different locations, with three locations being the standard. Each location is going to need its own network following the topology you selected, as shown in figure 10.5.

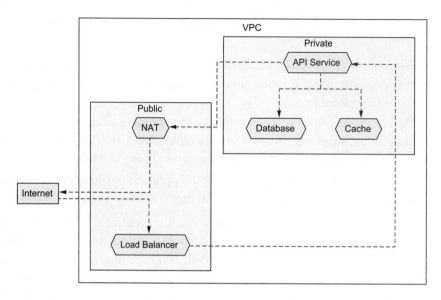

Figure 10.3   Two-segment network

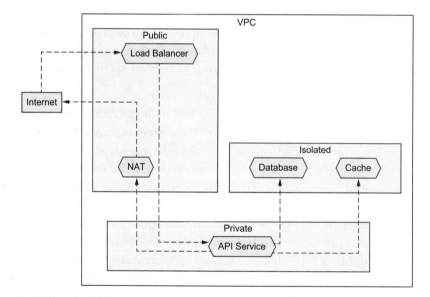

Figure 10.4   Three-segment network

The final element, the size of the network, is going to vary depending on your needs. This is the part we want to make dynamic by utilizing Terraform's built-in network functions to divide up any network that is provided to the module into the different subnets and zones, based on the parameters our users pass into the module.

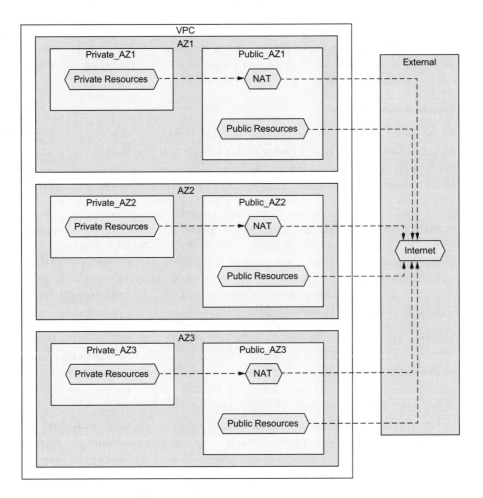

Figure 10.5   High availability

Now that we understand the needs of our network, we can go ahead and create a module (see figure 10.6). To keep things simple, we're going to define a high-level module with a few variables and let that module call out to submodules for building the actual networks with a topology selected by our module user. This has the benefit of being flexible while hiding the gory details of networking from the user themselves.

This is not the only way we could have structured this module. Some teams may prefer to manage their availability zone or location networks more

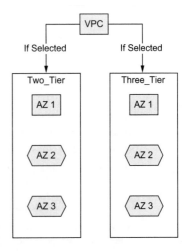

Figure 10.6 Module structure

directly and might simply publish these submodules as standalone modules. As with everything in software development, there are often multiple ways to solve any given problem. In this case, we're prioritizing ease of use over flexibility in network design, but for most developers this is a reasonable tradeoff.

10.2.3 *Location module*

We're going to start with the submodules that define our network in a single availability zone. As a general rule, I find it easier to start with the lowest-level component and get it working, rather than starting with the higher-level abstraction that we're going to build on top. Once we have our submodules built, it will be easier to wrap them up in a higher-level module.

> **NOTE** Since we're starting with the lower-level modules, there are some pieces that will be missing if we call these modules directly. In AWS, you cannot access the internet until an internet gateway is set up, but that's the responsibility of the high-level module that we'll be creating in the next section. In general, users will not be calling these submodules directly but will rely on the high-level module to call these instead.

The two-segment module, with a public and private network, is fairly straightforward. It takes in a CIDR block with the range of IP addresses it's allowed to use. Since we want to divide that block in two (one network for our public subnet and another for our private one), we need to use a single bit for our subnet. From there, we can use the cidrsubnet function to create our two subnets.

Our public subnet is going to get a special resource: a NAT gateway. NAT is a way that networks can allow private networks such as the ones we're creating to access the internet (or such as your home network, where your router translates between your local devices and the internet). This is created to enable our private subnet to have internet access. Also notice that we enable public IP addresses on the public subnet.

> **TIP** NAT gateways can be expensive, but they are the simplest way to set up NAT in most cloud providers. If you want to save money, you can use a NAT instance instead, but this is a much more involved process. If you'd like to see that in action, I have an open source NAT instance module (https://github .com/tedivm/terraform-aws-nat) for AWS you can review.

The private subnet is similar, although it has public IP addresses disabled. Unlike the public subnet though, we also create a route table for the public subnet, with a rule that pushes internet-based traffic to the NAT gateway. This is what allows the private subnet access to the internet without the internet being able to access the private subnet.

Listing 10.6 Public and private subnet module

```
variable "cidr_block" {
  description = "The CIDR block for the network."
  type        = string
```

```
}

variable "vpc_id" {
  description = "The ID of the VPC."
  type        = string
}

variable "availability_zone" {
  description = "The availability zone."
  type        = string
}

locals {
  private_subnet_cidr_block = cidrsubnet(var.cidr_block, 1, 0)
  public_subnet_cidr_block  = cidrsubnet(var.cidr_block, 1, 1)
}
```

Since we only need two networks we can use a single bit to split our network in half.

```
#
# Public Network
#

resource "aws_subnet" "public" {
  vpc_id                  = var.vpc_id
  cidr_block              = local.public_subnet_cidr_block
  map_public_ip_on_launch = true
  availability_zone       = var.availability_zone
  tags = {
    Network = "Public"
  }
}

resource "aws_eip" "nat" {
  tags = {}
}

resource "aws_nat_gateway" "main" {
  allocation_id = aws_eip.nat.id
  subnet_id     = aws_subnet.public.id
  tags          = {}
}

#
# Private Network
#

resource "aws_subnet" "private" {
  vpc_id            = var.vpc_id
  cidr_block        = local.private_subnet_cidr_block
  availability_zone = var.availability_zone
  tags = {
    Network = "Private"
  }
}
```

We pass the local for our public subnet to the cidr_block attribute.

We add a tag to our public subnet to make it easier to programmatically collect subnets when outside of Terraform.

This is the field that makes this a public subnet. All resources in this subnet will get a public IP address.

We create a NAT gateway to allow our private subnet to access the internet. A future goal would be to replace this with a NAT instance to save money.

We pass the EIP ID to the allocation_id attribute so our outbound traffic has a consistent IP address.

The NAT gateway needs to be in a public subnet so it can access the internet.

Since we left map_public_ip_on_launch off, resources in this subnet can not directly access the internet.

We pass the local for our private subnet to the cidr_block attribute.

Both of our subnets are in the same availability zone.

```
resource "aws_route_table" "private" {
  vpc_id = var.vpc_id
}
```

We create a route table for our private subnet so that internet traffic can be routed through the NAT gateway.

```
resource "aws_route_table_association" "private" {
  subnet_id       = aws_subnet.private.id
  route_table_id = aws_route_table.private.id
}
```

We have to associate the route table with the subnet.

```
resource "aws_route" "internet_access" {
  route_table_id            = aws_route_table.private.id
  nat_gateway_id            = aws_nat_gateway.main.id
  destination_cidr_block = "0.0.0.0/0"
}
```

Now we direct traffic to the NAT gateway.

This is the catch-all route. If the traffic is not going to a local IP address it will be sent to the NAT gateway.

```
output "private_subnet_id" {
  value = aws_subnet.private.id
}
```

We output the IDs of the private subnets so that we can use them in other modules.

```
output "public_subnet_id" {
  value = aws_subnet.public.id
}
```

We output the IDs of the public subnets so that we can use them in other modules.

The three-segment network includes an isolated network as well as the public and private networks. This network does not have internet access, which means we don't have to worry about routing to the NAT gateway.

However, this network presents a bit of a challenge for us. We were able to simply divide our first network in half, but dividing a network into thirds isn't something that can easily be done. Subnetting works by taking bits off of the network and using them to divide the network up, but that means they have to fit into powers of two. If we had four networks it would be easier, but there's no point in creating a network we have no use for.

We're going to get a bit creative to solve this problem without losing IP addresses. First, we're going to divide the network in half by taking a single bit. We'll use one of those subnets for the private network, as that network tends to have the most work in it. The other network we will then divide in half again, giving one to the isolated network and the other to the public network.

Listing 10.7   Public, private, and isolated subnet module

```
variable "cidr_block" {
  description = "The CIDR block for the network."
  type        = string
}

variable "vpc_id" {
  description = "The ID of the VPC."
  type        = string
}

variable "availability_zone" {
```

> We put the second half of the network in a local variable to make our code more readable.

> We are going to split our network in half, and then split it in half again. The first half is for our private network.

```
  description = "The availability zone."
  type        = string
}

locals {
  private_subnet_cidr_block = cidrsubnet(var.cidr_block, 1, 0)   ◄────
  intermediary_block        = cidrsubnet(var.cidr_block, 1, 1)   ◄────

  public_subnet_cidr_block   = cidrsubnet(local.intermediary_block, 1, 0)
  isolated_subnet_cidr_block = cidrsubnet(local.intermediary_block, 1, 1)
}
```

> We split the intermediary block in half to create our public and isolated networks. This will be smaller than our private network.

> Nothing really changes here compared to the two-segment network.

```
#
# Public Network
#

resource "aws_subnet" "public" {      ◄────
  vpc_id                  = var.vpc_id
  cidr_block              = local.public_subnet_cidr_block
  map_public_ip_on_launch = true
  availability_zone       = var.availability_zone
  tags = {
    Network = "Public"
  }
}

resource "aws_eip" "nat" {
  tags = {}
}

resource "aws_nat_gateway" "main" {
  allocation_id = aws_eip.nat.id
  subnet_id     = aws_subnet.public.id
  tags          = {}
}


#
# Private Network
#
```

> Nothing really changes here compared to the two-segment network.

```
resource "aws_subnet" "private" {      ◄────
  vpc_id            = var.vpc_id
  cidr_block        = local.private_subnet_cidr_block
  availability_zone = var.availability_zone
  tags = {
    Network = "Private"
  }
}

resource "aws_route_table" "private" {
```

```
    vpc_id = var.vpc_id
}

resource "aws_route_table_association" "private" {
  subnet_id       = aws_subnet.private.id
  route_table_id = aws_route_table.private.id
}

resource "aws_route" "internet_access" {
  route_table_id          = aws_route_table.private.id
  nat_gateway_id          = aws_nat_gateway.main.id
  destination_cidr_block = "0.0.0.0/0"
}
```

This is the catch-all route. If the traffic is not going to a local IP address it will be sent to the NAT gateway.

```
#
# Isolated Network
#
```

Not only do we leave map_public_ip_on_launch off, but we also don't have a NAT gateway. This network is completely isolated from the internet.

```
resource "aws_subnet" "isolated" {
  vpc_id            = var.vpc_id
  cidr_block        = local.isolated_subnet_cidr_block
  availability_zone = var.availability_zone

  tags = {
    Network = "Isolated"
  }
}

#
# Outputs
#

output "public_subnet_id" {
  value = aws_subnet.public.id
}
```

We output the IDs of the public subnets so that we can use them in other modules.

```
output "private_subnet_id" {
  value = aws_subnet.private.id
}
```

We output the IDs of the private subnets so that we can use them in other modules.

```
output "isolated_subnet_id" {
  value = aws_subnet.isolated.id
}
```

We output the IDs of the isolated subnets so that we can use them in other modules.

Now we have two modules that can create a different topology. Both modules take the same set of arguments and have the same outputs, which makes it easy to switch between them. Following this pattern, you can create additional topologies as your company needs them.

10.2.4　*High-level module*

If we only cared about hosting in a single location, we could potentially end there, but that would mean sacrificing our high availability goal. If our availability zone goes down, and our full application is hosted there, then our application goes down. So we need to spread things out a bit.

The problem is figuring out how to properly divide it up. We could create a module that always deploys to multiple availability zones, but there is a cost associated with high availability, and not every application needs that. You may want to host your development version in a cheaper environment, while using a more expensive environment for your production application.

At the same time, you don't want to use a different module for development than the one you use in production. Instead, we need to design a module that is flexible enough to deploy to a single location or to multiple locations depending on the need. To do this, we're going to allow the user to pass through the number of availability zones they want to use, and from there we'll calculate the subnets needed. This will require using a few of the fancier features of Terraform, such as `for` expressions and both the `math` and `network` functions. We'll also use the binary toggle technique we learned when introducing the count feature to switch between the two topology modules we've built.

TIP Since we allow people to select their own number of availability zones, we can't be sure that they will always pick a power of 2, which means we may have left over IP addresses. These extra ranges should be returned as an output so the module user can decide what to do with them.

Listing 10.8 Network module

```
variable "cidr_block" {
  description = "The CIDR block for the network. Can not be changed after
➥creation without the destruction of all resources."
  type        = string
}

variable "enable_isolated_subnet" {
  description = "Whether to create an isolated subnet. Can not be changed
➥after creation without the destruction of all resources."
  type        = bool
}

variable "availability_zones" {
  description = "The availability zones. Can not be changed after creation
➥without the destruction of all resources."
  type        = number

  validation {
    condition      = var.availability_zones > 0 && var.availability_zones
➥<= 4                                                              ◀──────┐
    error_message = "The number of availability zones must be at least 1   │
➥and no more than 4."                                                      │
  }                                    **To keep things simple we're**      │
}                                      **going to limit the number of**  ───┘
                                       **availability zones to 4.**

locals {
```

The number of subnets we create is
2 to the power of the subnet bits.
This may differ from the number of
availability zones.

It's always a good idea to leave helpful
comments for the next person.

If we are only in a single AZ, we don't
need to split our network up at all;
otherwise, we need either 1 or 2 bits.

```
    subnet_bits = var.availability_zones == 1 ? 0 : (var.availability_zones >
2 ? 2 : 1)
    #Reminder: pow(2, 0) = 1
    subnet_count = pow(2, local.subnet_bits)

    spare_subnet_cidr_blocks = [
      for i in range(var.availability_zones, local.subnet_count)
      : cidrsubnet(var.cidr_block, local.subnet_bits, i)
    ]
}
```

If we have more
subnets than we
need, return the
extra subnets as
a list.

```
data "aws_availability_zones" "available" {
  state = "available"
}
```

We use the data source to get the
availability zones for the region we are in.

We don't want to use zones that are not available.

```
resource "aws_vpc" "main" {
  cidr_block = var.cidr_block
}
```

The CIDR block for the VPC is the
one for the whole network.

```
module "two_tier_subnets" {
  source            = "./modules/az_2"
  count             = var.enable_isolated_subnet ? local.subnet_count : 0
  availability_zone = data.aws_availability_zones.available.names[
count.index]
  vpc_id            = aws_vpc.main.id
  cidr_block        = cidrsubnet(var.cidr_block, local.subnet_bits,
count.index)
}
```

Here we rotate through our
main network to identify the
CIDR for each availability zone.

```
module "three_tier_subnets" {
  source            = "./modules/az_3"
  count             = var.enable_isolated_subnet ? 0 : local.subnet_count
  availability_zone = data.aws_availability_zones.available.names[
count.index]
  vpc_id            = aws_vpc.main.id
  cidr_block        = cidrsubnet(var.cidr_block, local.subnet_bits,
count.index)
}
```

If we are creating an isolated
subnet, we should use this module.

```
output "vpc_id" {
  value = aws_vpc.main.id
}
```

Since we're using the count.index it doesn't
matter that we don't know this at plan time.

```
output "spare_subnet_cidr_block" {
  value = local.spare_subnet_cidr_blocks
}
```

We use count instead of foreach to
avoid relying on resources that
aren't known during plan time.

If we are not creating an isolated
subnet we use the two-tier module.

```
}
```

> We can use a local to store the active subnet module to make our code easier to read.

```
locals {
  subnet_module = var.enable_isolated_subnet ? module.three_tier_subnets :
module.two_tier_subnets
}
```

> The source of our outputs depends on which module we're using.

```
output "private_subnet_ids" {
  value = local.subnet_module[*].private_subnet_id
}
```

> We use the splat operator to get all of the private subnet IDs as a list.

```
output "public_subnet_ids" {
  value = local.subnet_module[*].public_subnet_id
}
```

> We do the same for the public subnet IDs.

```
output "isolated_subnet_ids" {
  value = var.enable_isolated_subnet ? local.subnet_module[*].
isolated_subnet_id : []
}
```

> We have to be a bit more careful here, as the az_2 module doesn't have isolated subnets.

Between the networking module itself and the submodules that go with it, we've built a pretty flexible system. As complicated as it looks from our perspective as the module developer, it's remarkably easy to use from the module user's perspective. It also allows our users to choose either high or low availability with variables they can pass through to their own top-level module, allowing them to deploy the same code in multiple environments without any code changes.

> **Listing 10.9 Network module example usage**

```
module "network" {
  source                 = "./top_level"
  enable_isolated_subnet = true
  availability_zones     = 3
  cidr_block             = "192.168.0.0/16"
}
```

> Change this to your module registry.

> Choosing either a two- or three-tier network is as simple as changing this variable.

> The CIDR block for our network

> We can choose how many availability zones we want to use and our module will dynamically create the subnets.

10.3 Provisioners

Provisioners are a way to create files and run commands either locally or remotely when Terraform creates or destroys resources. They can be used so Terraform can both deploy and configure (also known as "provision," hence the name) resources it creates. Provisioners are an advanced feature of Terraform that you are not likely to encounter in your day-to-day usage but that can act as a useful tool if you need to run commands from outside of Terraform either locally or on another machine.

> **WARNING** Using provisioners is most likely a bad idea. There is almost always a better alternative than using a provisioner, and we'll go over the most common of those at the end of this section. Using a provisioner creates points of failure, adds additional time to deployments, and introduces behavior that can be hard to predict. Modules that use provisioners are less portable and flexible and can be more difficult to debug. These should only be used when no other option is available to you.

10.3.1 Connections

If you are attempting to run commands or put files on your resources, you have to configure a connection first. This is done with the appropriately named `connection` block. The `connection` block is most commonly placed at the top level of the resource, which makes it apply to every provisioner on the resource. It's also possible to define a provisioner-specific connection, in which case you'd put the `connection` block inside of your `provisioner` block.

If you are connecting to your own resource, there is a special keyword, `self`, that allows you to reference attributes from the resource itself. For instance, if you have a connection to an `aws_instance`, you may want to pass through the IP address of that instance to your provisioner.

> **NOTE** In this example, we load an SSH key from the local filesystem. It is extremely important that you never commit your private SSH keys in with your code. Private keys should be considered sensitive, like passwords, and should be handled separately from your code.

Listing 10.10 `connection` **block examples**

```
resource "aws_instance" "direct" {
  ami           = data.aws_ami.ubuntu.id
  instance_type = "t2.micro"

  connection {
    type        = "ssh"
    user        = "ubuntu"
    private_key = file("~/.ssh/id_rsa")
    host        = self.public_ip
  }
}
```

This block is how we allow our provisioners to connect to the resource.

This is the type of connection we're making.

This is the user we're connecting as, which will depend on the system you're connecting to.

The self block is a reference to the resource being created. This will only work if the publc_ip is reachable by Terraform.

Connections are either WinRM if you're connecting to a Windows machine or SSH if you're connecting to a Unix machine. There are a lot of options for connecting, including passing your connection through a SOCKS5 proxy or a bastion host. This makes it easier for you to bridge the network that Terraform is running on (which will be the deployment orchestrator you picked in chapter 8) and the network where you're deploying things.

Listing 10.11   Bastion host

```
resource "aws_instance" "bastion" {
  ami           = data.aws_ami.ubuntu.id
  instance_type = "t2.micro"

  connection {
    type        = "ssh"
    user        = "ubuntu"
    private_key = file("~/.ssh/id_rsa")
    host        = self.private_ip

    bastion_host        = var.bastion_host
    bastion_user        = var.bastion_user
    bastion_private_key = file("~/.ssh/id_rsa")
  }
}
```

This block is how we allow our provisioners to connect to the resource.

Since the bastion host puts us inside of the network we can use the private IP address.

Bastion hosts are typically set up by a network team, so you'd have to get this information from them.

You may immediately notice a problem with this: you're essentially coding in a network detail to your module. While you can (and absolutely should) utilize variables and resource attributes to give yourself some flexibility, you still end up having to make decisions about whether to use a bastion host and then set that decision for all of your users or pass through quite a few variables. This makes using remote provisioners less portable than other options.

Connections do not have to be to the specific resource that was created. Any resource can use a provisioner, including resources where there isn't anything to connect to. The connection itself can define any machine at all. For example, you might create a provisioner on a Domain Name System record that logs into the machine it was created for and makes changes only after it was set.

Listing 10.12   Connection to different resource

```
resource "aws_instance" "other" {
  ami           = data.aws_ami.ubuntu.id
  instance_type = "t2.micro"
}

resource "aws_route53_record" "resource" {
  zone_id = data.aws_route53_zone.primary.zone_id
  name    = "example.com"
  type    = "A"
  records = [aws_instance.other.public_ip]

  connection {
    type        = "ssh"
    user        = "ubuntu"
    private_key = file("~/.ssh/id_rsa")
```

```
    host        = aws_instance.other.public_ip
  }
}
```

You can refer to other
resources in this block.

10.3.2 Command provisioners

There are two provisioners for running commands: `remote-exec` and `local-exec`. As you can probably guess, the `remote-exec` provisioner runs directly on the remote machine (and thus requires a connection be configured), while the `local-exec` provisioner runs on the same machine that Terraform is running on.

Despite doing very similar things, these provisioners are designed very differently. When using `remote-exec`, you have three parameters to use for selecting scripts, but you can only use one of them per `provisioner` block. The `script` parameter takes a relative path to a script file in your module, and the provisioner will then upload the script and run it. The `scripts` parameter is similar but takes a list of scripts to run in the specified order. The final parameter allows you to directly write scripts in your Terraform code as a direct string, without the need for a separate file (this is useful for small commands):

- `script` takes a path, relative to the file the block is defined in, to upload and run.
- `scripts` acts like `script` but takes a list of paths. The scripts will be uploaded and run in the order they were provided.
- `inline` allows you to pass through a string instead of a file. This is particularly useful if you just want to run a single command.

Listing 10.13   The `remote-exec` provisioner

```
resource "aws_instance" "main" {
  ami           = data.aws_ami.ubuntu.id
  instance_type = "t2.micro"

  connection {
    type        = "ssh"
    user        = "ubuntu"
    private_key = file("~/.ssh/id_rsa")
    host        = self.public_ip
  }

  provisioner "remote-exec" {
    inline = [
      "sudo apt-get update",
      "sudo apt-get install -y nginx"
    ]
  }
  provisioner "remote-exec" {
    script = "${path.module}/scripts/install.sh"
  }

  provisioner "remote-exec" {
```

The remote-exec provisioner runs
commands on the remote machine.

This is a list of commands that will
be run on the remote machine.

Multiple provisioners can exist in
a single resource and will run in
the order they are defined.

This script is defined locally
but will be copied to the
remote machine and executed.

```
    scripts = [
      "${path.module}/scripts/install.sh",
      "${path.module}/scripts/configure.sh"
    ]
  }
}
```

It's possible to provide a list of scripts as well.

The `local-exec` command runs on the same machine as Terraform and does not require any `connection` blocks. Unlike the `remote-exec` `provisioner`, you do not have the option of passing any `scripts` through, but instead can pass through single commands. That being said, you can always use your command to launch a `script` directly, or use the External provider, which we discuss in section 10.4.

Listing 10.14 The `local-exec` provisioner

```
resource "aws_instance" "main" {
  ami           = data.aws_ami.ubuntu.id
  instance_type = "t2.micro"

  provisioner "local-exec" {
    command = "echo '${self.id}' >> /tmp/instance_ids.txt"
  }
  provisioner "local-exec" {
    command = "bash ${path.module}/register_instance.sh '${self.id}'"
  }
}
```

We can run a command on the local machine.

It's possible to emulate the script parameter by calling scripts directly.

10.3.3 *File provisioners*

The `file` provisioner, as the name implies, allows you to create files on your remote instance. When using the `file` provisioner, you can have it upload a file from your own system by passing in a relative path to the `source` parameter or you can directly create the file by passing a string to the `content` parameter. A third parameter, `destination`, is used to tell Terraform where on the remote instance you want to place your file.

Listing 10.15 `file` provisioners content and source

```
resource "aws_instance" "main" {
  ami           = data.aws_ami.ubuntu.id
  instance_type = "t2.micro"

  connection {
    type        = "ssh"
    user        = "ubuntu"
    private_key = file("~/.ssh/id_rsa")
    host        = self.public_ip
  }

  provisioner "file" {
    destination = "/etc/hostname"
```

The file provisioner can be used to set the content of a file on a remote resource.

```
  content     = "api.${var.domain}"
}

provisioner "file" {
  destination = "/etc/nginx/nginx.conf"
  source      = "${path.module}/nginx.conf"
}

provisioner "remote-exec" {
  inline = ["sudo systemctl start nginx"]
}

}
```

It's also possible to copy a file directly from the local machine to the remote machine.

It's not uncommon to use the remote-exec provisioner to restart services after adding the configuration file.

It's also possible to upload entire directories with this method, although the destination directory has to already exist. Terraform will always run provisioners in the order they are defined, so you can use the `remote-exec` provisioner to create the directory before uploading the files and then again to set the permissions on the files.

Listing 10.16   Provisioner directory upload

```
resource "aws_instance" "main" {
  ami           = data.aws_ami.ubuntu.id
  instance_type = "t2.micro"

  connection {
    type        = "ssh"
    user        = "ubuntu"
    private_key = file("~/.ssh/id_rsa")
    host        = self.public_ip
  }

  provisioner "file" {
    destination = "/etc/nginx/sites-available/"
    source      = "${path.module}/sites-available/"
  }

  provisioner "remote-exec" {
    inline = ["sudo systemctl start nginx"]
  }

}
```

You can also copy entire directories from the local machine to the remote machine.

10.3.4 *Provisioner control*

Just as resources have `lifecycle` parameters, provisioners have their own parameters that can be used to change their behavior, such as when the provisioners run or how failures are handled.

By default, all provisioners run when a resource is first created. If you want a provisioner to run at destroy time instead, you can set the `when` parameter to `destroy`. This parameter is a little tricky though: just like the `prevent_destroy` parameter in our resource lifecycles, if you completely erase the resource from your code, then you also remove the parameter and its settings. This means you primarily want to use this for when a resource is naturally destroyed: that is, when you run `terraform destroy` or Terraform detects that the resource needs to be re-created.

Listing 10.17 `destroy time` **provisioner**

```
resource "aws_instance" "main" {
  ami           = data.aws_ami.ubuntu.id          Make sure you don't
  instance_type = "t2.micro"                       put this in quotes.

                                                   This script will be run when
  provisioner "local-exec" {                        the resource is destroyed.
    when    = destroy
    command = "bash ${path.module}/deregister_instance.sh '${self.id}'"
  }
}
```

Another parameter, `on_failure`, can be used to tell Terraform what to do in the event that a provisioner fails. The default value is `fail`, which means that Terraform will throw an error, stop the apply, and taint the resource so that it is destroyed and re-created in the next plan. If you do not want the application to stop, you can set this parameter to `continue` instead, and the error will be ignored.

Listing 10.18 Changing failure behavior

```
resource "aws_instance" "main" {
  ami           = data.aws_ami.ubuntu.id
  instance_type = "t2.micro"

                                              If the script fails, continue the run
  provisioner "local-exec" {                  anyways and ignore the failure.
    when       = destroy
    on_failure = continue
    command    = "bash ${path.module}/deregister_instance.sh '${self.id}'"
  }
}
```

10.3.5 *terraform_data*

The `terraform_data` resource is the famous "resource that does nothing" that we introduced in section 6.8.4. One of the more common uses for this resource is the ability to use provisioners without attaching them to a specific resource. Before the `terraform_data` resource was introduced, this was done with the `null_resource` instead, and it's not uncommon to run into examples that haven't been updated.

What makes the `terraform_data` resource useful for provisioners is its ability to take multiple triggers together and create a dependency on all of them. This allows you to create provisioners that run if any of the dependencies change while also limiting the script to run only once if any of them change.

Since triggers can also be any expression, it also allows for a lot more nuance than attaching a provisioner to a specific resource. You can trigger a `terraform_data`-based provisioner using any individual attribute of any resource or data source.

Listing 10.19   Using `terraform_data` for provisioning

```
resource "terraform_data" "provisioners" {            ◄────── The fact that terraform_data
                                                              doesn't actually do anything
  connection {                                                can be useful.
    type        = "ssh"
    user        = "ubuntu"
    private_key = file("~/.ssh/id_rsa")
    host        = aws_instance.main.public_ip    ◄────── We need to get the IP address
  }                                                       from the instance as there are
                                                          no self values we can use here.
  provisioner "remote-exec" {
    script = "${path.module}/scripts/initialize.sh"
  }

  depends_on = [                    ◄────── This resource, and thus it's provisioner,
    aws_instance.main,                      won't do anything until after the resources
    aws_db_instance.main                    it depends on have been created.
  ]
}
```

10.3.6 *Alternatives to using provisioners*

As mentioned at the start, provisioners should be an option of last resort. For most tasks, there really should be another option (see table 10.4).

One of the easiest ways to avoid using provisioners is with the concept of immutable infrastructure. Immutable infrastructure is a trend that has been very popular with the use of cloud-based infrastructure. Rather than attempt to keep running instances up to date, you replace them when you want to change their configuration or installed packages. This allows you to better test your images in advance of deploying them and prevents change-related failures from occurring with running machines.

With immutable infrastructure you build your machine images in advance with all of the software they need. During launch, you restrict yourself to just configuration, and even then just parts that can't be reasonably done in advance. When you do configure your individual machines, you do so with a tool like Cloud-Init.

Table 10.4   Provisioner purposes and alternatives

Purpose	Alternative
Software installation	Preinstall software on machine images that are used for the service.
Configure launched instance	Use Cloud-Init to pass configuration to the machine.
Add environment-specific files to the resource	Use Cloud-Init to create the files on launch.

Table 10.4 Provisioner purposes and alternatives (*continued*)

Purpose	Alternative
Add a custom shutdown sequence for destruction	Create a shutdown service for the machine and either bake it into the machine image or install the service with Cloud-Init.
Create a list of machine meta-data and save them to a file	Use output variables to return the metadata or the local provider to create files.

Cloud-Init is an open source system used to standardize configuration for cloud instances. It works by reading the Cloud-Init configuration and running commands or creating files based on that configuration. Each cloud vendor has its own way of passing this data in, but with Terraform it's typically a single parameter passed to a resource. Later in this chapter we discuss machine image building and give some examples.

While this does help us avoid provisioners in a number of cases, there are still going to be problems that users can run into outside of that. You may have a cloud service provider you're deploying to that doesn't have support for Cloud-Init (which is common when deploying Windows), for instance, and at that point provisioners could be helpful. When it comes to programming, there are always going to be extreme edge cases or areas where you need to get creative to solve a problem. Provisioners can be a tool in dealing with some of those problems, but make sure to always ask if there is a better way to solve the problem.

10.4 *External provider*

While provisioners allow you to run external commands when you create or destroy resources, they do have limitations. One particular problem is that they can't be used to load data for those resources. If you need to pull data in from a custom source that does not have a provider or data source for it, then provisioners won't help. Instead, you can use the external provider.

The external provider has a data source that can allow you to easily create custom data sources by calling external programs. The external provider works by calling programs on your local system and then feeding the results back to Terraform as an attribute. This means you have a lot of flexibility and can use any language you want to write a program to solve whatever problem it is you are trying to solve. On the other hand, that means your modules using it are less portable, as your users will have to ensure their delivery environment can actually run your program.

> **WARNING** As with provisioners, the external provider should only be used as an absolute last resort. While it doesn't have as many drawbacks as provisioners do, it does require extra maintenance and support. You have to build a script and ensure that your delivery environment has the programs necessary to run those scripts, both of which require a bit of extra work and maintenance.

10.4.1 *External datasource*

The external provider has a single data source: `external`. It does not have any resources, and that is for good reason. The external provider is meant to query for data; it is not meant to create and manage actual infrastructure, and so there is no need for any resources.

The `external` data source takes in three arguments. The first, `program`, is an array that starts with a command and takes in any options or arguments as additional elements. If you're familiar with Docker, this is basically the same structure as the `ENTRYPOINT` and `CMD` arguments in a `Dockerfile`. This is the only required parameter.

The second parameter is `query`. This is a map of strings (`map(string)`) that the provider converts into JSON and sends to your program through the standard input (`stdin`). If this optional parameter isn't set, then the provider will send an empty JSON array to your program.

The final parameter is `working_dir`. This allows developers to set the working directory for the program to run in. This defaults to the current working directory.

Your program is expected to return its own JSON object that `external` can convert into a map of strings. This map is available as the attribute `result`.

Listing 10.20   The external data source

```
data "external" "main" {
  program = ["bash", "${path.module}/script.sh"]
}

output "result" {
  value = data.external.main.result
}

output "specific_result" {
  value = data.external.main.result["specific_key"]
}
```

The external data source can be used to run custom-made scripts.

The script has to return a JSON object.

10.4.2 *Wrapper program languages*

Using the data source is pretty straightforward, but it does require that you write a program on top of just writing some HashiCorp Configuration Language. This is where the flexibility of the provider is both really powerful and potentially problematic, as you have to pick between several tradeoffs here.

On the one hand, you can use a language like `Bash` to write your program. This has the benefit of being extremely portable, as pretty much every unix-style system has the bash interpreter installed and the language has been very stable for a long time (this is similar to our reasoning for using Make as a job runner). This doesn't allow you to completely escape the concerns of environments though, as most Bash scripts still rely on underlying software being installed. As a minimum, you'll want a tool like `jq` to help manage the JSON going in and out of your script. The more complex your scripts are, the more tools they will need and the harder it'll be to maintain them with a language as primitive as Bash.

On the other hand, you could use a language such as Python, Java, or any other option that you are currently familiar with. These higher-level languages tend to be easier to understand and maintain for most teams, and they have a wide variety of libraries that can be used with them. This makes it easier on the team writing the module and makes it possible to build more complex applications than is feasible with Bash (at least for most teams: apologies if you happen to be a Bash guru). Unfortunately, most of these languages require a bit more setup for their applications, including potentially having to install dependencies on the system running it. This really reduces the portability of the module and puts more work on the people using it.

At the end of the day, the external provider is a bit of a hack anyway, and any module using it is likely to be designed for a very specific circumstance. In other words, there's a good chance that it's not a shared module but a system-specific one used to work around an problem. At that point, you likely have control over the delivery orchestrator and should do what is best for your team. However, if this is a module that is meant for redistribution, you should stick to Bash or avoid the external provider altogether.

> **TIP** Thinking about using Go? If that's the case, you can skip the external provider altogether and write a custom provider instead. Creating customer providers is the focus of chapter 12.

10.4.3 *Writing wrapper programs*

Regardless of the language you chose, the flow of your program is going to be the same. The program will get the contents of the query attribute as a JSON string from `stdin` and is expected to return the results back to Terraform with a JSON string using `stdout` (see figure 10.7).

Figure 10.7   External data source flow

Let's say we needed to calculate the square root of a number for a module we're working on. Terraform does not have a function to do this, so we decided to write a script for the external provider to use. In this case, we have an extremely simple example that only needs one argument, so we can get away without even needing to parse the query.

Listing 10.21   Square root script

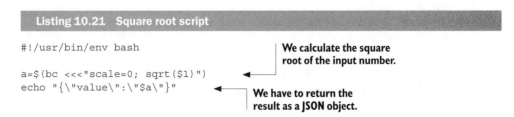

```
#!/usr/bin/env bash

a=$(bc <<<"scale=0; sqrt($1)")
echo "{\"value\":\"$a\"}"
```

We calculate the square root of the input number.

We have to return the result as a JSON object.

This type of extremely simple script is where the external provider can really excel, as it remains portable with no dependencies outside of Bash and requires minimal maintenance. It's also easy to use, as in this case we only have to use the program parameter of the data source.

Listing 10.22   Square root external data source

```
data "external" "main" {
  program = ["bash", "${path.module}/square_root.sh", "128"]
}

output "result" {
  value = data.external.main.result["value"]
}
```

We use command-line arguments to pass the number to the script.

Even though we only return a single value it is still wrapped in a JSON object.

For the most part, you can rely on arguments to avoid having to deal with parsing your input, but if your program isn't simple enough and requires a lot of arguments, then it can complicate things for the user trying to construct that program parameter. In that case, you have to rely on the `query` parameter instead. Building on our previous example, we can create a new program that lets users get the square root of any amount of numbers.

Listing 10.23   Square root query data source

```
data "external" "query" {
  program = ["python", "${path.module}/square_root.py"]

  query = {
    "0"      = "128"
    "1"      = "256"
    "2"      = "512"
    "random" = "1024"
  }
}

output "random" {
  value = data.external.query.result["random"]
}
```

We can send as many values as we want.

The keys are arbitrary and can be named anything.

In this case, we're going to try this with Python, as it's a bit easier to deal with loops. To keep our application as portable as possible, we are only going to use components from the Python standard library. Since we are using the `query` parameter, our program has to read from standard input and parse the JSON object that is being passed to it. Then we can iterate over the items in the query object to generate our return object, which we then encode with JSON.

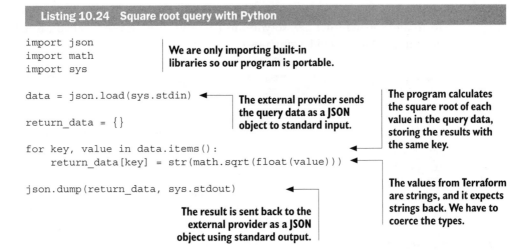

Listing 10.24 Square root query with Python

```python
import json
import math
import sys

data = json.load(sys.stdin)

return_data = {}

for key, value in data.items():
    return_data[key] = str(math.sqrt(float(value)))

json.dump(return_data, sys.stdout)
```

> We are only importing built-in libraries so our program is portable.

> The external provider sends the query data as a JSON object to standard input.

> The program calculates the square root of each value in the query data, storing the results with the same key.

> The values from Terraform are strings, and it expects strings back. We have to coerce the types.

> The result is sent back to the external provider as a JSON object using standard output.

10.4.4 Alternatives to external providers

The external provider is a great way to break out of Terraform to get data that you couldn't otherwise get, but, as shown, it does have some drawbacks. If possible, you should attempt to find another way to manage your problem.

For example, if your script is primarily to query a web service or make an API call, then you should consider using the HTTP provider instead. This provider lets you construct HTTP queries, similar to the command-line utility `curl`, and works directly in Terraform.

Now that Terraform supports custom functions in providers, it's also a good idea to look and see if a provider has implemented something you could use instead. If there is not a function, then at least confirm there are no data sources that accomplish the same thing, or close enough.

As a final option, you could also build your own Terraform provider. This is an especially appealing option for teams that already know Go, although it's likely overkill for teams without that experience. If this is something you're interested in, see chapter 12, where we break down how to create providers.

10.5 Local provider

Using provisioners, you can create files on remote systems, but what if you need to manage resources on your local system? As always, there is a provider for that—in this case the aptly named local provider.

10.5.1 Functions

The local provider is one of the first providers to take advantage of the new Terraform functionality that allows providers to define their own functions. Although it only defines a single function, it's a pretty useful one. While the `fileexists` function has been around basically as long as Terraform has, there has not been a way to detect if a directory exists. The local provider solves that with the `direxists` function.

NOTE   The ability to use functions from providers was introduced in Terraform and OpenTofu 1.8.0, so you must be using at least that version to take advantage of any provider functions.

Listing 10.25   Checking for the existence of a directory

> The fileexists function has existed
> in Terraform for a long time.

```
locals {
  file_exists = fileexists("${path.module}/example.txt")   ◄────┘
  dir_exists = provider::local::direxists("${path.module}/scripts/")   ◄────┐
}
```

> Starting in Terraform v1.8 we can use the provider
> prefix to access provider-specific functions.

10.5.2 Data sources

The local provider has two data sources that are practically identical: `local_file` and `local_sensitive_file`. They both take in a single parameter, filename, and they both have the same attributions. The difference is that `local_sensitive_file` will mark any attributes with the file contents as sensitive so that Terraform won't display it.

Listing 10.26   Local provider data sources

```
data "local_file" "foo" {
  filename = "${path.module}/config.txt"   ◄────┐
}
```

> The local_file data source is used to
> read the contents of a file, like the file
> function but with more attributes.

```
data "local_sensitive_file" "foo" {   ◄────┐
  filename = "${path.module}/private.key"
}
```

> The local_sensitive_file data source
> works like the local_file one except the
> content is marked as sensitive.

Both of these data sources read the contents of the file and make it available inside of Terraform. Unlike the file function, which is the most common way to read files, this allows provisioners, conditions, and dependencies to be created on the file. This data source also has additional attributes, such as checksums and base64 encoded versions of the content (see table 10.5).

Table 10.5 `local_file` and `local_sensitive_file` attributes

Attribute	Description
content	The actual content of the file. For `local_sensitive_file` this will be marked sensitive.
content_base64	The content of the file, encoded using base64. For `local_sensitive_file` this will be marked sensitive.

Table 10.5 `local_file` and `local_sensitive_file` attributes (*continued*)

Attribute	Description
content_base64sha256	The sha256 hash of the base64 content.
content_base64sha512	The sha512 hash of the base64 content.
content_sha1	The sha1 hash of the raw content.
content_sha256	The sha256 hash of the raw content.
content_sha512	The sha512 hash of the raw content.
content_md5	The md5 hash of the raw content.

If you know that you are going to need any of these attributes alongside the content itself, then you can simplify your code with these data sources.

10.5.3 Resources

The local provider also has the ability to create files with the `local_file` and `local_sensitive_file` resources. Just like the data sources, these resources have the same parameters and attributes, with the only difference being that the file content is considered sensitive.

> **WARNING** Creating local files with Terraform can be problematic. If your Terraform code is not run from the same location every time, then it won't be able to see the files between runs. If you don't find a way to restore the files between runs, Terraform will always detect drift.

The shortcomings of these resources means that it isn't particularly useful for most production cases. However, it can be useful for development purposes. If you are doing local development on a system, you can use this file to generate configuration files to connect to your environment. For example, you can use an open source module (https://github.com/tedivm/terraform-aws-dev-vpn) to attach a virtual private network to an environment and then drop the configuration file right into your module. This would be pretty useless in a production environment, since the file would immediately be thrown away, but can be useful when debugging systems.

Listing 10.27 Creating local files

```
resource "local_file" "main" {
  content  = "Hello World!"                    The local_file resource is used
  filename = "${path.module}/hello.txt"        to write content to a file.
}

resource "tls_private_key" "main" {
  algorithm = "ECDSA"
}                                               The local_sensitive_file
                                                resource is used to write
resource "local_sensitive_file" "key" {         sensitive content to a file.
```

```
    content  = tls_private_key.main.private_key_pem
    filename = "${path.module}/private_key.pem"
}
```

> **In this case, we take the content of our private key and save it to disk.**

10.6 Checks and conditions

In chapter 9, we covered testing Terraform modules as part of the development process, but Terraform also provides a way to run tests and assertions against long-running infrastructure. This allows you to provide additional safeguards to your modules and code while also providing another way to report back on the status of systems. In this section, we break down the major differences between checks and conditions so you can utilize these tools and increase your module quality and usability.

10.6.1 Preconditions and postconditions

The precondition and postcondition blocks exist inside of the lifecycle meta argument that exists on all resources and data sources. These blocks allow you to run validations before (precondition) or after (postcondition) a resource is created. If these validations fail, then it will block Terraform from going any further. This means these resources can be used as a safeguard to prevent misconfigurations from occurring.

Both of the condition blocks have two arguments: a condition parameter, which takes in any expression that evaluates to a boolean, and an error_message parameter, which will bubble up to the user if the condition field returns false. You can have any number of conditions, both precondition and postcondition, in a single resource.

Although you can refer to other resources in the condition, if you want to refer to the resource the condition is defined in, you have to use the self keyword. This is useful because it allows each resource created by a block that uses count or for_each to run the condition against each created resource individually without the developer having to manage indexes.

Listing 10.28 Preconditions as variable validation

```
resource "aws_lb" "example" {
  name               = "example"
  load_balancer_type = var.type
  ip_address_type    = var.ip_address_type
  subnets            = var.subnet_ids

  lifecycle {
    precondition {
      condition       = var.type == "application" ? true :
var.ip_address_type != "dualstack-without-public-ipv4"
      error_message = "The ip_address_type can only be set to
dualstack-without-public-ipv4 when the Load Balancer Type is
application."
    }
  }
}
```

> **This precondition will prevent Terraform from creating the resource if the condition is not met.**

> **The condition can be any valid expression, including multiple variables or even resource attributes.**

> **This error will be sent to the user if the condition is not met.**

Before Terraform v1.9.0 came out, it was common to use `precondition` blocks on resources inside of modules that had complex attributes in order to work around limitations with the variable block's validation system. Before this Terraform release, these `validation` blocks could only refer to themselves: if you had a `variable` whose acceptable values depended on how another `variable` was set, you couldn't enforce that with `validation` blocks. Since `precondition` blocks are attached to resources, they could refer to any number of variables or even attributes from other data sources or resources.

Listing 10.29 Variable validation in Terraform v1.9.0

```
variable "type" {
  type    = string
  default = "application"
}

variable "ip_address_type" {
  type    = string
  default = "dualstack"

  validation {
    condition      = var.type == "application" ? true : var.ip_address_type
    != "dualstack-without-public-ipv4"
    error_message = "The ip_address_type can only be set to
dualstack-without-public-ipv4 when the Load Balancer Type is
application."
  }
}
```

> This validation only works in Terraform v1.9.0 or later as it refers to other variables.

Although Terraform v1.9.0 makes variable `validation` blocks more flexible, this technique can still be useful, especially as it allows developers to keep their validations attached to the direct resources that they're affecting. However, you should consider using the variable validation itself as it's easier for developers to find.

The `postcondition` block has the same syntax as the `precondition` block but runs after a resource has been created or updated rather than beforehand. This allows you to stop execution if there is a problem with the resource or if the results of a data source lookup aren't what you expect.

Listing 10.30 Postcondition on data source

```
data "aws_ami" "ubuntu" {
  most_recent = true

  filter {
    name   = "name"
    values = ["ubuntu/images/hvm-ssd/ubuntu-focal-20.04-amd64-server-*"]
  }

  filter {
    name   = "virtualization-type"
```

```
      values = ["hvm"]
  }

  owners = ["099720109477"] # Canonical

  lifecycle {
    postcondition {
      condition     = timecmp(timestamp(), self.deprecation_time) == -1
      error_message = "Unable to find an AMI that is not deprecated."
    }
  }
}
```

> **Postconditions have to use self to refer to themselves. This is also one of the only valid uses for the timestamp function, as it won't cause state drift until the resource is deprecated.**

10.6.2 Checks

Checks are a way to ensure that your infrastructure is doing what you expect it to. They are similar to tests but are meant to run on all infrastructure, including long-lived infrastructure that lives in production environments. These can be used to validate the health of a system. They were introduced in Terraform v1.5.0.

At its simplest, the `check` block can be considered very similar to the `postcondition` block. You can use the `check` block to validate that a resource was created in the way you expected. What makes it unique is that, unlike the `postcondition` block, if a check fails, it will not stop Terraform from continuing. This allows you to use the `check` block to report back the health of your system without it impeding any changes to your system. The `check` block also allows you to run as many assertions as you like in a single block, while `postcondition` requires you to use multiple blocks.

Listing 10.31   `check` **block and** `postcondition` **comparison**

```
data "aws_ami" "ubuntu" {
  most_recent = true

  filter {
    name   = "name"
    values = ["ubuntu/images/hvm-ssd/ubuntu-focal-20.04-amd64-server-*"]
  }

  filter {
    name   = "virtualization-type"
    values = ["hvm"]
  }

  owners = ["099720109477"] # Canonical

  lifecycle {
    postcondition {
      condition     = timecmp(timestamp(), self.deprecation_time) == -1
      error_message = "Unable to find an AMI that is not deprecated."
    }

    postcondition {
```

> **If this fails, then execution will stop.**

> **To check multiple conditions, you can add multiple postcondition blocks.**

```
      condition       = self.imds_support == "v2.0"
      error_message = "Unable to find an AMI that enforces IMDSv2."
    }
  }
}

check "ami_check" {

  assert {
    condition       = timecmp(timestamp(),
  data.aws_ami.ubuntu.deprecation_time) == -1
    error_message = "Unable to find an AMI that is not deprecated."
  }

  assert {
    condition       = data.aws_ami.ubuntu.imds_support == "v2.0"
    error_message = "Unable to find an AMI that enforces IMDSv2."
  }
}
```

Unlike postconditions, the check block will not stop execution if an assertion fails.

The assert block has the same arguments as conditions do.

Unlike conditions there is no self object to refer to.

A single check block can contain multiple assert blocks.

What makes the `check` block really powerful is the use of scoped data sources. Inside of a `check` block, you can define as many data source blocks as you want, and they will only be available inside of your `check` block. If they happen to fail, this won't stop execution; it will just result in a warning.

Listing 10.32 `check` block with scoped data sources

```
check "health_check" {
  data "http" "api" {
    url = "${module.api.url}/health"
    request_headers = {
      Accept = "application/json"
    }
  }

  assert {
    condition       = data.http.api.status_code >= 200 &&
  data.http.api.status_code < 300
    error_message = "Healthcheck failed with status code
  ${data.http.api.status_code} and content ${data.http.api.request_body}."
  }
}
```

If this block fails it won't stop execution as it's part of the check block.

You can use attributes and variables inside of these blocks.

You refer to the data block just like you would outside of a check, but these are accessible only inside of the check.

Scoped data sources support both the `depends_on` and `provider` arguments, although they do not allow any other lifecycle arguments.

As a general rule, you should always try to use the `depends_on` argument if you don't already have an implicit dependency to a resource outside of the `check` block. If a check does not have any implicit dependencies, it will start running during your very first plan, even before you've created any resources. For example, if you ran a check to see if a web application was responding and just used the values from the input variable for the domain, then your check might run before the infrastructure has even had a chance to launch. Make sure you use the `depends_on` parameter and fill it with any resource you want to launch before the data source inside of the check actually runs.

> **Listing 10.33 check block with data source dependencies**

```
check "health_check" {
  data "http" "api" {
    url = var.healthcheck_endpoint
    request_headers = {
      Accept = "application/json"
    }

    depends_on = [module.api]
  }
  assert {
    condition      = data.http.api.status_code >= 200 &&
data.http.api.status_code < 300
    error_message = "Healthcheck failed with status code
${data.http.api.status_code} and content ${data.http.api.request_body}."
  }
}
```

Since we are using a variable there is no implicit dependency on this data source.

To prevent the first run of this check from failing we need to make this block depend on the module that launches the API.

10.7 *OpenTofu and Terraform compatibility*

Terraform and OpenTofu are remarkably compatible with each other. During the writing of this book, all examples were tested with both systems, and they simply worked without the need to change anything. That being said, the relationship between Terraform and OpenTofu is likely to evolve over time, with differences in functionality and implementation likely to occur.

10.7.1 *Tofu files*

The Tofu files feature was added in OpenTofu v1.8 and gives module developers a lot of power to write code that is compatible with both OpenTofu and Terraform while still being able to take advantage (or at least test out) new features available in one but not the other.

Terraform files all have the extension `.tf`, which is how Terraform knows to use them. OpenTofu has now added support for `.tofu` files as well. Terraform knows nothing about `.tofu` files, so it will always ignore them. OpenTofu knows about both Open-Tofu and Terraform files though, so if it sees a `.tofu` file with the same name as a `.tf` file, it will ignore the `.tf` file and use the `.tofu` file instead.

As a simple example, let's create a file named `compatibility.tf` and use it to define a local variable.

Listing 10.34 Populating `compatibility.tf`

```
locals {
  my_engine = "terraform"
}
```

◄─── **As long as compatibility.tofu exists this file will only be processed by Terraform, not OpenTofu.**

Now let's create a second file, `compatiblity.tofu`, and define that same local variable with a different value.

Listing 10.35 Populating `compatibility.tofu`

```
locals {
  my_engine = "tofu"
}
```

◄─── **This value will only be read from OpenTofu.**

Now when we refer to that local variable, the value will be different depending on whether we used Terraform or OpenTofu to run the code. When we use Terraform, it ignores `compatiblity.tofu`, and when we use OpenTofu, it ignores the matching `compability.tf` while still loading `compatibility.tofu`.

Listing 10.36 Identifying the engine

```
output "engine" {
  value = local.my_engine
}
```

◄─── **This will be "tofu" on OpenTofu and "terraform" on Terraform.**

10.8 When Terraform isn't appropriate

As fantastic as Terraform is, there are times when it is not the appropriate tool for the job. Sometimes this is because other tools exist that do it better, and other times it's because trying to get Terraform to manage it is too convoluted to be useful.

10.8.1 Kubernetes

Kubernetes is an open source container orchestrator that was initially developed by Google and has since taken off. While it originally focused mostly on containers, it has been expanded over the years and now includes plugins that let it control a variety of resources. Developers deploy to Kubernetes clusters using manifests, which are typically YAML files that define resources in a declarative way.

Although there are a lot of reasons why a team would use Kubernetes, it really shines for teams that have resources spread across multiple clouds or data centers as it provides a shared abstraction layer over those different providers. This allows developers deploying onto Kubernetes to define their configurations without worrying about the underlying vendor actually being used.

Listing 10.37   Example Kubernetes manifest

```
apiVersion: apps/v1
kind: Deployment
metadata:
  name: example-deployment
spec:
  replicas: 3
  selector:
    matchLabels:
      app: example-app
  template:
    metadata:
      labels:
        app: example-app
    spec:
      containers:
        - name: example-container
          image: nginx:1.14.2
          ports:
            - containerPort: 80
          resources:
            limits:
              cpu: "1"
              memory: "500Mi"
            requests:
              cpu: "500m"
              memory: "200Mi"
```

For the people maintaining the Kubernetes platform itself, Terraform can be a great tool. The most common way to use it is by creating modules for each cloud (GCP, AWS, Azure, etc.) that manage the infrastructure that Kubernetes runs on, including setting up any controllers and integrations between the cluster and the other cloud resources. This way, the platform engineers can spin up new clusters and manage old ones with all the benefits that infrastructure as code has.

The problem comes in for people attempting to deploy onto the cluster itself. While there is a Kubernetes provider, and it is technically possible to use Terraform to manage the resources being deployed onto a Kubernetes cluster, it is generally not a good idea. When you use Terraform with Kubernetes, you're putting an abstraction layer on top of an abstraction layer (see figure 10.8). This makes debugging problems a bit harder, as it requires you to debug through all the abstraction layers to figure out where a problem might be occurring.

Instead of using Terraform to manage the deployments onto Kubernetes, use the Kubernetes tools themselves. This can mean using the `kubectl` program as part of your normal continuous integration/continuous delivery operations or using a Kubernetes-specific tool like Helm or ArgoCD for managing complex applications.

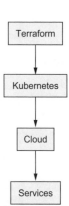

Figure 10.8 Abstraction layers

10.8.2 Container image building

These days, containers are an integral part of software development and deployment. Most applications will find themselves packaged up as a container image, pushed to a registry, and deployed to an orchestrator. It's only natural that some developers would consider building those container images as part of their infrastructure deployment process. In practice, this can be a problem for two primary reasons: it can greatly increase the time it takes to deploy changes, and it removes the loose coupling between application and infrastructure and turns it into a tight coupling.

The first problem is pretty easy to understand. Building containers takes time, and if you build your images as part of the Terraform deployment process then it can take a lot more time to run a deployment. This is the type of problem that tends to grow over time. As applications become more complex, they tend to take on more dependencies, giving them a longer build time, and larger applications may have multiple containers that have to be used (and thus built).

The other problem, that of coupling, is a bit more complicated. Containers and the infrastructure they run on almost always have a relationship. Depending on the application, you may be defining databases, streams, caches, or queues (among many, many other options). This infrastructure is defined in Terraform and linked to the containers, so there's always *some* level of coupling between container and infrastructure. This may make it seem like it's not a big deal to increase the strength of that dependency.

Most of the time, though, changes to an application don't need a change to infrastructure, unless a new feature is being added that calls for it. Infrastructure changes tend to include a lot of fine-tuning and functionality that the application itself doesn't care about. If you're increasing the number of containers running by default, redirecting logs to a new location, changing the hardware type of a database, or doing any number of other common tasks you don't need to make application changes. In these cases, you'd build and potentially deploy a new image for no reason.

Your images should have their own continuous integration/continuous delivery process so that you can push new versions up when you tag a new release. Your Terraform configuration can then refer to the versions you want to deploy. If you want to deploy a new version, you update your Terraform (typically via an input variable). This allows you to track upgrades inside of Git just like you do other changes, and rollbacks are as simple as reverting the commit.

Listing 10.38 Terraform container versions

```
variable "api_service_version" {          Make your version a variable
  type    = string                         so it can be changed.
  default = "latest"
}                                          You can always set it to use
                                           the latest tag by default.      Pass your version
module "api_service" {                                                     through to the module.
  source = "./modules/api_service"
  image  = "gcr.io/my-project/api-service:${var.api_service_version}"
}
```

Some teams also manage deployments of new containers outside of Terraform. If you're using a continuous deployment tool that supports features like progressive delivery (where new versions are slowly rolled out to more and more users, with a variety of different patterns to do so), you may want to rely on that system to upgrade your versions rather than Terraform. If this is something your team wants to do, then you'll want to tell Terraform to ignore any changes to your container version.

Listing 10.39 Terraform-ignoring container versions

```
resource "aws_ecs_task_definition" "this" {
  family               = "api"
  container_definitions = <<EOF
[
  {
    "name": "api",
    "image": "gcr.io/my-project/api-service:${var.api_service_version}"   ◄───┐
    "cpu": 256,
    "memory": 512,                          Since this is ignored the version
    "essential": true,                      will never be updated from inside
    "portMappings": [                       of Terraform after the first launch.
      {
        "containerPort": 80,
        "hostPort": 80
      }
    ]
  }
]
EOF
                                        Ignore changes to the
                                        container_definitions attribute
  lifecycle {                           to allow the version to be
    ignore_changes = [container_definitions]   ◄──┘  changed outside of Terraform.
  }
}
```

10.8.3 *Machine image building*

Terraform is regularly used to manage fleets of virtual machines. Virtual machines have a variety of uses, from providing NAT services to acting as the lower layer of a container orchestration system such as Kubernetes or EC2 Container Service. Regardless of what they're used for, there are two steps that these machines need to function: they need to have any required software installed, and they need to configure that software.

Although this may seem counterintuitive, the second task is actually much easier than the first. The vast majority of cloud service providers and virtual machine orchestrators support the `cloud-init` tool (https://cloudinit.readthedocs.io/en/latest/), which allows users to pass through data and scripts for machines to run when they are launched. This allows tools like Terraform, which has a Cloud-Init provider, to generate configurations that get passed to the machines when they're first launched.

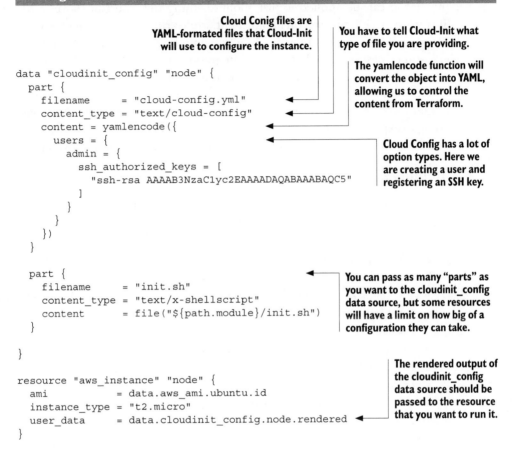

Listing 10.40 Cloud-Init and AWS Instances

Cloud Conig files are YAML-formatted files that Cloud-Init will use to configure the instance.

You have to tell Cloud-Init what type of file you are providing.

The yamlencode function will convert the object into YAML, allowing us to control the content from Terraform.

```
data "cloudinit_config" "node" {
  part {
    filename     = "cloud-config.yml"
    content_type = "text/cloud-config"
    content = yamlencode({
      users = {
        admin = {
          ssh_authorized_keys = [
            "ssh-rsa AAAAB3NzaC1yc2EAAAADAQABAAABAQC5"
          ]
        }
      }
    })
  }
```

Cloud Config has a lot of option types. Here we are creating a user and registering an SSH key.

```
  part {
    filename     = "init.sh"
    content_type = "text/x-shellscript"
    content      = file("${path.module}/init.sh")
  }

}
```

You can pass as many "parts" as you want to the cloudinit_config data source, but some resources will have a limit on how big of a configuration they can take.

```
resource "aws_instance" "node" {
  ami           = data.aws_ami.ubuntu.id
  instance_type = "t2.micro"
  user_data     = data.cloudinit_config.node.rendered
}
```

The rendered output of the cloudinit_config data source should be passed to the resource that you want to run it.

NOTE My first open source Terraform module (https://mng.bz/N1KD) is a wrapper around the `cloud-init` provider that makes it a bit easier to use. It takes in most of the Cloud Config options as parameters in Terraform, rather than requiring a full script to be defined, and it automatically compresses the script when it is too large.

This solves one of the problems—configuration—but leaves the problem of installing the required packages to the application. For that, you should consider using a tool such as Packer (https://www.packer.io/) to generate image templates that your team can use that already have the software installed. As we discussed in the section about provisioning, using prebuilt images has the advantages of being much easier to test and significantly quicker to launch.

10.8.4 Artifact management

At this point, you might be noticing a theme: packaging up "things" such as container or machine images should not be done inside of Terraform. Although container and machine images tend to be the more common areas where people make this mistake, this lesson can be applied to just about anything that you can shove into a registry. Terraform itself is focused on deployment, while artifact management is an integration concern. Whether it's deploying libraries, compiling applications, or building containers, you're best leaving that on the integration side of things and focusing on using Terraform to consume your already-generated artifacts.

Throughout this chapter, we explored various ways to use (or not use) Terraform to manage complex or rare use cases you might encounter. In the next chapter, we're going to explore how we can work with Terraform outside of Terraform itself, before we reach our final chapter on how to extend Terraform with custom providers.

Summary

- Giving your resources and domains easily decipherable names makes it easier for you to maintain your systems while also guaranteeing your resources have unique names.
- Although networking is complex, it's possible to use Terraform to abstract complicated network patterns behind easy-to-use modules.
- If you absolutely need to, you can use provisioners to run code outside of Terraform before or after a resource is created, but you should only use this as a last resort.
- The external provider can be used to create unique data sources without having to extend Terraform with a custom provider, but it makes the portability of your code more challenging.
- The local provider can be used to create files on your local machine, which is useful in some debugging and development scenarios.
- Checks and conditions are a way to increase code quality and resilience by running tests as infrastructure is deployed.
- It's possible to maintain compatibility between OpenTofu and Terraform by utilizing `tofu` files that are only run by OpenTofu.
- Terraform is great, but that doesn't mean you should use it for everything. There are a variety of use cases where other tools make more sense.

Alternative interfaces

11

This chapter covers

- Controlling Terraform from another language
- Breaking down the Terraform machine-readable UI into usable data structures
- Creating hooks to respond to Terraform streaming events as they occur
- Generating valid Terraform using JSON
- Using the CDK for Terraform project to generate valid Terraform from other languages

Terraform is both a tool and a language. The tool is the Terraform or OpenTofu binary itself: an engine and command line interface (CLI) application that is used to process code written in the Terraform language. The language, as we've seen throughout this book, is built on top of HashiCorp Configuration Language (HCL) and is populated with resources, data sources, and functions that are added with the use of providers.

What if you wanted to use Terraform without Terraform? As weird as that may sound, there are a lot of use cases where that comes up. Some teams simply don't want to learn Terraform and HCL, so they may want to develop their infrastructure as code (IaC) using a language they're more familiar with. Other teams may have a need to automatically generate Terraform, which is easier to do with JSON than it is with HCL. On the other side of things, teams may want to access the Terraform engine itself using their own language, with the goal of building their own tools on top of Terraform.

In this chapter, we explore the various ways of writing and operating Terraform from outside of Terraform. We start by focusing on how you can wrap the Terraform engine to use in any other language and then get into how you can write Terraform using JSON or, through the use of the Cloud Development Kit for Terraform (CDKTF) and Pulumi projects, use a completely different language altogether. We end the chapter with Terragrunt, a tool that wraps Terraform using some of the techniques in this chapter to give teams more control over their deployments.

NOTE   You'll need this when you need it. This chapter presents an extremely advanced topic: integrating Terraform into your own projects and tools. Just like creating providers, which we discuss in the next section, this content is not something you'd be expected to encounter on a regular basis. At the same time, if you do have a need to integrate Terraform into your tools programmatically, this chapter will be helpful to you.

11.1 Wrapping Terraform

Terraform does not have a traditional software development kit or library that can be used to control Terraform itself. Teams that want to build programs that run Terraform for them need to wrap the CLI to do so.

What does it mean to "wrap a CLI"? In general, this means creating a library that calls out to the CLI for you, processes the output from that CLI, and makes that output available to the developer in a useful way. This is called "wrapping" because you're surrounding the CLI tool with your own custom code and interfaces.

If you've gone through this book in order, then you've used multiple tools that have wrapped Terraform in its own package. Terragrunt wraps Terraform to allow you to manage deployments easier. Checkov and Trivy both are capable of reading state and plan files, so they've incorporated some of the data structures in Terraform into their own applications. Systems like HCP Terraform, Spacelift, Env0, Atlantis, and all of the other deployment tools wrap Terraform or OpenTofu.

Terraform was designed with this in mind and has a variety of features that make this easier.

TIP   Pay attention to licenses. Starting with Terraform v1.6, the HashiCorp version of Terraform is no longer open source and added limitations to what you are allowed to do with the Terraform engine. If you are building tools or products around this ecosystem, you may want to use OpenTofu, which has a very permissive open source license.

You have used the `terraform` and `tofu` programs throughout this book and are familiar with most of its commands, but you've been using it with the human-readable UI. These programs also have a machine-readable UI, triggered by passing in the `-json` flag to most commands. This UI follows a strict standard that programs wrapping Terraform can rely on, using JSON [which, despite its name (JavaScript Object Notation) is an open standard supported by most languages] to transfer data from Terraform into the native language wrapping it (see figure 11.1).

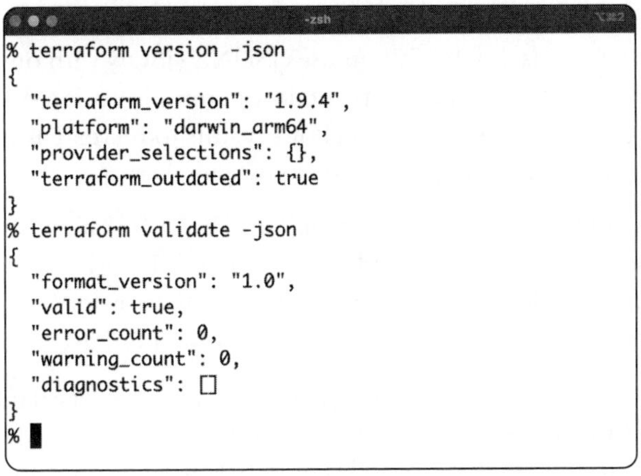

```
% terraform version -json
{
  "terraform_version": "1.9.4",
  "platform": "darwin_arm64",
  "provider_selections": {},
  "terraform_outdated": true
}
% terraform validate -json
{
  "format_version": "1.0",
  "valid": true,
  "error_count": 0,
  "warning_count": 0,
  "diagnostics": []
}
%
```

Figure 11.1   Terraform using JSON output

When building your wrapper, there are two primary concerns you have to consider. The first is actually running commands and getting the output. This generally means forming commands in your language, passing them to a library that executes them, retrieving the results, and dealing with any errors that come up.

The second consideration is parsing the results from the command and making those results available in a way that is useful and consistent with the language you're working with. In general, this means taking in your output, running it through a JSON parser, and structuring the data appropriately.

We're going to demonstrate this by building a wrapper for OpenTofu (which will also work with Terraform) using Python. You do not need to know Python to understand what we're doing here. The reason we're using Python is because of the simplicity and readability of the language. The goal here is to show you how to wrap Terraform in any language so that you can build tools in those languages to interact with Terraform and the data it produces.

11.1.1 *JSON output and machine-readable UI*

Terraform defines a set of data structures that you can use to read the output from Terraform when the `-json` flag is passed. These data structures are version controlled just like Terraform is and are extremely well documented. These data structures come in two flavors:

- JSON output format (https://mng.bz/DM2E) is used when a command returns a single response. The `terraform show`, `terraform validate`, and `terraform output` commands are examples of these. Each of them will return a single high-level JSON object with all of the data that would normally be displayed in a human-readable way.
- Machine-readable UI (https://mng.bz/IYGy) is used when a command returns a lot of responses. The `terraform plan` and `terraform apply` commands are the most common place for this. Each of them uses JSONL (JSON with one line per record), which means each line that is returned from our binary is a single JSON object that can be parsed on it's own. This allows results to be read as they come in instead of having to wait for the command to completely run.

The documentation for all of these fields is very robust, and both Terraform and Open-Tofu have done a great job at maintaining backward compatibility when introducing new features. That said, when building a wrapper you should always refer to the current documentation to see if any new fields have been added or old ones have changed.

> **TIP** The library that we're developing in this phase is available on GitHub at TerraformInDepth/tofupy (https://github.com/terraformInDepth/tofupy). If at any point you want to see the higher-level view of the project, you can take a look there.

11.1.2 *Initial Terraform client*

Our goal is to build a client library that someone writing Python can use to drive Terraform. The primary goal of this is to run commands, so we're going to need to gather a bit of information from our user and save it for our commands:

- The directory to run `tofu` in, since that defines what Terraform code to run
- Whether to use the `tofu` or `terraform` binary
- What level of logs we want to output
- Any environment variables we may want to pass

We're going to wrap these up into a simple class with a basic constructor. Since we need to rely on having the `tofu` or `terraform` binaries available, we can confirm they are there and raise an error if they aren't. We're going to create an initial class to load all of the values we'll need (such as the current working directory, whether we want Terraform logs to be more verbose, any environment variables we want to pass to OpenTofu, and the binary we want to use in case users want to switch from `tofu` to `terraform`).

Listing 11.1 Initializer in `tofupy/tofu.py`

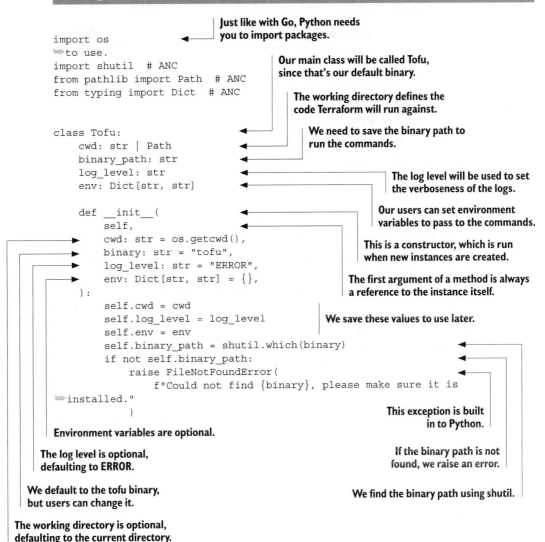

```
import os
to use.
import shutil   # ANC
from pathlib import Path   # ANC
from typing import Dict   # ANC


class Tofu:
    cwd: str | Path
    binary_path: str
    log_level: str
    env: Dict[str, str]

    def __init__(
        self,
        cwd: str = os.getcwd(),
        binary: str = "tofu",
        log_level: str = "ERROR",
        env: Dict[str, str] = {},
    ):
        self.cwd = cwd
        self.log_level = log_level
        self.env = env
        self.binary_path = shutil.which(binary)
        if not self.binary_path:
            raise FileNotFoundError(
                f"Could not find {binary}, please make sure it is
installed."
            )
```

Just like with Go, Python needs you to import packages.

Our main class will be called Tofu, since that's our default binary.

The working directory defines the code Terraform will run against.

We need to save the binary path to run the commands.

The log level will be used to set the verboseness of the logs.

Our users can set environment variables to pass to the commands.

This is a constructor, which is run when new instances are created.

The first argument of a method is always a reference to the instance itself.

We save these values to use later.

This exception is built in to Python.

Environment variables are optional.

The log level is optional, defaulting to ERROR.

If the binary path is not found, we raise an error.

We default to the tofu binary, but users can change it.

We find the binary path using shutil.

The working directory is optional, defaulting to the current directory.

Using our new client is simple. We have to import our library (which we're going to call `tofupy`) and create a new instance of our class, and we're good to go. At the moment, our class doesn't do anything, but we'll get to that.

Listing 11.2 Client usage

```
from tofupy import Tofu

workspace = Tofu(
```

We import our Tofu class from the tofypy package.

Create an instance of our class.

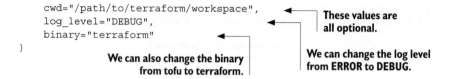

```
    cwd="/path/to/terraform/workspace",
    log_level="DEBUG",
    binary="terraform"
)
```

These values are all optional.

We can change the log level from ERROR to DEBUG.

We can also change the binary from tofu to terraform.

With our main entrypoint created, we can start running commands. As a quick refresher, running unix-style programs have several components:

- The command itself
- Standard output, which is how the program sends back data or messages
- Standard error, which the program can use for debugging purposes
- A return code, which is used to indicate that the command succeeded or to provide more detailed status responses

To make it easier for us to process commands, we're going to make a small little helper class. This class will collect all of the data from our command results and provide some extra methods (functions attached to classes) to make our lives easier. Specifically, we're going to make functions to parse any JSON or JSONL, as well as a method to easily throw a detailed error message when a command fails.

NOTE Python has a type of class known as a data class (https://realpython .com/python-data-classes/). These are used when the primary purpose of a class is to simply store data and share it around. We are going to be using data classes a lot, since the vast majority of what we're doing is simply parsing output from Terraform/OpenTofu.

Listing 11.3 Command results

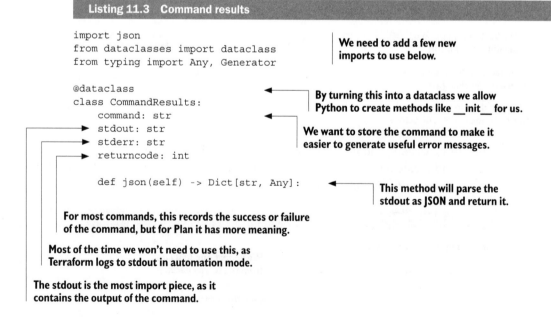

```
import json
from dataclasses import dataclass
from typing import Any, Generator


@dataclass
class CommandResults:
    command: str
    stdout: str
    stderr: str
    returncode: int

    def json(self) -> Dict[str, Any]:
```

We need to add a few new imports to use below.

By turning this into a dataclass we allow Python to create methods like __init__ for us.

We want to store the command to make it easier to generate useful error messages.

This method will parse the stdout as JSON and return it.

For most commands, this records the success or failure of the command, but for Plan it has more meaning.

Most of the time we won't need to use this, as Terraform logs to stdout in automation mode.

The stdout is the most import piece, as it contains the output of the command.

We parse each line as
JSON and yield it for use.

We split the stdout into lines,
since JSONL is line delimited.

This method will parse the
stdout as JSONL and return it.

```
        return json.loads(self.stdout)

    def jsonl(self) -> Generator[Dict[str, Any], None, None]:
        for line in self.stdout.splitlines():
            yield json.loads(line)

    def raise_error(self) -> None:
        try:
            for log in self.jsonl():
                if log.get("@level") == "error" and (
                    diagnostics := log.get("diagnostic")
                ):
                    raise RuntimeError(
                        f"Terraform command '{self.command}' failed:
{diagnostics.get('summary')}\n{diagnostics.get('detail')}",
                        diagnostics,
                    )
        except Exception:
            raise RuntimeError(
                f"Terraform command '{self.command}' failed: {self.stdout}."
            )
```

This helper command allows us to raise
an error with the command output.

Some errors come in
the form of JSONL, so
we parse it to improve
our messaging.

If we can't parse the logs as
JSONL, we raise a generic error.

Now that we have our `CommandResults` class, we can expand our initial `Tofu` client class with a new function to actually run commands against Terraform. Our goal here is to make it easy for us to call commands from other methods that we're going to create inside of our class.

On the outside, this function should look pretty simple. It should take a parameter for arguments we want to pass to the `tofu` command and a parameter to specify whether it should automatically raise an error when the command does not return a status code of 0.

Inside the function is a little bit more complicated. We have to convert any arguments passed in to strings, run our command, and send the results back. When constructing the command, we have to take our preferred binary, and then we need to pass in environment variables to control the behavior (`TF_IN_AUTOMATION` to tell Tofu not to expect any inputs, and `TF_LOG` to set our logging level) while also keeping the system- and user-provided environment variables. Finally, we need to wrap the responses up in a `CommandResults` class, raise any errors, and then return the results.

The good news is you only have to do this once; then the rest of your library can take advantage of it to call commands quickly and easily.

Listing 11.4 Command runner

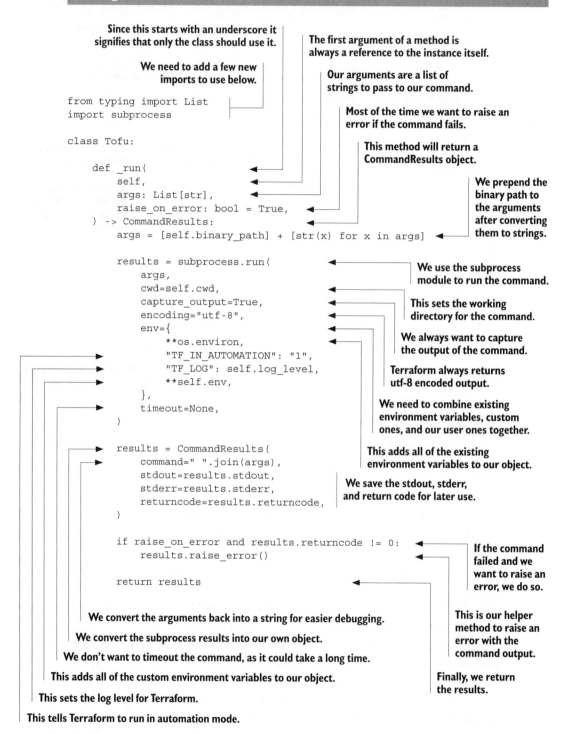

Since this starts with an underscore it signifies that only the class should use it.

We need to add a few new imports to use below.

The first argument of a method is always a reference to the instance itself.

Our arguments are a list of strings to pass to our command.

Most of the time we want to raise an error if the command fails.

This method will return a CommandResults object.

We prepend the binary path to the arguments after converting them to strings.

```python
from typing import List
import subprocess

class Tofu:

    def _run(
        self,
        args: List[str],
        raise_on_error: bool = True,
    ) -> CommandResults:
        args = [self.binary_path] + [str(x) for x in args]

        results = subprocess.run(
            args,
            cwd=self.cwd,
            capture_output=True,
            encoding="utf-8",
            env={
                **os.environ,
                "TF_IN_AUTOMATION": "1",
                "TF_LOG": self.log_level,
                **self.env,
            },
            timeout=None,
        )

        results = CommandResults(
            command=" ".join(args),
            stdout=results.stdout,
            stderr=results.stderr,
            returncode=results.returncode,
        )

        if raise_on_error and results.returncode != 0:
            results.raise_error()

        return results
```

We use the subprocess module to run the command.

This sets the working directory for the command.

We always want to capture the output of the command.

Terraform always returns utf-8 encoded output.

We need to combine existing environment variables, custom ones, and our user ones together.

This adds all of the existing environment variables to our object.

We save the stdout, stderr, and return code for later use.

If the command failed and we want to raise an error, we do so.

This is our helper method to raise an error with the command output.

Finally, we return the results.

We convert the arguments back into a string for easier debugging.

We convert the subprocess results into our own object.

We don't want to timeout the command, as it could take a long time.

This adds all of the custom environment variables to our object.

This sets the log level for Terraform.

This tells Terraform to run in automation mode.

With that we can finally call commands. To take advantage of that, let's expand our constructor to confirm that we're using a version of Terraform that we can actually support. We're going to do this by running the version command and parsing the results. Since v1 is the current version of Terraform, that's the one our wrapper is going to be designed for; we want to confirm our binary is also v1. If we pass the arguments version and -json to our _run function, it should return the results of Tofu version -json to us.

Listing 11.5 Terraform version

```
class Tofu:
    version: str          │ We can store the version
    platform: str         │ and platform for our users.

    def __init__(
        self,
        cwd: str = os.getcwd(),
        binary: str = "tofu",
        log_level: str = "ERROR",
        env: Dict[str, str] = {},
    ):
        'Truncated for brevity'

        results = self._run(["version", "-json"])
        version = results.json()
        self.version = version["terraform_version"]
        self.platform = version["platform"]

        ver_split = self.version.split(".")
        ver_major = int(ver_split[0])

        if ver_major != 1:
            raise RuntimeError(
                f"TofuPy only works with major version 1, found
{self.version}."
            )
```

We run the version command, making sure to pass the -json flag. This will raise an error if it fails.

We parse the JSON output of the version command.

We save the version and platform for later use.

We split the version string into its major and minor parts.

We convert the major version to an integer for comparison.

If the major version is not 1, we raise an error.

For the rest of our wrapper, we will continue to use the _run method and Command-Results to allow our class to run.

11.1.3 *Init*

The first method we need to add is also the first method most people run when using Terraform: the init command. When making our method, we should consider common use cases and make them easier for our developers. For instance, users may want to pass a backend configuration file or disable the backend altogether.

Terraform and OpenTofu evolve fairly regularly though, and we don't want to lock people out of options that we haven't considered. For that reason, most of our functions will have an `extra_args` parameter that developers can use to pass in any additional arguments or flags that they want.

Listing 11.6   Terraform `init`

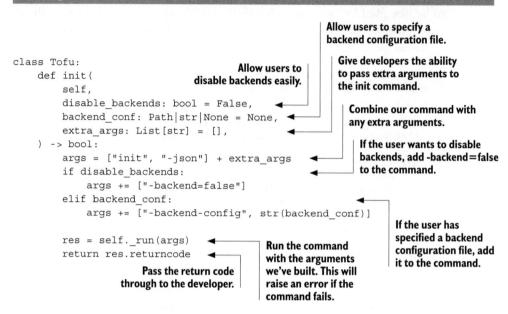

```python
class Tofu:
    def init(
        self,
        disable_backends: bool = False,
        backend_conf: Path|str|None = None,
        extra_args: List[str] = [],
    ) -> bool:
        args = ["init", "-json"] + extra_args
        if disable_backends:
            args += ["-backend=false"]
        elif backend_conf:
            args += ["-backend-config", str(backend_conf)]

        res = self._run(args)
        return res.returncode
```

Allow users to specify a backend configuration file.

Give developers the ability to pass extra arguments to the init command.

Allow users to disable backends easily.

Combine our command with any extra arguments.

If the user wants to disable backends, add -backend=false to the command.

If the user has specified a backend configuration file, add it to the command.

Run the command with the arguments we've built. This will raise an error if the command fails.

Pass the return code through to the developer.

Now that it's programmed, we need to confirm that it runs, and the best way to do that is with a test.

11.1.4 A detour into testing

Up until this point we didn't have anything to test. All of our previous work before the `init` function was preparation for creating command wrappers, which we now have. Now we just need to configure our test suite so we can go forward.

The first thing we need is a module we can test with. Everything in Terraform is about working with modules, and our commands are going to need a clean module to run. This module should have the basic components of any Terraform project (a data source, a resource, an input variable, output, and a check so we can use it for most of our testing). At the same time, we don't want a module that actually costs money to run or takes a lot of time. This is where our old friend `terraform_data` comes in handy.

Listing 11.7   Test module

```
variable "website" {
  type        = string
  description = "The url to pull data from."
  default     = "https://catfact.ninja/fact"
}
```

We need an input for testing input functionality.

This is a fun little API that returns random cat facts.

```
data "http" "site" {
  url = var.website
```
We use the **HTTP** data source to pull data from a website. Our default is a cat fact API.

```
  request_headers = {
    Accept = "application/json"
  }
}
```
This is our resource that does nothing, which is great for testing.

```
resource "terraform_data" "main" {
  input = data.http.site.response_body
}
```
We pass the attribute to our resource so there's a dependency to test.

```
check "example" {
  assert {
```
This puts a check in our state file for testing.

```
    condition     = length(terraform_data.main.output) > 0
    error_message = "HTTP lookup has content."
  }
```
Since this is just a test module the assertions don't really matter, the point is they exist.

```
  assert {
    condition     = data.http.site.status_code >= 200 &&
➥data.http.site.status_code < 300
    error_message = "HTTP lookup returned a success status code."
  }
}
```
Finally, we have an output so we can test that functionality as well.

```
output "site_data" {
  value = terraform_data.main.output
}
```
The output comes from our resource so it won't be known during plan.

We're going to place that module inside of the `tests/module` directory. Since we want each test to run independently, we're only going to use this folder as a template. We're going to create what's known as a fixture (a feature of `pytest` that allows us to generate environments for testing) to copy this module into a temporary directory for every test we run. While we're making our fixture, we'll also create a fixture that initializes the module so we don't have to manually do that for every test. Our fixtures will live in `tests/conftest.py`. To let Python know it's okay to look in that folder for code, add an empty file in `tests/__init__.py`.

Listing 11.8 Test fixtures

```
import shutil
from pathlib import Path

import pytest
from tofupy import Tofu
```
Our fixture generates a fresh root-level model by using another fixture, tmpdir, to get a temporary directory.

This marks the function as a fixture.

We make a copy of our module directory in the temporary directory.

```
@pytest.fixture
def tofu_rlm(tmpdir):
    shutil.copytree(
        Path(__file__).parent.absolute() / "module",
        tmpdir,
```
This is the path to our module on disk.

This is the path to the temporary directory.

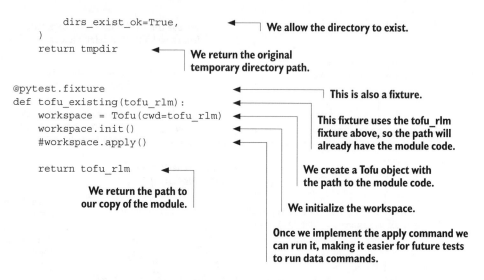

```
        dirs_exist_ok=True,        We allow the directory to exist.
    )
    return tmpdir                  We return the original
                                   temporary directory path.

@pytest.fixture                    This is also a fixture.
def tofu_existing(tofu_rlm):
    workspace = Tofu(cwd=tofu_rlm)    This fixture uses the tofu_rlm
    workspace.init()                  fixture above, so the path will
    #workspace.apply()                already have the module code.

    return tofu_rlm                We create a Tofu object with
                                   the path to the module code.
        We return the path to
        our copy of the module.    We initialize the workspace.

                                   Once we implement the apply command we
                                   can run it, making it easier for future tests
                                   to run data commands.
```

Now we can write our first test. In `tests/test_init.py`, we'll create a test that uses our `tofu_existing` fixture to create and initialize a module and then confirms that the `.terraform` directory exists.

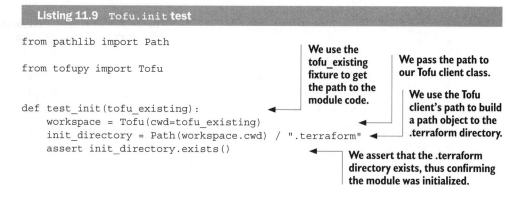

Listing 11.9   `Tofu.init` **test**

```
from pathlib import Path

from tofupy import Tofu                 We use the           We pass the path to
                                        tofu_existing        our Tofu client class.
                                        fixture to get
                                        the path to the      We use the Tofu
                                        module code.         client's path to build
def test_init(tofu_existing):                                a path object to the
    workspace = Tofu(cwd=tofu_existing)                      .terraform directory.
    init_directory = Path(workspace.cwd) / ".terraform"
    assert init_directory.exists()      We assert that the .terraform
                                        directory exists, thus confirming
                                        the module was initialized.
```

We'll be able to use our fixtures for all of our tests going forward. To run our tests, we should run the command `pytest` from our project directory.

11.1.5 *Validating*

Our next command to wrap is the `tofu validate` command. Before we begin, let's run this command and see the output. If you make a copy of your test workspace and run `terraform validate` without first initializing it, you get a JSON string that includes an error.

> **TIP**   Running commands is a great way to see the data structure, but it can sometimes give you an incomplete picture and requires you to create Terraform code for a variety of scenarios to get all the possible iterations. The documentation for each data structure is the ideal place to look.

Listing 11.10 Validate JSON example

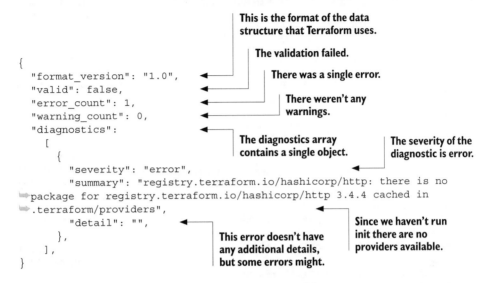

```
{
    "format_version": "1.0",          ◄────  This is the format of the data
    "valid": false,                          structure that Terraform uses.
    "error_count": 1,                ◄────  The validation failed.
    "warning_count": 0,              ◄────  There was a single error.
    "diagnostics":                   ◄────  There weren't any
        [                                    warnings.
            {                               The diagnostics array          The severity of the
                "severity": "error",        contains a single object.      diagnostic is error.
                "summary": "registry.terraform.io/hashicorp/http: there is no
package for registry.terraform.io/hashicorp/http 3.4.4 cached in
.terraform/providers",
                "detail": "",        ◄────                         Since we haven't run
            },                            This error doesn't have   init there are no
        ],                                any additional details,   providers available.
}                                         but some errors might.
```

The structure is pretty simple. We have the `format_version`, which describes the version of the data structure used and is on most JSON messages from Terraform. In our example, we purposely did not initialize the workspace so we could see an error with the `validation` command. As a result, in the JSON response we can see that our test code is not currently `valid` as that field is set to `false`. Since there were errors in the code that we're running, we can see the number of errors and warnings. The `diagnostics` list contains objects with much more detail on what those errors are, in our case telling us that we need to run the `init` command to download providers.

We need to map these fields to objects in our language. In this case, we need two objects: `Validate` and `Diagnostic`. We're going to use a `dataclass`, just like we did with our `CommandResult`. We want to keep our logic for parsing the data structure near to our classes, as it makes maintenance easier, so we're going to pass through the full data we get to the class and allow it to process that data into the appropriate fields.

This can get a bit recursive. One object may have another object inside of it, like how our validate class will have a list of diagnostic items inside of it. When this happens, we have to convert the data from our high-level object into the lower-level types. We can use the same technique of passing the data through and allowing the child object to fill out its own fields.

Listing 11.11 Validate and diagnostic structures

```
from dataclasses import field

@dataclass
class Diagnostic:
    # Format: https://developer.hashicorp.com/terraform/cli/commands/
```

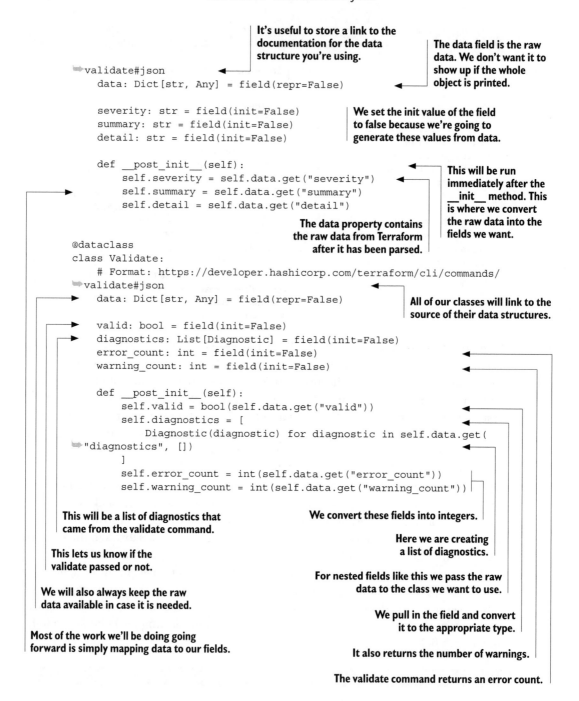

It's useful to store a link to the documentation for the data structure you're using.

The data field is the raw data. We don't want it to show up if the whole object is printed.

```
validate#json
    data: Dict[str, Any] = field(repr=False)

    severity: str = field(init=False)
    summary: str = field(init=False)
    detail: str = field(init=False)
```

We set the init value of the field to false because we're going to generate these values from data.

```
    def __post_init__(self):
        self.severity = self.data.get("severity")
        self.summary = self.data.get("summary")
        self.detail = self.data.get("detail")
```

This will be run immediately after the __init__ method. This is where we convert the raw data into the fields we want.

The data property contains the raw data from Terraform after it has been parsed.

```
@dataclass
class Validate:
    # Format: https://developer.hashicorp.com/terraform/cli/commands/
validate#json
    data: Dict[str, Any] = field(repr=False)

    valid: bool = field(init=False)
    diagnostics: List[Diagnostic] = field(init=False)
    error_count: int = field(init=False)
    warning_count: int = field(init=False)

    def __post_init__(self):
        self.valid = bool(self.data.get("valid"))
        self.diagnostics = [
            Diagnostic(diagnostic) for diagnostic in self.data.get(
"diagnostics", [])
        ]
        self.error_count = int(self.data.get("error_count"))
        self.warning_count = int(self.data.get("warning_count"))
```

All of our classes will link to the source of their data structures.

This will be a list of diagnostics that came from the validate command.

This lets us know if the validate passed or not.

We will also always keep the raw data available in case it is needed.

Most of the work we'll be doing going forward is simply mapping data to our fields.

We convert these fields into integers.

Here we are creating a list of diagnostics.

For nested fields like this we pass the raw data to the class we want to use.

We pull in the field and convert it to the appropriate type.

It also returns the number of warnings.

The validate command returns an error count.

That was the hard part. Since all of the logic lives inside of the `dataclasses` we created, our actual `validate` function ends up being very small. One thing to note is that in this case we don't want our `_run` function to raise an error, since a failed validation will return 1 instead of 0. In this case, our command didn't fail, but the configuration was invalid, so we want to return the normal `Validate` object.

Listing 11.12 `Tofu.validate` **method**

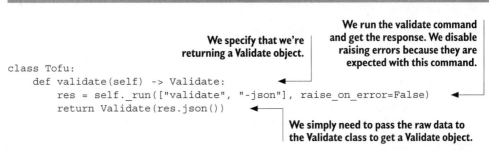

We specify that we're returning a Validate object.

We run the validate command and get the response. We disable raising errors because they are expected with this command.

```
class Tofu:
    def validate(self) -> Validate:
        res = self._run(["validate", "-json"], raise_on_error=False)
        return Validate(res.json())
```

We simply need to pass the raw data to the Validate class to get a Validate object.

The final step is to write some tests. In this case, we need two tests: one for when the validate command succeeds and another when it fails so we can confirm that our diagnostic objects are properly created. We're going to do the same thing we did earlier to generate an invalid configuration and run our command on a module that had not been initialized. Then we'll test against one that has been initialized and confirm that returns no errors.

Listing 11.13 `Tofu.validate` **tests**

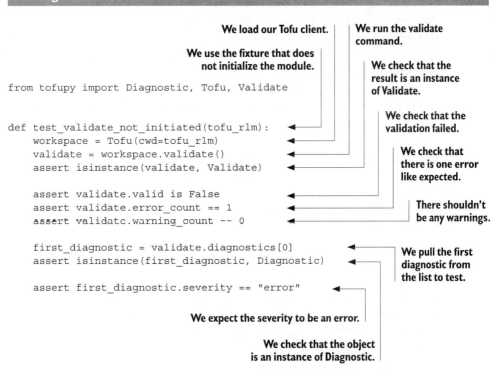

We load our Tofu client.

We use the fixture that does not initialize the module.

We run the validate command.

We check that the result is an instance of Validate.

We check that the validation failed.

We check that there is one error like expected.

There shouldn't be any warnings.

We pull the first diagnostic from the list to test.

```
from tofupy import Diagnostic, Tofu, Validate


def test_validate_not_initiated(tofu_rlm):
    workspace = Tofu(cwd=tofu_rlm)
    validate = workspace.validate()
    assert isinstance(validate, Validate)

    assert validate.valid is False
    assert validate.error_count == 1
    assert validate.warning_count == 0

    first_diagnostic = validate.diagnostics[0]
    assert isinstance(first_diagnostic, Diagnostic)

    assert first_diagnostic.severity == "error"
```

We expect the severity to be an error.

We check that the object is an instance of Diagnostic.

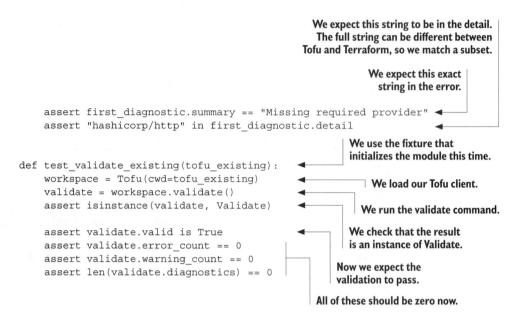

We expect this string to be in the detail.
The full string can be different between
Tofu and Terraform, so we match a subset.

We expect this exact
string in the error.

```
assert first_diagnostic.summary == "Missing required provider"
assert "hashicorp/http" in first_diagnostic.detail
```

We use the fixture that
initializes the module this time.

```
def test_validate_existing(tofu_existing):
    workspace = Tofu(cwd=tofu_existing)
    validate = workspace.validate()
    assert isinstance(validate, Validate)

    assert validate.valid is True
    assert validate.error_count == 0
    assert validate.warning_count == 0
    assert len(validate.diagnostics) == 0
```

We load our Tofu client.

We run the validate command.

We check that the result
is an instance of Validate.

Now we expect the
validation to pass.

All of these should be zero now.

With that, our validate wrapper is complete. Between the `init` and `validate` functions, we now can do something useful with our library!

11.1.6 *State*

Programmatically accessing state has many benefits. It allows developers to build tools that analyze existing infrastructure for a variety of reasons, such as finding security vulnerabilities, estimating pricing, validating compliance, or comparing different state versions to see what changed. That said, state is also one of the more complicated data structures we have to work with.

There are two ways to read state from Terraform and OpenTofu, each with their own downsides. In chapter 6, we used `terraform state pull` to view the state for a specific project. This showed us the internal representation that Terraform uses for state. This is the most complete data structure we can find for looking at state, but it also isn't as well documented and is not considered part of the machine-readable UI.

The other command we can use is the `terraform show` command, which allows us to read plans or state files and output them in JSON. The output of this command is defined in the machine-readable UI, which makes it much easier for us to work with, and the data structure that comes out of it is nested in the plan data structure so we will need to parse it no matter what. The problem is that it isn't a complete representation: it misses the `serial` and `lineage` fields. This command also expects the state file to exist as an actual file (including with the appropriate file extension, `tfstate`). This means we have to run `terraform state pull` before we can run `terraform show`.

Since we have to run both commands anyway, we can combine the data from our `terraform state pull` with the output of `terraform show` to generate a more complete picture. This really just means adding two additional fields (`lineage` and `serial`) to our data structure. These fields should be optional, since we want to reuse the state data model when we build out plan representation.

This makes our logic a bit more complicated, but it's still very straightforward. We run `terraform state pull` and save the results to a temporary file and then run `terraform show` on that file. We then pass the entire output of `terraform show` to our state model, alongside the two pieces of missing data.

Listing 11.14 `Tofu.state` **method**

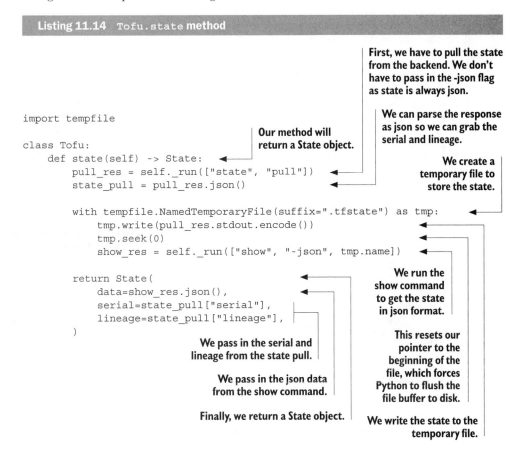

```
import tempfile

class Tofu:
    def state(self) -> State:
        pull_res = self._run(["state", "pull"])
        state_pull = pull_res.json()

        with tempfile.NamedTemporaryFile(suffix=".tfstate") as tmp:
            tmp.write(pull_res.stdout.encode())
            tmp.seek(0)
            show_res = self._run(["show", "-json", tmp.name])

        return State(
            data=show_res.json(),
            serial=state_pull["serial"],
            lineage=state_pull["lineage"],
        )
```

First, we have to pull the state from the backend. We don't have to pass in the -json flag as state is always json.

Our method will return a State object.

We can parse the response as json so we can grab the serial and lineage.

We create a temporary file to store the state.

We run the show command to get the state in json format.

This resets our pointer to the beginning of the file, which forces Python to flush the file buffer to disk.

We write the state to the temporary file.

We pass in the serial and lineage from the state pull.

We pass in the json data from the show command.

Finally, we return a State object.

Just like our previous wrappers, we rely on our data model to interpret the data that came back from the command. The state has the fields we've already discussed, along with a Terraform version. The two most important fields are `root_module` and `outputs`, each of which has its own data structure. When you create the `State` class, make sure to put it toward the bottom of your file, as it depends on the `Output` and `Resources` classes and needs those defined first.

Listing 11.15 State data structure

```
@dataclass
class State:
    # Format: https://developer.hashicorp.com/terraform/internals/
```

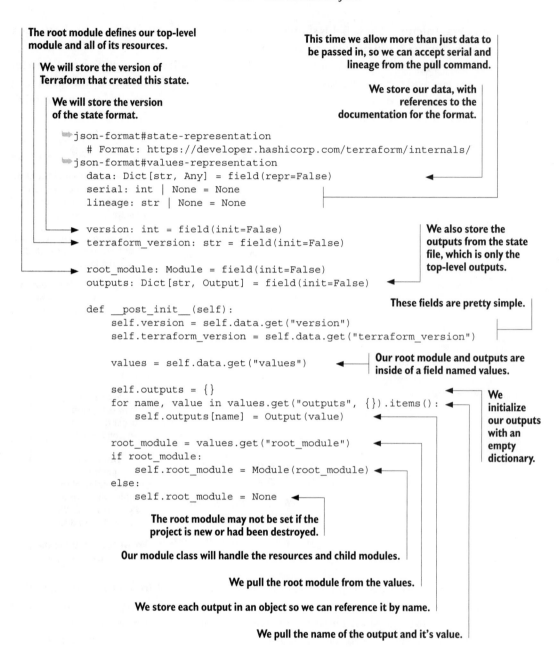

The root module defines our top-level module and all of its resources.

This time we allow more than just data to be passed in, so we can accept serial and lineage from the pull command.

We will store the version of Terraform that created this state.

We store our data, with references to the documentation for the format.

We will store the version of the state format.

```
json-format#state-representation
    # Format: https://developer.hashicorp.com/terraform/internals/
json-format#values-representation
    data: Dict[str, Any] = field(repr=False)
    serial: int | None = None
    lineage: str | None = None

    version: int = field(init=False)
    terraform_version: str = field(init=False)

    root_module: Module = field(init=False)
    outputs: Dict[str, Output] = field(init=False)

    def __post_init__(self):
        self.version = self.data.get("version")
        self.terraform_version = self.data.get("terraform_version")

        values = self.data.get("values")

        self.outputs = {}
        for name, value in values.get("outputs", {}).items():
            self.outputs[name] = Output(value)

        root_module = values.get("root_module")
        if root_module:
            self.root_module = Module(root_module)
        else:
            self.root_module = None
```

We also store the outputs from the state file, which is only the top-level outputs.

These fields are pretty simple.

Our root module and outputs are inside of a field named values.

We initialize our outputs with an empty dictionary.

The root module may not be set if the project is new or had been destroyed.

Our module class will handle the resources and child modules.

We pull the root module from the values.

We store each output in an object so we can reference it by name.

We pull the name of the output and it's value.

The output data structure is pretty simple. It has a name, a value, and a flag to mark the data as sensitive or not.

Listing 11.16 Output data structure

```
@dataclass
class Output:
```

```
    # Format: https://developer.hashicorp.com/terraform/internals/
⮕json-format#values-representation
    data: Dict[str, Any] = field(repr=False)

    value: Any = field(init=False)
    type: str = field(init=False)
    sensitive: bool = field(init=False)

    def __post_init__(self):
        self.value = self.data.get("value")
        self.type = self.data.get("type")
        self.sensitive = self.data.get("sensitive")
```

The value of the output, which can be of any type.

The type of the output.

Whether the output is sensitive or not.

This is perhaps the simplest class we have to create.

The module data structure is a recursive data structure: one of its fields represents the child modules, which in turn can have their own child modules. We can work with those the same way we do with the top-level module and simply pass the data in, allowing each module to build the objects for its children modules.

Listing 11.17   Module data structure

Modules contain child modules, making this a recursive structure.

We will store the resources in a dictionary, keyed by their address.

The Terraform address of the module.

```
@dataclass
class Module:
    # Format: https://developer.hashicorp.com/terraform/internals/
⮕json-format#values-representation
    data: Dict[str, Any] = field(repr=False)

    address: str | None = field(init=False)
    resources: Dict[str, Resource] = field(init=False)
    child_modules: List[Dict[str, "Module"]] = field(init=False)

    def __post_init__(self):
        self.address = self.data.get("address")

        self.resources = {}
        for resource in self.data.get("resources", []):
            self.resources[resource.get("address")] = Resource(resource)

        self.child_modules = {}
        for child_module in self.data.get("child_modules", []):
            self.child_modules[child_module.get("address")] =
⮕Module(child_module)
```

Initialize the resources dictionary.

Iterate over the resources in the module.

Store each child module in the dictionary.

Iterate over the child modules in the module.

Initialize the child modules dictionary.

Store each resource in the dictionary.

Modules also have resources, which of course are the entire point of using Terraform. Resources have a lot of fields but are otherwise pretty simple, with no nesting.

Listing 11.18   Resource data structure

```
@dataclass
class Resource:
    # Format: https://developer.hashicorp.com/terraform/internals/
    json-format#values-representation
    data: Dict[str, Any] = field(repr=False)

    address: str = field(init=False)
    mode: str = field(init=False)
    type: str = field(init=False)
    name: str = field(init=False)
    index: int | None = field(init=False)
    schema_version: int = field(init=False)
    provider_name: str = field(init=False)
    values: Dict[str, Any] = field(init=False)
    sensitive_values: Dict[str, bool] = field(init=False)

    def __post_init__(self):
        self.address = self.data.get("address")
        self.mode = self.data.get("mode")
        self.type = self.data.get("type")
        self.name = self.data.get("name")
        self.index = self.data.get("index")
        self.schema_version = self.data.get("schema_version")
        self.provider_name = self.data.get("provider_name")
        self.values = self.data.get("values")
```

> Resources have a lot of fields but they are all pretty straightforward.

> Resources are a matter of simply mapping fields to values.

With that we have the ability to represent the state inside of our language. From there we can go on to build tools to analyze or validate the state of our project.

11.1.7   *Apply*

So far, everything we've done relies on commands that run quickly and return a full JSON object. The `apply` command is a bit different though. It can run over long periods of time and output a lot of different messages. When using the `-json` flag, these results come in with a full JSON object on each line. These lines each have five standard fields, plus additional fields depending on the type:

- `@level`—This is normally `info` but can be `error` or `warn` when something goes wrong.
- `@message`—This is a human-readable message.
- `@module`—This will be either `tofu.ui` or `terraform.ui` depending on our engine.
- `@timestamp`—The time the message was sent out.
- `type`—The most important field, the type defines what other optional fields are available. We'll talk about this field in a bit.

In our next example, we reformat the event lines to make it easier to see them, but when you're actually running an `apply` or `plan`, each JSON object will only be a single line.

Listing 11.19   Event lines

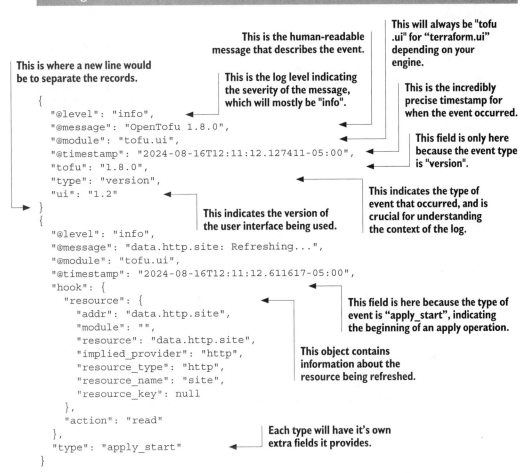

The first thing we need to do is create a new function to wrap our commands in. The existing one works great as long as we want all of our results at once, but if we want the results as they come in, we need to be able to process them line by line. We're going to use a language feature called generators, which allows our function to `yield` a single line at a time for our caller function to iterate over.

Listing 11.20   Streaming process results

```
class Tofu:
    def _run_stream(
        self,
```

This function yields events from Terraform commands that return JSONL.

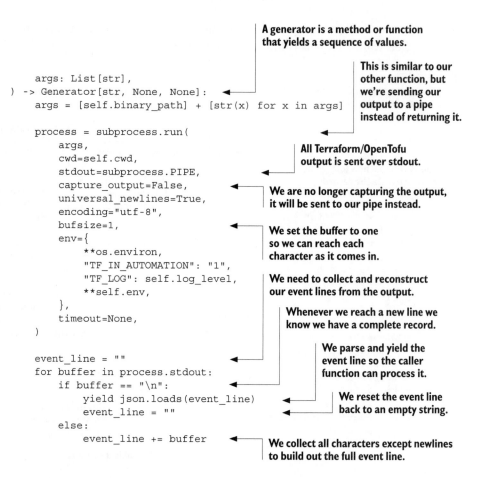

A generator is a method or function that yields a sequence of values.

```
        args: List[str],
    ) -> Generator[str, None, None]:
        args = [self.binary_path] + [str(x) for x in args]

        process = subprocess.run(
            args,
            cwd=self.cwd,
            stdout=subprocess.PIPE,
            capture_output=False,
            universal_newlines=True,
            encoding="utf-8",
            bufsize=1,
            env={
                **os.environ,
                "TF_IN_AUTOMATION": "1",
                "TF_LOG": self.log_level,
                **self.env,
            },
            timeout=None,
        )

        event_line = ""
        for buffer in process.stdout:
            if buffer == "\n":
                yield json.loads(event_line)
                event_line = ""
            else:
                event_line += buffer
```

This is similar to our other function, but we're sending our output to a pipe instead of returning it.

All Terraform/OpenTofu output is sent over stdout.

We are no longer capturing the output, it will be sent to our pipe instead.

We set the buffer to one so we can reach each character as it comes in.

We need to collect and reconstruct our event lines from the output.

Whenever we reach a new line we know we have a complete record.

We parse and yield the event line so the caller function can process it.

We reset the event line back to an empty string.

We collect all characters except newlines to build out the full event line.

Now we can write our `apply` method. We're going to add parameters to our method for common arguments, such as a plan file if one exists or variables to pass through if we expect to also run a `plan`. We're also going to have a high-level data struct that we return at the end of our method, just like we have with the others.

Where we differ is by adding a new parameter, `event_handlers`, which expects user-provided functions. This will allow users of our library to trigger events based off the responses from OpenTofu as those messages come in, rather than waiting until the entire process has finished. This can be used, for instance, to stream the results to a logging server or a user console as they come in.

Listing 11.21   `Tofu.apply`

```
from typing import Callable

class Tofu:
    def apply(
        self,
        plan_file: Path | None = None,
```

If we have a plan file, we add it to the args.

We always want auto-approve and JSON output.

```python
    variables: Dict[str, str] = {},
    destroy=False,
    event_handlers: Dict[str, Callable[[Dict[str, Any]], bool]] = {},
    extra_args: List[str] = [],
) -> ApplyLog:
    args = ["apply", "-auto-approve", "-json"] + extra_args
    if plan_file:
        args += [str(plan_file)]

    for key, value in variables.items():
        args += ["-var", f"{key}={value}"]

    if destroy:
        args += ["-destroy"]

    output = []
    for event in self._run_stream(args):
        output.append(event)
        if event["type"] in event_handlers:
            event_handlers[event["type"]](event)
        if "all" in event_handlers:
            event_handlers["all"](event)

    return ApplyLog(output)
```

We convert the plan file to a string.

Convert any variables into arguments.

If destroy is set to true, we add the -destroy flag.

We need to collect the events to pass to the ApplyLog.

We catch the yielded events from the _run_ stream method.

We append each event to our output list to pass to the ApplyLog.

Check if we have a handler for the event type.

If we have a handler for the event type, we call it.

We pass our list of events to the ApplyLog to return.

If we have a handler for all, then we call it on every event.

Check if we have a handler for all event types.

Although users can build their own handlers for real-time responses, there will also be cases where it's useful to have a high-level object in response. For that we're going to build a data structure that represents the apply, but instead of having a simple object we're going to have to construct it from our event logs. We do this by iterating over the logs to look for specific types and then saving the data from those types in our object.

There are a few dozen message types, but they all follow the same pattern. You can find the message type by looking at the type field and then mapping that back to the machine-readable UI documentation for the type. Once you have that, you can map the unique fields to your Python code.

Here we focus on the three types that are most commonly considered: version, outputs, and change_summary. From the change summary, we can retrieve the number of items changed, removed, imported, or added as well as the type of operation. We'll also look for diagnostic messages, which indicate an error. We already built the

Diagnostics class when we wrote the method for validate and the Outputs class when we wrote our state wrapper, so we can reuse those here.

Both apply and plan use a very similar structure for streaming logs, so we'll create a parent class to store the logic for both.

Listing 11.22 ApplyLog **data structure**

```
@dataclass
class StreamLog:
    # Format: https://developer.hashicorp.com/terraform/internals/
    machine-readable-ui
    data: List[Dict[str, Any]] = field(repr=False)

    terraform_version: str = field(init=False)

    outputs: Dict[str, Output] = field(init=False)
    added: int = field(init=False)
    changed: int = field(init=False)
    removed: int = field(init=False)
    imported: int = field(init=False)
    operation: str = field(init=False)

    errors: List[Diagnostic] = field(init=False)
    warnings: List[Diagnostic] = field(init=False)

    def __post_init__(self):
        self.outputs = {}
        self.errors = []
        self.warnings = []

        for line in self.data:
            if line.get("type") == "version":
                self.terraform_version = line.get("version")
                continue

            if line.get("type") == "diagnostic":
                if line.get("@level") == "error":
                    self.errors.append(Diagnostic(line))
                if line.get("@level") == "warning":
                    self.warnings.append(Diagnostic(line))
                continue

            if line.get("type") == "outputs":
                for key, value in line.get("outputs").items():
                    self.outputs[key] = Output(value)
                continue

            if line.get("type") == "change_summary":
```

This comes from event types of "version".

These come from event types of "outputs".

These come from event types of "change_summary".

We reuse the Diagnostic class to store errors and warnings.

Iterate over every event log.

We need to initialize our objects and lists.

If we have a log of the version type, we pull the version out and save it.

Logs only have one type so we can restart our loop.

If we have a diagnostic log, we check for errors and warnings.

If we have an outputs log, we pull the outputs out of it.

We pull out each key value pair.

We append the warning to our warnings list.

The change_summary is one of the last events to output.

We create an Output object for each output.

We append the error to our errors list.

```
        changes = line.get("changes", {})
        self.added = changes.get("add", 0)
        self.changed = changes.get("change", 0)
        self.removed = changes.get("remove", 0)
        self.imported = changes.get("import", 0)
        self.operation = changes.get("operation", None)
        continue
```

> We can pull all the values out and save them.

> We create a new class that inherits from StreamLog.

```
class ApplyLog(StreamLog):
    pass
```

> This signifies that we are not adding any new functionality to the ApplyLog class.

While we covered the most commonly used types, the event log has a lot of other types available.

11.1.8 Plan

Writing a `plan` wrapper is the most complicated component we need to build. Just like our `state` method, we have to run `terraform show` against a `plan` file to actually build the `plan` method, which means running more than one command. Running a plan is also a longer-running operation, which means that we have to process event log messages like we did with the `apply` method. Finally, the data structure for a plan is one of the more complex structures to deal with (although we're already written many of the components).

While it may be complicated, we can at least build on top of what we have already written. To start with, our `PlanLog` can look just the like the `ApplyLog` (in fact, since `apply` can also run a plan, when a `plan` file isn't provided, the apply log will often contain components from a plan) we wrote, which is why we gave both classes a common parent to contain all of our logic. That way, when we add more supported event types, both data structures will get updated. That leaves us with a very boring `PlanLog`, but keeping them as different structures will help anyone using our library distinguish between the two.

Listing 11.23 `PlanLog` **data structure**

```
class PlanLog(StreamLog):
    pass
```

> We extend the StreamLog class to create our PlanLog class.

```
class ApplyLog(PlanLog):
    pass
```

> Since all apply logs are also plan logs, we can extend PlanLog to create ApplyLog.

Our actual `plan` method is going to look similar to our `apply` method. We need to allow variables, and we can optionally allow a user to specify where to save the `plan` file so it can be passed to future steps. However, if we want to return the actual plan data structure (as opposed to just the log), we need to make sure to save a copy of the plan even if the user doesn't specify a place to do so, since we need to pass that file to `terraform show` to get the full plan.

Listing 11.24 `Tofu.plan`

Plan files have to have the tfplan extension.

If our users don't specify a plan_file, we create a temporary directory to create one in.

We always return a PlanLog and optionally a Plan.

```python
from typing import Tuple

class Tofu:
    def plan(
        self,
        variables: Dict[str, str] = {},
        plan_file: Path | None = None,
        event_handlers: Dict[str, Callable[[Dict[str, Any]], bool]] = {},
        extra_args: List[str] = [],
    ) -> Tuple[PlanLog, Plan | None]:
        try:
            temp_dir = None
            if not plan_file:
                temp_dir = tempfile.TemporaryDirectory()
                plan_file = Path(temp_dir.name) / "plan.tfplan"

            args = ["plan", "-json", "-out", str(plan_file)] + extra_args

            for key, value in variables.items():
                args += ["-var", f"{key}={value}"]

            output = []
            for event in self._run_stream(args):
                output.append(event)
                if event["type"] in event_handlers:
                    event_handlers[event["type"]](event)
                if "all" in event_handlers:
                    event_handlers["all"](event)

            plan_log = PlanLog(output)

            if plan_file.exists():
                show_res = self._run(["show", "-json", plan_file])
                return plan_log, Plan(show_res.json())

            return plan_log, None

        finally:
            if temp_dir:
                temp_dir.cleanup()
```

We build our command-line arguments.

We add the variables to the command-line arguments.

Handlers also function the same way as apply.

Plan files are only created with successful plans, so there may not be one.

After our code finishes we clean up any temporary directories we created.

We create our PlanLog from the output.

If there is no plan file, we return None for the Plan.

Just like with apply, we save the output for our PlanLog.

We return the PlanLog and the Plan.

We run the show command to get the Plan.

The plan data structure has a lot of fields. These are split between metadata about the plan itself, a copy of the state used to generate the plan, multiple lists of changes, and an example of the planned root module. We've already defined a lot of these classes: `module`, `output`, and `state` already exist. Everything else is either a change, which we'll get to in a moment, or a simple data type that we can directly define.

Listing 11.25 Plan data structure attributes

```
@dataclass
class Plan:
    # Format: https://developer.hashicorp.com/terraform/internals/
    json-format#plan-representation
    data: Dict[str, Any] = field(repr=False)

    resource_changes: Dict[str, ChangeContainer] = field(init=False)
    resource_drift: Dict[str, ChangeContainer] = field(init=False)
    output_changes: Dict[str, Change] = field(init=False)
    prior_state: State = field(init=False)

    planned_root_module: Module = field(init=False)
    planned_outputs: Dict[str, Output] = field(init=False)
    relevant_attributes: Dict[str, List[str]] = field(init=False)

    format_version: str = field(init=False)
    terraform_version: str = field(init=False)
    applyable: bool = field(init=False)
    complete: bool = field(init=False)
    errored: bool = field(init=False)
    variables: Dict[str, Any] = field(init=False)
```

Plans contain Changes, ChangeContainers, and States.

These are attributes which change or affect the plan.

Any known outputs from the plan.

These fields are all metadata about the plan.

This is what Terraform plans to do.

Now that we have our attributes configured, we can create the data processing method to populate them.

Listing 11.26 Plan data structure function

```
@dataclass
class Plan:

    def __post_init__(self):
        self.format_version = self.data.get("format_version")
        self.terraform_version = self.data.get("terraform_version")
        self.applyable = self.data.get("applyable")
        self.complete = self.data.get("complete")
        self.errored = self.data.get("errored")

        self.variables = {}
        for variable_key, variable_data in self.data.get("variables",
        {}).items():
            self.variables[variable_key] = variable_data["value"]
```

Resource changes are the
primary reason to run Terraform.

We can reuse our State object for this,
although it will be missing lineage and serial.

The Module structure is recursive
and contains a lot of data.

```
        planned_values = self.data.get("planned_values", {})
        self.planned_root_module = Module(planned_values.get(
"root_module"))

        self.planned_outputs = {}
        for output_name, output_data in self.data.get("output_changes",
{}).items():
            self.planned_outputs[output_name] = Output(output_data)

        self.relevant_attributes = {}
        for attribute in self.data.get("relevant_attributes", []):
            self.relevant_attributes[attribute["resource"]] =
attribute["attribute"]

        self.prior_state = State(self.data.get("prior_state"))

        self.resource_changes = {}
        for resource_change in self.data.get("resource_changes", []):
            address = resource_change.get("address")
            self.resource_changes[address] = ChangeContainer(
resource_change)

        self.resource_drift = {}
        for resource_drift in self.data.get("resource_drift", []):
            address = resource_drift.get("address")
            self.resource_drift[address] = ChangeContainer(resource_drift)

        self.output_changes = {}
        for output_name, output_change in self.data.get("output_changes",
{}).items():
            self.output_changes[output_name] = Change(output_change)
```

Unlike other changes, output changes
are not wrapped in ChangeContainers.

Resource drift is a separate concept from resource
changes, but are common in refresh-only plans.

Now we need to review changes. We have multiple fields that use changes, but you may have noticed that we called those fields ChangeContainers rather than just change. This is because there's a hidden data structure in our plan that isn't documented as part of the change itself. This structure contains a bunch of metadata about the change, such as what resource it applies to, and then has the change embedded in it. Not all of these fields will be defined for every change, so we need to allow some to be empty.

Listing 11.27 `ChangeContainer` **data structure**

```
@dataclass
class ChangeContainer:
    # Format: https://developer.hashicorp.com/terraform/internals/
    json-format#change-representation
    data: Dict[str, Any] = field(repr=False)

    address: str = field(init=False)
    previous_address: str | None = field(init=False)
    module_address: str | None = field(init=False)
    mode: str = field(init=False)
    type: str = field(init=False)
    name: str = field(init=False)
    index: int | None = field(init=False)
    provider_name: str | None = field(init=False)

    disposed: str | None = field(init=False)
    action_reason: str = field(init=False)

    change: Change = field(init=False)

    def __post_init__(self):
        self.address = self.data.get("address")
        self.previous_address = self.data.get("address")
        self.module_address = self.data.get("address")
        self.mode = self.data.get("mode")
        self.type = self.data.get("type")
        self.name = self.data.get("name")
        self.index = self.data.get("index")
        self.provider_name = self.data.get("provider_name")
        self.disposed = self.data.get("disposed")
        self.action_reason = self.data.get("action_reason")
        self.change = Change(self.data.get("change"))
```

> These fields may not exist in the data.

> Index is only defined for resources that use count or for_each.

> Change is a separate object that contains the actual change data.

> These fields map directly to the data structure.

> We create a Change object from the change data.

Now we can finally build the change data structure. Most of this is really straight-forward. We have a list of actions (as a single change can have multiple actions: for instance, replacing a resource involves both a `delete` and a `create` action). The change data structure also has a `before sensitive` and `after_sensitive` object to tell you what attributes in the `before` and `after` objects are sensitive, so you can avoid printing those values out.

The `before` and `after` objects are where things can get confusing. These are actually extremely straightforward: each key points to an attribute of the object being changed, along with the value it was before the change and the value it's expected to be after the change. Attributes with no changes are left out. What makes this confusing is that the documentation on the Terraform site does not appear to be correct, as it describes a much more complex data structure here that is really only used in state.

Listing 11.28   Change data structure

Whether the field itself or
any attributes are sensitive.

A list of any currently unknown attributes
that will be set during the apply.

This contains the attributes after the
change, and it may be empty for deletions.

Whether the field itself or
any attributes are sensitive.

This contains the attributes before
the change, and it may be empty.

There is at least one
action, sometimes two.

```python
@dataclass
class Change:
    # Format: https://developer.hashicorp.com/terraform/internals/
    json-format#change-representation
    data: Dict[str, Any] = field(repr=False)

    actions: List[str] = field(init=False)
    before: Dict[str, Any] | None = field(init=False)
    after: Dict[str, Any] | None = field(init=False)

    before_sensitive: Dict[str, bool] | bool = field(init=False)
    after_sensitive: Dict[str, bool] | bool = field(init=False)

    after_unknown: Dict[str, bool] = field(init=False)

    def __post_init__(self):
        self.actions = self.data.get("actions", [])
        self.before = self.data.get("before")
        self.after = self.data.get("after")
        self.before_sensitive = self.data.get("before_sensitive")
        self.after_sensitive = self.data.get("after_sensitive")
        self.after_unknown = self.data.get("after_unknown")
```

All of these
fields can
pass straight
through to
our object.

Although there was a lot of data to manage there, it puts us in a great place. With this we can programmatically review any plan using our native language. This can allow teams to build tools that evaluate those plans, which in turn can provide custom safeguards for deployments. We will show you how that looks in section 11.1.10.

11.1.9 Output

Our final command to map is the output command. This is our easiest example to write, as we've already written the output class in a previous example

Listing 11.29   `tofu.Output`

```python
class Tofu:
    def output(self) -> Dict[str, Output]:
        res = self._run(["output", "-json"])
```

This method returns a
dictionary of Output objects.

This runs the command to get
the output in JSON format.

```
ret = {}
for key, value in res.json().items():
    ret[key] = Output(value)
return ret
```

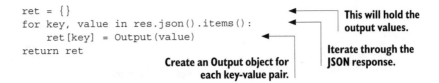

This will hold the output values.

Iterate through the JSON response.

Create an Output object for each key-value pair.

At this point you're ready to run the vast majority of commands from Terraform inside of your language and manage the results, enabling you to build a variety of tools on top of the Terraform (or OpenTofu) project.

11.1.10 Using our library

Now that our library is built, let's see it in action. One of the examples we gave at the start of the chapter was the idea of building a security scanner. While there are existing security scanners out there, this type of scanning can be used for more than just security. You could use this to validate that plans follow certain rules to look up the resource types to estimate pricing.

For our example, we'll use a Python library called Typer which makes it very easy to build command-line applications. We use Typer to create a single command application that takes in a path to a module as its own argument. Inside of that code, we'll use our library to initialize the project and run a plan. Then we'll iterate over the plan object to look for any changes that would violate our rules.

To start, we add a single rule to our code: if we are managing any security groups, we want to make sure we don't accidentally create an ingress rule that allows traffic from anywhere to hit the resources attached to the security group. In our code, we have a statement to look for the appropriate resource type and then look to see if the plan changes violate our rule.

Listing 11.30 Security scanner

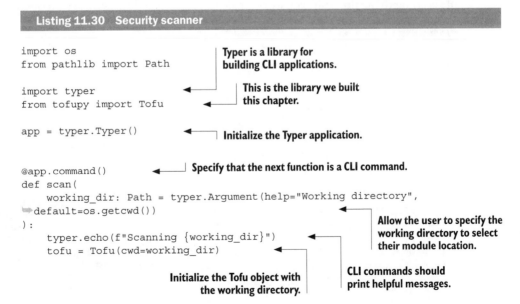

```
import os
from pathlib import Path

import typer
from tofupy import Tofu

app = typer.Typer()

@app.command()
def scan(
    working_dir: Path = typer.Argument(help="Working directory",
default=os.getcwd())
):
    typer.echo(f"Scanning {working_dir}")
    tofu = Tofu(cwd=working_dir)
```

Typer is a library for building CLI applications.

This is the library we built this chapter.

Initialize the Typer application.

Specify that the next function is a CLI command.

Allow the user to specify the working directory to select their module location.

CLI commands should print helpful messages.

Initialize the Tofu object with the working directory.

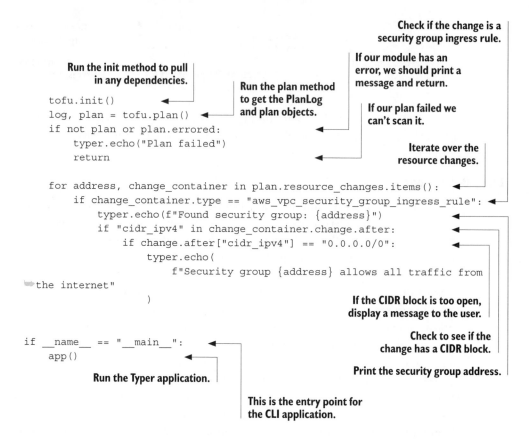

Run the init method to pull in any dependencies.

Run the plan method to get the PlanLog and plan objects.

Check if the change is a security group ingress rule.

If our module has an error, we should print a message and return.

If our plan failed we can't scan it.

Iterate over the resource changes.

```
tofu.init()
log, plan = tofu.plan()
if not plan or plan.errored:
    typer.echo("Plan failed")
    return

for address, change_container in plan.resource_changes.items():
    if change_container.type == "aws_vpc_security_group_ingress_rule":
        typer.echo(f"Found security group: {address}")
        if "cidr_ipv4" in change_container.change.after:
            if change.after["cidr_ipv4"] == "0.0.0.0/0":
                typer.echo(
                    f"Security group {address} allows all traffic from
the internet"
                )

if __name__ == "__main__":
    app()
```

If the CIDR block is too open, display a message to the user.

Check to see if the change has a CIDR block.

Print the security group address.

Run the Typer application.

This is the entry point for the CLI application.

Now let's create a new module in the module directory next to our scanner. This module is going to purposefully violate our rule by creating an ingress rule with open access.

Listing 11.31   Example failing module

```
data "aws_vpc" "default" {
  default = true
}
```
For this example, we're going to use the default VPC.

```
resource "aws_security_group" "example" {
  name   = "example_group"
  vpc_id = data.aws_vpc.default.id
}
```
Create a security group for our test.

```
resource "aws_vpc_security_group_ingress_rule" "example" {
  security_group_id = aws_security_group.example.id
  cidr_ipv4         = "0.0.0.0/0"
  from_port         = 443
  ip_protocol       = "tcp"
  to_port           = 443
}
```
Add a rule that allows all traffic to port 443.

This is a security risk since it allows all traffic, but it's just for testing.

We're just about ready to run our command, but first we need to install our dependencies. You're going to run one command to do that:

```
python -m pip install typer tofupy
```

> **NOTE** You might have noticed that we're installing `tofupy` directly from the Python registry. This is because the library we wrote in this chapter has been open sourced and uploaded for your use.

Now that we have everything installed, we're good to go! You should run the command `python scanner.py ./module` to run our code against our test module and see the output.

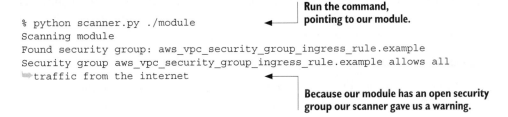

Listing 11.32 Security scanner usage

```
% python scanner.py ./module                          ◄─┐  Run the command,
Scanning module                                          pointing to our module.
Found security group: aws_vpc_security_group_ingress_rule.example
Security group aws_vpc_security_group_ingress_rule.example allows all
⇒traffic from the internet                            ◄─┐
                                                         Because our module has an open security
                                                         group our scanner gave us a warning.
```

As you can see, it detects the resource type, and then we're able to see that the attribute changed to violate our rule. This type of programmatic introspection can be applied to standalone tools around security and cost control, or it can be applied to full-scale applications like those covered in chapter 8.

11.2 Using JSON instead of HCL

In the last section, we went over how to programmatically control Terraform from other languages, but what if you wanted to write Terraform configurations from another language instead? You might be asking yourself: Why would anyone ever want to generate Terraform programmatically? It turns out that there are a lot of reasons someone may consider this. Once you can programmatically generate Terraform, it opens up some interesting possibilities:

- Create an application that allows you to draw diagrams and have them converted into infrastructure
- Create a tool that reads existing infrastructure and converts it into Terraform so it can be replicated
- Use another language to define your infrastructure without having to build the engine to launch it (you'll see an example of this is in section 11.3)

As we discovered in the last section, Terraform was designed to allow both humans and machines to interact with it. We learned that you can output JSON from Terraform so it can be read directly. Terraform also allows developers to programmatically generate their configuration by creating JSON files.

When a human writes Terraform, they use HCL files, the syntax we've used throughout this book. HCL was designed to be human friendly, with a very easy-to-read format. This format isn't as easy for computers to write though, and it certainly isn't universal in the way that JSON is. For this reason, Terraform also supports JSON as an alternative to HCL.

The process for both formats is the same: you create resources, data sources, and other objects and place them into files for Terraform to read. Just like with HCL, you can split things into multiple files and Terraform will reach each of them to construct the graph. It's even possible to mix HCL and JSON files in the same directory and Terraform will reach each of them. The only difference is that instead of your file containing a bunch of HCL blocks, it contains a JSON object that represents the same items.

With this method, you can create Terraform projects that are written by computers instead of humans. In this section, we'll go over the differences between the HCL and JSON format so you can understand how to structure your JSON files when you create your Terraform code generators.

11.2.1 *JSON structure*

Code written for Terraform in JSON should have a filename ending in `tf.json` (or `tofu.json` if you're using the compatibility features of OpenTofu from the previous chapter). You can have as many of these files as you'd like, and you can even mix HCL and JSON files together in the same project.

Each JSON file is a single JSON object. At the top level, you can specify keys that correspond to the HCL block types: `resource`, `data`, etc. Each of these keys has different objects nested underneath. Where you would have previously defined a `resource` block, you instead create an object under the resources key.

To see this in action, let's convert our test case from the previous section, listing 11.7, into JSON. We'll do this in a single file and include our variable, data source, resource, checks, and outputs.

> **WARNING** Be careful about comments. When copying any of the example JSON, remember that JSON itself does not support comments, so any of the comments in the listings have to be removed before your code can run. In section 11.2.3, we discuss how Terraform lets you work around this problem.

Listing 11.33 Test module as JSON

```
{
  "variable": {
    "website": { // This is the name of the variable.
      "type": "string",
```

The top-level keys correspond to HCL blocks.

We have to specify the type as a string, not a keyword.

```
        "description": "The url to pull data from.",
        "default": "https://catfact.ninja/fact"
    }
  },
  "data": {
    "http": {
      "site": {
        "url": "${var.website}",
        "request_headers": {
          "Accept": "application/json"
        }
      }
    }
  },
  "resource": {
    "terraform_data": {
      "main": {
        "input": "${data.http.site.response_body}"
      }
    }
  },
  "output": {
    "site_data": {
      "value": "${resource.terraform_data.main.output}"
    }
  }
}
```

In JSON, keys can not be repeated, so all data sources in this file have to be defined here.

The data source type.

The name of the data source.

Attributes have to be referenced using the string template syntax.

All of our resources in this file are defined here.

The resource type.

The name of the resource.

Attributes have to be referenced using the string template syntax.

Our resource output is passed through as an output.

The JSON format supports all of the major HCL blocks that you're used to while following the same pattern as our previous example. This means you can define all of these blocks as high-level keys in your JSON object:

- Resource
- Data
- Variable
- Output
- Locals
- Module
- Provider
- Terraform

Let's take a look at another block, the `provider` block. The `provider` block in HCL can be defined multiple times in a single module, even using the same name. When writing this out in JSON, we have to use a list to represent these different blocks. For example, if we wanted to create an alias for the AWS provider, we'd have to define a list of options to include our default provider configuration and that alias.

Listing 11.34 `provider` alias in JSON

```
{
  "provider": {
    "aws": [
      {
        "region": "us-east-1"
```

Since the provider block doesn't have names but can be used multiple times it is a list.

Even if you did not have two blocks you would still use a list.

```
    },
    {
      "alias": "backups",
      "region": "us-west-2"
    }
  ]
 }
}
```

11.2.2 Expressions and keywords

In the JSON language, there are a lot of limitations around the use of expressions. JSON itself does not understand what an expression is and has no concept of functions or keywords, and it doesn't have a way to refer to other fields such as variables or resource attributes. Instead, you have to use the Terraform string template format (as discussed in section 3.7.1) for any values that need strings, even if your expression is simply using the value from a resource.

Listing 11.35 Expressions with interpolation

```
{
  "locals": {
    "config": "${upper(var.config)}"    ◄─────  String templates can be used for
  }                                               interpolation and to run functions.
}
```

This can be used for some levels of logic, although it is limited. The ternary statement can only be used if all of the arguments are strings and can't easily be used to distinguish between other types such as booleans. You're basically stuck using logic to generate strings when writing expressions.

Listing 11.36 Logical expressions

```
{
  "locals": {
    "config": "%{ if var.option == null }default%{ else }${var.option}%{
  endif }"                      ◄─────
  }                                      Limited logic can be used, but only for strings.
}
```

Although a minor detail, this also extends to fields like `provider` or `depends_on`, which normally take a direct resource. For these you can simply refer to the resource but place it in quotes so it's a valid JSON string.

Listing 11.37 Keywords

```
{
  "resource": {
    "terraform_data": {
```

```
      "main": {
        "input": "${data.http.site.response_body}",
        "depends_on": [
          "data.http.site"          ◄─── Dependencies have to
        ]                                be specified as strings.
      }
    }
  }
}
```

11.2.3 Comments

The JSON format does not have a concept of comments. Most of the time this isn't a problem, as humans shouldn't be writing JSON directly anyway. You may still want to provide context from your code. For instance, you may find it useful to add a comment telling developers not to manually edit a file or provide comments to help debug how your configuration was generated. To do this you can create a field with the attribute `//` in any object in your JSON, with the value being any comment you want to write.

Listing 11.38 Comments

```
{
  "//": "This file was automatically generated and should not be manually
▬►edited.",                                    ◄───  You should add a header
  "resources": {                                     comment to generated code.
    "terraform_data": {
      "main": {
        "//": "This resource was generated in example.py line 38.",  ◄───
        "input": "${data.http.site.response_body}"
      }                                              Debugging information
    }                                                can also be helpful.
  }
}
```

11.3 Cloud Development Kit for Terraform

The Cloud Development Kit for Terraform (CDKTF) is a framework and tool built on top of Terraform that allows developers to define their infrastructure using one of a handful of standard software languages. CDKTF is built by HashiCorp, and it supports Typescript, Python, Java, C#, and Go.

NOTE CDKTF is Terraform only. The CDKTF doesn't directly support OpenTofu.

CDKTF works by taking the programs written in traditional languages and converting them to Terraform using the JSON pattern we discussed in the previous section. This allows developers to utilize all of the providers that Terraform has without the need to use HCL or JSON. It does this by starting with your main language, passing it through the CDKTF library, converting it to JSON, and then passing it to Terraform. Terraform, of course, gives you access to all of the providers. What you end up with is an abstraction layer on top of your abstraction layer (see figure 11.2).

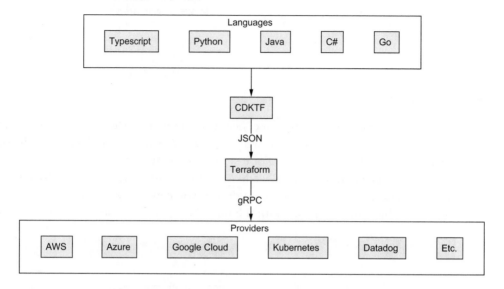

Figure 11.2   CDKTF abstraction layers

CDKTF has two components: a CLI (named `cdktf`) that developers run to generate their projects (similar to the `terraform` and `tofu` binaries) and a set of libraries for each language. Each supported language has its own libraries, but they all follow the same pattern and structure.

CDKTF works by translating what was written in any of these languages to the Terraform JSON format we discussed throughout section 11.2. This is done with the `cdktf synth` command, which synthesizes the code from your starting language into the language Terraform can read. After running that command, you can then run `cdktf deploy` to run through the Terraform `plan` and `apply` cycle (see figure 11.3).

Figure 11.3   CDKTF development cycle

11.3.1 *Should I use CDKTF?*

CDKTF has one major use case: developers want to define their IaC but don't want to learn another language to do so. This is an extremely common use case, as developers often have limited time and have to pick and choose what to spend it on. Many teams will select CDKTF because they believe it will increase their ability to adopt IaC techniques.

I am very skeptical that teams actually achieve any time savings or productivity benefits by using CDKTF over native Terraform. The reality is that most of learning Terraform is not about the language but about the concepts around IaC and how to properly manage and test it. This book is a reflection of that: the first third of the book was about the language itself, while the remainder of the book was about how to utilize IaC to the fullest. Switching from HCL to Typescript doesn't change the need to adapt continuous integration or continuous delivery techniques to the unique use cases of IaC or change the intricacies of state management. Testing with IaC still has the same pitfalls whether you're using CDKTF or HCL.

For teams that are simply managing their infrastructure, Terraform with HCL is the best option. The ecosystem is more developed, there are a lot more tutorials and online lessons to be found, and using Terraform directly removes another abstraction layer that may make debugging more difficult.

CDKTF does have its uses though. If you are building a tool or product that generates plans for infrastructure, then you may decide that CDKTF is the right choice. For example, if you were to build an application that attempted to read someone's code and automatically generate the infrastructure to host that project, then using CDKTF to generate a configuration that can be read with Terraform might be the way to go.

11.3.2 *CDKTF setup*

Before we begin, we need to install the CDKTF CLI. CDKTF is written in Typescript and uses npm (the Node Package Manager) for installation, so if you don't already have Node installed you should go ahead and do that. Once done, run the following command:

```
npm install --global cdktf-cli@latest
```

Like most command-line tools, you can learn more about the CLI and its commands by running cdktf help. Although CDKTF is written in Typescript, it supports multiple languages. To keep things simple and readable, we'll continue on with Python.

11.3.3 *Apps, stacks, and resources*

CDKTF divides things into apps, stacks, and resources. Stacks and resources are both pretty straightforward, as they have corresponding components in Terraform. Resources are, as you could probably guess, resources (which includes data sources). Where you would create a resource block in HCL, you'd create a resource object in CDKTF.

Listing 11.39 CDKTF resources

```
from cdktf_cdktf_provider_random.uuid import Uuid

my_uuid = Uuid(
```

We import the Uuid resource from the random provider.

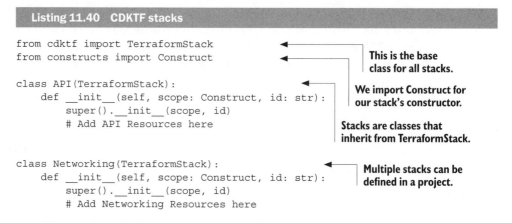

```
        scope=scope,
        id="my_unique_id",
        keepers={
            "keeper": "value"
        },
)
```

The scope comes from
the stack's constructor.

Each resource must have a unique
identifier within the stack.

This is the keepers attribute, just like with the
Terraform random_uuid resource.

Keepers are used to
generate a new **UUID**
when the value changes.

Stacks roughly correspond to a top-level module or workspace. It's inside of stacks that you define all of your resources, including calls to modules. Every stack has its own state, just like every instance of a top-level module will have its own state.

Listing 11.40   CDKTF stacks

```
from cdktf import TerraformStack
from constructs import Construct

class API(TerraformStack):
    def __init__(self, scope: Construct, id: str):
        super().__init__(scope, id)
        # Add API Resources here


class Networking(TerraformStack):
    def __init__(self, scope: Construct, id: str):
        super().__init__(scope, id)
        # Add Networking Resources here
```

This is the base
class for all stacks.

We import Construct for
our stack's constructor.

Stacks are classes that
inherit from TerraformStack.

Multiple stacks can be
defined in a project.

Apps are where we break out of the Terraform world and build an abstract on top. Apps are essentially a collection of different stacks. You always have an app, even if you only have a single stack, and the app is what lets `cdktf` know how to work with your code.

Once you have your app ready, you can pass your stacks to it. If you forgot to do this, then the app will be completely unaware of your stack. Since stacks are simply classes, you can store them in other files and import them in. Once you've added the stacks to the app, you have to run the `app.synth` function so the CDKTF library can build its internal data structures.

Listing 11.41   CDKTF apps

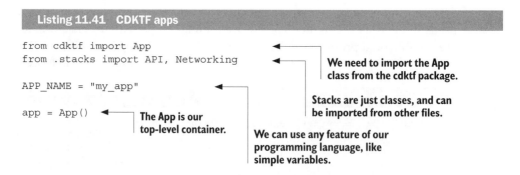

```
from cdktf import App
from .stacks import API, Networking

APP_NAME = "my_app"

app = App()
```

We need to import the App
class from the cdktf package.

Stacks are just classes, and can
be imported from other files.

The App is our
top-level container.

We can use any feature of our
programming language, like
simple variables.

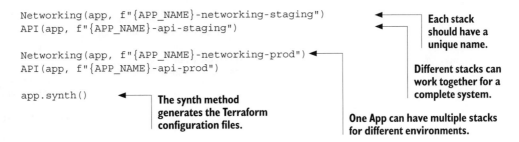

```
Networking(app, f"{APP_NAME}-networking-staging")
API(app, f"{APP_NAME}-api-staging")

Networking(app, f"{APP_NAME}-networking-prod")
API(app, f"{APP_NAME}-api-prod")

app.synth()
```

Each stack should have a unique name.

Different stacks can work together for a complete system.

One App can have multiple stacks for different environments.

The synth method generates the Terraform configuration files.

11.3.4 CDKTF usage

One nice thing about CDKTF is that it has a built-in project initializer, which will generate a project in your choice of language using the CLI you just installed. By running the command `cdktf init`, you'll kickstart an interactive program that will ask you questions about your project that it will use to customize your initial project structure.

Once that's done, you'll have a working project, although it won't do very much just yet. To get us going, we'll use the `random` and `null` providers for some experimentation. You'll have to explicitly add these to your project using the `cdktf provider add` command (so `cdktf provider add null` and `cdktf provider add random`). This installs the libraries needed into your language. Once your libraries are available you can build out your first project.

Listing 11.42 CDKTF example project

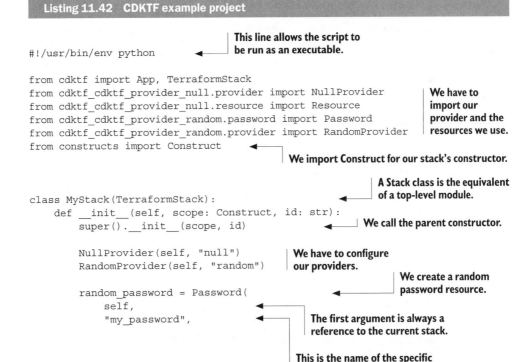

```python
#!/usr/bin/env python

from cdktf import App, TerraformStack
from cdktf_cdktf_provider_null.provider import NullProvider
from cdktf_cdktf_provider_null.resource import Resource
from cdktf_cdktf_provider_random.password import Password
from cdktf_cdktf_provider_random.provider import RandomProvider
from constructs import Construct

class MyStack(TerraformStack):
    def __init__(self, scope: Construct, id: str):
        super().__init__(scope, id)

        NullProvider(self, "null")
        RandomProvider(self, "random")

        random_password = Password(
            self,
            "my_password",
```

This line allows the script to be run as an executable.

We have to import our provider and the resources we use.

We import Construct for our stack's constructor.

A Stack class is the equivalent of a top-level module.

We call the parent constructor.

We have to configure our providers.

We create a random password resource.

The first argument is always a reference to the current stack.

This is the name of the specific resource, similar to a block label.

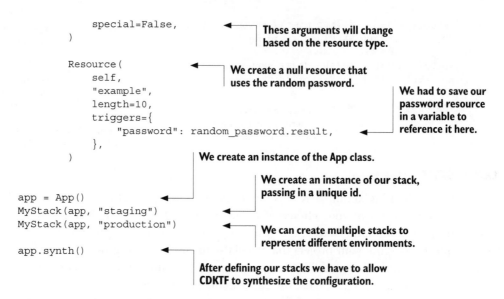

```
            special=False,              ◄──┐ These arguments will change
        )                                  │ based on the resource type.

        Resource(                  ◄──┐ We create a null resource that
            self,                      │ uses the random password.
            "example",                                        We had to save our
            length=10,                                        password resource
            triggers={                                        in a variable to
                "password": random_password.result,   ◄──┐    reference it here.
            },
        )                          ┌──► We create an instance of the App class.

                                   │    We create an instance of our stack,
                                   │    passing in a unique id.
app = App()              ◄─────────┘
MyStack(app, "staging")     ◄──┐
MyStack(app, "production")  ◄──┘ We can create multiple stacks to
                                 represent different environments.

app.synth()              ◄──┐
                            │ After defining our stacks we have to allow
                            │ CDKTF to synthesize the configuration.
```

Now we jump into the typical development cycle. Once you've made changes to your project, you have to convert your code into a language Terraform can read using the `cdktf synth` command. By default, it converts your program to JSON, but the latest version of CDKTF has an option to convert to HCL instead. We're going to run that so we can see how our Python code looks in HCL.

Listing 11.43　CDKTF example generated HCL

```
terraform {                       ◄──┐
  required_providers {            ◄──┤ This entire file was generated
    null = {                         │ programmatically by CDKTF.
      version = "3.2.2"
      source  = "null"               These providers from the our
    }                                NullProvider and RandomProvider
    random = {                       declarations.
      version = "3.6.2"
      source  = "hashicorp/random"
    }                                              Since we didn't configure a
  }                                                backend the state will be
  backend "local" {                           ◄── stored locally.
    path = "/Users/robert/testing/cdktf/terraform.staging.tfstate"
  }


}

provider "null" {            ◄──┐
}                               │ Since we didn't pass any
                                │ configuration to the provider
provider "random" {             │ this block is empty.
}
resource "random_password" "my_password" {
```

```
    length = 16                        We set a length of 16 and disabled
    special = false                    special characters on the CDKTF side.
}
resource "null_resource" "example" {                        CDKTF created the
    triggers = {                                            relationship between
        password = "${random_password.my_password.result}"  ◄───  the two resources.
    }
}
```

Other than some interesting formatting choices, this is completely valid HCL code that Terraform can run. Unfortunately, generating HCL presents some problems: if you try to run the cdktf deploy command, Terraform will see both the HCL and a JSON file, triggering an error due to both files defining the same block. For now, delete the cdktf.out directory if you happened to generate an HCL file before attempting to deploy.

Deploying happens with the cdktf deploy command. If you only have one stack then one will automatically be selected, but if you have more than that (like in our example) you have to pick one to deploy (e.g., cdktf deploy staging). Unless you pass the -skip-synth flag, this command will synthesize your code again; then it will run the normal terraform plan and terraform apply steps.

To destroy that environment, you can run cdktf destroy staging.

At this point, you've learned how to wrap Terraform and OpenTofu in your own language, build your own language generator for Terraform, or use the CDKTF project to generate Terraform for you. Now that you've mastered the external ways to extend Terraform, we're ready to explore how you can extend Terraform internally by creating a custom provider.

Summary

- Terraform and OpenTofu are both built with the idea that they would be run programmatically, so they both utilize JSON as an optional output for most commands.
- Terraform and OpenTofu have two outputs meant to be read by machines: the machine-readable UI for streaming events and the JSON output format for quick responses.
- Both applications also are able to read JSON files instead of HCL to allow Terraform configurations to be generated programmatically.
- JSON is available in pretty much every programming language available.
- Humans should not write Terraform using JSON, instead relying on the more user-friendly HCL.
- CDKTF is another option for generating Terraform code from inside another programming language, although it is only available for a subset of languages.

12

Terraform providers

This chapter covers

- Using the Terraform Provider Scaffolding template to bootstrap your development
- Using Terraform Plugin Framework to build a provider
- Utilizing the `provider`, `data`, `resource`, and `function` interfaces
- Creating your development environment and enabling local use
- Signing and publishing your module to a registry

Writing a Terraform provider is not something the average user of Terraform will ever have to do. The reality is that there are a huge number of providers already out there, and most developers can make do with what's there. That being said, there are several reasons why a developer may decide to build a provider:

- If a team is building a platform they want other developers to use, then there's a big advantage in allowing them to control that platform with Terraform.

Most companies that are selling a developer-focused platform are likely to consider this, but it can also be true of teams building internal platforms.

- Teams that are using open source platforms without a provider already written may find themselves writing one. This is what we will be doing in this chapter.
- Now that it's possible to create functions in providers, teams may find it useful for certain types of data processing. The open source Terraform Core Functions (https://mng.bz/BX2J) provider is a great example of this.

If your use case happens to fit in one of those areas (or you just really like exploring systems and want to build one for fun), then you are probably wondering what it takes to build a provider. In this chapter, we walk through the simplest way to approach this task.

TIP Writing a provider requires knowledge of the Go language. While we can go over the Terraform-specific components here, anyone who has to maintain a provider should, at a minimum, go through the tour of Go (https://go.dev/tour/welcome/1).

Unlike the Terraform language itself, which has strong guarantees of compatibility, Terraform internals are regularly evolving. There have been multiple software development kits and protocols (the language spoken between Terraform and providers over gRPC) over the years, with the current state of the art being the Terraform Plugin Framework, which supports Protocol version 6.

The Terraform Plugin Framework builds on top of the protocol in such a way that you really don't need to understand the protocol itself to build a plugin (with providers being the most common form of plugin). As I'll show in this chapter, creating a provider with the Plugin Framework can be a pretty straightforward task by implementing a simple provider for the Mastodon service. Terraform will communicate with our provider using gRPC (although this is mostly abstracted away from us by the plugin framework), and our provider will use an existing open source library to speak with a Mastodon server using its HTTPS-based API (see figure 12.1).

Figure 12.1   Terraform Mastodon provider flow

12.1   Design

Before we begin any development, it's important to make a plan for what we want to build. Terraform providers are primarily interfaces in Terraform to other systems. When we build modules, we put a lot of thought and effort into maintaining compatibility, or only breaking it when needed, and that is even more important when it comes to providers. Changing a provider in a backward incompatible way has the potential to be far more disruptive than changing a module, as an individual provider can be used by a significant number of modules.

For this reason, I like to start by defining my interfaces first: What are the resources, data sources, and functions that I want to make available to users, and how do I want them to use them? Before we write a single line of code, we should consider this.

In this chapter, we build a provider to work with a system called Mastodon. Mastodon is a microblogging platform very similar to sites like Twitter, except that instead of being run by a single corporation, it is an open source platform that anyone can run on their own. Each instance of Mastodon can speak to other instances, creating a federated social network. Our goal is to be able to post messages to Mastodon from Terraform.

NOTE The entire project developed in this chapter has been published to GitHub at https://mng.bz/dXyQ.

To start, we'll create a resource for posting, a data source to look up users, and a function that can be used to validate the username structure that Mastodon uses. Our goal is to make these new items available to developers so they can use them as shown in following listing.

Listing 12.1   Mastodon provider examples

```
terraform {
  required_providers {
    mastodon = {
      source = "terraformindepth/mastodon"
    }
  }
}

provider "mastodon" {        ◄──┐  Users will probably use environment
  host = "https://hachyderm.io"   │  variables, but we should also allow
}                                  │  for provider blocks.

data "mastodon_account" "me" {  ◄──┐  Users will likely want to be
  username = "tedivm"              │  able to look up accounts.
}

resource "mastodon_post" "this" {  ◄──┐  Users will also want
  content = "Hello, World!"            │  to manage posts.
}
```

By starting with what we want our users to do, we ensure that their experience is centered in the rest of our design process.

12.2 *Developer environment*

Before we begin, we need to make sure we're ready for development. Thus far, we've primarily been working with Terraform, but now we're going to transition into the world of Go. This means that the very first thing we need to do is install the Go language tools themselves (https://go.dev/doc/install). How exactly you do that depends on your specific system.

It's also a good idea, if you haven't already, to install any extensions for your IDE that will help you with the language. For example, if you're using VSCode, then you want to install the Go language extension (https://mng.bz/rKrX). Once that's installed, you're ready to begin setting up your specific project.

12.2.1 Template

Now we need to create our initial project. HashiCorp maintains a template project (https://mng.bz/VVg5) that we can use to get started, so the first thing we want to do is clone that repository locally and give it a quick review. Since this repository is an active project, it's important to go through the instructions in its README file, as things may have changed. In particular, pay attention to the minimum version of Go supported to make sure you have that installed and that the Terraform version supported is in line with what you plan to support.

Now we need to do a small amount of cleanup. Since this template isn't a Cookiecutter template like our module template, it isn't going to have the values you expect, and there may be things that have to be changed. As a general rule, I suggest the following:

1 Update the `./github/dependabot.yml` file to make sure all actions get updated. There is a `@TODO` comment in the file where this needs to be done.

2 Erase or replace the contents of `.github/CODEOWNERS` and `.github/CODE_OF_CONDUCT.md` to match your organization's policies and teams.

3 Erase `.copywrite.hcl` as that is a file used internally by HashiCorp to maintain its repositories.

4 Rename the module to match what you are building by running `go mod edit -module github.com/YOUR_ORGANIZATION/terraform-provider-YOUR_SERVICE _NAME`. The module name should refer to your repository on GitHub, even if you haven't created it yet.

5 Run `go mod tidy`.

6 Update the description of the project in `README.md`. You may want to leave all of the instructions on using the project.

7 In `main.go`, update the name of the module, including in the comments so that the `go generate` command properly functions.

12.2.2 Developer overrides

Once that's done, we need to prepare our system itself. This primarily means letting Terraform know to use our locally developed provider, rather than attempting to download one off of the internet. This can be done by editing the `~/.terraformrc` file, but first you need to know where to point it. When you run `go install`, the Go command-line interface will build your provider and place it in the GOBIN directory.

Run `go env GOBIN`, and if that returns a result, save it, but if it returns blank, save the results of `echo $HOME/go/bin` instead.

Now that we know where our provider is going to be installed we can update `~/.terraformrc` to point Terraform at our new location by updating the `dev_overrides` option for our provider.

Listing 12.2   Local provider with `.terraformrc`

```
provider_installation {           The dev_overrides block allows us
                                  to use locally built providers.         This folder will
    dev_overrides {                                                       be different on
        "terraformindepth/mastodon" = "/Users/tedivm/go/bin/"            your system.
    }

    # For all other providers, install them directly from their origin provider
    # registries as normal. If you omit this, Terraform will _only_ use
    # the dev_overrides block, and so no other providers will be available.
    direct {}
}
```

That's it! You are now ready to begin development of your provider.

12.3 *Terraform Plugin Framework features*

Before we get into the specifics of creating a provider, we'll talk about some of the features available in the Terraform Plugin Framework that will be used throughout the rest of the process. In particular, we discuss how you can define parameters and attributes for the different components you create and how you can make it easier for users of your provider to debug problems they may encounter.

12.3.1 *Schemas*

A common feature when using the Terraform Plugin Framework is the use of schemas. Schemas are data structures in the framework that are used to expose parameters, attributes, and configuration values through the framework. They can be used to specify what type a parameter is, whether it's required or computed, the default value, and other important metadata about the parameter such as documentation.

Providers, resources, and data sources all use schemas as part of their definition. When we go over each of these components, I'll show you how to build schemas for them.

Listing 12.3   Schema example

```
func (p *MastodonProvider) Schema(ctx context.Context, req
    provider.SchemaRequest, resp *provider.SchemaResponse) {          Schemas are
    resp.Schema = schema.Schema{                                       defined in their
        Attributes: map[string]schema.Attribute{                       own functions.

                                  Schemas are maps of
                                  schema attributes.
```

All schemas have to map
to a type, such as String.

```
            "host": schema.StringAttribute{
                MarkdownDescription: "Mastodon host to connect to.",
                Optional:            true,
                Default:             stringdefault.StaticString(
    "mastodon.social"),
            },
            "email": schema.StringAttribute{
                MarkdownDescription: "Username to connect to the server as.",
                Optional:            true,
                DeprecationMessage:  "Use access token instead.",
            },
            "password": schema.StringAttribute{
                MarkdownDescription: "Password to use for connecting to the
    server.",
                Optional:            true,
                Sensitive:           true,
                DeprecationMessage:  "Use access token instead.",
            },
            "access_token": schema.StringAttribute{
                MarkdownDescription: "Password to use for connecting to the
    server.",
                Optional:            true,
                Sensitive:           true,
            },
        },
    }
}
```

It's possible
to mark an
attribute as
deprecated.

Schemas can have default values.

Sensitive attributes are
filtered out from logs.

While this covers schemas in an overall way, we'll get into some of the specific functionality and fields in the next sections.

12.3.2 *Error handling and logging*

Before we get into the implementation of your provider, we need to have a brief discussion on logging and error handling. If you are familiar with the Go language already,
you might be familiar with tools such as the Go log package and logger functions. The
Terraform Plugin Framework provides its own logging tools, and it's important that
you use them.

One of the most important things about making a provider is to make it user friendly.
That includes all sorts of things such as great documentation, but one of the most
important pieces can be around logging and error messages. You want to return good
error messages and log events in a way that makes it easy for your users to understand
and correct their code, as nothing is more frustrating to developers than errors they
can't interpret and resolve.

The Terraform Plugin Framework handles this in two ways:

- The resp object passed to most functions includes a Diagnostics object that can
  be used to add custom errors to bubble up to your users. The functions on this
  object can be called multiple times, so it's possible to populate multiple error

messages in a single function call. This means you should avoid returning on the first error and instead return after processing everything you can for the user. You'll see this in the provider `Configure` function in the next section.

- The `tflog` package should be used instead of the `log` package. This package has features that are specific to Terraform, and the various log-level functions (`tflog.Debug`, `tflog.Error`, etc.) map to the levels Terraform displays based on the `TF_LOG` variable. There are also features of these packages such as log filtering that you can potentially use.

Listing 12.4 Logging and error messaging

> The logging lines help to understand what's happening in the provider, but aren't displayed by default.

```
func (p *MastodonProvider) Configure(ctx context.Context, req
 provider.ConfigureRequest, resp *provider.ConfigureResponse) {
    var data MastodonProviderModel
    tflog.Debug(ctx, "mastodon_provider configure")          ◄──┘
    resp.Diagnostics.Append(req.Config.Get(ctx, &data)...)

    if data.AccessToken.IsUnknown() {
        resp.Diagnostics.AddAttributeError(    ◄───┐
            path.Root("user-access-token"),
            "Unknown Mastodon User Password",
            "The provider cannot create the Mastodon API client as there
 is an unknown configuration value for the Mastodon User Password. "+
                "Either target apply the source of the value first, set
 the value statically in the configuration, or use the
 MASTODON_USER_PASSWORD environment variable.",
        )
    }
    access_token := os.Getenv("MASTODON_ACCESS_TOKEN")
    if !data.AccessToken.IsNull() {
        access_token = data.AccessToken.ValueString()
    }

    // Repeat for user_email and user_password

    if access_token != "" {
        ctx = tflog.SetField(ctx, "mastodon_access_token", access_token)  ◄─┐
        ctx = tflog.MaskFieldValuesWithFieldKeys(ctx,
 "mastodon_access_token")                              ◄──
    } else if user_email != "" && user_password != "" {
        ctx = tflog.SetField(ctx, "mastodon_user_email", user_email)
        ctx = tflog.SetField(ctx, "mastodon_user_password", user_password)
        ctx = tflog.MaskFieldValuesWithFieldKeys(ctx,
 "mastodon_user_password")
    } else {
        resp.Diagnostics.AddAttributeError(    ◄───
            path.Root("user-access-token"),
            "Missing Mastodon Credentials",
```

> We can provide errors about attributes to the Diagnostics object, which will be displayed to the user.

> We can also make sure to filter out the value from the logs.

> We can log the access token to help with debugging.

> We can provide more than one error on the same flow.

```
            "The provider cannot create the Mastodon API client as neither
⇒the Access Token or the Username and Password fields are set.",
        )
    }

    if resp.Diagnostics.HasError() {        ◄─────┐  Before moving on we can check
        return                                    │  for errors and return early.
    }

    // Continue to configure client
}
```

The most important thing about error handling and logging that you should keep in mind is that you should never use any of the `Fatal` methods of the `log` package. If your provider exits early, it will not return the appropriate errors back to Terraform for your users and may even leave you with corrupted state. If you encounter a problem that requires you to stop processing, then store the error messages in `Diagnostics`, use `tflog` to print out an immediate log, and then return from the function.

12.3.3 Testing

In many ways, writing tests is similar to how you would write tests for modules using Terratest, as both Terraform Plugin Testing and Terratest are extensions of the Go testing package. Just like with Terratest, testing your provider includes writing code using the Terraform language and then examining what happens when you run that code.

The big difference between Terratest and the Terraform Plugin Testing frameworks is that with the plugin testing framework you often define your Terraform code in your tests themselves, and instead of testing entire modules you typically test a single resource or data source at a time.

> **NOTE** One major consideration when running tests is that they can cost real money, depending on what service you're building. If you were making a provider for one of the major cloud vendors, for instance, you'd have to pay for resources used. In our case this is less of a concern, as the Mastodon service is free to use. To make this easier to manage, the testing packaging makes a distinction between unit tests and acceptance tests.

Unit tests are completely isolated tests that don't rely on any other outside service. These are primarily useful for testing logic but don't actually test how a provider interacts with the service it's connecting to. You'll primarily see unit tests run against functions created by the provider, although they are also useful if your provider has any shared logic.

Acceptance tests, on the other hand, are used to explicitly test against the service the provider is managing. These are always used for resources and data sources created by your provider. You can always mark a test as an acceptance test by naming the test function with the prefix `TestAcc`, while unit tests just start with `Test`.

Acceptance tests will only be run if the environment variable TF_ACC is set to 1., which is set automatically in our template when you run the command make testacc. When you're testing functions, you may find it's worth skipping the acceptance tests and only running the unit tests, as this will save you both time and potentially money.

As we go through this chapter, I'll show you how to create tests for resources, functions, and data sources.

12.4 Provider interface

The first thing we need to do is configure the entry point package to our provider. In this case, we do so by implementing the provider.Provider interface. This interface includes a few functions and structures that tell Terraform what your provider ships with and how they can be used (see table 12.1).

Table 12.1 Provider interface

Function	Purpose
Metadata	Manages the version and type prefix for the provider
Schema	Returns the schema that defines the configuration for the provider
Configure	Configures the client and any other libraries needed by the provider and makes them available to the resource and data sources
Resources	Returns a list of resource constructors
DataSource	Returns a list of data source constructors
Functions	Returns a list of function constructors
New	Creates an instance of the provider

Since we started with a template, we already have the boilerplate in the file internal/provider/provider.go.

Listing 12.5 Template boilerplate

```
// Copyright (c) HashiCorp, Inc.
// SPDX-License-Identifier: MPL-2.0

package provider                          Most of these imports will be useful later on.

import (                        ◄─────┐   We will replace the http
    "context"                             client with one to the      All of these are types that
    "net/http"                  ◄─────┘   service we're building.     we will use in this project.

    "github.com/hashicorp/terraform-plugin-framework/datasource"
    "github.com/hashicorp/terraform-plugin-framework/function"
    "github.com/hashicorp/terraform-plugin-framework/provider"
    "github.com/hashicorp/terraform-plugin-framework/provider/schema"
    "github.com/hashicorp/terraform-plugin-framework/resource"
    "github.com/hashicorp/terraform-plugin-framework/types"
)
```

We will have to replace all of the "Scaffolding" names.

```go
// Ensure ScaffoldingProvider satisfies various provider interfaces.
var _ provider.Provider = &ScaffoldingProvider{}
var _ provider.ProviderWithFunctions = &ScaffoldingProvider{}

// ScaffoldingProvider defines the provider implementation.
type ScaffoldingProvider struct {
    // version is set to the provider version on release, "dev" when the
    // provider is built and ran locally, and "test" when running acceptance
    // testing.
    version string
}
```

This struct will eventually contain all of our provider's attributes.

```go
// ScaffoldingProviderModel describes the provider data model.
type ScaffoldingProviderModel struct {
    Endpoint types.String `tfsdk:"endpoint"`
}
```

This struct maps our provider fields back to Terraform.

```go
func (p *ScaffoldingProvider) Metadata(ctx context.Context, req
provider.MetadataRequest, resp *provider.MetadataResponse) {
    resp.TypeName = "scaffolding"
    resp.Version = p.version
}
```

This is the name of the provider, which we'll set in the next section. This will also be the prefix for all of our resources.

```go
func (p *ScaffoldingProvider) Schema(ctx context.Context, req
provider.SchemaRequest, resp *provider.SchemaResponse) {
    resp.Schema = schema.Schema{
        Attributes: map[string]schema.Attribute{
            "endpoint": schema.StringAttribute{
                MarkdownDescription: "Example provider attribute",
                Optional:            true,
            },
        },
    }
}
```

The provider schema is where we define the provider's configuration.

```go
func (p *ScaffoldingProvider) Configure(ctx context.Context, req
provider.ConfigureRequest, resp *provider.ConfigureResponse) {
    var data ScaffoldingProviderModel

    resp.Diagnostics.Append(req.Config.Get(ctx, &data)...)

    if resp.Diagnostics.HasError() {
        return
    }

    // Configuration values are now available.
    // if data.Endpoint.IsNull() { /* ... */ }

    // Example client configuration for data sources and resources
    client := http.DefaultClient
    resp.DataSourceData = client
    resp.ResourceData = client
}
```

This is where we'll configure our API client.

The example uses the HTTP client.

We have to pass the client to the DataSource and Resource so they can use it.

```
func (p *ScaffoldingProvider) Resources(ctx context.Context) []func()
resource.Resource {
    return []func() resource.Resource{
        NewExampleResource,
    }
}
```

This is where we'll register the constructors for our resources.

```
func (p *ScaffoldingProvider) DataSources(ctx context.Context) []func()
datasource.DataSource {
    return []func() datasource.DataSource{
        NewExampleDataSource,
    }
}
```

This is where we'll register the constructors for our data sources.

```
func (p *ScaffoldingProvider) Functions(ctx context.Context) []func()
function.Function {
    return []func() function.Function{
        NewExampleFunction,
    }
}
```

This is where we'll register the constructors for our functions.

```
func New(version string) func() provider.Provider {
    return func() provider.Provider {
        return &ScaffoldingProvider{
            version: version,
        }
    }
}
```

This is the constructor for our provider.

12.4.1 *Template cleanup*

Although it's great to have an example to start with, there are a few things we'll want to change in this file. For one, we don't want to actually ship the example functions, resources, or data sources. For the functions `Resources`, `DataSources`, and `Functions`, we should erase the examples from the object that is returned.

The next thing we want to do is rename our provider. The starter template uses the name `ScaffoldingProvider`, so we should simply find and replace all instances of that with our new name. Since our example is for a Mastodon provider, we should name it `MastodonProvider`. We also need to update the `TypeName` in the `Metadata` function. This name is what our users will see and use when creating `provider` blocks. We'll go with the obvious and name it `mastodon`.

Listing 12.6   **Metadata update**

```
func (p *MastodonProvider) Metadata(ctx context.Context, req
provider.MetadataRequest, resp *provider.MetadataResponse) {
    resp.TypeName = "mastodon"
    resp.Version = p.version
}
```

The provider name is now "mastodon".

Notice we are referring to the MastodonProvider now.

12.4.2 *Provider model and schema*

Now we need to define configuration options our provider will expose. This is going to be very specific to your provider. A provider that is only functions may not expose any options, while those that connect to an external API will typically include parameters for authentication.

For our Mastodon provider, we use the Go library (https://github.com/mattn/go-mastodon). To add that dependency to our project, we need to run the command `go get github.com/mattn/go-mastodon` followed by `go mod tidy`. When you're working on your own provider, you will likely add at least a client library for the service you're connecting to.

To use that library, we'll need a host, client ID, client secret, and either a username and password or a token to represent the user. We define these both on our high-level provider struct as part of our schema, where we can also add a description for our users or mark a parameter as sensitive.

You'll notice that we set these parameters as optional. This is because we plan on allowing them to be set by environment variables as well as the `parameter` block. This is a good practice that most providers tend to follow, since it makes it easier for most users of the provider to switch between different credentials without needing any code changes.

Listing 12.7 Provider schema

```
func (p *MastodonProvider) Schema(ctx context.Context, req
provider.SchemaRequest, resp *provider.SchemaResponse) {
    resp.Schema = schema.Schema{
        Attributes: map[string]schema.Attribute{
            "host": schema.StringAttribute{
                MarkdownDescription: "Mastodon host to connect to.",
                Optional:            true,
            },
            "client_id": schema.StringAttribute{
                MarkdownDescription: "Client ID for Mastodon App.",
                Optional:            true,
            },
            "client secret": schema.StringAttribute{
                MarkdownDescription: "Client Secret for Mastodon App.",
                Optional:            true,
                Sensitive:           true,
            },
            "email": schema.StringAttribute{
                MarkdownDescription: "Username to connect to the server as.
Can not be used with `access_token`.",
                Optional:            true,
            },
            "password": schema.StringAttribute{
```

We allow this and other fields to be Optional so we can read from the environment variables if it isn't set.

This is a sensitive value, so we'll mark it as such.

We allow either email/password or access_token to be used for authentication, so we have to add all of them to the schema.

```
                MarkdownDescription: "Password to use for connecting to
  the server. Can not be used with `access_token`.",
                Optional:            true,
                Sensitive:           true,
            },
            "access_token": schema.StringAttribute{
                MarkdownDescription: "Token to use for connecting to
  the server. Used instead of `email` and `password`.",
                Optional:            true,
                Sensitive:           true,
            },
        },
    }
}
```

We also need to define our provider model, which is the struct inside of Go that we use to pass these values around.

Listing 12.8   Provider model

This struct is used to hold the configuration values for the provider.

```
type MastodonProviderModel struct {
    Host         types.String `tfsdk:"host"`
    ClientID     types.String `tfsdk:"client_id"`
    ClientSecret types.String `tfsdk:"client_secret"`
    Email        types.String `tfsdk:"email"`
    Password     types.String `tfsdk:"password"`
    AccessToken  types.String `tfsdk:"access_token"`
}
```

Each of the fields have to map back to their name in our Schema.

12.4.3   *Provider configuration*

Finally, we're going to use the `Configure` function of our provider to configure the Mastodon client for use by any data source or resource that we build in our provider. The actual creation of the Mastodon client is pretty straightforward, with the bulk of the `Configure` function focusing on validating the user input and giving back useful error messages. For every parameter we add, we adopt the same pattern:

1   Check to see if the value is `Unknown`. This is a very special state that will only occur if a user defines a `provider` block with a derived value. For example, if you were using the Kubernetes provider with Amazon Elastic Kubernetes Service, you might first create the cluster with the AWS provider before then using the attributes from the cluster resource to feed into the Kubernetes provider. If Terraform attempts to configure the client before the values needed to configure it are available, those parameters will show up as `Unknown`. When that happens, we want to give the user some useful advice.

2   Populate the internal function value from an environment variable. If the environment variable isn't set, then this will be an empty string.

3 Pull any value from the `provider` block and use that value if it is not `null`. This will override any environment variable.

4 Run any of the complex validation that you want to occur and register any errors.

That should be done for every parameter that we've defined in our schema. Depending on your provider, you may want to do additional validation: for example, you could validate that any URL is appropriately formatted, or you may only care about some variables if other ones aren't set.

When you encounter an error, do not immediately stop processing, and definitely do not attempt to kill the program. Keep processing and collect all of the errors by passing them to `resp.Diagnostics.AddAttributeError`. Once you've processed all of your values, you should check `resp.Diagnostics.HasError` and return immediately if there are errors.

Listing 12.9 Provider configure attribute validation

> We have to update our import statement to include github.com/hashicorp/terraform-plugin-framework/path.

> If the variable is in the special "unknown" state, we can't use it and need to register an error.

```
func (p *MastodonProvider) Configure(ctx context.Context, req
provider.ConfigureRequest, resp *provider.ConfigureResponse) {
    var data MastodonProviderModel
    tflog.Debug(ctx, "mastodon_provider configure")
    resp.Diagnostics.Append(req.Config.Get(ctx, &data)...)

    if data.Host.IsUnknown() {
        resp.Diagnostics.AddAttributeError(
            path.Root("host"),
            "Unknown Mastodon API Host",
            "The provider cannot create the Mastodon API client as there
is an unknown configuration value for the Mastodon API host. "+
                "Either target apply the source of the value first, set
the value statically in the configuration, or use the MASTODON_HOST
environment variable.",
        )
    }
    host := os.Getenv("MASTODON_HOST")
    if !data.Host.IsNull() {
        host = data.Host.ValueString()
    }
    if host == "" {
        resp.Diagnostics.AddAttributeError(
            path.Root("mastodon-host"),
            "Missing Mastodon Credentials",
```

> First load the value from environment variables. This will default to an empty string.

> Now if the value is set in the configuration, we'll use that instead.

> If the value isn't set anywhere we need to register an error.

> This is the title of the error.

> We should call out the specific attribute that is missing.

```
            "The provider cannot create the Mastodon API client as the
Host is not set.",
        )
    }
```
This is the description
of the error.

```
    /* client-id, client-secret, user-email, user-password, and
user-access-token follow the same pattern */
    /* These blocks were excluded for brevity, but you should add them in
if you're running this locally. */

    if access_token == "" && (user_email == "" || user_password == "") {
        resp.Diagnostics.AddAttributeError(
            path.Root("user-access-token"),
            "Missing Mastodon Credentials",
            "The provider cannot create the Mastodon API client as neither
the Access Token or the Username and Password fields are set.",
        )
    }
```

Now we have to confirm
that we have either the
access token or the
username and password.

```
    if resp.Diagnostics.HasError() {
        return
    }
}
```

If we have any errors, we need to
stop here. By waiting until the end
we can collect all of the errors and
present them to the user at once.

Now that we have our parameters, we can actually create our client. This will depend on the library you use, but for our Mastodon example it's as simple as creating a client and then authenticating it. There are two ways for Mastodon to authenticate though (a token or with user credentials), so we need to branch our logic slightly depending on which method was used.

Once the `resp` parameter is created, we can use it to populate `DataSourceData` and `ResourceData`, making the client available to the resources we create in the next sections. Note that we don't configure the client to be used for functions: this is because functions should always be logic only and should never reach out to an external service, so Terraform does not even have a `FunctionData` option.

Listing 12.10   Provider configure client creation

The client configuration section
tends to be unique to each provider.

Since we have two different ways
to authenticate, we need to check
which one is being used.

```
    var config mastodon.Config
    if access_token != "" {
        tflog.Debug(ctx, "mastodon_provider configure with access token")
        config = mastodon.Config{
            Server:       host,
            ClientID:     client_id,
            ClientSecret: client_secret,
            AccessToken:  access_token,
        }
    } else {
```

We need to add the github.com/mattn/
go-mastodon library to our imports.

```
        tflog.Debug(ctx, "mastodon_provider configure without access token")
        config = mastodon.Config{
            Server:       host,
            ClientID:     client_id,
            ClientSecret: client_secret,
        }
    }

    c := mastodon.NewClient(&config)
    user, err := c.GetAccountCurrentUser(context.Background())
    if err != nil {
        tflog.Error(ctx, "GetAccountCurrentUser Error: "+err.Error())
        resp.Diagnostics.AddError(
            "Mastodon GetAccountCurrentUser Failed, API is not usable.",
            err.Error(),
        )
    }

    tflog.Debug(ctx, "mastodon_provider current user: "+user.Acct)

    if access_token == "" {
        tflog.Debug(ctx, "mastodon_provider configure authenticate
user based")
        err := c.Authenticate(context.Background(), user_email,
user_password)
        if err != nil {
            tflog.Error(ctx, "Authentication Error with User Based Auth:
"+err.Error())
            resp.Diagnostics.AddError(
                "Mastodon User Based Login Failed",
                err.Error(),
            )
        }
    }

    if resp.Diagnostics.HasError() {
        return
    }

    // Example client configuration for data sources and resources
    resp.DataSourceData = c
    resp.ResourceData = c
}
```

> We create the client with the configuration we've built.

> We test the client by getting the current user. This will fail if the client is not configured correctly.

> We add an error to the diagnostics if the client is not usable.

> If we're not using an access token, we need to authenticate the user.

> It's useful to log the current user of the client for debugging purposes.

> If there are any errors, we should return.

> Finally, we pass the client to our data sources and resources.

At this point, our provider is ready to go. The only changes we'll need to make are to update the responses from the functions `DataSources`, `Resources`, and `Functions` as we add new items to our provider.

12.4.4 *Provider testing*

Our first and immediate concern is to configure our provider so that other tests, such as on our resources or data sources, can be done. We do this by configuring a factory function that returns a new instance of our provider server. This factory function will be used in all of our test cases going forward.

Outside of that, there isn't always a lot to do on the provider side itself. Since other tests depend on the provider working and being configured, we can add a check in place that the environment variables we require are actually set and fail early if they are not.

> **TIP** When running your tests, your provider needs to be able to access credentials to actually function. The easiest way to do this is with the environment variables that we've built into the provider.

Listing 12.11 Testing providers

```
package provider

import (
    "os"
    "testing"

    "github.com/hashicorp/terraform-plugin-framework/providerserver"
    "github.com/hashicorp/terraform-plugin-go/tfprotov6"
    "github.com/stretchr/testify/assert"
)

var testAccProtoV6ProviderFactories = map[string]func() (
tfprotov6.ProviderServer, error){
    "mastodon": providerserver.NewProtocol6WithError(New("test")()),
}

func testAccPreCheck(t *testing.T) {
    client_host := os.Getenv("MASTODON_HOST")
    assert.NotEmpty(t, client_host, "MASTODON_HOST must be set for
acceptance tests")

    client_id := os.Getenv("MASTODON_CLIENT_ID")
    assert.NotEmpty(t, client_id, "MASTODON_CLIENT_ID must be set for
acceptance tests")

    client_secret := os.Getenv("MASTODON_CLIENT_SECRET")
    assert.NotEmpty(t, client_secret, "MASTODON_CLIENT_SECRET must be set
for acceptance tests")

    client_token := os.Getenv("MASTODON_ACCESS_TOKEN")
    assert.NotEmpty(t, client_token, "MASTODON_ACCESS_TOKEN must be set
for acceptance tests")
}
```

This is a map of provider names to factory functions that create a new provider server.

We have to import a couple of packages to enable our provider to be used in testing.

We need to register our provider with the provider factory so it can be used in future tests.

If the environment variable is not set, the test will fail with a message.

Each important environment variable should be retrieved and checked for existence.

This function is used to check that the environment variables needed for acceptance tests are set.

12.5 Data source

To write a data source, we have to implement that interface for data sources and then add it to our provider. Unlike our provider entry point that we wrote earlier, we can expect to have multiple data sources in each project.

The data source interface (see table 12.2) is pretty similar to the provider interface. We have a `Metadata` to give our data source a name, a `DataSourceModel` and corresponding `Schema` function where we define our parameters and attributes, and a `Configure` function where we pull in our client from the provider `Configure` function. We also have a function called `Read`, which is where the bulk of our logic is going to go.

Table 12.2 Data source interface

Function	Purpose
Metadata	Returns the name of the data source
Schema	Returns the Schema for the data source
Configure	Configures the data source, typically by getting the client from the provider instance
Read	Uses the parameters set by the user to look up the associated data and populate the state

We'll use the boilerplate that came with our template. To begin, copy the file `internal/provider/example_data_source.go` to a new file with a name appropriate to your data source. For the Mastodon provider, we'll start with `mastodon_account`, so we'll create the file `internal/provider/account_data_source.go`. Now update the name by searching for `Example` and replacing it with `Account` (or the name of your specific data source).

12.5.1 Data source schema

Next, we need to define our `Schema` and `Model` (`AccountDataSourceModel` in our example). This is what defines the parameters and attributes for our new data source. This data source is going to have a parameter with an account name, and it'll have attributes that it pulls down from the server. The way we distinguish this is with the `computed`, `required`, and `optional` keys in our schema, which lets Terraform know which values are `computed` (potentially generated by our provider, rather than provided by a user as a parameter). Values that are `computed` may not be known during plan time.

Listing 12.12 Data source schema and metadata

```
// AccountDataSource defines the data source implementation.
type AccountDataSource struct {
    client *mastodon.Client
}

// AccountDataSourceModel describes the data source data model.
```

We need to switch from the http.Client to the mastodon.Client.

Just like providers, data
sources have a model that
holds the configuration values.

```go
type AccountDataSourceModel struct {
    Username    types.String `tfsdk:"username"`
    Id          types.String `tfsdk:"id"`
    DisplayName types.String `tfsdk:"display_name"`
    Note        types.String `tfsdk:"note"`
    Locked      types.Bool   `tfsdk:"locked"`
    Bot         types.Bool   `tfsdk:"bot"`
}
```

Each of the fields have
to map back to their
name in our Schema.

```go
func (d *AccountDataSource) Metadata(ctx context.Context, req
datasource.MetadataRequest, resp *datasource.MetadataResponse) {
    resp.TypeName = req.ProviderTypeName + "_account"
}
```

This is the
type name
that will be
used in the
Terraform
configuration.
It's built from
our provider
name.

```go
func (d *AccountDataSource) Schema(ctx context.Context, req
datasource.SchemaRequest, resp *datasource.SchemaResponse) {
    resp.Schema = schema.Schema{
        // This description is used by the documentation generator and
the language server.
        MarkdownDescription: "Account data source",

        Attributes: map[string]schema.Attribute{
            "username": schema.StringAttribute{
                MarkdownDescription: "Account username that we want to
look up.",
                Optional:            false,
                Required:            true,
            },
```

This field is required since
we need it for the lookup.

```go
            "id": schema.StringAttribute{
                MarkdownDescription: "Account identifier",
                Optional:            false,
                Required:            false,
            },
```

This value is one
of the ones we
want to up, so it
should not be
set by the user.

```go
            "display_name": schema.StringAttribute{
                MarkdownDescription: "Account display name.",
                Optional:            false,
                Required:            false,
            },
            "note": schema.StringAttribute{
                MarkdownDescription: "Account note or profile bio",
                Optional:            false,
                Required:            false,
            },
```

Note that this field is a
boolean, not a string.

```go
            "locked": schema.BoolAttribute{
                MarkdownDescription: "Whether the account is locked.",
                Optional:            false,
                Required:            false,
            },
            "bot": schema.BoolAttribute{
                MarkdownDescription: "Whether the account is a registered
bot.",
                Optional:            false,
```

```
            Required:              false,
          },
        },
      }
  }
```

Now we can look to creating our `Read` function. For our purposes, we'll use the `AccountLookup` function from the `go-mastodon` library. We use the `Configure` function to get that provider-level client and bring it into our data source. We do this by creating a new instance of the model we created, using APIs to pull in the data we need to populate it, and then saving the data to state.

12.5.2 Configure

The next thing we need to do is configure our data source. This is important because it's how we make the client configured in our provider available to the rest of our functions. In general, the content of the `configure` function is going to look identical between our different data sources, but the signature will be unique.

> **Listing 12.13 Data source `configure`**

```
func (d *AccountDataSource) Configure(ctx context.Context, req
 datasource.ConfigureRequest, resp *datasource.ConfigureResponse) {
    // Prevent panic if the provider has not been configured.
    if req.ProviderData == nil {
        return
    }

    client, ok := req.ProviderData.(*mastodon.Client)

    if !ok {
        resp.Diagnostics.AddError(
            "Unexpected Data Source Configure Type",
            fmt.Sprintf("Expected *mastodon.Client, got: %T. Please report
 this issue to the provider developers.", req.ProviderData),
        )

        return
    }

    d.client = client
}
```

Pluck the client out of the ProviderData object. Notice we changed the client type to *mastodon.Client.

If the client is not the expected type, we add an error to the diagnostics.

Assign the client to the data source client field.

12.5.3 Read

The `read` function is the heart of any data source. It exists to take the user-provided parameters, run some code, and then store the results in state. Most of the time this means using a client to call an API and return the results, but there are data sources (the `cloudinit_config` data source, for instance) that simply perform local operations and return those results.

The first thing we do is parse the data we're provided into an instance of our model. This will be a common pattern for most of the `data source` and `resource` functions. Once we have that model, we can read parameters from it to refine our search. After the search is complete, we populate that object with the new results and store them in state.

Listing 12.14   `Data source read`

```go
func (d *AccountDataSource) Read(ctx context.Context, req
datasource.ReadRequest, resp *datasource.ReadResponse) {
    var data AccountDataSourceModel

    tflog.Debug(ctx, "mastodon_account data source read")

    // Read Terraform configuration data into the model
    resp.Diagnostics.Append(req.Config.Get(ctx, &data)...)

    if resp.Diagnostics.HasError() {
        return
    }

    account, err := d.client.AccountLookup(ctx,
data.Username.ValueString())
    if err != nil {
        resp.Diagnostics.AddError(
            "Failed to lookup account",
            fmt.Sprintf("Failed to lookup account: %s", err),
        )
        return
    }

    data.Id = types.StringValue(string(account.ID))
    data.DisplayName = types.StringValue(account.DisplayName)
    data.Note = types.StringValue(account.Note)
    data.Locked = types.BoolValue(account.Locked)
    data.Bot = types.BoolValue(account.Bot)

    // Write logs using the tflog package
    // Documentation: https://terraform.io/plugin/log
    tflog.Trace(ctx, "read the mastodon_account data source")

    // Save data into Terraform state
    resp.Diagnostics.Append(resp.State.Set(ctx, &data)...)
}
```

We start by pulling in what the user themselves configured.

If the user provided invalid data, we return early.

We use the client to look up the account from the user-provided data.

If we fail to look up the account, we return an error.

We include the error message from our client in the diagnostics.

We then populate the data model with the values we got back from the client. This may require some type coercion.

We log that we successfully read the data source.

We save the data we got back from the client into the state.

The final step before we can test our data source is to register it with our provider. Going back to our `provider.go` file, we need to add the `constructor` function to the response from the `DataSource` function.

12.5.4 Registration

Finally, we need to make our data source available to our users. We do this by going back to our provider and updating the `DataSources` function to include the constructor for our data source. The constructor came as part of our boilerplate and, outside of the name changes, didn't require us to change it.

Listing 12.15   Data source registration

```
func (p *MastodonProvider) DataSources(ctx context.Context) []func()
datasource.DataSource {
    return []func() datasource.DataSource{
        NewAccountDataSource,
    }
}
```

> We add the constructor of the data source to the list so the provider will make it available to Terraform.

Now our data source should be ready for use. We need to install our new version by running `go install`. Next, we should go to the `examples/data-sources` folder and create a new folder named `account`. Inside of that, we can write a simple example of our data source, which has the benefit of also working as documentation.

12.5.5 Usage

Since we've already configured our developer overrides, we simply need to install our provider to test it. We can do this with the command `go install`. As long as there aren't any errors when compiling the provider, we should be able to test it.

Listing 12.16   Data source example

```
terraform {
  required_providers {
    mastodon = {
      source = "terraformindepth/mastodon"
    }
  }
}

provider "mastodon" {}

data "mastodon_account" "me" {
  username = "tedivm"
}
```

> Make sure to require our specific provider, or it will default to hashicorp/mastodon, which doesn't exist.

> We don't have any required configuration because we're using environment variables instead.

> This is our new object!

> We're looking up the account for the user "tedivm", which is the author's account on hachyderm.

That's it! Now we can run the normal `terraform init` (ignoring any errors about it not being able to find our provider) and `terraform apply` commands to see our data source in action.

12.5.6 Testing

Now we need to write a test for our data source. We're going to use the resource helper to build our test. This makes our jobs a lot easier, as the `resource.Test` function will handle the work of spinning up a provider server, running our test by literally calling the Terraform binary to make our tests as realistic as possible, and finally cleaning up any resources after it is finished.

The `resource.Test` function takes the testing context and a `resource.TestCase` as its primary arguments. The bulk of your testing logic will be in the `resource.TestCase` struct, which takes several arguments. The `PreCheck` and `ProtoV6ProviderFactories` arguments allow us to pass through the functions we created in section 12.4.4 to give our test the ability to launch our provider. These two arguments will be the same every time you use `resource.Test` for your project.

The steps argument is where we define our real logic. This argument takes a list of `resource.TestStep` structs. Each step is run one at a time following the previous step, but for most data sources there will only be a single step (we'll see multiple steps when looking at later resources). This is because data sources primarily exist to look up data, which is a fairly simple process.

Most `resource.TestStep` steps will have a `Config` and a `Check` argument (although there are a lot of other options: make sure to review the documentation for this struct to see everything it is capable of). The `Config` field takes a string that contains the Terraform/HCL code to run for the test. For the most part, this should be an extremely simple example of the specific data source being tested (in this case, a single `data` block for `mastodon_account`).

The check argument is where you write your actual assertions. It expects you to pass a `resource.TestCheckFunc`, but there are a few ways to do that:

- Use a `resource.TestCheck*` helper function to generate your test function for you. For example, you can use `resource.TestCheckResourceAttr` to return a function that confirms a resource attribute is the value you expect.
- Use `resource.ComposeTestCheckFunc` or `resource.ComposeAggregateTest-CheckFunc` to group many functions together into a single function. The first example will fail when any of the functions passed to it fail, while the second will run all tests and aggregate the results.

Although that might seem like a lot to take in, it's actually pretty straightforward once you see it in code. For our example, we're going to look up a Mastodon account and confirm that one of the attributes is what we expect it to be. To do that, we'll use a known account (my own) and confirm it isn't marked as a bot.

Listing 12.17   Testing data sources

```
package provider

import (
    "testing"

    "github.com/hashicorp/terraform-plugin-testing/helper/resource"
)

func TestAccAccountDataSource(t *testing.T) {
```

The resource package is used for resources and data sources.

We pass our provider factories in so the test can
spin up a provider server to test against.

We pass our provider precheck function in to
confirm our needed environment variables are set.

```
resource.Test(t, resource.TestCase{
    PreCheck:                    func() { testAccPreCheck(t) },
    ProtoV6ProviderFactories: testAccProtoV6ProviderFactories,
    Steps: []resource.TestStep{
        {
            Config: testAccAccountDataSourceConfig,
            Check: resource.ComposeAggregateTestCheckFunc(
                resource.TestCheckResourceAttr(
    "data.mastodon_account.test", "bot", "false"),
            ),
        },
    },
})
}

const testAccAccountDataSourceConfig = `
data "mastodon_account" "test" {
  username = "tedivm@hachyderm.io"
}
`
```

We check that the bot
attribute is set to false.

Now we specify the checks that we
want to run against the data source.

The configuration value
is a string of pure HCL.
We define this in a
separate constant.

We set the username to a known
value so we can test the output.
This is the author's account.

This is a list of steps that the
test will take. For data sources,
this is usually just a single step.

This is the configuration that
we will use for our test.

Now we can run `make acctest` and our tests will run (assuming we remember to set the environment variables for the provider, otherwise we'll get an error)! Just like when using the provider in real life we do have to make sure it's configured using the environment variables we defined when creating the provider interface. If we haven't set those required environment variables our testing precheck will fail.

12.6 Resources

Adding resources to our provider is the only way to allow our provider to actually *do* something. They have the same starting point as data sources (`Metadata`, `Schema`, `Configure`, and `Read` functions) but also have three additional functions to allow for actions: the `Create`, `Update`, and `Delete` functions. The combination of `create`, `read`, `update`, and `delete` is known as CRUD and is a key feature of many storage and REST-based APIs (see table 12.3).

Table 12.3   Resource interface

Function	Purpose
Metadata	Returns the name of the resource
Schema	Returns the schema for the resource

Table 12.3   Resource interface (*continued*)

Function	Purpose
Configure	Configures the data source, typically by getting the client from the provider instance
Create	Creates the resources from the user-provided parameters and updates the state
Read	Uses the ID saves in state to look up the associated data and populate the state
Update	Takes the ID from an existing resource and updates it with the passed-in data
Delete	Deletes the resource using the ID stored in state
ImportState	Imports an existing resource into state by taking an ID and storing the contents in state

12.6.1 Resource schema

Just like with our data source, we need to define a model and schema. The schema for resources tends to be a bit more complex, as you have to also consider what resources can be changed and which would instead trigger a replacement, but overall it's the same process as used previously.

For our Mastodon provider, we start with the most important resource, `mastodon_ post`. This resource will allow us to create new posts on our Mastodon server from inside of Terraform—for example, to post an update whenever a service is deployed. To do this, we have to create a schema that exposes a few parameters: `status` (the text of the post), `sensitive` (a filter people can apply to their posts as a sort to notify people that the message may contain sensitive content), and `visibility` (whether the post is `public`, `unlisted`, `private`, or `direct`). We're going to copy the example from our scaffolding template over to `port_resource.go` and `post_resource_test.go` to begin.

Listing 12.18   Resource schema

```
// PostResourceModel describes the resource data model.
type PostResourceModel struct {
    Id         types.String `tfsdk:"id"`
    CreatedAt  types.String `tfsdk:"created_at"`
    Account    types.String `tfsdk:"account"`
    Content    types.String `tfsdk:"content"`
    Visibility types.String `tfsdk:"visibility"`
    Sensitive  types.Bool   `tfsdk:"sensitive"`
}

func (r *PostResource) Metadata(ctx context.Context, req
resource.MetadataRequest, resp *resource.MetadataResponse) {
    resp.TypeName = req.ProviderTypeName + "_post"
}

func (r *PostResource) Schema(ctx context.Context, req
resource.SchemaRequest, resp *resource.SchemaResponse) {
    resp.Schema = schema.Schema{
```

> This should be familiar, as it is the same as data source and provider models.

> This will translate to mastodon_post.

**The Required and Optional fields are
both false because this field is read only.**

```
        // This description is used by the documentation generator and
    the language server.
        MarkdownDescription: "Post resource",

        Attributes: map[string]schema.Attribute{
            "id": schema.StringAttribute{
                Computed:            true,
                Required:            false,
                Optional:            false,
                MarkdownDescription: "Post identifier",
                PlanModifiers: []planmodifier.String{
                    stringplanmodifier.UseStateForUnknown(),
                },
            },
            "created_at": schema.StringAttribute{
                MarkdownDescription: "Post creation timestamp",
                Computed:            true,
                Required:            false,
                Optional:            false,
                PlanModifiers: []planmodifier.String{
                    stringplanmodifier.UseStateForUnknown(),
                },
            },
            "account": schema.StringAttribute{
                MarkdownDescription: "Account that created the post",
                Computed:            true,
                Required:            false,
                Optional:            false,
                PlanModifiers: []planmodifier.String{
                    stringplanmodifier.UseStateForUnknown(),
                },
            },
            "content": schema.StringAttribute{
                MarkdownDescription: "Post content, must be provided by
    the user.",
                Required:            true,
            },
            "visibility": schema.StringAttribute{
                MarkdownDescription: "Post visibility (public, unlisted,
    private, direct).",
                Optional:            true,
                Computed:            true,
                Default:             stringdefault.StaticString("public"),
            },
            "sensitive": schema.BoolAttribute{
                MarkdownDescription: "Post sensitive",
                Optional:            true,
                Computed:            true,
                Default:             booldefault.StaticBool(false),
            },
        },
    }
}
```

**This plan modifier
prevents us from
displaying "Attribute
known after apply"
for fields that won't
change.**

**When it can't
calulate the value
of the field it will
use the value
stored in state.**

**This field is also
computed and read only.**

**This field is has to be marked
as computed because it
has a default value.**

**This field is
computed because it
has a default value.**

**Default value for the sensitive field. This requires we
import github.com/hashicorp/terraform-plugin
-framework/resource/schema/booldefault**

12.6.2 Resource configure

We also have to define the `configuration` function, very much like we did with the data source. The only real difference is that we're pulling from a different value when we grab our client from the provider.

Listing 12.19   Resource configuration

```
func (r *PostResource) Configure(ctx context.Context, req
   resource.ConfigureRequest, resp *resource.ConfigureResponse) {
   // Prevent panic if the provider has not been configured.
   if req.ProviderData == nil {
      return
   }

   client, ok := req.ProviderData.(*mastodon.Client)

   if !ok {
      resp.Diagnostics.AddError(
         "Unexpected Resource Configure Type",
         fmt.Sprintf("Expected *mastodon.Client, got: %T. Please report
   this issue to the provider developers.", req.ProviderData),
      )

      return
   }
   r.client = client
}
```

This is almost identical to the data source configure functions.

Just like in other configure functions, we check if the client is of the expected type.

Note that we're passing this to the resource and not a data struct.

Now we get into the functions that have a real effect on the world. The `Create` function should only be called once for any specific resource, after which the `Update` and `Delete` functions will be used to modify the resource.

12.6.3 Resource create

We are starting to get into unique territory. Unlike data sources, resources actually create and manage infrastructure. The very first time a new resource is created Terraform will call the `Create` function. This means that this function will only be called once per resource, and we can generally assume that it is not trying to update an existing resource. This also means that we don't have to worry about getting any existing values from state.

The `create` function starts by creating a model for the specific resource and then populating that model with the data from the plan. Once you have that, you can create the resource using the method and library specific to your platform. In our case, we utilize the `PostStatus` function from the Mastodon client.

Once you've created the new object, you should store all of the attributes from that creation back into the model. Some of these fields likely didn't exist before, such as the `CreatedAt` field in our example, and will be populated for the first time. Updating fields that did exist may seem weird, but it helps you figure out if the data is being changed by the server in strange ways and will present a message to the user if that is occurring.

TIP If the platform you're working with does modify a field compared to how you passed it in, then you should do everything you can to normalize the return result so it matches expectations or you will have eternal state drift. In our Mastodon example, the server adds HTML to the message, so we have to strip that out.

Listing 12.20 Resource `Create` function

```
func (r *PostResource) Create(ctx context.Context, req
  resource.CreateRequest, resp *resource.CreateResponse) {
    var data PostResourceModel

    // Read Terraform plan data into the model
    resp.Diagnostics.Append(req.Plan.Get(ctx, &data)...)

    if resp.Diagnostics.HasError() {
        return
    }

    toot := mastodon.Toot{
        Status:     data.Content.ValueString(),
        Visibility: data.Visibility.ValueString(),
        Sensitive:  data.Sensitive.ValueBool(),
    }

    post, err := r.client.PostStatus(context.Background(), &toot)

    if err != nil {
        resp.Diagnostics.AddError("Client Error", fmt.Sprintf("Unable to
  create post, got error: %s", err))
        return
    }

    p := bluemonday.NewPolicy()

    // Update the model with the created post data
    data.Id = types.StringValue(string(post.ID))
    data.CreatedAt = types.StringValue(post.CreatedAt.String())
    data.Account = types.StringValue(string(post.Account.ID))
    data.Content = types.StringValue(p.Sanitize(post.Content))
    data.Visibility = types.StringValue(post.Visibility)
    data.Sensitive = types.BoolValue(post.Sensitive)

    // Write logs using the tflog package
    // Documentation: https://terraform.io/plugin/log
    tflog.Trace(ctx, "created a resource")

    // Save data into Terraform state
    resp.Diagnostics.Append(resp.State.Set(ctx, &data)...)
}
```

We populate our Toot struct with the data from the Terraform plan.

If we get an error, we add it to the diagnostics and return.

We create a new post using the client.

We initialize the bluemonday package, which requires us to import github.com/microcosm-cc/bluemonday.

Since the server adds HTML to our content we get a mismatch between what we sent and what we get back. This normalizes it so we don't get an error or state drift.

Finally, we add our resource to state.

12.6.4 *Resource read*

The resource Read function is very similar to that of a data source, with the big difference being that there is an existing object in state for you to read from. This means our function looks pretty similar to our data source, with the exception that we start by pulling in that state for our lookup.

If we had to do any normalization in our Create function, then it's important to also do that here; otherwise, you'll see state drift after every read.

Listing 12.21   Resource Read function

```
func (r *PostResource) Read(ctx context.Context, req resource.ReadRequest,
    resp *resource.ReadResponse) {
    var data PostResourceModel

    // Read Terraform prior state data into the model
    resp.Diagnostics.Append(req.State.Get(ctx, &data)...)

    if resp.Diagnostics.HasError() {
        return                                           We pull the post data back in
    }                                                    from the ID we saved in state.

    post, err := r.client.GetStatus(context.Background(), mastodon.ID(
    data.Id.ValueString()))

    if err != nil {
        resp.Diagnostics.AddError("Client Error", fmt.Sprintf("Unable to
    read post, got error: %s", err))
        return                          Just like in our other
    }                                   functions we need to strip
    p := bluemonday.NewPolicy()         HTML from the content.        If we didn't
                                                                      normalize
    data.Id = types.StringValue(string(post.ID))                     the content,
    data.CreatedAt = types.StringValue(post.CreatedAt.String())      this read
    data.Account = types.StringValue(string(post.Account.ID))        would cause
    data.Content = types.StringValue(p.Sanitize(post.Content))       state drift.
    data.Visibility = types.StringValue(post.Visibility)
    data.Sensitive = types.BoolValue(post.Sensitive)                 Finally, we update
                                                                      the state with any
    // Save updated data into Terraform state                        changes that may
    resp.Diagnostics.Append(resp.State.Set(ctx, &data)...)           have occurred.
}
```

12.6.5 *Resource update*

The Update function is what is called whenever the desired state does not match the existing state. Unlike the Create function, this will only be called on a resource that exists, but the pattern is still similar. The big difference is that you'll already have an ID for your resource that you can use to update it in place, rather than having to create a new one. Just like with `Create`, you'll also want to read the server results back into the model before storing it in state.

Listing 12.22 Resource `Update` function

```
func (r *PostResource) Update(ctx context.Context, req
  resource.UpdateRequest, resp *resource.UpdateResponse) {
    var data PostResourceModel

    // Read Terraform plan data into the model
    resp.Diagnostics.Append(req.Plan.Get(ctx, &data)...)

    if resp.Diagnostics.HasError() {
        return
    }

    toot := mastodon.Toot{
        Status:     data.Content.ValueString(),
        Visibility: data.Visibility.ValueString(),
        Sensitive:  data.Sensitive.ValueBool(),
    }

    post, err := r.client.UpdateStatus(context.Background(), &toot,
      mastodon.ID(data.Id.ValueString()))

    if err != nil {
        resp.Diagnostics.AddError("Client Error", fmt.Sprintf("Unable to
  read post, got error: %s", err))
        return
    }

    p := bluemonday.NewPolicy()

    data.Id = types.StringValue(string(post.ID))
    data.CreatedAt = types.StringValue(post.CreatedAt.String())
    data.Account = types.StringValue(string(post.Account.ID))
    data.Content = types.StringValue(p.Sanitize(post.Content))
    data.Visibility = types.StringValue(post.Visibility)
    data.Sensitive = types.BoolValue(post.Sensitive)

    // Save updated data into Terraform state
    resp.Diagnostics.Append(resp.State.Set(ctx, &data)...)
}
```

The Update function is often very similar to the Create function.

This is similar to create, but we're passing in the existing ID to update our existing post.

Just like everywhere else we need to normalize our content field.

After the update we need to update our state with the new values.

We save the updated data back to the state.

12.6.6 Resource delete

The final part of our CRUD pattern is the `Delete` function. This is most likely the simplest function here, as it simply takes in the ID of the resource and makes the API call needed to delete it. As long as the function completes successfully, then Terraform will handle removing it from state.

Listing 12.23   Resource `Delete` function

```
func (r *PostResource) Delete(ctx context.Context, req
    resource.DeleteRequest, resp *resource.DeleteResponse) {
    var data PostResourceModel

    // Read Terraform prior state data into the model
    resp.Diagnostics.Append(req.State.Get(ctx, &data)...)

    if resp.Diagnostics.HasError() {
        return
    }

    err := r.client.DeleteStatus(context.Background(), mastodon.ID(
    data.Id.ValueString()))

    if err != nil {
        resp.Diagnostics.AddError("Client Error", fmt.Sprintf("Unable to
    delete post, got error: %s", err))
        return
    }

}
```

Deleting tends to be one of the more simple actions as there is no need to update state.

Once we delete the post we're done.

12.6.7 *Registration*

Just like with our data source, we have to register our new resource. This is done in the same way: go to the provider and update the `Resources` function to also return the constructor for the resource. Once done, you can install it with `go install`.

Listing 12.24   Registering resources

```
func (p *MastodonProvider) Resources(ctx context.Context) []func()
    resource.Resource {
    return []func() resource.Resource{
        NewPostResource,
    }
}
```

We add our new resource constructor to the list of resources the provider exposes.

12.6.8 *Testing*

Testing resources is very similar to testing data sources. You use the same functions and structs as a data source test does. Unlike data sources, however, you have more to test. Besides simply creating and destroying your resource, you need to also make sure you're testing the updating and importing process as well. This is where the ability to add multiple steps to a test case can come in handy.

Since resources often have a variety of configurations you'll need to test with, it is a common pattern to create a function to generate your Terraform/HCL code with different attributes. When testing a Mastodon post, for instance, you're likely going to run the same configuration with different post content. Rather than hardcoding every variant as a unique string, we can generate it with a function instead.

Listing 12.25 Testing resources

Here we test that the content matches what we passed to our resource.

We're going to test that the content matches and that our default visibility is used.

This time we're going to have multiple steps.

These two parameters are the same as our data source example.

```go
package provider

import (
    "fmt"
    "testing"

    "github.com/hashicorp/terraform-plugin-testing/helper/resource"
)

func TestAccPostResource(t *testing.T) {
    resource.Test(t, resource.TestCase{
        PreCheck:                 func() { testAccPreCheck(t) },
        ProtoV6ProviderFactories: testAccProtoV6ProviderFactories,
        Steps: []resource.TestStep{
            {
                Config: testAccPostResourceConfig("First Test Post"),
                Check: resource.ComposeAggregateTestCheckFunc(
                    resource.TestCheckResourceAttr("mastodon_post.test",
"content", "First Test Post"),
                    resource.TestCheckResourceAttr("mastodon_post.test",
"visibility", "public"),
                ),
            },
            {
                ResourceName:      "mastodon_post.test",
                ImportState:       true,
                ImportStateVerify: true,
            },
            {
                Config: testAccPostResourceConfig("Post After Update"),
                Check: resource.ComposeAggregateTestCheckFunc(
                    resource.TestCheckResourceAttr("mastodon_post.test",
"content", "Post After Update"),
                ),
            },
        },
    })
}

func testAccPostResourceConfig(content string) string {
    return fmt.Sprintf(`
resource "mastodon_post" "test" {
  content = %[1]q
}
`, content)
}
```

Now we test that the visibility used the default value.

This test is a bit different, as we're going to test that our resource can be imported.

Our final test is to test an update to make sure it works.

This function generates a configuration for our test, allowing us to pass in values to change the configuration.

We're using the go fmt package to add our attribute values to the configuration.

As you can see, testing resources is not a whole lot more complicated than testing data sources. Although you're doing a bit more in your tests, you're using the same tools that you've used already to accomplish the task.

12.7   *Functions*

Functions themselves take in parameters, process those parameters in a unique way to the function, and return the result. Writing functions is much simpler than resources or data sources, as you don't have to worry about clients or state (see table 12.4).

The ability to write custom functions for Terraform is very new and is not supported by older versions of Terraform. However, even if your provider contains functions, it can still be used in older versions of Terraform. When that occurs, Terraform will simply ignore the functions in your provider and give an error if anyone tries to use them.

Table 12.4   Function interface

Function	Purpose
Metadata	Returns the name of the function
Definition	Returns the function definition, which is similar to a schema but specifc to functions
Run	Runs the function and returns the results

12.7.1 *Function definition*

The function definition is very similar to a schema but much simpler. It has a summary and description for documentation, a list of parameters, and then the return type of the function.

Listing 12.26   Function definition

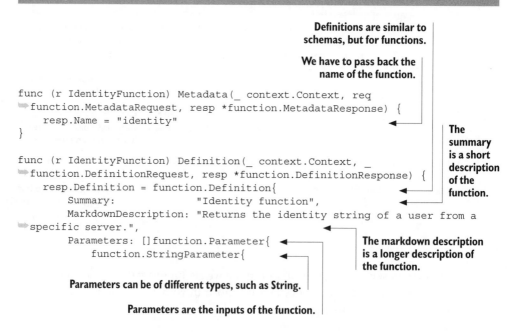

Definitions are similar to schemas, but for functions.

We have to pass back the name of the function.

```
func (r IdentityFunction) Metadata(_ context.Context, req
  function.MetadataRequest, resp *function.MetadataResponse) {
    resp.Name = "identity"
}

func (r IdentityFunction) Definition(_ context.Context, _
  function.DefinitionRequest, resp *function.DefinitionResponse) {
    resp.Definition = function.Definition{
        Summary:            "Identity function",
        MarkdownDescription: "Returns the identity string of a user from a
  specific server.",
        Parameters: []function.Parameter{
            function.StringParameter{
```

The summary is a short description of the function.

The markdown description is a longer description of the function.

Parameters can be of different types, such as String.

Parameters are the inputs of the function.

```
            Name:                  "username",
            MarkdownDescription: "The username to generate the
⇒identity from.",
          },
          function.StringParameter{
            Name:                  "server",
            MarkdownDescription: "The server the user is hosted on.",
          },
        },
        Return: function.StringReturn{},          ◄──────  This is where you define the
    }                                                      return type of the function.
}
```

12.7.2 Function run

The Run function is used to define how the Terraform function will actually run. All of the functions follow the same pattern: load in any parameters that were set, run your data transformation, and then return the results.

Listing 12.27 Function Run

```
func (r IdentityFunction) Run(ctx context.Context, req
⇒function.RunRequest, resp *function.RunResponse) {          We define the variables to
    var username string                                      store the arguments.
    var server string

    resp.Error = function.ConcatFuncErrors(req.Arguments.Get(
⇒ctx, &username, &server))         ◄──────  We get the arguments from the
                                            request and store any errors.
    if resp.Error != nil {         ◄──────
        return
    }                              If there are any errors, we return early.

    resp.Error = function.ConcatFuncErrors(resp.Result.Set(
⇒ctx, "@"+username+"@"+server))    ◄──────
}                                            We set the result of the
                                             function  and check for errors.
```

12.7.3 Registration

The final step is to register the function with the provider. This is done by updating the return results of the provider Functions function to return the function constructor.

Listing 12.28 Function register

```
func (p *MastodonProvider) Functions(ctx context.Context) []func()
⇒function.Function {
    return []func() function.Function{
        NewIdentityFunction,           ◄──────
    }                                  Add the new function constructor to
}                                      the list of functions returned.
```

Now the function will be available to run by calling `provider::mastodon::identity` from inside of Terraform.

12.7.4 Testing

Although this may seem counterintuitive, testing functions tends to be a bit more complicated than testing resources. This isn't because the tests themselves are all that more complicated, but there's several more use cases that come up when testing functions. Not only do you have to test the happy path (where the user passes in the appropriate values), but you also have to test for some additional options, such as a user passing `unknown` or `null` values instead.

Unlike our previous examples, we're going to be using the `resource.UnitTest` function instead of `resource.Test`. This is because testing functions qualify as unit testing, not acceptance testing, as functions never reach out to a service to function. That being said, the `resource.UnitTest` function is very similar to the `resource.Test` function, with the biggest difference being that it doesn't need a `Precheck` parameter.

Another thing to note is that we're setting a minimum version of Terraform to run our tests with. This is important because the ability to add functions did not exist until Terraform v1.8, so we do not want to test our functions with earlier versions as we know they will fail.

Listing 12.29   Testing functions

```
package provider

import (
    "regexp"
    "testing"

    "github.com/hashicorp/terraform-plugin-testing/helper/resource"
    "github.com/hashicorp/terraform-plugin-testing/tfversion"
)

func TestIdentityFunction_Known(t *testing.T) {        ◀── Test that the function works when passed known values.
    resource.UnitTest(t, resource.TestCase{
        TerraformVersionChecks: []tfversion.TerraformVersionCheck{
            tfversion.SkipBelow(tfversion.Version1_8_0),
        },
        ProtoV6ProviderFactories: testAccProtoV6ProviderFactories,
        Steps: []resource.TestStep{
            {
                                                       Functions don't save attributes in state, so we're using an output to test the function.
                Config: `
                output "test" {
                    value = provider::mastodon::identity("tedivm",
"hachyderm.com")
                                                       We're testing that the function returned the expected value.
                }
                `,
                Check: resource.ComposeAggregateTestCheckFunc(
                    resource.TestCheckOutput("test",
"@tedivm@hachyderm.com"),
```

```
            ),
          },
        },
      })
  }

  func TestIdentityFunction_Null(t *testing.T) {
    resource.UnitTest(t, resource.TestCase{
        TerraformVersionChecks: []tfversion.TerraformVersionCheck{
            tfversion.SkipBelow(tfversion.Version1_8_0),
        },
        ProtoV6ProviderFactories: testAccProtoV6ProviderFactories,
        Steps: []resource.TestStep{
            {
                Config: `
                output "test" {
                    value = provider::mastodon::identity(null, null)
                }
                `,
                ExpectError: regexp.MustCompile(
`argument must not be null`),
            },
        },
    })
  }

  func TestIdentityFunction_Unknown(t *testing.T) {
    resource.UnitTest(t, resource.TestCase{
        TerraformVersionChecks: []tfversion.TerraformVersionCheck{
            tfversion.SkipBelow(tfversion.Version1_8_0),
        },
        ProtoV6ProviderFactories: testAccProtoV6ProviderFactories,
        Steps: []resource.TestStep{
            {
                Config: `
                resource "terraform_data" "test" {
                    input = "tedivm"
                }

                output "test" {
                    value = provider::mastodon::identity(
terraform_data.test.output, "hachyderm.com")
                }
                `,
                Check: resource.ComposeAggregateTestCheckFunc(
                    resource.TestCheckOutput("test",
"@tedivm@hachyderm.com"),
                ),
            },
        },
    })
  }
```

Test that the function fails when passed a null value. → (points to `func TestIdentityFunction_Null`)

Confirm that the function returned an error when passed a null value. → (points to `ExpectError` block)

Test that the function works when passed unknown values. → (points to `func TestIdentityFunction_Unknown`)

This is our most complex config, as our function needs a resource to depend on. → (points to `Config:`)

State-only resources are very useful for testing. → (points to `resource "terraform_data" "test"`)

Our output won't be available until after the apply phase. → (points to `value = provider::mastodon::identity(`)

12.8 *Publishing*

Now that you've written your provider, you want to make it available to your users. Since our Mastodon client is built on open source software, we can publish it to a public registry. If your project isn't open source, you should look into the systems your company uses: for example, if you have an instance of Artifactory, you can look up the specific instructions for publishing there.

12.8.1 *Updating documentation*

After all of the changes you've made, there's a good chance your documentation is not up to date. The good news is this can be done in an automated way. By running `go generate`, the template will use the `tfplugindocs` plugin, which reads the schemas from your provider (including the `markdownDescription` fields) to generate consistent documentation for your provider and all of its data sources, resources, and functions. You may want to consider installing the pre-commit framework in this repository and automating this.

Just like when using `terraform-docs`, you are still required to write your own examples, and it's very common to provide extra details around provider configuration. The scaffolding template has a folder, `examples`, that you can use as a starting point, and as long as you follow the structure in the `examples/README.md` file, the examples you write will get included in the generated documentation.

12.8.2 *Creating a GPG key*

Whether you're using Terraform or OpenTofu, you need to sign your releases with a registered key pair for users to install your provider. Creating and registering your key pair only has to happen once, and you can reuse the same key for any of your providers. The easiest way to create a key pair is with the GPG utility, which should be available on your system package manager (`brew`, `apt`, etc.).

Once you have it installed, run `gpg --full-generate-key`. This will create an interactive session and present options. For the type of key, select the first option, `RSA` and `RSA` (the other options are not supported by Terraform). When asked for the keysize, select `4096`. From there, just hit Enter to select the default options, then `y` to accept them.

Next, the interactive system will ask for user information: enter your name or the name of the company you work for and then an email. Record the final `USER-ID` that it outputs for the next steps.

Once you've completed these steps, you'll have one last chance to confirm, and then you'll be asked to enter a `passphrase`. This phrase will be needed to unlock the keys for use and act as a security measure in case the keys are leaked. You should save this value somewhere securely, alongside your keys.

Now export your public and private keys:

```
$ gpg --armor --export "USER-ID" > public.pem
$ gpg --armor --export-secret-keys "USER-ID" > private.pem
```

Finally, we want to make these keys available inside of GitHub Actions, as we'll be publishing directly from there. The template we used to start our project includes a release workflow that expects the key to exist as a secret with the name GPG_PRIVATE_KEY and the passphrase as PASSPHRASE. Go ahead and add those to your GitHub repository as secrets (https://mng.bz/xKrB) for the next steps.

12.8.3 Registering the provider

Before we can actually publish our provider, we have to register it. This process is different for Terraform and OpenTofu. For Terraform, you have to go to the Terraform Registry. Once there, go to User Settings and Signing Keys. In that window, add your public key. Now users can validate that you signed your provider releases.

Once your key is registered, you can register your provider. On the top right of the website select Publish, then Provider. Then just follow the forms to select your repository as the source for the provider. When you publish a new release, it will show up in the registry automatically.

With OpenTofu, you have to submit your provider and key through their GitHub Issues. Go to their registry site (https://github.com/opentofu/registry) and follow the links to submit a signing key, and then follow the link for submitting a Provider.

12.8.4 Creating a release

Now for the easy part. To build a new provider version, simply go to your repository on GitHub, select Releases, and create a new release. As long as you use a semantic version for your tag, the GitHub Actions workflow in `.github/workflows/release.yml` will handle the rest. It will read the configuration in `.goreleaser.yml` and build all of the appropriate architectures of your plugin, uploading them back up to your release in GitHub. From there those provider builds will get pulled down by users when they run `terraform init`.

At this point, our journey through Terraform and OpenTofu has come to an end. Throughout this book you've learned not only about writing Terraform but also the best practices around infrastructure as code as a whole. You should now have the ability to define all of your infrastructure programmatically, complete with testing and even the ability to extend Terraform for use cases it may not currently support. With this knowledge, you can bring resiliency, repeatability, and confidence when deploying and managing infrastructure.

Summary

- Creating a provider is not something that most Terraform developers will need to do.
- Terraform providers are written in Go and require that you have a developer environment setup to support that language.
- Data sources, resources, and functions can be created with the Terraform Plugin Framework.

- Rather than start from scratch, you can use the Terraform Provider Scaffolding template available from HashiCorp.
- Building a provider is a process of implementing interfaces in Go and can be surprisingly simple.
- Once finished, you can publish your provider to a registry for others to use.

index